Ra[illegible] Outlook

FLAT RACING GUIDE 2017

Interviews • Statistics • Results
Previews • Training centre reports

Raceform

Contributors: Richard Birch, James Burn, Graham Dench, Steffan Edwards, Jack Haynes, Dylan Hill, Tony Jakobson, Andrew King, David Milnes, Oliver O'Donoghue, Justin O'Hanlon, John O'Hara, Ed Quigley, Colin Russell, Mark Storey, Nick Watts

Designed and edited by Nick Watts and Dylan Hill

Published in 2017 by Raceform Ltd
27 Kingfisher Court, Hambridge Road, Newbury RG14 5SJ

A catalogue record for this book is available from the British Library.

ISBN 978-1-910497-21-0

Printed by CPI Group (UK) Ltd, Croydon, CRO 4YY

Est. 1909 RACING & FOOTBALL OUTLOOK

Contents

Est. 1909
RACING & FOOTBALL OUTLOOK

Editor's introduction

LAST year will be remembered most for two great forces who will hopefully be locking horns on the racecourse for many years to come.

The first, of course, was Aidan O'Brien. The master of Ballydoyle has achieved some unbelievable feats during his tenure but nothing to top 2016 when he became the most prolific Group/Grade 1-winning trainer of all time (worldwide) and sent out the first three in the Prix de l'Arc de Triomphe as Found beat stablemates Highland Reel and Order Of St George.

It was very nearly even better as he came within just over a length and an unfortunate stumble of winning all five British Classics, US Army Ranger coming up just short in the Derby behind Harzand and Idaho's St Leger exit allowing Harbour Law to claim a shock victory.

Minding was responsible for two of O'Brien's Classic victories and it's great to see the mighty filly back for another season as a four-year-old, while O'Brien also holds a typically strong hand in the Classics again with Churchill and Rhododendron to the fore.

For the first time, though, we will now

MINDING: back to spearhead Aidan O'Brien's team as a four-year-old

FRANKEL: a legend on the racecourse and off to a fine start as a sire

get to see Frankel's progeny in the Classics and perhaps the greatest Flat horse of all time can level the playing field after the huge advantage supplied by Coolmore's legendary stallions.

Frankel certainly made a fine start as a sire and tracking his newcomers became one of the stories of the year. There's still a way to go for him yet – he didn't land a Group 1 in Europe and he obviously had access to an outstanding book of mares – but it bodes well and our expert Steffan Edwards looks upon them favourably as he weighs up the Classic markets in his ante-post preview.

Pedigree expert Oliver O'Donoghue also looks at Frankel's start as well as identifying the best of the sires whose first crops hit the track this year.

We've got plenty more top writers to guide you through all the likely plotlines for 2017.

Our regional reporters have scoured the yards in their area to bring you all the best prospects from all over Britain and Ireland, while Nick Watts has searched far and wide for his list of 30 horses to follow.

As well as that, we have invaluable stable insight from trainers Dean Ivory and Jim Boyle; there are the unique views of Ed Quigley and Richard Birch; Time Test brings you all the key speed figures; and Dylan Hill guides you through last season's leading form.

Then there are the stats, reams and reams of winner-finding numbers detailing the top trainers and jockeys also broken down course by course so you know who to follow at your local track.

Once again we have every base covered for a year packed with bumper profits, and don't forget to buy your copy of the RFO every week for the very latest news and tips.

Profiles for punters
Dean Ivory

DEAN IVORY: has gone from strength to strength in recent seasons

Profile by John O'Hara

THE Ivory family have been training horses for decades, but Dean Ivory, having taken over the licence at Harper Lodge Farm in Radlett, Hertfordshire in 2002, has moved the operation to a higher level in recent seasons.

Ivory's father Ken peaked with 29 winners in 1997 and Ivory beat the total just twice in his first 11 years at the helm, but the last four years have seen him break through the 30-winner barrier three times even as the number of horses in his care remains roughly the same.

"I have 51 horses in training, with around another nine or ten more around the place," he says. "I don't want any more. It is important to me that I have a one-on-one relationship with each horse and if I increased my string I couldn't."

The difference, therefore, is the quality of the horses, backed up by a remarkable increase in the prize-money the yard has earned in recent years. Having won £200,000 for the first time in 2013, Ivory passed the half-million mark two years later and topped that again last year with almost £620,000.

"Last year we had without doubt our best team, and that was with our big star Tropics on the sidelines. Librisa Breeze flew the flag for us as he improved enormously for coming here and I hope we can get a little more out of him this season. If we do then he will be looking at the major races.

"Librisa Breeze is actually a particular favourite of mine and often on a Sunday when everyone has done their jobs and gone home I'll go into his box with him and just sit next to him, stroking him and talking to him. These horses are my best friends and I treat them as if they are.

"Of course we were delighted to bring in more winnings, but that is the end product of a long process. I've turned down owners many times when I think they're not going to give me a free rein at looking after their horses. It's hugely important they have faith in me and let me do the job.

"Actually," he adds, "I always tell any new owner that their horses' interests will come before theirs. I'm all about getting the best out of every horse and nothing will change how I operate. Not all horses learn at the same rate, just as children don't, and you can't rush them. You have to tip away or you are going to be playing catch-up, but only as quick as the horse will allow you. The one thing about training horses is you can't steal time as you will only have to pay it back later. But in fairness we have some wonderfully patient owners here and the strength of the string has grown year on year."

Ivory first fell in love with horses when he hung out with his grandfather, who kept broodmares.

"I was very close to him and he taught me so much about horses. When I was a teenager I started helping my father out around his stables. Dad built his own gallops here with my help and since he retired I have added to and improved them.

"The main one is almost a mile to the top which has an S-bend and heal on it. There are lots of figures of eight; part of the gallop is a figure of nine. We have a mile-and-a-half gallop and a nice little two-furlong gallop to educate the babies on as well as a few hurdles."

LIBRISA BREEZE: flew the flag

The horses are also regularly given a break from the norm as Ivory loves to get them out to enjoy a pick of grass in the paddocks whenever possible.

"You can't keep them locked up all that time and it is good for their minds to be out as much as possible," he says.

"During the winter I send most of them to Max and Shelly Weston's Childwickbury Stud. I know the stud is excellent as it was originally part of Jim Joel's set-up. It is only 15 minutes up the road and has been a real boon for us."

All trainers tell you they can't do their job without good staff and Ivory is no different, emphasising the importance of assistant and head lad Chris Scally.

"We have a great understanding with the horses. We are on the gallops a lot and when I go racing he stays here and doesn't miss a thing. He helps me go through some of the decisions on the races. He sees things that I don't and vice-versa."

As Ivory starts his 16th year in charge, there are high hopes for another good campaign.

"I don't like to set targets but if we can maintain the level of the last two seasons, or even improve on it, I will be a happy man. I have the owners and horses so I'm very hopeful."

The horses

Artscape 5yo gelding
Iffraaj – Artisti

We got him last year from Jim Bolger's yard and he hadn't been able to run due to lots of little issues, but we finally managed to get him out at Chelmsford in September and he ran a very encouraging race in fourth over a mile. He then got off the mark at Kempton in February when we dropped him to 6f, winning by a nose, which was brilliant for such an inexperienced horse. He's clearly quite capable and could be a decent sprint handicapper, but we have to treat him very carefully.

Blaze Of Hearts 4yo gelding
Canford Cliffs – Shesthebiscuit

He's still a maiden after six starts, but he's been improving all the time and we had him gelded over the winter which should bring him on again. He's been taking on horses with more experience and he's been a little green, but he's still been second once and third three times. He should also do better as he goes up in trip. He's doing well at home but I'm in no hurry with him.

Cappananty Con 3yo gelding
Zebedee – Fairmont

I remember when we bought him he looked to have funny feet, but the guy selling him told me he was fine and he wanted to keep a share so that was good enough for me. I'm glad we took the chance as he's a very nice horse and he's really done well since the penny dropped. We taught him to settle by fitting him with a hood at home and we were able to step him up to 6f at Wolverhampton in January when he got off the mark. The extra furlong really helped him there and he could be a real dark horse this season.

GOLDEN AMBER (right): struggled after this win but is down in the weights

Fighting Temeraire 4yo colt
Invincible Spirit – Hot Ticket

Invincible Spirit is a sire I like a lot and this is a lovely colt. He won as a two-year-old despite needing time to grow into his frame and I always knew he'd progress last year. He was second in good handicaps on his first two runs and then showed real grit and determination when he won at Newmarket. His problem is that he doesn't do rough races - some horses are like bad drivers, they just barge out without using their mirrors, but he's a gentleman and would never bump and barge another horse. However, when a race works out for him, he's very good.

Forever Yours 4yo gelding
Canford Cliffs – Gilded

His mother won the Queen Mary but he's a big, backward sort. He had a couple of growing spurts last season which meant he had a stop-start campaign and we were able to run him only twice. We dropped him to 6f for his last run at Yarmouth in September and he was a good third at 66-1, which suggests he should be able to win soon. Everything he does at home suggests he wants further, but he just wants to get on with it on a racecourse and if you tried to settle him he'd pull your arms out so we'll keep him to 6f for now.

Golden Amber 6yo mare
Holy Roman Emperor – Time Of Gold

She's a lovely genuine mare. She didn't win last year after going up to a mark of 100 for her last win in a handicap at Newmarket and she hasn't quite got black type yet, but she still runs more good races than bad and has come down in the weights again now. She needs plenty of pace in the race so she can be delivered late.

Goldslinger 5yo gelding
Gold Away – Singaporette

He's a real staying sort, which is a little odd as his mother was a sprinter. He shot up in the weights when winning four times in 2015 and that made life difficult for him last year, but he could have more to offer. He's still rather immature for a five-year-old and can lose interest quickly when things don't go right for him – if he gets an uncontested lead he has a real chance. But he was also much too keen when he first went over hurdles and did better in that discipline this winter, so he's getting better.

Incredible Dream 4yo gelding
Vale Of York – Finnmark

He could be an improver this year. He made his debut at Kempton in February and finished ninth over a mile. The trip was too short for him as he's got a middle-distance pedigree, but it was all about education for him and he learned a lot. He'll do well when he steps up in trip.

Kadrizzi 4yo gelding
Hurricane Cat – Kadiania

He did well last season and had a great win at Ascot in August when everything went perfectly for him. A straight track like that is the one thing he needs and he also likes to go at his pace and then run through horses at the end, which is what happened as he came from last to first. That was on good to firm ground, which we always knew he liked, but he's also won on soft as a two-year-old which gives us another string to our bow. He's gone up to a mark of 102 now and life will be tough, but he's impossible to read as he never works as well as his mark suggests he should anyway. He's as good as ever and a year stronger so hopefully he'll pay his way again.

Lancelot Du Lac 7yo gelding
Shamardal – Dodie Mae

He's a real favourite around the yard and seems to be just as good as ever at the age of seven. We've had our difficulties getting him right and he didn't show anything in his three runs on turf last year, but

NEZAR: has had problems since these heady days in 2013 but Ivory is confident he has sorted those out

he bounced back on the all-weather earlier this year. His next big aim will be the 6f race on all-weather finals day in April, in which he was second last year, if I can get him qualified. When we get the all-weather business out of the way I'd like to think we might have another crack at the July Cup, although I'd have to talk it over with his owners first. He was beaten only four lengths in 2015 and I think he's got better since then. He's been a real money-spinner for us and I don't think he's finished.

Librisa Breeze 5yo gelding
Mount Nelson – Bruxcalina

What a lovely horse he was to be sent to us. He came here at the end of 2015 having been bought for 90,000gns and it quickly became apparent that he was pretty useful, but never in my wildest dreams did I think I could improve him by a stone and a half. I decided to take a few chances with him, one by dropping him in trip even though his sire is a jumps stallion, and we actually managed to turn a 1m2f horse into a bit of a sprinter. You put yourself in the firing line when you make a decision like that, but I thought it was what he needed and thankfully he proved me right. He started off over a mile, winning at Wolverhampton in April, and he would have won the Hunt Cup if he hadn't had such a bad draw. He then won two big 7f handicaps and was sixth in the Champions Sprint. He's done well over the winter and he could be even better this term. We're working backwards from Royal Ascot, where the Diamond Jubilee would be the logical target, and he could start in the Abernant at Newmarket. He's a very exciting horse.

Lucymai 4yo filly
Multiplex – Miss Lesley

I trained this filly's dam to win over 6f and she's inherited plenty of that speed, although she surprised even us when winning at Kempton at 50-1 as a two-year-old. She ran well after that without winning until she suffered a chip in her knee which ruled her out for most of last year. She came back this winter and took a while to find her feet again, but she has more to offer and I'd be disappointed if we couldn't squeeze another win or two out of her.

Nezar 6yo gelding
Mastercraftsman – Teddy Bears Picnic

We got him from John Quinn's yard out of a Ripon claimer last June. He won that race over 6f, which was his first victory since 2013. I knew he had had his problems, but we quickly sorted them out. We decided to put him away and take our time with him after that and hopefully that will help him to come back to his best. He's been working well.

Soaring Spirits 7yo gelding
Tamayuz – Follow My Lead

He's a quirky horse and we're forever trying different things with him, but I think we've finally worked him out. Last summer

STAKE ACCLAIM: picked out by Dean Ivory as his horse to follow this year

he won three races in three weeks - two at Brighton and one at Leicester - and then ran some big races in defeat. It seems he loves to run from the front and tracks where he has to think, like Brighton with its switchback, are ideal for him.

Stake Acclaim 5yo gelding
Acclamation – Golden Legacy

I keep waiting for him to really take off and progress as he just hasn't fulfilled his potential yet. He's been a bit weak and, like some of Acclamation's stock, he can be moody and isn't the most genuine, but he definitely has the ability to be better than he's shown. Last year he won first time out at Windsor but then he didn't really go on from there. He should certainly win races this season and if I had to pick one from the yard to follow this season he'd be the one.

Tangramm 5yo gelding
Sakhee's Secret – Tripti

I must say we've done very well with this horse. When he came to us in 2015 he'd run three lifeless races over sprint distances, but to me he just looked like he was crying out for further and he went on to win seven races out of eight, with a second in the middle. That took his mark up from 54 to 83 and his improvement has pretty much levelled off now as he has a few aches and pains that keep catching up with him. However, I'm sure he can still win a couple more races.

Tropics 9yo gelding
Speightstown – Taj Are

He's been a brilliant horse, winning eight times and twice finishing second in the July Cup, the last time by a nostril which was heartbreaking. Unfortunately he missed all of last season as he sprained his tendons just as he was starting to canter and then, when we got him going again, he injured his ligament. He's nine now and obviously won't be getting any faster, but I still have high hopes he can win again this year. His enthusiasm is certainly as good as ever because as soon as sees the horsebox leave the yard he wants to go with them. He still holds the Windsor track record and I'll definitely be looking to sending him back there for the Listed race at the start of June he won two seasons ago.

Profiles for punters
Jim Boyle

JIM BOYLE: hoping for the green light this summer to redevelop his yard

Profile by Dylan Hill

THE slow workings of government have frustrated people in all walks of life for time immemorial and one of the latest victims is Jim Boyle – but things are finally starting to look better for the Epsom trainer.

Boyle can certainly train winners – he sent out 59 in 2009, his best season since taking out a licence at South Hatch Stables seven years earlier – but they have been harder to come by since then due to the infrastructure of the yard.

"It's hard work," says Boyle. "The yard is old and rundown and it's very labour-intensive. We've been able to do the job but not at a level I'd like to be at. For five or six years we haven't felt able to market ourselves either because if anyone came to see the yard they wouldn't see what we'd like them to see.

"We've been having ongoing discussions with the council in that time about redeveloping it, but things have gone painfully slowly and it's been incredibly frustrating."

However, Boyle was finally able to put in a pre-planning application before Christmas and a decision is expected by the summer. He then hopes, all being well, to have a new yard in 2018 with much-improved facilities.

There's already a more positive vibe around the yard, though, following Boyle's best season since 2012 last year. Perhaps, having admitted it had been hard to push themselves during the dark days of making no progress with the council, that light at the end of the tunnel is already having an effect.

Boyle set himself a target of 20 winners and just about reached it.

"I thought that was a very fair figure," he reflects, "and it was nice to get there. For the last five years we've been around the 20-horse mark and we'd had a steady enough stream of winners, albeit without the higher-profile successes we'd have liked, but last year was certainly as good as any in that time"

Things may well improve again now Boyle has managed to keep hold of all five of his two-year-olds from last season, who included highly promising pair El Torito and Silver Penny, having in recent times been forced to sell many of his better youngsters – a "fact of life" for trainers lower down the ladder, as he has put it.

Boyle also gives a positive mention to his five two-year-olds for 2017 – two colts by Kyllachy and Camacho plus three fillies by Lethal Force, Foxwedge and Footstepsinthesand.

"They're a nice bunch," he says, "and it gives us plenty to look forward to for the future. The colts are both nicely forward and you should be seeing them by May or June. The fillies might need a little bit longer."

Now things are looking more positive, did Boyle ever consider leaving Epsom?

"It's always been the right place, it's just been the wrong facility for us. We've had options to go elsewhere but we're very keen to make a go of it in Epsom. I love training here, I think it's a superb place to train with fantastic gallops. The only thing missing is the yards."

A WINTER'S MORNING: Jim Boyle's string walk to the gallops in 2010

The horses

Baby Gal 3yo filly
Royal Applause – Our Gal

We got her this year from Giles Bravery's yard after she'd lost her way a bit and I was pleased with her debut fourth at Kempton in February. She has some promise and should be a decent handicapper. She's shown she handles Brighton, finishing second there last year, and we'll try to find her races at Epsom as well.

Black Bess 4yo filly
Dick Turpin – Spring Clean

She's the stable star and means a lot to us as she's a home-bred. She's worked her way up and won three times last season before not being beaten far at Epsom on her last run. She's a big, tall, rangy filly who was always going to improve with age and I'd like to think we can get more improvement out of her this year.

Cordite 6yo gelding
Footstepsinthesand – Marion Haste

We got him out of Mick Appleby's yard early last year when he was still too high in the weights – he'd been fourth in a Group 3 as a youngster and was rated 104 at one point. However, he came down to 72 before his last run in October and that was right up there with his best as he finished second at Windsor over 1m2f. He'd been headstrong when he arrived and my head girl Louisa Allen deserves huge credit as she taught him to settle. We'd always thought about stepping him up in trip, but that Windsor race was the first time we felt able to do it and he saw it out well, so he'll probably stick to middle distances now. He should be competitive this year.

Duke Of North 5yo gelding
Danehill Dancer – Althea Rose

He won at Salisbury and Brighton last year and didn't get a clear run when he wasn't beaten far back at Brighton in August. He picked up a little injury after that so he's had a nice break, but he's back in good order. He wants cut in the ground.

Ebbisham 4yo gelding
Holy Roman Emperor – Balting Lass

He's slightly frustrating. He can look really

EL TORITO: a fine fourth in this nursery at Glorious Goodwood last year

GIOVANNI DI BICCI: all-weather winner who can also do well on turf

good when he wins, as he did at Kempton in November, but he doesn't always back it up and can be in and out. He's best when fresh and we'll avoid quick ground with him.

El Torito 3yo colt
Tagula – April Green

He's a lovely horse. He won at Windsor in June and his owners are great sports who wanted some good days out, so we took him to Glorious Goodwood and the Ebor meeting after that and he wasn't disgraced at all, finishing fourth of 17 and ninth of 19 in good races. We were a bit disappointed with him after his last run at Yarmouth, but it was the end of a long season and probably one race too many. He's grown nicely over the winter and we'll step him up to 7f, which he should appreciate.

Giovanni Di Bicci 5yo gelding
Medicean – Marula

He's done all his winning on the all-weather but I thought he ran some nice races on turf as well last year. His last run at Epsom was really promising as he missed the break but ran on to finish third. That was over 7f and all his wins have been over a mile, so hopefully he can build on that.

Inke 5yo mare
Intikhab – Chifney Rush

She's a tough handicapper who won her third race out of four first time out at Lingfield last season and was second at Epsom after that. However, she got jarred up at Glorious Goodwood and we just got her back for two runs at the backend when I didn't think she ran badly at all in good races. I think she's still capable of more but she prefers ease in the ground.

Lemon Drop 3yo filly
Paco Boy – Zia

She was weak and backward last year but showed glimpses of ability in her three maidens before getting lost on the all-weather last time. She's grown over the winter, although not quite as much as I'd hoped she would. However, there's some leeway in her mark and she ought to win a race or two this year.

Moonstone Rock 3yo filly
Rock Of Gibraltar – Komena

She's a tough filly. After running okay in three maidens, she was given a mark of 63 and ran very well on her handicap debut at Leicester when third, but she just

PERFECT PASTIME (centre): grand old boy who can win again

couldn't handle the all-weather next time. She should be better this year and hopefully she'll build on her promise back on turf. She can win off her mark.

Onorina 5yo mare
Arcano – Miss Honorine

She's a big mare who needed time to mature but has got better and better as she's gone further. She won at Lingfield and Newbury last year and I was pleasantly surprised she ran as well as she did when fourth at Salisbury on her last run. The ground was soft and she hadn't handled that in the past, but she did really well even though it wasn't to her liking and that will open more doors for her. She's strengthened up again over the winter and will get 2m.

Perfect Pastime 9yo gelding
Pastoral Pursuits – Puritanical

He's a grand old boy who wins a couple of races each year when things fall right for him. He's best on soft ground and needs to be rated in the low 60s – any higher and he struggles. He's quirky and has just started getting a bit funny in the stalls but I'm sure he'll be fine.

Rattle On 4yo gelding
Pivotal – Sabreon

He took time to find his feet, but he got better through last year and was unlucky to bump into one on his penultimate run at Chelmsford in October. He was favourite back there next time and we were disappointed he was only fifth, but I think he was over the top. He's had a nice break and starts on the right mark to have a good season.

Silver Penny 3yo filly
Hellvelyn – Pennyspider

She won her maiden at Windsor last season, coming on bundles for her debut run, which all mine do. She was then beaten a length in a nursery at Bath and has gone up 1lb to 69. We don't have any big plans for her but we'll see how she progresses in handicaps. She loves soft ground so that will determine her programme a bit.

Est. 1909
RACING & FOOTBALL OUTLOOK

Pedigrees for punters by Oliver O'Donoghue

FRANKEL fever swept last year's Flat season and his 54 per cent winners-to-runners strike-rate and tally of six black-type scorers was impressive, even taking into account he covered a high number of exceptional racemares and producers in his debut book.

Highlights in Europe were the classy fillies Fair Eva, Queen Kindly and Toulifaut, while Frankuus showed admirable toughness and Soul Stirring became the sire's first top-level winner when she won the Hanshin Juvenile Fillies in Japan. There were also a number of exciting maiden winners.

It will be fascinating to see how Frankel's first crop progresses at three – he had his first three-year-old winner 27 days into the new year – and whether his second crop can match or even better the performance of his first crop.

There is also much intrigue about the 25 stallions who joined the ranks a year later, the most notable of which are discussed below.

Camelot
Montjeu – Tarfah (Kingmambo)

Camelot came agonisingly close to being the first horse since Nijinsky to land the English Triple Crown and it is hardly surprising that his progeny have been garnering plenty of attention at the sales.

A champion at two and three, the son of Montjeu went unbeaten in his first five starts, three of which were Classics.

Considering his runners have yet to hit the racecourse, his stud fee jumped significantly from €25,000 to €35,000 in 2017, indicating just how popular his foals and yearlings have been.

Seventy-four of his yearlings sold last year for an average of 98,296gns, with 400,000gns paid by MV Magnier for a yearling colt out of Iowa Falls, a three-parts sister to New Bay, which is one of at least eight two-year-olds by Camelot in the care of Aidan O'Brien.

Dawn Approach
New Approach – Hymn Of The Dawn (Phone Trick)

One sire who may get plenty of early two-year-olds is Dawn Approach.

Trained by Jim Bolger, Dawn Approach was six from six as a juvenile, including victories in the first juvenile race of the year in March, the Coventry Stakes, the National Stakes and the Dewhurst Stakes, in a year that saw him crowned champion two-year-old.

The son of New Approach also landed the 2,000 Guineas in 2013 before running too keen in the Derby, but he then confirmed his prowess as a miler by beating Toronado by a short-head in the St James's Palace Stakes.

By mid-February 38 of his two-year-olds had already been named, again indicating that he will have a strong early presence, while 36 of his yearlings sold last year for an average of 83,667gns. That included an unnamed half-brother to Hungerford Stakes scorer Breton Rock in training with Richard Hannon, picked up for 275,000gns by Peter and Ross Doyle at Book 1.

Declaration Of War
War Front - Tempo West (Rahy)

Declaration Of War was a late-maturing two-year-old and did not appear until November in France when he won back-to-back juvenile contests.

Switched to Aidan O'Brien, he rewarded his trainer's patient handling by landing a Group 3 race at Dundalk. Continuing to improve at four, he won the Queen Anne Stakes at Royal Ascot and the Juddmonte International at York from Irish Derby winner Trading Leather.

The son of War Front covered 171 mares in his first and only season at Coolmore in Ireland, including 46 black-type winners, and his yearlings were well received in the sales ring. Seven of them made six-figure prices at Book 1 of the October Yearling Sale at Tattersalls and 380,000gns was the price paid by Al Shaqab Racing for a yearling colt out of Silver Star.

Five of his two-year-olds are in the care of his former trainer Aidan O'Brien, whose son Joseph has another.

Farhh
Pivotal - Gonbarda (Lando)

Farhh was a rather late-maturing type, winning a maiden on his only start at two and a 20-runner handicap on his only start at three over a mile.

As a four-year-old, though, Farhh finished runner-up in no fewer than four Group 1 contests, twice to Frankel, and third in another, while also managing to win the Thirsk Hunt Cup. He then broke through at the top level at five, winning the Lockinge Stakes at Newbury and the Champion Stakes at Ascot, in which he saw off Cirrus Des Aigles and Ruler Of The World.

Farhh covered a relatively small book compared to the other big guns, with 81 mares, yet among them were Bianca Nera, who won the Moyglare Stakes; Something Exciting, who won the Nassau Stakes and was third in the Oaks; and Zahrat Dubai, who was second in the Oaks.

Bred off a fee of £17,500, 19 of his yearlings changed hands last year for an average of 42,890gns. Expect his runners to progress with age.

INTELLO (right): two of his yearlings made 300,000gns at Book 1

LETHAL FORCE: should get some nice early two-year-olds

Intello
Galileo – Impressionnante (Danehill)

Bred on the same cross as Frankel, Intello won both his races at two over a mile in France, where he was trained by Andre Fabre. His most notable success the following year came in the Prix du Jockey Club at Chantilly when he saw off Morandi by two lengths.

He covered a book of 139 mares in his first season at Cheveley Park and it is noteworthy that 32 per cent of those mares were black-type winners. Among the mares he covered were Prix de Diane winner Millionaia and Cheveley Park Stakes scorers Hooray and Pas De Reponse. Also included are the dams of Nassau Stakes scorer Sultanina, Prix de l'Opera winner Lily Of The Valley and Prix du Cadran conqueror Mille Et Mille.

Two of his yearlings made 300,000gns at Book 1, including Gabr, who is out of the 1,000 Guineas second Spacious and in training with Sir Michael Stoute, and an unnamed colt out of Seal Of Approval's dam Hannda in training with John Gosden.

Others to note

Al Kazeem was retired to stud in 2014 but was put back into training after he was found to be subfertile. From the 76 mares he covered, only 23 foals were registered, yet his yearlings have been well received with five selling for an average of 124,000gns.

Lethal Force is fancied to get some nice early two-year-olds having placed on all four starts at two. He later developed into a top-class sprinter, winning the Diamond Jubilee Stakes from Society Rock. Sixty-seven of his yearlings sold last year for an average of 35,517gns, with 160,000gns paid for a colt at Book 2 named Jet Pilot who has since gone to France.

The ill-fated **Society Rock** won the same race as Lethal Force when it was known as the Golden Jubilee Stakes. Ninety of his yearlings sold last year for an average of 30,994gns, with Armando Duarte going to 210,000gns at Book 1 to secure an unnamed colt out of the Listed-placed Strange Magic, now in the care of Hugo Palmer.

Ante-post preview by Steffan Edwards

2,000 Guineas

ANOTHER 2,000 Guineas, another short-priced Aidan O'Brien favourite. Last year I was happy to take on Air Force Blue, because as a precocious May foal I thought he might not train on. This year I have no such concerns about **Churchill**.

The bare form of his Chesham Stakes win was nothing special, but the money for him that day spoke volumes about the regard in which he was held. The workmanlike nature of his subsequent successes in the Tyros Stakes and Futurity Stakes did not get everybody that excited either, but he's clearly the type who never does more than he has to.

A more convincing win in the National Stakes and a comfortable victory in the Dewhurst now see him as 6-4 favourite for the Guineas and it's hard to pick holes in him.

His form is solid, having accounted for the likes of subsequent Group 1 winners Thunder Snow and Rivet as well as smart pair Mehmas and Lancaster Bomber, who has been beaten by Churchill three times but gave his form a boost by finishing second at the Breeders' Cup.

The Galileo-Storm Cat cross has already produced a 2,000 Guineas winner in Gleneagles as well as a couple of Irish 1,000 Guineas winners in Marvellous and Misty For Me. Last year's 1000 Guineas runner-up Ballydoyle is another example, so it's clear it's a winning formula, and I expect Churchill to be very difficult to beat.

That said, he's not an ante-post price and I prefer to look for one or two at much bigger odds.

Indeed, apart from Churchill the race is pretty open because his stablemate **Caravaggio** is the only other horse priced less than 16-1 and there must be a doubt about getting him the mile.

Unbeaten in four starts last year, he was an impressive winner of the Coventry Stakes when winning despite being drawn on the wrong side and then bolted up in the Phoenix Stakes.

An American-bred son of Scat Daddy, he's clearly a very speedy sort (Aidan O'Brien has described him as the fastest 2yo he's ever had) and might run in a 7f trial in the spring to help connections decide whether he goes to the Guineas or heads down the sprinting route. I expect it will be the latter.

The Vintage Stakes produced last year's winner Galileo Gold and **War Decree** has the potential to follow in his footsteps.

He's bred to be a miler and beat a solid yardstick in Thunder Snow at Goodwood. If Churchill was to fail to make the gig, he has the look of a super sub and I'm not overly concerned by his absence from the racecourse after July.

Interestingly, however, Highland Reel also missed the second half of his juvenile campaign after taking the Vintage Stakes and he was sent to the French Guineas on his reappearance as Gleneagles and Ol' Man River represented the yard at Newmarket. I wouldn't be surprised if War Decree ended up at Deauville even though he's more likely to get his ground at Newmarket. Where he goes will hint at the confidence the stable has in Churchill.

There was plenty to like about the way **Cliffs Of Moher** won his maiden as the time was fast and they were strung out behind him. A son of Galileo who has the speed for a mile, he could take in a Guineas trial according to O'Brien, but with other candidates higher up the pecking order it remains to be seen if he can force his way on to the Newmarket bus.

The home defence is arguably led by **Rivet**, who took the Racing Post Trophy last year. He won well enough that day, but of course he was up against staying types in general and he had been put in his place by Churchill in the Dewhurst.

His trainer, William Haggas, didn't think he handled the track at Newmarket and was more comfortable on the flat terrain at Doncaster, which puts a bit of a question mark over his participation in the Guineas. In addition, the partnership that owns him includes Michael Tabor and John Magnier, so they are likely to have a say in whether he takes on Churchill.

I still think it's likely he runs at Newmarket, but I have a feeling a mile will be a minimum for him this year and that he'll do better over further. The Guineas might work as a nice prep for Epsom.

Thunder Snow has done nothing but advertise the Dewhurst form since chasing home Churchill at Newmarket. A five-length win in the Criterium International has been followed by a successful spell in Dubai and he has the form to be in the mix.

Best Solution didn't take to the dirt at Meydan anywhere near as well as Thunder Snow. He might do better back on turf but has a bit to find on the pick of last year's form.

Superlative Stakes winner **Boynton** also spent the winter in Dubai. An American-bred who is suited by a quick surface, he was a solid third in the Vintage Stakes when giving 3lb to the first two. He's a smart colt, but Charlie Appleby expects him to be suited by 1m2f this year so maybe the Guineas will be a bit sharp for him.

Syphax has been bought by Godolphin.

CHURCHILL (centre): hard to pick holes in the form of his Dewhurst victory

LARCHMONT LAD: should relish the mile and is worth an each-way play

He overcame greenness to win on his debut at Musselburgh and then came from a long way back to beat Best Of Days in the Acomb Stakes. He looks a promising colt, but he's a May foal and the Guineas might just come too soon for him.

Barney Roy had some issues which delayed his debut, but when he finally made it to the track in September he won in taking style at Haydock. He probably lacks the experience required at the moment, but he's highly rated by the Richard Hannon stable and if he takes in a trial he could well take a big step forward. A strongly run mile should suit him well.

However, the more solid option from the yard is **LARCHMONT LAD**, who may not be a particularly sexy selection but is a big price for a horse who had a progressive profile last season and promises to be even better this year.

Strong at the finish on his debut at Sandown in a race that worked out well, he then took a step up when third in a three-way photo to a Listed race at Doncaster next time. Considering he'd been off for two months prior to that (suffered an infection behind his hoof wall), was expected to need the run and didn't settle in the race itself, he ran really well.

He showed the benefit when taking the Group 3 Tattersalls Stakes on his final start. The form is pretty solid, with the runner-up Whitecliffsofdover going off favourite but only managing third in a bit of a tactical affair in the Lagardere next time out, the third, Sir Dancealot, winning a Listed race next time before finding the mile too far in the Racing Post Trophy and the fourth, Best Solution, winning the Autumn Stakes on his next start.

Larchmont Lad needs to improve, but at Newmarket he was again at his best at the finish, seeing out the trip well, and he looks sure to relish stepping up to a mile in the Guineas. By Footstepsinthesand out of a half-sister by King's Best to an Italian 2,000 Guineas winner, he's got miler written all over him and I think he's worth an each-way play at 50-1.

The disappointing favourite in the Tattersalls Stakes was **Escobar**. He had looked promising in his first two starts, though, and returned a dirty scope after bombing out at Newmarket. He's another who will now likely take in a Guineas trial and it shouldn't come as a surprise if he bounces back in a big way given his trainer, Hugo Palmer, said he had "carried all before him" at home – strong words given the yard also housed the Royal Lodge winner **Best Of Days**.

It's harder to forgive a couple of Dewhurst flops.

South Seas had improved through the ranks on softer ground and still has to prove he can act on a quicker surface, while **Seven Heavens** seemed to go the wrong way last season, not settling at all in the Dewhurst, and is a late May foal. He's not for me.

The latter was a rare letdown for Frankel that day as the 2011 winner of this race has made a great start to his career at stud and is well represented among the dark horses for the Guineas.

John Gosden said that **Cracksman** would start off over 1m2f this year, and Roger Charlton has suggested the same with **Atty Persse**, so that probably rules them out, but the likes of Swiss Storm, Eminent and Mirage Dancer have the potential to make a splash in one of the trials and stake a claim.

The one who makes most appeal of that trio is David Elsworth's **SWISS STORM**.

The word was out before his debut that he was highly regarded as he was sent off odds-on. Unfortunately he proved far too green and could finish only seventh that day, but he showed his true ability next time at Newbury, travelling well throughout and galloping on strongly to win in impressive style. That was over 7f and a mile should be right up his street this year – his dam was speedy but Frankel should pass on the stamina required.

He was due to contest the Racing Post Trophy after winning his maiden but picked up a bug and had to miss the race. He's light on experience, but he is on course for the Greenham, has any amount of potential and it wouldn't be a surprise to see him win at Newbury – over a course and distance he's already proven over – and shorten considerably for the Guineas. Godolphin bought out Elsworth's share in the colt over the winter so he'll be racing in blue this season.

Roger Varian said a Guineas trial might be in the offing for **Cape Byron** after he quickened away to win his maiden in

SWISS STORM: the son of Frankel has any amount of potential

TITUS: seems more likely to wait for the Irish 2,000 Guineas

impressive style. A son of Shamardal, he's another who could be anything.

The French challenge could be led by **National Defense**, who made all to win the Prix Jean Luc-Lagardere and seems to enjoy being out in front. Criquette Head-Maarek has yet to choose which Guineas he goes for.

Andre Fabre's **Al Wukair** is another who could travel or stay at home. He looked a talented colt when quickening up to win a Listed race at Deauville in October and would be an interesting candidate if making the trip.

Jim Bolger's **Zorion** didn't beat a great deal on his debut, but he couldn't have won much easier and is well regarded. He's a brother to Zip Top, who was runner-up in the Racing Post Trophy, and it'll be interesting if he makes it to a trial in the spring. He looks more of a miler in the making than stablemate **Dubai Sand**, who has already won over 1m1f.

The Irish Guineas looks a likelier target for impressive debut winners **Titus**, trained by Dermot Weld, and **Glastonbury Song**, trained by Ger Lyons, while the likes of **Blue Point**, **Dreamfield** and **Harry Angel** all look sprinters in the making and are likely to have the Commonwealth Cup as their target rather than the Guineas.

2,000 Guineas

Newmarket, 6 May

	Bet365	*Betfred*	*Betway*	*Boyles*	*Coral*	*Hills*	*Lads*	*PPower*
Churchill	**6-4**	**6-4**	**6-4**	5-4	5-4	5-4	5-4	**6-4**
Caravaggio	**7**	**7**	**7**	6	**7**	**7**	6	6
War Decree	14	14	**16**	**16**	**16**	**16**	12	12
Rivet	**16**	**16**	**16**	**16**	**16**	**16**	**16**	**16**
National Defense	**20**	**20**	16	16	16	-	**20**	**20**
Cliffs Of Moher	16	**20**	**20**	**20**	-	**20**	-	**20**
Thunder Snow	16	**25**	20	**25**	20	**25**	20	16
Swiss Storm	**33**	25	**33**	**33**	25	**33**	**33**	25
Mirage Dancer	**33**	-	**33**	-	**33**	**33**	**33**	**33**
Best Solution	20	-	33	25	33	**40**	33	33
Eminent	**40**	-	33	33	25	**40**	33	25
South Seas	33	33	25	33	25	**40**	25	25
Escobar	40	-	25	20	33	33	33	**50**
Larchmont Lad	40	-	33	-	40	**50**	40	33

each-way 1/4 odds, 1-2-3

Others on application, prices correct at time of going to press

1,000 Guineas

PRIOR to last year the record of fillies Aidan O'Brien had sent to the 1,000 Guineas without a prep race was not good – they had finished 059807890300 – whereas six of the 17 who had been given a run beforehand made the first three at Newmarket, including two winners.

That all changed last year when Minding led a one-two-three for the yard and the third, Alice Springs, was the only one coming off a prep race. This suggests there was a change in policy at Ballydoyle and a decision made to get their best fillies ready to run first time out rather than build them up gradually.

On the assumption that this change of focus remains in place, it becomes harder to oppose impressive Fillies' Mile winner **Rhododendron**. She took a real step up for the quicker ground and step up to a mile at Newmarket and comprehensively turned around Moyglare Stakes form with her stablemate **Hydrangea**.

However, to my eyes they both look likely to want further this year and both have siblings who were best over middle distances. That doesn't mean that one of them can't win, but I expect them to be ridden to run the finish out of their rivals and for that reason I'm looking for fillies who can travel off a good pace and do them for speed at the finish.

It's also worth remembering that their main market rivals in the Fillies' Mile both disappointed. **Sobetsu** scoped dirty and something presumably amiss with **Spatial** as well as she stopped quickly and Andrea Atzeni looked down. Both could bounce back, although in Sobetsu's case it will probably be over further.

Promise To Be True also disappointed when a short price for the Moyglare. She ran a better race when second in the Prix Marcel Boussac but was then comfortably beaten in the Criterium International.

The softish ground at the Curragh and Saint-Cloud may have been against her and O'Brien described her as a bit of a baby on Arc weekend, so it's likely she'll progress well from two to three and appreciate the likely quicker terrain at Newmarket, but she is a May foal and no winner has been that young in the last 28 years.

Intricately was a surprise winner of the Moyglare, reversing earlier form with the three Ballydoyle fillies, but she's another who will probably be suited by middle distances this year.

The Boussac winner **Wuheida** also looks more of an Oaks filly on paper. Charlie Appleby has said he plans to start her off in the Guineas, but the reason he gave was that he's "old school" and believes it's the best Oaks trial.

Dabyah tried to make all in the Boussac, getting a gap on her field when quickening up but run down inside the last. She's a half-sister to a 1m6f winner, but he was by Teofilo whereas she's by the Australian sprinter Sepoy. I expect she'll be suited by a mile but will just come up short.

Senga and **Toulifaut** had their excuses at Chantilly, being held up further back than ideal given the stop-start pace and, in the case of the latter, being badly hampered as well, but my guess is they'll stay at home for the Pouliches.

Fair Eva was the Guineas favourite for some time last year but may not be quite that good after all. The conclusion seemed to be that she needed 7f when beaten in the Lowther and the market agreed, sending her off odds-on when up in trip in the Rockfel, but again she was beaten.

Brave Anna and **Roly Poly** were first and second in the Cheveley Park and showed their best form by far when they got to race on fast ground last season, which is so important to their sire War Front's progeny.

Both have the potential to get a mile this year, but there's a bit of a question-mark over how well War Fronts progress from two to three. His sons War Command, Giovanni Boldini, Hit It A Bomb and Air Force Blue have all failed to carry top two-year-old form over to their Classic season.

Queen Kindly, who beat Roly Poly in the Lowther, was below her best in the

CRISTAL FIZZ: showed a smart turn of foot to win the Radley Stakes at Newbury

Cheveley Park and is probably better judged on her York win. However, she looks pretty speedy to me and I expect her to prove best over sprint trips like her mother Lady Of The Desert.

I was quite taken by **Sea Of Grace**'s win in the Flame of Tara as she showed great determination to get the better of Eziyra, but her owner has since moved all his horses to France, which must make a trip to Newmarket less likely.

Eziyra gave that form a bit of a boost when taking another Group 3 at the Curragh next time, but Dermot Weld said afterwards that he'd aim her at the Irish 1,000 Guineas. Weld also nominated Guineas trials for **Tempera** and the Killavullan Stakes winner **Making Light**, but he hasn't exactly made a habit of bringing one over for this race in the past.

Only three times in the last 35 years has the winner of the 1,000 Guineas not had Group-race form at two but, given the doubts over all the fillies discussed already, there may be more of a chance for something to emerge this year.

One of the three who bucked that trend was the Barry Hills-trained Ghanaati, who won the Guineas first time out in 2009 on the back of just a Kempton maiden win, and Owen Burrows, who took over the licence from Barry Hills at Kingwood House Stables, has a fascinating contender in **TALAAYEB**.

Attractively bred, being by Dansili out of a half-sister to Ghanaati, she could not have made a more eyecatching debut last September, travelling strongly in behind and, despite clipping heels as she challenged between horses, quickening up smartly to win going away.

It was a seriously impressive performance and it's worth taking the chance that her trainer, who sent out Massaat to finish second in last year's 2,000 Guineas, can get her ready for the big day. It's possible she could take in a trial beforehand, but she's quite a neat filly and might be best going straight to the Guineas.

The other one to back is **CRISTAL FIZZ**, who has achieved more than Talaayeb having won a Listed race at Newbury last season. That form is rock-solid as the runner-up, Glitter Girl, had filled the same spot in the Oh So Sharp and Cristal Fizz really impressed on both her starts.

She apparently doesn't show a lot at home, which explains why she was sent off at 16-1 for her debut at Ascot, but she quickened up in fine style despite being slowly away and having her path continually blocked until she finally got daylight.

Second-favourite to win at Newbury, she was again held up off the pace and picked up strongly despite having to be switched more than once. She won a shade cosily and the time was marginally quicker than the earlier Horris Hill and the later 0-95 handicap for older horses.

By Power out of a 1m2f winner by Galileo, she should be suited by a mile this year and sitting off a good gallop and being delivered late looks just the way to get the best out of her, so I can see the Guineas setting up nicely for her.

She is twice the price of the Oh So Sharp winner **Poet's Vanity**, who did it well that day, building on a 10l maiden win at Salisbury on her previous start. She's got the size to improve from two to three and shapes like a mile will suit her, for all that her pedigree wouldn't guarantee it.

I also wouldn't give up on the Oh So Sharp fifth **Double Lady**, who was one of a few caught out by the steady early gallop at Newmarket. Andre Fabre had brought her over with a view to testing her Guineas credentials, just as he did with Miss France a few years ago, and she'll be interesting if returning as her maiden form (split a couple of subsequent Group/Grade 3 winners on debut before winning easily second time out) reads well.

Aneen ran out a clear winner on her second start. She's a half-sister to last year's Irish 2,000 Guineas winner Awtaad and a mile should prove ideal this season, so she'd be of some interest if making the journey for Kevin Prendergast, but her owner does have Talaayeb as well so maybe they will be kept apart and Aneen held back for the Irish Guineas.

Shutter Speed saw out the mile well to make a winning debut on soft ground at Yarmouth. John Gosden feels she'll be better on a quicker surface and it's easy to concur given her pedigree (by Dansili out of an Oasis Dream mare). She does shape like she'll be suited by further than a mile this year, though.

The same could be true of stablemate **Icespire**. She came from the back of the field to win by four lengths on her debut over 7f at Salisbury and, although she probably didn't beat a great deal, Robert Havlin was very complimentary. She's certainly bred to be good, being by Frankel out of a half-sister to 1,000 Guineas winner Special Duty, but she's another with the negative of being a May foal.

Rockfel winner **Spain Burg** is now trained in the USA and **Delectation**, who won the Firth of Clyde for Bryan Smart, is now being trained in Germany. It's now unlikely either of those will be contesting the Guineas. The same no doubt goes for **Terrakova**, the second foal of Goldikova, who won well on her debut on the Polytrack at Chantilly. I expect she'll stay in France for the Pouliches.

1,000 Guineas

Newmarket, 7 May

	Bet365	*Betfred*	*Betway*	*Boyles*	*Coral*	*Hills*	*PPower*	*188bet*
Rhododendron	**9-2**	7-2	4	4	7-2	**9-2**	**9-2**	**9-2**
Wuheida	12	12	12	**14**	10	9	12	12
Fair Eva	**16**	**16**	14	14	**16**	12	**16**	12
Dabyah	**16**	**16**	14	**16**	**16**	12	14	**16**
Talaayeb	**20**	16	16	**20**	14	16	16	16
Brave Anna	**20**	**20**	**20**	16	**20**	16	**20**	18
Poet's Vanity	**20**	16	**20**	**20**	16	**20**	16	18
Queen Kindly	**20**	**20**	**20**	**20**	**20**	16	**20**	**20**
Roly Poly	16	16	16	14	**20**	16	16	16
Promise To Be True	16	**20**	16	16	16	**20**	**20**	18
Hydrangea	20	14	14	20	**25**	12	16	18
Intricately	20	20	**25**	20	**25**	14	20	18
Spatial	**33**	**33**	20	**33**	25	**33**	**33**	**33**
Cristal Fizz	33	-	33	-	25	33	-	**40**

each-way 1/4 odds, 1-2-3

Others on application, prices correct at time of going to press

Derby

WHILE I think Churchill will be difficult to beat in the Guineas, the Derby is another matter. I think he showed plenty of speed last year and may well stay 1m2f, but there has to be a question-mark over him being as effective over 1m4f.

There must even be a chance Churchill doesn't go to the Derby, sticking instead to a mile for the Irish Guineas and St James's Palace Stakes.

Aloft, who won the Queen's Vase, is a peculiar exception in terms of a Galileo-Storm Cat cross producing a horse at its best beyond 1m2f and that colt had at least hinted at being a strong stayer in the making in three starts over a mile at two. In contrast, Churchill has yet to run beyond 7f and to my eyes looks to have much more in common with the likes of 2015 Guineas winner Gleneagles.

Aidan O'Brien isn't short of other candidates for Epsom, though. For starters, he had the first three home in the Beresford Stakes.

The winner, **Capri**, went on to finish third in the Criterium de Saint-Cloud next time out and he was probably value for better than the bare form given he raced on a slower part of the track in the straight.

Runner-up **Yucatan** went on to fill the same position in the Racing Post Trophy, while the third, **Exemplar**, is a half-brother to Blue Bunting, who won the Irish and Yorkshire Oaks, so can't be knocked on his pedigree.

O'Brien also has **Sir John Lavery**, who was green on his debut but improved next time to win his maiden by seven lengths. He could be a potential contender.

So could **Venice Beach**, who made a most promising debut when second to **Titus** in a backend Leopardstown maiden. Dermot Weld considers the winner a potential Classic prospect, but with the Derby in mind the runner-up could be the one to take from the race as he looked far less streetwise but was eating up the ground at the finish. He's bred to be smart, being a half-brother to Arc and King George winner Danedream.

I think John Gosden holds a strong hand.

In a truly run race and a fast time, **CRACKSMAN** ran out an impressive winner on his debut at Newmarket last back end. Gosden said afterwards that he sees him as a 1m2f horse and might start him off in the conditions race at Newbury over that trip at the April meeting.

The question of the Derby was left open,

CAPRI (right): raced on a slower part of the track when winning the Beresford

GLENCADAM GOLD: one of several exciting entries for John Gosden, but could he be the one to wait for the King Edward VII like his sire Nathaniel?

but that Newbury race is one he's won in recent years with Western Hymn and the filly Star Of Seville, both of whom went on to run at Epsom, and it's early enough in the year to be able to fit in a Derby trial afterwards and give a horse more experience before the big day.

Cracksman is by Frankel, who seems to be getting his progeny to stay quite well, out of a mare who won a Listed race over 1m1f in heavy ground and is a half-sister to Halla San, who was placed in a Northumberland Plate and a couple of Chester Cups, so there's enough stamina there to suggest the Derby trip will by no means be beyond him.

As we know, trainers are often creatures of habit, so the route taken by Gosden with **Glencadam Glory** was interesting.

Back in 2010 he sent out Nathaniel to finish runner-up to Frankel on his debut at Newmarket and he chose the same race to introduce this son of Nathaniel. Glencadam Glory also finished second, seeing his race out well, and then went to Doncaster to run in the same maiden in which Nathaniel was narrowly beaten second time up.

This time Glencadam Glory came away with a win, benefiting from a good front-running ride from Frankie Dettori, and it was interesting to hear Gosden compare him favourably to his sire afterwards. At the time he held entries in the Royal Lodge and Racing Post Trophy but, as with Nathaniel, his trainer decided to put him away for the winter after two runs.

Nathaniel returned in the spring with a wide-margin maiden win followed by a narrow defeat in the Chester Vase. He then skipped the Derby for Royal Ascot, where he bolted up in the King Edward VII, and followed up in the King George. Whether Glencadam Glory will continue to take the same path remains to be seen, but let's just say it wouldn't be a shock to see him return in the Chester Vase in May.

The Nottingham maiden Gosden won

with Golden Horn in 2014 was named in honour of the Derby winner last year. There were two divisions and the stable won the first of them with **TARTINI**, who was surprisingly an unconsidered outsider.

There looked to be no fluke about his win, though, the time being significantly faster (3.53sec) than the second division and the first three finishing well clear of the fourth and fifth, who both went on to win their maidens next time out.

Despite showing signs of greenness, Tartini finished powerfully, stretching out really well, and there can be little doubt he will relish stepping up to middle distances this year. A half-brother to Derby fourth and St Leger winner Lucarno, Derby fourth and Great Voltigeur winner Thought Worthy and Long Distance Cup winner Flying Officer, he won't be short of stamina, but he's also by Giant's Causeway – his three siblings were all by Dynaformer – and that may have given him a little more speed, giving him a chance to improve on their Derby performances.

The other division of the Golden Horn maiden was won well by **Youmkin**, but the race was a bit of a sprint following a fairly steady early pace and it's hard to know what he achieved. He wouldn't be sure to stay 1m4f on pedigree either, being a brother to Champagne Stakes winner Saamidd.

Godolphin have one or two others to fire at the race, though. The Hugo Palmer-trained **Best Of Days**, who won the Royal Lodge and is bred to stay well, is the one with the form in the book and, being by Azamour out of a High Chaparral mare, he looks an obvious candidate.

There are some less exposed types waiting in the wings as well, although Jim Bolger's **Zorion** might just find the Derby trip stretching him a bit.

In contrast, the Roger Charlton-trained **Atty Persse** should be suited by going up to at least 1m2f this year. A son of Frankel, he impressed in winning at Sandown on his debut and was strong at the finish that day.

Big Challenge, trained by Saeed bin Suroor, won a backend Nottingham maiden in good style. He's a son of Sea The Stars and should also relish stepping up in distance.

Whether Sir Michael Stoute has a contender this year is hard to tell. **Crystal Ocean**, who is closely related to Crystal Capella and a half-brother to Hillstar, shaped quite well when narrowly beaten on his debut, while stablemate **Elucidation**, a half-brother to Unnefer, won his

Derby

Epsom, 3 June

	Bet365	*Betfred*	*Betway*	*Boyles*	*Coral*	*Hills*	*Lads*	*PPower*
Churchill	**6**	**6**	5	5	5	5	5	5
Waldgeist	16	16	**20**	-	16	16	16	**20**
Capri	**20**	16	16	14	16	**20**	16	**20**
Rivet	16	**20**	**20**	16	**20**	16	16	16
Yucatan	**20**	**20**	**20**	16	16	16	**20**	**20**
Sir John Lavery	**20**	**20**	**20**	**20**	16	**20**	**20**	14
Tartini	16	16	**25**	-	16	20	16	**25**
Cracksman	25	-	25	-	**33**	**33**	25	25
South Seas	**33**	-	25	25	25	-	25	-
Exemplar	**33**	**33**	25	-	**33**	-	25	20
Best Of Days	**33**	25	**33**	25	25	**33**	**33**	25
Mirage Dancer	**33**	-	**33**	**33**	**33**	**33**	**33**	**33**
Venice Beach	**33**	-	-	-	-	**33**	-	25
Atty Persse	**40**	-	33	-	33	**40**	33	33

each-way 1/4 odds, 1-2-3

Others on application, prices correct at time of going to press

TEMPLE CHURCH: the form of this Newbury win worked out well

maiden second time out at Leicester, but neither make strong appeal.

Temple Church and **Raheen House** drew clear of the other two runners in the Haynes, Hanson & Clark Stakes at Newbury and Brian Meehan's runner-up did the form no harm by winning his maiden next time up and then finishing fourth in the Racing Post Trophy.

Hughie Morrison suggested Temple Church would return in a Derby trial and both have the potential to make the Derby line-up, but to my eyes they look likelier candidates for the St Leger when their stamina will really come to the fore.

In contrast, I think 1m2f will be as far as **Eminent** wants to go and there must also be stamina doubts about the likes of **South Seas**, **Mirage Dancer**, **Cliffs Of Moher** and **Best Solution**.

I can see **Rivet** staying the Derby trip (the Fastnet Rock-Galileo cross has already produced an Epsom Classic winner in Qualify, who took the Oaks in 2015) but his connections' plans seem a bit up in the air at the moment and whether he gets the chance to prove it remains to be seen.

Andre Fabre has several horses entered including promising maiden winners **Aim True** and **Pharaonic** (half-brother to New Bay), while Group 3 winner **Akihiro** would be interesting if supplemented, but it appears the one he's planning to bring over is **Waldgeist**, who took the Group 1 Criterium de Saint-Cloud in October.

Coming at the end of the season and usually run in soft ground, the 1m2f invariably takes some getting and the form doesn't always work out, but Fabre clearly believes that Waldgeist is a Derby horse in the making. After the race, he said: "He is obviously a Derby type. I can see him performing well at the Curragh (in the Irish Derby), but he will be prepared for the Epsom Derby as well."

His pedigree leaves no doubt about his stamina and, from those comments, it seems it might just be the track at Epsom that slightly concerns his trainer.

Fabre also has an interesting unraced horse entered in **Meistersinger**, who's a half-brother to eight winners including Moonlight Magic and Masterstroke.

Two other unraced horses to look out for are the Gosden-trained 750,000gns purchase **Erdogan**, who's by Frankel out of Dar Re Mi and so a half-brother to So Mi Dar, and O'Brien's **Wisconsin**, who's by Deep Impact out of Peeping Fawn, a multiple Group 1 winner for the stable.

RHODODENDRON: won the Fillies' Mile well but now looks a bit too short

Oaks

RHODODENDRON heads the market for the Oaks but, with the form book suggesting there's not much between her and **Intricately** it's tempting to side with the latter at a much bigger price.

It was windy when Joseph O'Brien's filly won the Moyglare, the ground was on the soft side and Hydrangea wound the pace up from a fair way out, which I think suited Intricately's stamina. Her pedigree (by Fastnet Rock out of a Galileo mare) also suggests she'll be suited by middle distances this year and it's easy to see why the sharp mile on fast ground at Santa Anita didn't suit her on her final start.

The problem is that on balance I think **Rhododendron** is the better filly having improved on quicker ground when she beat Hydrangea in the Fillies' Mile. That said, the fact those three fillies kept beating each other last season might suggest none of them should be feared that much and the value lies elsewhere.

Coronet is shortest of the British-trained runners. She won well on her debut at Leicester and did what was required to take the Zetland Stakes next time. That bare form isn't anything special, but John Gosden said afterwards that he sees her as an Oaks filly and would target the Musidora with her, so she has to be respected.

Gosden also trains **Shutter Speed**, **Astronomy's Choice** and **Enable**, who all made winning debuts in backend maidens.

Shutter Speed isn't sure to stay 1m4f but the other two ought to get every yard. The Pretty Polly was mentioned as a likely starting off point for Astronomy's Choice, although it's worth noting that Gosden said he wasn't sure she'd be an Epsom type as she's a big, tall filly. Enable is by Nathaniel out of a Sadler's Wells mare and 1m4f might even turn out to be on the short side for her.

Backing Godolphin horses for the Classics hasn't exactly been a road to riches in recent seasons, but last year's merger of the Darley breeding operation with Godolphin racing under the stewardship of John Ferguson was intended to help get things back on track and they could well get a big boost this year because Charlie Appleby holds a strong hand in the Oaks.

WUHEIDA looked a smart sort when getting the better of Spatial on her debut at Newmarket and proved she was indeed a high-class filly when taking the Marcel Boussac second time out. While it's true she benefited from sitting close to the pace in a race that became a bit of a dash, she did well to overhaul the speedier Dabyah and it's worth remembering that she was the least experienced in the line-up.

She's by Dubawi out of a Singspiel mare who won the Ribblesdale, so her pedigree suggests she can only improve for a step up to middle distances this year, and while her trainer plans to start her off in the Guineas, it'll probably then be straight to Epsom, where she should excel.

SOBETSU seems to be held in similarly high regard to Wuheida and it's easy to see why. She bolted up by ten lengths in a fast time on her second start in a Newmarket maiden that's been won by some smart fillies in the past, including Midday and Taghrooda, and was given her Group 1 assignment in the Fillies' Mile.

Initially put in as a hot favourite, she did drift on the day (some observers said she was beginning to go in her coat) and was eventually sent off joint-favourite with the winner Rhododendron. In the event she failed to run her race, but she scoped dirty afterwards so it's easy to forgive her that.

She's another daughter of Dubawi and her dam, from the family of Generous, won at up to 1m3f and stayed even further, so she looks a real middle-distance prospect. It wouldn't be a surprise if she reappeared in the Pretty Polly or Musidora.

Really Special, trained by Saeed bin Suroor, had the speed to win over 6f on her debut but then stepped up to a mile to win the Listed Montrose Stakes. She's bred to stay, being out of a 2m winner, but isn't short of pace, as she showed when scoring over 7f out in Dubai earlier this year. It's hard to see her as an Oaks filly.

The maiden **Crimson Rock** won at Newbury last backend proved a real stamina test, the pace picking up from some way out in tacky ground. The first three finished clear and she did well to get off the mark at the first attempt after being carried right leaving the stalls.

A $1,000,000 purchase, she's closely related to Peeping Fawn, who was second in the Oaks and won four Group 1s over middle distances. She's clearly bred to be smart and stamina shouldn't be an issue, but Ralph Beckett said she would always appreciate a bit of cut and, while watering means that's not the huge issue it has been in the past, it makes me wonder whether the track will be ideal for her.

The third-placed finisher in that race, **Serenada**, is a sister to Musidora winner Liber Nauticus, who went on to finish fifth in the Oaks. She travelled best of all but just ran a bit green when asked to pick up. There's plenty more to come from her and she could easily become a contender on the back of a reappearance maiden win.

Rich Legacy, another trained by Beckett, didn't build on her May Hill win, finishing a well-beaten fourth in the Fillies' Mile and then beating only one home in the Criterium de Saint-Cloud, but perhaps she'd just had enough for the year by that stage. There's certainly enough stamina on her dam's side to balance out the speed from her sire Holy Roman Emperor and she might bounce back in a trial this season.

Luca Cumani doesn't have many winning debutantes, so there was plenty to like about **Aljezeera**'s first-time-out win at Doncaster. A 450,000gns daughter of Frankel out of a dual US Grade 1 turf winner, she was sent off odds-on and drew nicely clear in the closing stages. She's well regarded and could be anything.

Horseplay improved second time out for a step up in trip on soft ground, winning by 13 lengths. She may not have beaten much but it was still an eyecatching performance. Bred to stay well, being out of a mare who won at up to 1m5f and was runner-up in the Sagaro Stakes, she wouldn't be one to write off if the ground came up unseasonably testing in June.

On pedigree **Eziyra** has a fair chance of staying the Oaks trip as there's plenty of stamina on the dam's side, but Dermot Weld thinks she's a miler in the making.

The same goes for **Making Light**, who is by Tamayuz out of a 1m4f winning sister to Ribblesdale winner Irresistible Jewel but showed plenty of pace last year.

Others likely to fail on the stamina front include **Fair Eva**, **Spatial** and **Dabyah** as well as **Talaayeb**, who has prospects of staying on paper (dam is a Park Hill runner-up) but showed plenty of dash on her debut over 7f.

Sea Of Grace would have made some appeal but for being switched to be trained in France at the end of last year, while David Wachman's retirement from training has led to his impressive maiden winner **White Satin Dancer** joining her in being shipped across the Channel to France.

Another ex-Wachman filly, **Rain Goddess**, may still make the race as she's gone to Aidan O'Brien. She caused a bit of a surprise when winning on her debut at 50-1, but there was no fluke about it and, by Galileo out of a Danehill Dancer mare, she's bred along similar lines to Minding.

New stablemate **Promise To Be True** could come good this year, but as a sister to Maybe, who didn't convince on the stamina front when fifth in the Oaks, the distance must be a question mark.

Another Ballydoyle filly, **Longing**, is currently unraced, but she's a 1,000,000gns daughter of Galileo out of a French 1m2½f winner and worth looking out for.

There are also a couple of unraced Frankel fillies worth noting. **Mori**, trained by Sir Michael Stoute, is the second foal of Midday and therefore a half-sister to Midterm, who spent last winter as Derby favourite, while Roger Varian's **Nothing But Dreams** is the first foal of Danedream.

Portfolio

2,000 Guineas

Swiss Storm 1pt e-w 33-1
(generally)

Larchmont Lad 1pt e-w 50-1
(Hills)

1,000 Guineas

Talaayeb 2pts 20-1
(bet365, Boyles)

Cristal Fizz 1pt 40-1
(188Bet)

Derby

Cracksman 2pts 33-1
(Coral, Hills)

Tartini 1pt e-w 25-1
(Betway, Paddy Power)

Oaks

Sobetsu 2pts 33-1
(bet365, Paddy Power)

Wuheida 1pt 16-1
(Ladbrokes, Paddy Power)

Oaks

Epsom, 2 June

	Bet365	*Betfred*	*Betway*	*Boyles*	*Coral*	*Hills*	*Lads*	*PPower*
Rhododendron	7	7	6	**8**	**8**	6	6	7
Coronet	10	10	10	**12**	**12**	**12**	**12**	**12**
Wuheida	14	14	14	14	14	12	**16**	**16**
Crimson Rock	**20**	**20**	16	16	**20**	16	16	16
Hydrangea	14	14	14	12	16	12	**20**	12
Intricately	**20**	-	**20**	**20**	-	-	**20**	**20**
Talaayeb	**20**	-	**20**	**20**	14	-	16	16
Eziyra	**20**	**20**	**20**	**20**	16	**20**	16	**20**
Really Special	16	-	**20**	**20**	-	**20**	16	**20**
Promise To Be True	16	16	20	16	16	**25**	20	20
Rich Legacy	**25**	-	**25**	**25**	20	-	**25**	**25**
Sea Of Grace	**25**	**25**	**25**	**25**	20	20	20	**25**
Aljezeera	25	25	25	25	25	25	25	**33**
Sobetsu	**33**	-	20	16	25	25	25	**33**

each-way 1/4 odds, 1-2-3

Others on application, prices correct at time of going to press

Est. 1909
RACING & FOOTBALL OUTLOOK

Nick Watts's horses to follow

BLUE POINT 3 b c

Shamardal – Scarlett Rose (Royal Applause)
112123-

The Commonwealth Cup is already on the agenda for this horse and you can understand why. He ran well in the Dewhurst on his last start, but the 7f trip definitely stretched him, so it makes sense to keep him doing what he does best. Before that he had won three of his five starts, producing his best performance in the Gimcrack at York when he scored to victory over Mokarris by three lengths. This is a top sprinter in the making.

Charlie Appleby, Newmarket

BREAKABLE 6 ch m

Firebreak – Magic Myth (Revoque)
635412115-

It was a tale of two halves for this mare last season. For the first half of the campaign she promised but didn't quite deliver. However, in the second half there was no stopping her as she won three times, twice under Rachel Richardson and once under David Allan. All of her wins came at around the mile mark and she is one to bear in mind for the latter part of the season when the ground has a bit of cut in it. Thoroughly genuine, she starts the season on a mark of 96 and her winning hasn't stopped yet.

Tim Easterby, Great Habton

BRUTAL 3 b c

Pivotal – Loreto (Holy Roman Emperor)
42215-

This useful colt has entries in the Irish 2,000 Guineas and the Derby and, while he needs to improve to win either of those, it's possible he might. He ran well on his first three starts last season but then put it all together on his fourth run, winning a Leopardstown maiden easily. That display earned him a crack at the Racing Post Trophy and, although he was sent off at 40-1, he ran a cracker to finish fifth, beaten a shade over three lengths. He might just have been a late bloomer.

Ger Lyons, Co Meath

CAPTAIN POWER 5 b g

Captain Rio – Invincible Power (Invincible Spirit)

0521705-

A horse who has won his fair share but always gives the impression he has more left in him. He was first past the post twice last season, although he was disqualified after victory at Naas in August for causing interference. That seemed harsh, but he soon made amends by winning next time out at Leopardstown. A nervy type who gets on well with Robbie Downey, he is most effective over 6f and handles cut in the ground. His trainer is a dab hand with sprinters and could have another useful one on his hands.

Edward Lynam, Co Meath

CRACKSMAN 3 b c

Frankel – Rhadegunda (Pivotal)

1-

Not all of Frankel's progeny went on last season, but this one looks like he'll get better and better with time. He is out of a Listed winner and carries the same colours as Golden Horn. Last season he was restricted to just one appearance, but it was a winning one as he took a Newmarket maiden comfortably, beating Wild Tempest by a length and a quarter. The fourth, Stradivarius, has won since and the form should work out. This year he should be effectiver over 1m2f and possibly a Derby trip.

John Gosden, Newmarket

DON'T TOUCH 5 b g

Dutch Art – Expressive (Falbrav)

151045-

This gelding may not quite be top-class yet but he's not far off and still on an upward curve. He won at Listed level last season, beating the useful Danzeno, and wasn't disgraced in two hot races towards the end of the season. Fourth behind Shalaa in a Group 3 in October, he then dropped a place in the Champions Sprint on his last start but was beaten only a length and three-quarters by The Tin Man at the line. A Group 1 may not be out of the question this season, possibly the Sprint Cup at Haydock.

Richard Fahey, Musley Bank

DUTCH CONNECTION 5 ch h

Dutch Art – Endless Love (Dubai Destination)

2921560-

A rock-solid Group 2 performer, this horse ended last season on a negative, but he was probably slightly overfaced and is better judged on his earlier form. He won the Lennox Stakes at Goodwood, a perfect race for him (7f Group 2) and wasn't disgraced in the Summer Mile when second behind Mutakayyef. It's debatable as to whether he truly sees out a mile, but with another year on his back he might do and that would open up many more options. If nothing else, though, make sure you back him to retain his Lennox title at Goodwood.

Charlie Hills, Lambourn

EZIYRA 3 ch f

Teofilo – Eytarna (Dubai Destination)

2121-

Dermot Weld, the master of Galway, always lines up a useful filly up for the 7f fillies' maiden at Galway and 2016 was no different. Eziyra was just 2-5 to win it, but there was strength in depth to the race, with runner-up Hydrangea later placing in the Moyglare and Fillies' Mile. She wound up her season with an easy win in the Group 3 Weld Stakes at the Curragh and there's little doubt that on pedigree she will be well suited to middle distances this year. An Oaks, whether domestically or at Epsom, must be on the agenda.

Dermot Weld, The Curragh

FRANKUUS 3 gr c

Frankel – Dookus (Linamix)

1534118-

After making a winning debut at Haydock, this Frankel colt then didn't appear to go on, being beaten in his next three outings. However, he got the show back on the road with a Listed win at Haydock in September and then repeated the feat in a Group 3 at Chantilly on his next start. Those wins may have taken a toll on him as he was below par on his final start of the campaign at Saint-Cloud, but this strong stayer has more Group success in him this season. He seems to handle any type of ground.

Mark Johnston, Middleham

GLASTONBURY SONG 3 ch c

Casamento – Nesmeh (More Than Ready)

1-

More and more Irish horses are using Dundalk in the formative stages of their careers and this Casamento three-year-old did exactly that in September last year. The word was out about him beforehand as he was sent off at 4-6 and he won like an odds-on shot should do, beating Chelsea Corsage by two and a quarter lengths. Jockey Colin Keane admitted they had hoped for a performance like that and it will be fascinating to see how his career develops. The Irish 2,000 Guineas may be his first big target.

Ger Lyons, Co Meath

IDAHO 4 b c

Galileo – Hveger (Danehill)

23321U5-

Last year's Derby third may well have landed the St Leger but for unseating Seamie Heffernan when poised to challenge. Earlier on he had won the Great Voltigeur having shown tremendous consistency to finish placed in the Ballysax, Derrinstown, Derby and Irish Derby. His brother, Highland Reel, really came of age as a four-year-old, so it is to be hoped that Idaho can do the same. All middle-distance races should be on his agenda, although there's always the possibility he might get a Cup trip in time.

Aidan O'Brien, Ballydoyle

LOST IN SILENCE 3 b f

Holy Roman Emperor – Suitably Discreet (Mr Prospector)

218-

From one of the best Moyglare families, this filly was promising last season if you ignore an obviously below-par run at Listowel on her final start of the season. Prior to that she had been a good second at Limerick on her debut behind the useful Ellery Lane before getting off the mark on her next outing at the Galway Festival, edging out Delegating by half a length. She doesn't have any fancy entries but might not be badly handicapped off a mark of 79 and could make her mark in the summer on quick ground.

Dermot Weld, Co Kildare

MASSAYAN 4 ch c

Iffraaj – Masiyma (Dalakhani)

611-

This lightly raced four-year-old made a low-key debut at the Curragh but won both his subsequent starts by a neck and a head. That shows how tough he is and there should be plenty more to come from him this season. His dam was a 1m4f winner and he is also related to plenty of stayers, so he should be perfectly at home over 1m6f or further this year. It's difficult to tell how far he can go, but Listed/Group 3 races might be an option for him and, although both his wins came on soft ground, he should handle better conditions.

Dermot Weld, Co Kildare

MIRSAALE 7 ch g

Sir Percy – String Quartet (Sadler's Wells)

3711308-

This dual-purpose performer might need a rest after a busy jumping campaign, but he was expertly nurtured back to top form on the Flat last season, winning at Catterick and Ripon. He then went for the Ascot Stakes shortly afterwards and, while he didn't cut much ice there, he did regain the winning thread when transferred to jumps in the autumn, winning twice at Perth. Officially rated 97, he may need to drop a few pounds before becoming effective again, but you can be assured his shrewd trainer will find some winning opportunities for him.

Keith Dalgleish, South Lanarkshire

MOONLIGHT MAGIC 4 b c

Cape Cross – Melikah (Lammtarra)

5106363-

A season that promised much after a convincing win in the Derrinstown never really delivered thereafter. He finished last in the Derby and wasn't much better in the Irish Derby or the Irish Champion Stakes. Either side of those efforts he did perform slightly better, with a brace of thirds in the Royal Whip and the Prix Daniel Wildenstein. Maybe with a bit of time off and another year on his back, his wily trainer can coax him back to his best. The Derby can take some getting over and he is a superbly bred horse whose time may come again.

Jim Bolger, Co Carlow

MOOTAHARER 4 b c

Dubawi – Tahrir (Linamix)

21/-

Charlie Hills must have been deeply disappointed that he was unable to get this half-brother to the brilliant Muhaarar on to the track at all last season. However, his patience can be rewarded now. Mootaharer showed promise in a brief two-year-old career, winning easily at Newmarket on his second start, but is a different sort to his illustrious sibling in that he will be fine over a mile and possibly further in time. There's not much racecourse evidence to go on, but it's entirely possible he'll be up to Group 1 class by the time the autumn comes around.

Charlie Hills, Lambourn

MULK 4 ch g

New Approach – Nannina (Medicean)

219-

A daughter of Group 1 winner Nannina, Mulk began the season well, finishing second in a strong edition of the Wood Ditton, splitting Sky Kingdom (a subsequent Group 3 winner) and Muntahaa (fourth in the St Leger). He then thrashed Exoteric at Chester's May meeting and that earned him a crack at the Tercentenary Stakes, in which he disappointed when finishing only ninth. Sir Michael Stoute didn't run him again but is a master at bringing horses back at four-year-olds and this one is still worth following on the evidence of that early-season promise.

Sir Michael Stoute, Newmarket

ORDER OF ST GEORGE 5 b h

Galileo – Another Storm (Gone West)

111234-

As long as this horse stays fit, he could win the Ascot Gold Cup for many years to come. On the day that mattered he was far too good for the best stayers around, showing a great turn of foot up the centre of the track to beat Mizzou by three lengths. Although beaten at odds of 1-7 in the Irish Leger, he again showed his class in the Arc on his next outing when third behind Found. It wouldn't be surprising if he was feeling the effects of that by the time he ran at Ascot on Champions Day and that defeat shouldn't be held against him. A truly top-class stayer.

Aidan O'Brien, Ballydoyle

PRECIOUS RAMOTSWE 3 b f

Nathaniel – Miss Pinkerton (Danehill)

1-

John Gosden isn't averse to introducing a top newcomer in the middle of winter and he may have done it again here with this daughter of Nathaniel. She made her debut just before Christmas at Kempton and won easily, defeating Flight Of Fantasy by upwards of two lengths. She is well bred, out of a daughter of Rebecca Sharp, and while a lack of big-race entries makes it difficult to know exactly how good she might be, the visual evidence of her debut victory was very convincing. She should be noted carefully.

John Gosden, Newmarket

RAINBOW LEGACY 3 b c

Frankel – Gift Range (Spectrum)

0-

This is a slightly speculative suggestion as he beat only one horse home on his only racecourse start and the losing margin was almost 20 lengths. However, he was only 7-2 to win that day so clearly better was expected and it could have been the good to soft ground that wasn't to his liking. He is in the 2,000 Guineas and Derby and his breeding is exceptional – his dam is a full-sister to Golan and Derby runner-up Tartan Bearer – so let's put that debut down to experience and expect better when we next see him.

Sir Michael Stoute, Newmarket

RIBCHESTER 4 b c

Iffraaj – Mujarah (Marju)

531312-

It's amazing to think that this horse went off at 33-1 when third in the 2,000 Guineas. He made relentless improvement thereafter, winning the Jersey on his next start and almost taking the Sussex Stakes. Continuing to progress, he then notched his first Group 1 win in the Jacques le Marois before winding up with a second to Minding in the QEII. That is a top-class season and there's no reason why he won't be better still this year with another year on his back. Redemption in the Sussex Stakes might be his first objective.

Richard Fahey, Musley Bank

SEA WOLF 5 b g

Amadeus Wolf – Rose De France (Diktat)

21010-

This gelding moved to Ireland from the Michael Dods stable last season and it paid immediate dividends with a handicap win over 7f at the Curragh. Although below-par at Galway on his next start, he then went back to the Curragh again for the Irish Cambridgeshire and showed his liking for the venue when taking the race by half a length at the expense of Sikandarabad. He again failed to back up that run on his final start in an Ascot handicap behind Yuften, but look out for him back at the Curragh, possibly in a Listed race.

Ger Lyons, Co Meath

TWILIGHT PAYMENT 4 b c

Teofilo – Dream On Buddy (Oasis Dream)

423121-

This is a stayer definitely going places. He was a 20-1 shot for the Queen's Vase at Royal Ascot, but he ran a cracker to finish third behind Sword Fighter and never looked back thereafter. He shed his maiden tag at the Curragh on his next start and then gave Order Of St George a good race in a Group 3. On his final start of the campaign he took the scalp of Forgotten Rules in a Listed event. While it's a pity he never went for the St Leger, he should be fresh to do battle this season in all Listed/Group contests over 1m6f or further.

Jim Bolger, Co Carlow

SHUTTER SPEED 3 br f
Dansili – Photographic (Oasis Dream)
1-

Yarmouth has sometimes witnessed the debut of some great horses – Raven's Pass and Noble Mission to name but two. Shutter Speed could be the latest after she won there last October. Apparently she had gone in her coat and wouldn't have enjoyed the soft ground, so she was pretty much winning on talent alone. She has entries in the 1,000 Guineas and the Oaks and, while she has a way to go before justifying either of those, this well-bred daughter of Dansili could be a smart horse in the making.

John Gosden, Newmarket

SNOANO 5 b g
Nayef – White Dress (Pivotal)
0426414260518-

This gelding was kept very busy last season with 13 outings, but he responded by winning twice – in the Queen Mother's Cup at York and later in the season at Ayr. Interestingly, both of his victories came on good to soft ground, so he is definitely one to look out for when there is a bit of cut. He starts the season on a mark of 95 – 3lb higher than his last winning mark – but he took a while to hit top form last year and if it is the same story this time around then he will be well treated by the time his turn comes.

Tim Easterby, Great Habton

VENICE BEACH 3 b c
Galileo – Danedrop (Danehill)
2-

This half-brother to Arc winner Danedream must have been slow to come to hand last season as he didn't make his debut until October in a mile maiden at Leopardstown. He was the outsider of Aidan O'Brien's five runners, too, so it seems fairly obvious that not much was expected of him. However, he ran a cracker to be beaten half a length into second by Titus and that augurs well for the future. The first half of the season may come too soon for him, but maybe a Queen's Vase/Gordon Stakes/St Leger kind of season may be in store.

Aidan O'Brien, Ballydoyle

WAR DECREE 3 b c
War Front – Royal Decree (Street Cry)
121-

This horse has slightly gone under the radar, but he didn't do a lot wrong as a juvenile, winning two of his three starts, with the only blemish coming at Newmarket in the Superlative Stakes when beaten by Boynton. He recovered from that on his last start when beating Thunder Snow comfortably in the Vintage Stakes at Goodwood, after which his jockey Ryan Moore said he was "a colt with a good future". He has all the right entries for this season and might be one for the Irish 2,000 Guineas at the end of May.

Aidan O'Brien, Ballydoyle

WINGS OF DESIRE 4 ch c

Pivotal – Gull Wing (In The Wings)

311429-

This colt came a long way in a short space of time last season, winning a Wolverhampton maiden in April before contesting the Derby barely a month later. In between he had won the Dante, thereby justifying his trip to Epsom. He didn't fare badly there, finishing fourth, and he backed that up with a great effort when second to Highland Reel in th King George. Below-par in the Juddmonte International on his latest start, he is still very much one to watch this season and is a genuine Group 1 horse.

John Gosden, Newmarket

YUFTEN 6 b g

Invincible Spirit – Majestic Sakeena (King's Best)

2104941-

This six-year-old has always been a useful horse despite being moved round the houses a bit. He started off life with William Haggas, moved to Johnny Murtagh and has finished up with Roger Charlton, who did well with him in two runs last season. He finished fourth in a Newmarket handicap before winning at Ascot in October when he comfortably won the Balmoral Handicap, beating Remarkable by a length. Charlton is very adept with these older horses and will place him to advantage this season, probably in big handicaps.

Roger Charlton, Beckhampton

ZORION 3 b c

Smart Strike – Zofzig (Danzig)

1-

Although it was only a maiden at Roscommon he won last August, there's every chance that Zorion is a lot better than that and will prove that to be the case this season. He's well-bred, being a brother to Zip Top, and he attracted some positive quotes after his victory, with the trainer's representative stating "he's a colt we like and one with a future". Entries in the Irish 2,000 Guineas and Irish Derby indicate the esteem in which he is held and, although there's not much talk about him at the moment, there might be before too long.

Jim Bolger, Co Carlow

Top ten horses

Blue Point
Frankuus
Idaho
Massayan
Order Of St George
Rainbow Legacy
Shutter Speed
Twilight Payment
Venice Beach
Wings Of Desire

JACK HOBBS: the brilliant 2015 Irish Derby winner can make up for lost time

Newmarket by Aborigine

IRISH Derby winner **Jack Hobbs** heads a strong Clarehaven team that can enable *JOHN GOSDEN* to regain the trainers' championship crown wrested from him by Aidan O'Brien last year.

As a three-year-old Jack Hobbs ran a tremendous race to finish second to Golden Horn in the Derby before crossing the Irish Sea to win the Curragh equivalent by five lengths.

Things did not go so well for him as a four-year-old because he was sidelined after not firing and being pulled up in the Jockey Club Stakes at Newmarket.

Gosden nursed him back during the summer and his one run in the autumn produced a highly creditable third to Almanzor in the Champion Stakes at Ascot.

He's all set to run in the Sheema Classic in Dubai and that should provide him with a launching pad to all the top 1m2f-1m4f races this year.

Gosden has a sure touch with quality fillies and is full of optimism about his Classic hopeful **Coronet**.

This unbeaten daughter of Dubawi had always looked the part in her work and confirmed that promise with an impressive winning debut at Lingfield in September. After that confidence booster she won a Listed race at Newmarket as she pleased and was then put away for the winter.

Gosden will not be rushing her and tells me the plan is to wait for the Musidora, in which she will not carry a penalty, and then on to Epsom for the Oaks if she fulfils her promise.

The Dansili filly **Shutter Speed** is more of a dark horse after her one run resulted in a smooth success at Yarmouth in October. Despite running green, she stayed on to beat Song Maker by a neck over a mile on soft ground and she adds further strength to Gosden's team of three-year-old fillies, as does the Prix Marcel Boussac third **Dabyah**, who could return to France for the Prix D'Essai des Pouliches.

Among the older horses, Gosden will be looking to last year's Musidora winner **So Mi Dar** as one of main weapons.

Last year his Dubawi filly did her owner-breeders, the Lloyd-Webbers proud with three wins despite a mid-season injury that caused her to miss the Oaks.

The intention is to get her ready for the Middleton Stakes back at York and then go in search of Group 1 success at home and abroad.

WILLIAM HAGGAS holds out high hopes for **Dal Harraild**, who isn't yet fully appreciated.

The Champs Elysees gelding was precocious enough to score as a juvenile but progressed even more as a three-year-old with three wins from six starts. Two of those were gained in handicaps at Musselburgh and Goodwood, but it was his final effort at Newmarket that marked him as a budding star when, stepped up to Listed company at Newmarket, he readily pulled clear of Barsanti.

Haggas reports that he has thrived during the winter and the plan is to start him off in the Yorkshire Cup. Though Dal Harraild won on soft ground as a juvenile, his trainer insists he will prove most formidable on fast summer ground.

Haggas also singled **Zwayyan** out for a favourable mention.

The good-looking son of Pivotal took some time to come to hand and did not run as a juvenile. It was not until his fourth appearance that he revealed his potential, showing his appreciation of a step up in trip to take a Lingfield maiden by two lengths from Prosecute before winning a handicap at Haydock.

His final run resulted in a creditable fifth

SO MI DAR: goes for the Middleton Stakes before tackling Group 1 company

DAL HARRAILD (right): will start off in the Yorkshire Cup and is exciting

to God Willing on the Rowley Mile, where he did not handle the Dip.

His progress over the winter has been significant and he can work his way through handicaps into Pattern races.

Haggas knows a decent filly when he sees one having landed the 2011 Oaks with Dancing Rain, who made all the running to win under Johnny Murtagh, and **Dynamic** could earn herself a tilt at the Epsom Classic.

There was a lot to like about her only juvenile run at Newbury, where she was putting in all her best work in the closing stages to finish a neck third to Di Alta over a mile on soft ground. Considering she met trouble in running, that was highly promising and, once she is stepped up in trip, she will start fulfilling her immense potential.

SIR MICHAEL STOUTE has his usual strong team of older horses.

Arab Spring has had a busy start to the year, finishing second in the Winter Derby Trial at Lingfield before a trip to Qatar, and he could be in for an exciting year.

Convey paid his way last year with a Listed win at Pontefract and his work on the Waterhall gallop in the early months of the year confirmed that he has another profitable campaign ahead of him.

ROGER VARIAN has moved into the Carlburg Stables formerly owned by Clive Brittain up the Bury Road.

Varian has already proved himself with a steady stream of top-class winners, most notably **Postponed**.

The winner of the 2015 King George for Luca Cumani, he was then switched to Varian, who sent him out to win his first four races last year including the Juddmonte International before a lacklustre display when only fifth to Found in the Arc.

Varian is plotting a similar route, with his trip to Dubai for the Sheema Classic followed by the Coronation Cup, but thistime he can hopefully take in the King George,which he missed last year following a setback.

LUCA CUMANI holds out high hopes for **Gorgeous Noora**, whose one run last year was a staying-on third to Really Special at Chelmsford.

That might not seem particularly encouraging, but the way she has developed during the winter indicates she will rise to far greater heights. She is an exciting prospect.

WILLIAM JARVIS has a couple of hard-hitting handicappers in Cold Snap and Wimpole Hall, who could pick up some decent prizes as the season progresses.

Jarvis is particularly keen on the four-year-old **Cold Snap**.

Unraced as a juvenile, he quickly started making up for lost time when he won a decent 6f Windsor maiden by three-quarters of a length from He's My Cracker. He has had his issues but has wintered well and is well handicapped.

Jarvis feels that he will develop into a top sprinter, but he will be at his best on fast ground.

Wimpole Hall will need further but contributed to his keep last season with wins at Kempton in June and Sandown in August. You can forget his last run when down the field on the Rowley Mile as he was feeling the effects of a busy season.

He has been gelded and a valuable handicap around the 1m2f mark should be well within his capabilities.

MARTYN MEADE has made an immediate impression since his arrival in Newmarket a couple of years back and his handling of **Aclaim** was commendable, allowing him to work his way up through handicaps into Pattern company.

After winning a hot Ascot handicap in September, he justified market support with a smooth length win over Lumiere in the Group 2 Challenge Stakes here on the Rowley Mile.

Looking at him on the Heath, it is evident he has strengthened during the winter and the bold decision to step him up in class could pay handsome dividends in the Lockinge back at Newbury.

DAVID ELSWORTH believes that **Swiss Storm**, now part-owned by Godolphin along with Trevor Harris's Lordship Stud, has a bright future.

This son of Frankel is a fine, strong sort – like his sire – and went in comfortably over 7f at Newbury after finding 6f too sharp on his debut at Haydock.

All being well, Elsworth will use the Greenham Stakes on the Berkshire course as a stepping stone to a tilt at the 2,000 Guineas.

Sir Dancealot, another fine, strong colt, should also pay his way, starting off in the Free Handicap.

ED DUNLOP is pleased with the way **Amazing Red** has wintered.

This half-brother to the stable's globe-trotting hero Red Cadeaux is also the type to improve with age. Unraced as a two-year-old, his win over Timekeeping at Pontefract on his second start augured well for the future, as does the work he has been putting in up the Al Bahathri Polytrack.

Mudallel is another to follow from Dunlop's yard as the 380,000gns son of Invincible Spirit is clearly going the right way at home.

JAMES TATE has quickly established himself as an up-and-coming young trainer and **Via Via** is one to watch.

She was a 6-1 winning nap at Newmarket in the autumn and Tate tells me he will use her favourable handicap mark before going for Listed races.

ALAN BAILEY works wonders with the moderate material at his disposal and his useful sprinter **Go Far** can bring 'the Captain', as he is affectionately known, further sprinting success this year.

A winner of the Ayr Bronze Cup in 2015, his work confirms he has retained his sparkle and he is at his best on fast ground.

PAUL D'ARCY'S multiple all-weather winner **Spring Loaded** suffered a minor stress fracture in January, so D'Arcy has had to bypass the Sprint on Good Friday at Lingfield.

He's very smart on his day and well handicapped back on turf, though D'Arcy may forego that initially, pencilling in a Listed race at Chester for his possible comeback in midsummer.

MARK TOMPKINS enjoyed some good results on the all-weather over the winter and two of his winners, **Lost The Moon** and **Bracken Brae**, have the ability to continue their progress on grass.

Hot off the Heath

Coronet

Gorgeous Noora

Swiss Storm

Ireland by Jerry M

AIDAN O'BRIEN has his usual strong team of three-year-olds and the headline act, as the short-priced favourite for the Qipco 2,000 Guineas and winter favourite for the Derby, is **Churchill**, who looks a more robust colt than Air Force Blue 12 months ago.

Winner of five of his six starts last season, he gradually improved through the season and his victory in the Dewhurst was outstanding. Not a lot went right for him in the race, but he stayed on strongly to beat a quality field which included subsequent Breeders' Cup Juvenile Turf runner-up Lancaster Bomber as well as subsequent Group 1 winners Thunder Snow and Rivet.

He has none of the stamina doubts of Air Force Blue last year and, if he's at his best, the question will not be whether he wins but whether he does so in a manner that puts him forward as a realistic contender to follow up at Epsom.

Caravaggio has more in common with Air Force Blue but connections can avoid the same pitfalls by training him for a sprint campaign. Brilliantly impressive in an unbeaten juvenile campaign which included victories in the Coventry Stakes and Phoenix Stakes, he will surely be aimed at the Commonwealth Cup.

Instead the other Guineas candidates from Ballydoyle will probably be **War Decree**, not seen since beating Thunder Snow in the Vintage Stakes at Goodwood in July, and the totally unexposed **Cliffs Of Moher**, impressive winner of a backend Leopardstown maiden.

Apart from Churchill, the most obvious Derby prospect from the stable is the Galileo colt **Capri**.

He enjoyed a good season last year with three wins and the attitude he showed in grinding out those victories bodes well. The doubt is whether he is quick enough to win a Derby – he seemed to get a little outpaced in the 1m2f Criterium de Saint-Cloud when last seen in October – but he should certainly be a leading St Leger contender.

Yucatan has every chance of being a Derby horse, even though he is out of the brilliant miler Six Perfections and has little stamina on that side of his pedigree. A late starter last year, he made rapid progress to chase home Capri in the Beresford Stakes and Rivet in the Racing Post Trophy so there is every chance he could improve further this year.

Expect a good bit of improvement as well from the twice-raced **Sir John Lavery**, a runaway winner of a Gowran maiden and a good middle-distance prospect.

Quite where **Lancaster Bomber** fits in is more difficult to ascertain and a US Classic bid could be considered for a horse likely to excel over at least 1m2f.

Nothing among O'Brien's fillies looks like another Minding, but **Rhododendron** is certainly consistent and, on good ground or quicker, she would be the most convincing 1,000 Guineas contender.

A gradual improver last season, she put up her best performance when tackling the Guineas trip for the first time in readily landing the Fillies' Mile in October from her stablemate Hydrangea, looking far better than when beating the same rival on much softer ground in the Debutante Stakes at the Curragh.

Brave Anna boasts the same official rating (116) as Rhododendron, 1lb ahead of stablemate Roly Poly after a short-head separated them in the Cheveley Park Stakes at Newmarket. Both fillies are in the 1,000 Guineas betting but there would have to be some doubt about either getting the mile.

Promise To Be True could do very well

ACAPULCO (right): has joined Ballydoyle from the Wesley Ward yard

over middle distances. Her dam was a sprinter and she's a sister to a pair of good winners who failed to get further than a mile, but she is a close relative of Oaks winner Dancing Rain and Derby winner Dr Devious. She came up short in Group 1 company, but her excellent and perhaps slightly unlucky second in the Prix Marcel Boussac at Chantilly gives hope that she could be effective over further.

The hole left in the Ballydoyle older brigade with the retirement of Found is more than filled by the news that **Minding** will come back for a four-year-old campaign.

This filly is top-class over a wide range of trips, but she is likely to be aimed at all the top 1m-1m2f races, with the latter perhaps her optimum trip.

The return of high-class fillies **Seventh Heaven** and **Alice Springs** means that the strength in depth among the stable's older fillies is impressive and will probably free up Minding to take on the boys.

Over 1m4f, the globetrotting **Highland Reel** might just be kept at home a little more for prizes such as the Coronation Cup and the King George, while it will also be interesting to see what Derby runner-up **US Army Ranger** can achieve this season as he is yet to fulfil his true ability.

O'Brien's team of sprinters is greatly boosted by the arrival of **Acapulco**, the breathtaking 2015 Queen Mary winner who has joined from Wesley Ward. She will be aimed at the King's Stand before heading off to the paddocks.

Washington DC is also back for more having finished second in the Prix de l'Abbaye last season.

Also staying in training is the Ascot Gold Cup winner **Order Of St George**, who will defend his crown, while **Idaho** is another fascinating staying prospect as he should get two miles without any problems.

The retirement of dual Derby winner Harzand and Champion Stakes winner Fascinating Rock leaves a huge hole at the top of *DERMOT WELD*'s team, so hopes seem to rest a good deal on the return in full health of **Zawraq**.

The one-time leading Derby hopeful made no more than a satisfactory return in the Trigo Stakes at Leopardstown last autumn, but that second place at least gives Weld something to build upon after all the five-year-old's injury problems.

The 2015 Ascot Gold Gup third **Forgotten Rules** is another horse bidding to

TWILIGHT PAYMENT: beat Forgotten Rules last season and is an Irish Leger type

make up for lost time. His campaign never really got off the ground last year, but at his best he can still be a force in the staying division.

The Aga Khan's filly **Eziyra** could well be the best of Weld's three-year-olds. She progressed through the season, culminating in a taking success on heavy ground in the Park Stakes at the Curragh in September. She may well be equally efficient on better ground and looks likely to be prepared for the Irish 1,000 Guineas.

Making Light is another promising filly having won two of her three starts, including when beating the colts in the Group 3 Killavullan Stakes at Leopardstown, while **Tempera** and **Titus**, both backend maiden winners at that track, could also make a mark.

JIM BOLGER has an interesting team and his three-year-olds look strong over middle distances.

The Eyrefield Stakes winner **Dubai Sand** is likely to stay well and could be aimed at the Irish Derby, while **Holistic Approach** did extremely well to win a Curragh maiden over an inadequate trip in October and can make an impact despite a very disappointing effort at Leopardstown.

Very impressive Roscommon maiden winner **Zorion** should be effective at a mile and is likely to be seen in an early Classic trial, as is Curragh maiden winner **Vociferous Marina**.

The prospects for the older horses from Coolcullen should be enhanced by the return of the filly **Turret Rocks**. She disappointed after her initial effort in last season's 1,000 Guineas but much better is expected this season.

Tribal Beat could make a mark over a mile. His disappointing effort at Leopardstown on Champions Weekend should not detract from what he achieved in winning last summer's Desmond Stakes after ten months off and he could still be exciting.

Twilight Payment could be an Irish St Leger horse on the strength of his win over Forgotten Rules in the Loughbrown Stakes in September.

Only Aidan O'Brien had more individual juvenile winners last season than *GER LYONS* and, while quite a few of those will not be returning to Glenburnie this season, some significant ones do.

Psychedelic Funk was the best of Lyons's early-season juveniles and did very little wrong apart from a sub-standard effort in the National Stakes. He may get another chance to see if he can do anything over 7f but may well be best over sprint trips.

Glastonbury Song showed an impressive turn of foot to win his sole start at Dundalk and may well have a spring Classic trial on his radar.

Among the older brigade, it is good to see **Ardhoomey** back. He came through a busy campaign well last year and looks likely to acquit himself well in the better sprints this season.

MICHAEL HALFORD looks as though he will have a very nice bunch of three-year-olds this season, headed by the unbeaten **Ambassadorial**.

This Godolphin colt could be exciting on the basis of winning twice at Dundalk last year, the second of which was a convincing success in the Listed Star Appeal Stakes in October.

Rehana was impressive when beating Rhododendron in a Curragh maiden in June. She didn't really repeat that form on softer ground later in the season but could be a different proposition on quicker ground over the summer.

A dark horse from the stable could be **Yulong Xiongyin**, an unextended winner of a Dundalk maiden in December on his sole start.

Irish 2,000 Guineas winner Awtaad will not be an easy one for *KEVIN PRENDERGAST* to replace, but he has a potentially exciting filly in **Aneen**.

Unlucky on her debut in a hot maiden at Leopardstown on Champions Weekend, she put a big field to the sword in a Curragh maiden the following month and could be very good.

The flagbearer for *JOSEPH O'BRIEN* in his first full season as a Flat trainer is unquestionably the filly **Intricately**.

She provided the young trainer with his first Group 1 winner when landing the Moyglare Stud Stakes in September and her pedigree suggests she will be best at about a mile.

Invincible Irish

Aneen

Churchill

Zorion

ANEEN: won at the Curragh last season and could be very good

Berkshire by Downsman

CLIVE COX enjoyed his finest season in 2016 and the good news for the Sheepdrove trainer is that the aces from his annus mirabilis will again be among his pack this year.

Cox was Lambourn's leading Flat trainer and racked up a career-best 65 winners in Britain last term to go alongside record prize-money of just over £1.5 million.

Profitable and **My Dream Boat** were the biggest contributors to that pot and promise to be headliners once more.

Now in the colours of Godolphin, Profitable is the first horse Cox will train for Sheikh Mohammed's operation and notching another Group 1 to go with his King's Stand Stakes victory will be top of the five-year-old's agenda.

Versatile with regards to ground but perhaps more lethal with cut underfoot, he will be aimed at all of the top-level sprints, with the King's Stand and Nunthorpe primary targets, but the son of Invincible Spirit is also effective at 6f, as shown by his fourth in last year's July Cup.

A step up in trip is on the cards for My Dream Boat, whose finest hour came when he denied subsequent Prix de l'Arc de Triomphe heroine Found in the Prince of Wales's Stakes at Royal Ascot.

With Cox feeling the five-year-old is settling better in his races, a move up to 1m4f has been mooted, with the Arc a possible end-of-season dream for him.

A consistent sort with a preference for easy ground, he could start off over 1m2f in the Prix Ganay or Tattersalls Gold Cup.

Sovereign Stakes winner **Zonderland**, a colt Cox has always held in high regard, will also be part of the team of older horses and is rated an exciting prospect with another winter on his back. He could emerge into a force in the big mile races.

As for the Classic generation, Cox could give Mill Reef Stakes winner **Harry Angel** an entry in the 2,000 Guineas, but a sprinting campaign is more likely for a horse

MY DREAM BOAT (right): takes the scalp of Found at Ascot last season

LIMATO: set for another great sprinting campaign for Henry Candy

who promises to go to the top. The Commonwealth Cup at Royal Ascot is the race for him.

Either with Profitable or Harry Angel, Cox could be running into **Limato**, *HENRY CANDY's* joint-world champion sprinter of 2016.

A class act, he had a wonderful time when bolting up in the July Cup and Prix de la Foret, with a second in the Nunthorpe sandwiched in between.

He started last term over a mile in the Lockinge and ended it in the Breeders' Cup Mile and connections may consider another crack down that route, but races such as the July Cup could be there for the taking.

Star sprinter Muhaarar, who brushed Limato aside in the 2015 Commonwealth Cup, provided trainer *CHARLIE HILLS* with four Group 1 wins and, while the trainer went without success at the top table last year following the retirement of the Oasis Dream colt, he has the ammunition to put that right this season.

Among his big hopes is **Magical Memory**, who could start off in the Duke of York at the Dante meeting, a race he won last year, before another crack at the Diamond Jubilee Stakes. He went off favourite for that last summer when the easy ground went against him and Hills has not lost faith.

Confidence is also high in **Cotai Glory**, who was second to Profitable in the King's Stand. He has thrived at Highclere Stud this winter and looks a bigger horse this time around to the delight of his trainer.

Mootaharer, Muhaarar's half-brother, also has Hills purring after a frustrating 2016 campaign when he failed to make the track because of a sinus problem. A spell at Shadwell Stud has done the son of Dubawi the world of good.

Lennox Stakes winner **Dutch Connection** also has another big race in him on quick ground.

Of the three-year-olds, Windsor maiden winner **Barrington**, last seen finishing sixth to Mehmas in the July Stakes, is rated a nice prospect who could start in the Greenham.

OWEN BURROWS, like Hills, can count on the support of Hamdan Al Maktoum and it is not impossible that the owner could be rewarded with Classic success courtesy of **Talaayeb**, who impressed when denying a well-regarded Hills inmate at Newmarket in September.

A daughter of Dansili, she could go for the 1,000 Guineas and is bred to get further.

Burrows began training only last year but is no stranger to the Classics having saddled **Massaat** to finish second in last season's 2,000 Guineas.

A crack at the Derby did not work out for the son of Teofilo and a problem emerged after he was well beaten in the Sovereign Stakes, but that has been sorted and Burrows is relishing getting him back on track.

The same could be said of Dante fourth **Muntazah**, who also had a problem after the Princess of Wales's Stakes. He has been back in since before Christmas and is a big, scopey sort who should do better as a four-year-old.

Akhlaaq, who won on his debut at Salisbury, is another for notebooks when lining up on decent ground.

The arrival of *ED WALKER*, who has replaced David Lanigan at Kingsdown, is a major boost for Lambourn and the trainer has made a bright start to his new base, which he will be hoping continues when his leading lights come out.

Last year's Craven winner **Stormy Antarctic** has wintered well and is a bigger, stronger horse. He will probably run in a Listed race in France in March before a crack at the Group 1 Champions Mile in Hong Kong on May 7.

His second in the Prix Jean Prat entitles him to be a player in that and Walker will be disappointed if he does not win a Group 1.

Ultimate Avenue is another to follow haing filled his big frame this winter, developing into a stunning looker. The Greenham could be a starting point and there are options in France, but the Craven is unlikely as Walker feels the three-year-old did not handle the Dip when sixth in the Tattersall Stakes.

Glorious Impact is another horse Walker feels can make an impact over 1m2f this term, while **Indian Blessing** is described as exciting and may be aimed at a Classic trial.

Classics won't be on the agenda for **Mrs Danvers**, but *JONATHAN PORTMAN* will certainly be aiming his flying filly at some top sprints.

The three-year-old was the revelation of 2016 when unbeaten in five races, progressing from an authoritative win in the Weatherbys Super Sprint to landing the Group 3 Cornwallis Stakes.

All of her races have been over 5f, but Portman could try to stretch her stamina out to 6f with a tilt at the Commonwealth Cup in mind, with the path to that race starting in the Prix Sigy at Chantilly or Ascot's Pavilion Stakes.

HARRY DUNLOP also has a pair of three-year-old fillies to follow but, unlike Mrs Danvers, **Flight Of Fantasy** and **Assanilka** are more about stamina than speed, so they could come into the reckoning for Oaks trials.

Robin Of Navan, who gave the trainer his first Group 1 winner when landing the Criterium de Saint-Cloud in 2015, is also expected to be a leading light. He is likely to be campaigned in France over 1m-1m2f as he is best with cut in the ground.

In contrast, a sound surface is essential for **Early Morning**, who could be a player in the right conditions in some of the summer's big mile handicaps.

WILLIAM MUIR is another trainer familiar with the French programme and could aim Restorer at the Prix d'Harcourt at Chantilly on April 9.

However, **Phijee** is undoubtedly the horse exciting Muir most ahead of the season. A winner of two of his starts last year, the Sepoy colt was on his way to Hong Kong, but the sale fell through and Muir now has the 2,000 Guineas on his mind.

Willytheconqueror is an older horse who should also make his mark. He won twice during his three-year-old campaign, which can be a tricky time for sprinters, and has done well during the off-season. He may be pointed at the Palace House Stakes at Newmarket on Guineas weekend.

Muir also thinks plenty of **Calvados Spirit**, another who has the potential to do well at four having filled into a big, strong horse.

MRS DANVERS: Commonwealth Cup could be on the agenda for her

HUGHIE MORRISON is planning to treat **Temple Church** as a Group horse until he is proved otherwise. The son of Lawman won the Haynes, Hanson and Clark Stakes at Newbury last season from subsequent Racing Post Trophy fourth Raheen House and, being part of a staying family, the Derby could even be a possibility.

The shrewd Morrison can also count on smart stayers **Sweet Selection**, **Marmelo**, **Nearly Caught** and **Vent De Force**, who should continue to perform with credit.

Runners from the yard of *JOSE SANTOS* are often worth a second look.

The Brazilian was responsible for Dandy Flame striking at 200-1 at Wolverhampton last summer and reckons **Lady Valdean** will be his leading light this term.

The three-year-old improved in each of her four runs last season, finishing a close second at Nottingham on her final run at 20-1. She could even be aimed at an Oaks trial, though she will not be rushed after a setback towards the end of last year.

Stable star **Litigant** is still around for *JOE TUITE* and must be feared if the trainer can keep him right because there is a big engine under his fragile bonnet, but there is also a new wave coming through at Felstead Court.

Machine Learner won two of his last three for Michael Bell in the autumn, both 1m4f handicaps, and was subsequently bought for 70,000gns, while **Surrey Hope** should not have much trouble winning a maiden.

That is also the object for *RICHARD HUGHES* when it comes to **Angel's Quest**, who may be pointed to France with owners' premiums in mind, while **Nathania** and **Meteoric Riser** are other names to note from the Hughes yard.

ARCHIE WATSON, Lambourn's youngest trainer, has made a fine start to his new career and could make a name for himself in 2017, with **Plead** and **Calvinist** possibly the two standouts among his squad.

Finally, not content with being the leading jumps trainer in the region, *NICKY HENDERSON* likes to have a few Flat runners and reckons his smart hurdler **Beyond Conceit** could have a decent prize in him.

Berkshire's best

Limato

Mrs Danvers

My Dream Boat

The North by Borderer

IT doesn't seem that long ago that the north was being written off as a wasteland for Flat racing, with many claiming that only the powerful *MARK JOHNSTON* yard was likely to house horses capable of competing at the highest level.

How times have changed as Johnston, despite sending out close to 200 winners yet again, wasn't even the most prolific trainer in the area and one of four different northern stables producing winners at the highest level.

Johnston's Group 1 winner The Last Lion has been retired to stud after landing the Middle Park, but one other leading juvenile who should progress further as a three-year-old is **Yalta**.

The son of Exceed And Excel is something of an enigma having disappointed on his final three starts last year, but he's clearly very smart on his day as he won his first two races over 6f last year and produced an amazing performance to thrash The Last Lion when dropped down to the minimum trip in the Molecomb Stakes at Goodwood. He will be worth bearing in mind for decent three-year-old sprints.

Two lesser-known Johnston horses likely to shine this season are the well-bred filly **Khamaary**, who won on her debut at Redcar in October and should start her second season on a fair mark in handicaps, and **Makkaar**, who won a Newmarket maiden over 7f on his third and final start last season and is expected to fare even better as he steps up in trip.

The other big northern powerhouse is the yard of *RICHARD FAHEY*, who has sent out more than 100 winners in each of the last nine years, and looks to have the stronger hand this time with Group 1 win-

YALTA: Mark Johnston's speedball looked exceptional at Goodwood

QUEEN KINDLY: the daugher of Frankel may be going for the 1,000 Guineas

ner **Ribchester** his flagbearer.

The Godolphin-owned four-year-old mixed it with the best in 2016. After finishing third in the 2,000 Guineas at Newmarket, he won the Jersey Stakes at Royal Ascot and the Group 1 Prix Jacques le Marois at Deauville as well as being placed in the Sussex and Queen Elizabeth II Stakes.

He starts his the new season in Dubai in March but after that he will again contest all the big mile races, perhaps starting off in the Lockinge at Newbury in May. He might even step up to 1m2f at some stage so a race like the Coral-Eclipse could well feature on his agenda as well.

Birchwood, who also runs in the Godolphin colours, managed just one win in 2016, a Listed event at Chester, and overall had a rather disappointing campaign given he was a Group 2 winner as a juvenile. However, he is thought to be in much better form this time around.

A new addition to the Fahey team from Godolphin this year is the sprinter **Toscanini**, who was formerly with Mick Halford in Ireland.

His primary task is to act as lead horse for Birchwood and Ribchester, but he's a pretty smart performer in his own right and could well make his mark in Group sprints.

Queen Kindly, who was Fahey's star juvenile last season with three wins including the Sky Bet Lowther Stakes, will be aimed at the Qipco 1,000 Guineas, but she was such a speedy filly there must the doubts as to whether she will stay a mile. Sprinting is more likely to be her forte and she should go well in a race like the Commonwealth Cup.

There are no shortage of good sprinters in the Fahey team as the 2015 Ayr Gold Cup winner **Don't Touch**, who ended last season with a career-best fifth in the Champions Sprint, and **Growl**, who was second in both those races last year, will both pay their way in decent 6f races, with Don't Touch perhaps also stepping up to 7f.

The unbeaten **Brian The Snail** looks an exciting sprint three-year-old. Though he may start off in a handicap or two, he is considered a Group performer.

Two other lightly raced Fahey horses to follow are **Forest Ranger**, who won a Redcar maiden before finishing third in a Pontefract Listed contest, and **Andok**, who won two out of three in 2016 and met his sole defeat when second to the

INTISAAB: a progressive sprinter

progressive Masham Star on his final start.

Despite changing yards at the start of last year, *DAVID O'MEARA* sent out another 103 winners. One of his main contributors to that tally was the sprinter **Intisaab**, who won three races over 6f, the first off 80 at Ayr and the third off 100 at York.

Although he'll be starting the new turf season on another career-high mark, he is a progressive sort who should find further winning opportunities, with a step up to 7f also on the cards.

However, the main one to note from the O'Meara yard is the once-raced four-year-old **Kharbetation**. He was sent off at 11-2 for his debut in a Thirsk maiden last summer and breezed home by five lengths from an odds-on shot who won a maiden by five lengths on his next start.

The Dream Ahead gelding met with a slight setback after that so failed to run again, but he is considered a pretty useful prospect and is expected to win some decent handicaps this year.

KARL BURKE reports his Group 1 winner **Quiet Reflection** to be in excellent order, the filly having spent the winter with her trainer.

Burke is planning to start Quiet Reflection back in May, after which she will be aiming to add to her highly successful 2016 campaign at the top level when she won the Commonwealth Cup at Royal Ascot and the Sprint Cup at Haydock.

Although the Duke of York Stakes at the Dante meeting would seem the obvious starting point for her, Burke feel that could turn out to be a red-hot contest, so he is contemplating dropping her back to 5f for the Temple Stakes at Haydock later in the month.

After that she is likely to run in all the good 6f sprints like the Diamond Jubilee at Royal Ascot, Newmarket's July Cup and the Sprint Cup again at Haydock, although the Nunthorpe could also be on the cards.

Although she acts on good ground, the four-year-old seems a better filly when there is some cut, so that might determine her programme to some extent.

A couple more Burke horses to look forward to are **Lost At Sea** and **San Sebastiano**.

Lost At Sea, an £80,000 breeze-up buy, won in good style on his debut at Doncaster's St Leger meeting and, though he failed to add to his tally in much better company after that, he is the sort to improve as he matures.

San Sebastiano cost a mere 7,000gns as a yearling but showed useful form when winning a Doncaster maiden at 50-1 in July. Although she was well beaten on her only subsequent start, she is far better than she showed that day and, being by the Irish 2,000 Guineas winner Power out of a Rainbow Quest mare, is likely to be seen to her better advantage when stepped up to 1m or 1m2f.

Although without two of his star performers of last year, Mecca's Angel and Easton Angel, *MICHAEL DODS* has a few interesting three-year-olds to run, most notably **Kings Gift**, who was second to

SYPHAX (left): Godolphin now own this colt, who has Classic ambitions

the well-regarded Andok on his debut and then went at Ayr and Redcar before finishing runner-up in the Horris Hill at Newbury. He looks set for another good season.

Chipping is another from the Dods yard who should have no problems winning a race or two this year as he will be starting on a really handy mark. A son of the tough Dark Angel, he won a maiden at Redcar on his second and final start of 2016 and is capable of proving much better than that level.

Bamber Bridge is another unexposed three-year-old capable of plenty of improvement. He was off the mark straight away last season, winning at Hamilton, and was then more seriously tested in a couple of valuable sales races, his better effort being when fourth in a £300,000 contest at Doncaster.

Another three-year-old who looks set for a good season is **Syphax** from the *KEVIN RYAN* yard. He made it two wins from two runs when landing the competitive Acomb Stakes at York's Ebor meeting and the form was franked when the runner-up went on to win the Royal Lodge.

Now owned by Godolphin, he is likely to be aimed at the 2,000 Guineas.

DAVID BARRON didn't have the best of years in 2016, but his Two-Year-Old Trophy winner **Wick Powell** has been given a real chance by the handicapper on a mark of 85 and should find further opportunities.

We have also yet to see the best of Barron's **Rodden Rainbow**, who looked a fair prospect when winning a Ripon maiden last August.

Angels of the north

Birchwood

Quiet Reflection

Yalta

The West by Hastings

THE *RICHARD HANNON* team's modus operandi has long been about nippy two-year-olds and for many years that stood them in good stead, but last season there seemed to be a marked shift away from that angle with more emphasis being placed on longevity.

Under the guidance of Hannon junior, the speedy juveniles have been augmented by several horses with the scope to make a mark over middle distances as they get older and, while the tally of winners has dipped as a result, Hannon has plenty of smart prospects for the season.

The most exciting three-year-old in the yard is **Larchmont Lad**, who went into many notebooks last year as he gave the distinct impression the best would not be seen of him until he had filled his frame and was faced with more of a stamina test.

Larchmont Lad did not make his debut until July when readily coming clear of Maths Prize in a Sandown maiden and the form was well franked when the runner-up went on to record a couple of nice wins.

He was slightly unlucky next time at Doncaster when meeting trouble in running and improved again on his final run with an eyecatching victory in the Group 3 Tattersalls Stakes at Newmarket, seeing off Aidan O'Brien's Whitecliffsofdover in the style of a youngster going places. He is likely to need more than a mile as his career progresses and is definitely one to follow.

Promising is an unexposed type who lived up to her name last season despite not winning and can make the grade as the season unfolds.

TABARRAK: back to spearhead Richard Hannon's team of older horses

ATTY PERSSE: will be seen in the Godolphin blue this year and should do well

Stepped up to Group 3 level despite her maiden status, she bustled up the more experienced and streetwise Kilmah in the Prestige Stakes at Goodwood last August and can only get better with age.

Eqtiraan is more of a dark horse as he was beaten at 1-2 on his final outing last year, but he has since been gelded and could reap the benefits of that operation.

Eqtiraan made a winning debut at Ascot last July despite running very green, after which Hannon described him as a "gorgeous horse" who would be looked after with 2017 in mind. Third in the Solario before his Salisbury flop, he certainly looks the part and could be one for top races over 6f and 7f.

Tabarrak is now a four-year-old but has had only six runs and should have plenty more to offer this season.

A winner at Ascot on his last run in May, he missed the rest of the season due to a few niggling problems, but Hannon reports him to be in good heart again now and he has also been gelded since he last ran.

Tashaar was a bit disappointing last season, failing to fulfil the promise of a 2015 campaign that saw him win three times up to Listed level, but he has also been gelded and could do much better this time around.

Although *ROGER CHARLTON* will be without flagship horse Time Test, who has been transferred to race in the US, the master of Beckhampton still has a number of horses of plenty of interest for the season ahead and prime among them are Atty Persse and Fair Eva.

Atty Persse is a son of Frankel and won his only start at Sandown in the colours of his breeder Bjorn Nielsen, but he will sport the Godolphin blue this year.

His debut victory marked him down as a horse of considerable potential and as he was sent off a well-supported favourite to beat a Godolphin-owned horse in Hamada, so it is no real surprise that Sheikh Mohammed's operation swooped to purchase the youngster.

He is likely to start off in one of the Guineas trials this spring but could also be a

YUFTEN: won the Balmoral Handicap on his second start for Roger Charlton

Derby contender given stamina did not appear to be a problem.

Whatever the distance, there is no doubt he has the potential to go right to the very top and jockey George Baker's assertion that he "should make a nice three-year-old" may well look like one of the understatements of all time by the autumn.

With all the focus on Frankel's first crop last year, it was inevitable that **Fair Eva** would garner plenty of attention for becoming his first Pattern winner in the Princess Margaret Stakes at Ascot.

She didn't quite live up to the hype after that and was beaten at odds-on in the Lowther and the Rockfel, but she certainly didn't run badly either time, especially when stepped up to 7f at Newmarket, and will be much better with another winter on her back as she needed to mature. She can still make the grade at the top level.

Yuften was switched to Charlton's yard last autumn and immediately made an impact when taking the Balmoral Handicap at Ascot on only his second start for the trainer.

In doing so the six-year-old leapt into the reckoning for the Lincoln this April, for which he is very prominent in the betting, and he looks set for a good season regardless of what happens at Doncaster.

Charlton has worked his magic on similar horses in the past as the change of scenery at Beckhampton often has many beneficial effects and Yuften looks to be another who will prosper in his new surroundings.

Projection and Quest For More are two more older horses who should pay their way over the year.

Great things were expected of **Projection** last term, but his season was limited to just three appearances and he failed to win. However, he was far from disgraced in any of those runs and, being a son of the speedy Acclamation, he should be a force in some of the big summer handicaps over 6f on slick ground.

The Charlton team are certainly confident there are races to be won with him and the same goes for **Quest For More**, who is not getting any younger at seven but still retains plenty of enthusiasm.

Even Charlton was amazed at the way he took his racing last autumn, finishing his season in terrific form in top staying races, and he should go well in similar contests.

Although the *BRIAN MEEHAN* yard is probably not the force of old, the winners still flowed last year and it should be the same this time around.

One horse certain to carry plenty of stable confidence throughout the spring and summer will be **Raheen House**.

Described by the trainer as "a proper horse" after winning at York last October, the youngster went on to finish a staying-on fourth behind Rivet in the Group 1 Racing Post Trophy at Doncaster later that month.

The feeling at the Meehan yard is that Raheen House has really grown into his frame since last autumn and he can make up into a very decent middle-distance prospect this season before taking in the top races over the autumn.

A dark horse to follow from the Meehan yard is **Giovanni Battista**, who made all to make a winning debut over 7f at Newmarket last October. He did that easily and will get a mile.

ROD MILLMAN might not be a high-profile name but his Devon yard regularly turns out winners every season and there is no reason why that should not be the case once again.

Master Carpenter struggled last season having been forced into Group company by the handicapper, who raised him to a mark of 110 for his victory in the John Smith's Cup at York in 2015.

However, he is now down to 99 and that more realistic level gives him every chance of a more successful campaign, perhaps starting in the Lincoln, although he's possibly better over further.

Similar races will also be on the agenda for **Sir Roderic** after a stellar campaign which saw him win five handicaps, rising from a mark of 67 to 97. He was twice well beaten off that mark at the backend of the season but had been on the go for a long time.

Champagne Champ will also pay his way once again when the ground is riding on the softer side of good.

Western wonders

Atty Persse
Larchmont Lad
Quest For More

QUEST FOR MORE: won the Prix du Cadran and is a top-class stayer

The South by Southerner

RALPH BECKETT has always excelled with his middle-distance fillies and several of his best have been kept in training this year to give him a strong hand in the older division.

The most notable is **Simple Verse**, who famously won the St Leger on appeal in 2015 having initially been disqualified on the day.

Now a five-year-old, she found things a bit tougher last year but still did well when stepped back up in trip, winning the Park Hill Stakes on a return to Doncaster in September before finishing third in the Long Distance Cup at Ascot the following month.

The plan this time around was to take her out to Dubai in late March to contest the Dubai Gold Cup on World Cup night before she returns to England to tackle all the top staying events through the summer.

Another high-class mare back at Beckett's Andover base is **Moonrise Landing**, who racked up five straight wins last winter, the highlight of which was her success in the Marathon on all-weather finals day at Lingfield.

After that the six year-old won a Listed race at York on the turf and she is now on the way back after a spell on the sidelines.

Diamonds Pour Moi and **She Is No Lady** both struck in Listed races at Saint-Cloud at the backend of last year and could make their mark in Group company this time around.

Diamonds Pour Moi's extended 1m4f success was particularly impressive as it was her first run since going wrong in the Oaks and only the fourth of her life, so she should have a lot more to come.

Crimson Rock is a typical Beckett three-year-old who may well get the chance to stake her claim as an Oaks filly.

This staying type won her only start over a mile at Newbury last October and is likely to step up in trip for an Epsom trial.

Yet another filly, **Bletchley**, will be campaigned over much shorter trips having been an excellent second to subsequent Group 1 winner Brave Anna in the Albany Stakes at Royal Ascot last summer. Her form tailed off after that, but she is expected to make up into a smart performer this year.

Among the boys, there are high hopes that Leicester maiden winner **Sound Bar** can progress.

Beckett was included in the Juddmonte roster for the first time last year and this son of Oasis Dream should develop with time, as much of the Khalid Abdullah stock tend to do. He looks a miler.

Long-term patrons Qatar Racing are responsible for **Chemical Charge**, who has been through a few hoops since winning on his debut for Beckett at Salisbury in 2014.

After following up on the all-weather, the son of Sea The Stars spent 18 months off with injury until resurfacing in Ireland last year under the care of Ger Lyons, but he was sent back to Beckett last autumn.

Second in a Group 3 at the Curragh for Lyons, Chemical Charge has finished runner-up in two Listed races since his return, latterly at Toulouse in December, and could have more to give in 2017.

A filly of a rather different type to most of those in training with Beckett was the success story for *ANDREW BALDING* last season as the lightning-quick **Dancing Star** won four of her five handicaps, culminating in victory in the Stewards' Cup at Goodwood.

It's always touch and go whether even a top-notch three-year-old makes the cut for such big handicaps these days and Dancing Star squeezed in last of the 28 runners

HARBOUR LAW: Laura Mongan hopes he will be a Cup horse this season

despite being penalised for a tremendous victory in the same Newmarket handicap won by Magical Memory before his 2015 triumph.

Once again the flying filly ran out a comfortable winner at Goodwood, evoking memories of her owner Jeff Smith's wonderful Lochsong.

She's a Group horse on that evidence and, while her first crack at the top level went awry in the Sprint Cup, the ground was desperate that day so it's easy to forgive. She is sure to do better this year.

Another horse who surely has more to offer than when tried in Group 1 company last year is **South Seas**.

The son of Lope De Vega completed a hat-trick when running away with the Solario Stakes, but he then managed only sixth in the Dewhurst and was perhaps over the top when easily seen off by Thunder Snow in France.

His three wins all came with plenty of cut in the ground and that could be the key to him – it was good when he disappointed in the Dewhurst – so he might be the sort to spring a surprise when we get some rain. Balding also expects him to stay at least 1m2f, so he will have plenty of options.

Poet's Vanity stands out among the young fillies. A ten-length maiden winner at Salisbury, she went on to land the Rockfel Stakes at Newmarket in good style.

Plenty of horses don't act on the Rowley Mile, so course form will stand her in good stead when it comes to the 1,000 Guineas, which is unsurprisingly her first big target and she is likely to go straight there.

After the Rockfel, Balding said Poet's Vanity was so good at home she was demoralising his other fillies, which is some statement considering **Horseplay** was among them.

She came out that same month for her second outing and ran away with a Nottingham maiden by 13 lengths. She should get middle distances and, while the ground was soft, there's nothing to say she won't be equally effective when it's quicker.

One of the most remarkable stories of last season was provided by Epsom trainer *LAURA MONGAN*, who upset all the big guns when **Harbour Law** won the St Leger at Doncaster.

Mongan told Southerner that, quite incredibly, Classic success hasn't brought a single new horse to the yard, although she has some lovely two-year-olds in the same ownership as Harbour Law.

As for the stable star himself, Mongan said: "Harbour Law has done really well through the winter and I was delighted with the way he looked when he came-back in. He's always been an impressive individual, with plenty of size, but he looks even better now than he did at three. He's a beautiful horse.

"There are a few options for him, but I think the most likely race for his reappearance is the Sagaro Stakes at Ascot, before which he'll probably have a racecourse gallop at Kempton, as he did before the St Leger. The main target is the Ascot Gold Cup and he looks like a proper Cup horse to me. Not that I've had many!"

If there is to be another small stable punching above their weight in the Classics this season, perhaps it will be that of *DAVID MENUISIER*.

Having made the bold decision to take out a licence when he had just four horses in 2014, John Dunlop's former assistant has made rapid strides and sent out 15 winners last season at a strike-rate of 15 per cent and a £21 profit to £1 level stakes.

Menuisier even found himself in the enviable position of working out how to shuffle the deck before the Racing Post Trophy when he had two entries at the five-day stage.

In the end **Contrapposto** got the nod for Doncaster and could manage only ninth, but that will be a valuable learning experience for a colt described by his trainer as a "big baby" last year. Placed in the Convivial Maiden at York, he had won well at Nottingham and a mark of 92 can surely be exploited before he steps up in class.

CONTRAPPOSTO: more to come

Menuisier ultimately decided **Make Time** was too backward for that sort of test as a two-year-old, which makes it all the more impressive that he had romped home by five lengths at Salisbury in September.

That was on soft ground, but it had been good to firm when he came within a nose of making a winning debut at 50-1 at Ascot so he is clearly versatile and should also make a smart three-year-old.

Rising star Menuisier also has a nice four-year-old on his hands in **Saunter**, who won his first two starts for the yard last season after being bought from France. A non-stayer when stepped up in trip next time at Newmarket, he rounded off his campaign by finishing second in a 1m2f Listed race at Le Croise-Laroche and should be competitive at that level.

AMANDA PERRETT had another good season despite the death of stable star Astronereus, with **You're Hired**'s Glorious Goodwood success among the highlights. He won another handicap at Yarmouth on his final start and should have more to offer.

Perrett reports that **Arch Villain**, who hasn't run since winning the stayers' race on Shergar Cup day, won't be back until June, but he could be one for a decent staying handicap at the end of the season.

GARY MOORE doesn't have the same stars he has acquired over jumps, but he will still send out plenty of Flat winners this year.

Asked for one to follow, Moore picked out **Jacob's Dream**. Last of 12 on his only run as a two-year-old last season, he is an awful lot better than that.

Southern stars

Contrapposto

Harbour Law

You're Hired

Midlands by John Bull

JAMES GIVEN enjoyed a successful year with his two-year-olds in 2016 and, while Prince Of Cool has been sold to Qatar, he is hoping prolific juvenile winner **Tawny Port** can continue his progress at three.

The son of Arcano won four of his last six starts last season, including a Class 2 nursery at Ayr in September, and has plenty of size and scope, with Given reporting the 85-rated colt to do have developed over the winter.

Given said: "Tawny Port looks well and is much stronger. He is now 20kg heavier and has certainly done well physically.

"If he continues his progress and rises another 10lb he won't be far off Listed class. We'll look for a three-year-old handicap over 6f or 7f to start off with him and he's better when there's cut in the ground. His style of racing suggests he'll be fine over a mile as the season goes on."

Another three-year-old with potential Listed class is **Savannah Slew**, who won at Thirsk and Yarmouth last year and starts the season on a mark of 79.

Given said: "She's a little bit quirky but quite talented. She missed the break badly on her final start of last year at Doncaster but flew past all bar three of her rivals to finish fourth. It's not beyond the realms of possibility that we may try to pinch some black type with her – it would be very important as she is owned by her breeders, Dachel Stud."

Starboard Watch, an unraced three-year-old daughter of Harbour Watch, is another to follow when she makes her debut on the track having narrowly missed out on running last season, while among the older horses the consistent sprinter **Sign Of The Kodiac** should once again

HARBOUR WATCH: his daughter Starboard Watch is one to make a note of

be returning to the winner's enclosure in the summer, with a return to Newmarket in June among his possible targets.

Given will be hoping for more of the same with his juveniles this time around and he nominated two youngsters that are showing promise.

He said: "On a short-term basis, **Mistress Of Venice** should be a nice early type. She is by Bated Breath, is strong and forward and could be on the track quite early on.

"On a long-term basis, **Reactive** is a lovely colt by Cityscape. He is related to Trick Or Treat, who we know so well, and although he won't be seen early on we're hoping he will progress nicely through the year."

IVAN FURTADO has assembled a team of 30 horses for the forthcoming campaign and is hopeful a few new recruits can provide a big day for the yard in leading handicap company.

Normal Equilibrium, formerly trained by Robert Cowell, has joined Furtado and the Brazilian-born trainer is aiming the seven-year-old at the Epsom Dash, in which he finished a close ninth last year.

Furtado said: "Normal Equilibrium is a nice horse and his best form is on the turf. He's well handicapped on the pick of his form and he will contest some nice handicaps during the summer, with the Epsom Dash the ultimate aim."

An early-season assignment is in mind for fellow new addition **Dutch Art Dealer**, who scored in a first-time visor at Newcastle on his yard debut at the start of January.

Furtado said: "He disappointed at Kempton on his second start for us but I shouldn't have run him back that quickly. We've given him a break and the Lincoln meeting at Doncaster is the target, although I'd have thought he's more likely to get in the consolation race."

Furtado believes there is more to come from Intensical, who has been acquired from Jim Bolger, and also feels three-year-old **Frank's Legacy** will be winning on turf over 6f and 7f.

TONY CARROLL enjoyed his best season yet on turf last year, notching 25 winners, and three of his leading lights should be shining once more this time around.

Stable star **Boom The Groom** won sprint handicaps at Glorious Goodwood and York last campaign and, despite the six-year-old starting on a career-high mark of 107, he should once again do connections proud.

German recruit **Quixote** ran with promise in some hotly contested handicaps last season and has been running with credit on the all-weather in the past few months. The former Listed scorer certainly retains plenty of ability and should be visiting the winner's enclosure.

BOOM THE GROOM (far side): should do well despite career-high mark

POUR LA VICTOIRE (right): ought to do well at Brighton again this summer

Consistent seven-year-old **Pour La Victoire** is the proverbial standing dish having handled the unique undulations at Brighton to win in each of the last four seasons and should be seen to best effect there once again this year.

SCOTT DIXON'S horses have returned to form on the all-weather during the winter months and, after a slightly indifferent campaign last year, he may well have several well-handicapped horses this season.

Boots And Spurs is definitely capable of winning on turf off a mark of 79, with the straight 7f at Leicester and Doncaster suiting him well.

Crosse Fire, **Coiste Bodhar** and **Socialites Red** have all been performing well on the all-weather and are also worth following on turf.

MICK APPLEBY moved yards towards the end of last year and his string have also been running creditably during the winter.

Stable star **Danzeno** was unlucky not to get his head in front last season and clearly retains plenty of ability, while **Hakam** is worth following. Bought for £26,000 in August, he has been plying his trade successfully on the all-weather and remains unexposed on turf.

The Colin Bacon-owned trio of **Poyle Vinnie**, **House Of Commons** and **Faithful Creek** have all been running well on the all-weather and can score during the summer, with the owner also recently nominating three-year-old Cryptonite as one to follow.

Cropredy-based trainer *PAUL WEBBER* would not be the first name to spring to mind ahead of the summer Flat season, but in **Blue Revelation** he has a talented recruit who is certainly worth keeping on your side.

The four-year-old son of Exceed And Excel finished fourth on his debut in a fair 7f maiden at Naas, won by subsequent Group 2 scorer Herald The Dawn, in 2015.

He wasn't seen again until winning a run-of-the-mill mile maiden at Lingfield in November on his first run for Webber and, off a mark of 78, it would be no surprise to see the unexposed gelding go well in handicaps this campaign.

Webber may also give **Gwafa**, winner of the Swinton Hurdle last year, a Flat campaign in the coming months after running him over jumps this spring.

Midlands magic

Normal Equilibrium

Reactive

Tawny Port

Est. 1909
RACING & FOOTBALL OUTLOOK

Tipping Point Ed Quigley

Gosden leading resistance against O'Brien

AIDAN O'BRIEN carried all before him last season and bookmakers are clearly expecting more of the same this time around as he trains the favourite for all the British and Irish Classics and is not only a certainty for the Irish trainers' title but 1-5 to retain his British crown as well.

O'Brien looks well stocked again, with Churchill, favourite for the 2,000 Guineas and the Derby, and the explosive Caravaggio in his artillery, not to mention the mighty filly Minding coming back for more.

Any list of horses to follow at Pattern level or similar this season must surely include at least one from Ballydoyle, but with the bookmakers giving little away – and unlikely to do so at any stage – I've suggested one potentially flying a little more under the radar.

It won't be easy for other trainers to get in on the act, but John Gosden has made as good a fist of it as anyone in recent seasons and that may well be the case again.

The master of Clarehaven looks to have assembled a particularly nice team of three-year-olds and I've suggested who could make their mark at the top level over contrasting trips.

Among the older horses, even O'Brien and Gosden will be hard pushed to topple the French great Almanzor, who is finally likely to get his chance in the Arc after connections swerved the race last year to concentrate on the Champion Stakes.

The international scene is packed with great mares at the moment and, while it looks like we'll have to watch Winx from afar as she's set for another all-Australian campaign, it looks like last season's Queen Anne winner Tepin could head back to Royal Ascot.

On the jockeys' front, it will be fascinating to see how the new champion, Jim Crowley, gets on in his new role as number one to Sheikh Hamdan Al Maktoum.

The man he displaced as champion, Silvestre de Sousa, and the man he replaced in the Hamdan job, Paul Hanagan, will both be snapping at his heels in the race to be champion this year, while Ryan Moore and Frankie Dettori remain the men to follow in the big races.

Have an enjoyable and profitable Flat season. Fingers crossed the following six horses can be a part of it.

Algometer 4yo colt
21716- (David Simcock)

Winner of three of his seven starts, Algometer has the potential to make up into a really smart stayer this season.

He wasn't disgraced when seventh in the Derby and improved to win a Group 3 winner at Newbury in September.

There should be a lot more to come when he steps up in trip and it looks like he will gallop all day.

He should really come into his own when the ground is on the softer side and, granted his preferred conditions, he can land a blow in all the top staying events, perhaps even the Ascot Gold Cup with a wet spell in June.

Dreamfield 3yo colt
11- (John Gosden)

You won't see many more impressive winners of a maiden than Dreamfield routing the opposition at Nottingham in October and, having made it two out of two next time at Newmarket, he could be a force to be reckoned with.

He wasn't totally in love with the ground and possibly the 7f trip when scrambling home by a head on the second occasion and it looks like John Gosden will wisely drop him back to sprint trips rather than be tempted into a Guineas trial.

On quick ground over 6f, he can have a big say wherever he turns up and he could be value at 20-1 for the Commonwealth Cup at Royal Ascot.

Exemplar 3yo colt
213- (Aidan O'Brien)

Exemplar is perhaps one of the less heralded representatives from the Ballydoyle stable, but a lot more can be expected from the colt when tackling middle distances this season.

He is a half-brother to Irish and Yorkshire Oaks winner Blue Bunting and related to a host of other performers with plenty of stamina in their blood.

He's encountered only testing ground in Ireland so far and his pedigree also suggests he will be much more at home on a sound surface, so it wouldn't be a big surprise were he to end up outshining some of his more illustrious stablemates by the end of the season.

ALGOMETER: should have a lot more to offer when he steps up in trip

Rivet 3yo colt
21151- (William Haggas)

Rivet didn't fire on all cylinders in the Dewhurst last year, but the son of Fastnet Rock still won three of his five starts overall, including the Racing Post Trophy when he bounced back in style to beat Yucatan.

Connections indicated that the colt didn't really handle the Dip at Newmarket and a track with a flatter configuration would be more to his liking.

With that in mind, it would be no surprise to see him start off in the Irish 2,000 Guineas and then step up to 1m2f sooner rather than later. He rates an exciting prospect for the season.

Syphax 3yo colt
11- (Kevin Ryan)

Winner of the Acomb Stakes when last seen, Syphax has displayed greenness on both starts on the racecourse but clearly has gears under the bonnet.

Having won at Musselburgh on his debut, he was thrown in at the deep end at York but justified Kevin Ryan's faith by storming home once the penny dropped.

Connections resisted a crack at the Breeders' Cup with him as they felt he wasn't ready for the challenge and that could prove a wise move as he has been given time to mature both physically and mentally. He looks to be learning on the job and can make an impact in some of the top mile events this summer.

Tartini 3yo colt
1- (John Gosden)

Tartini came home with a wet sail to win on his debut in a Nottingham maiden in October – the same one won by Golden Horn – and should make up into a smart three-year-old.

Hooded for his first start, he was weak in the betting but got the job done in good style.

Clearly not the most straightforward, he looks to have plenty of ability and is from a good family as a half-brother to 2007 St Leger winner Lucarno.

He can make up into a smart middle-distance/staying performer and could be the best hope of getting the Derby back on home soil.

RIVET: the Irish 2,000 Guineas could be the race for him

RACING & FOOTBALL OUTLOOK
Est. 1909

Richard Birch

Read Richard every week in the RFO

Hoping to complete the circle afer a curtailed holiday in the autumn

I CUT short a Florida holiday last autumn by two days because of a long-held intention to place the biggest bet of my life on **Magic Circle** in the Cesarewitch.

Imagine my dismay when the plane touched down at Gatwick and I learned that Ralph Beckett hadn't declared the gelding for the 2m2f Newmarket marathon, presumably on account of the forecast good ground.

As things turned out I am not sure Magic Circle, who appreciates plenty of give in the ground, would have beaten the three-length Cesarewitch winner Sweet Selection, so the money saved from that October afternoon is ready to be invested on the five-year-old at some stage this season.

Who knows? He might even have his year planned around the Cesarewitch again, although I fear he will be too highly rated by then.

Winner of five of his 13 career starts, Magic Circle is a richly talented – and still underrated – stayer who should improve again in 2017 and make his mark in minor Group company when underfoot conditions are in his favour. Once more he is at the top of my list of horses to follow for the campaign.

Another who could progress from smart handicapper to Group-race contestant this year is Paul Midgley's five-year-old sprinter **Giant Spark**.

A huge stamp of a horse with a Rolls Royce engine, Giant Spark won four races in 2016, signing off with his best performance in taking a Navan 6f handicap off a mark of 89.

The son of Orientor possesses a conspicuously high cruising speed on soft ground and added to his appeal by showing admirable battling qualities in Ireland.

He starts the season on 95, but I doubt that is the ceiling of his ability and confidently expect there to be plenty more to come.

Mazzini, brought along with trademark patience and skill by James Fanshawe, capped a fine four-year-old campaign by impressively landing a 6f Kempton handicap off 84 in November.

It would be no surprise if this Exceed And Excel gelding, who comes from a late-maturing family that his trainer knows well, makes further significant progress this term and graduates into a Stewards' Cup horse.

Brian Ellison, one of the best trainers of handicappers around, is responsible for two of my list, namely Robero and Big Time Dancer.

Robero thrived for Ellison's tutelage last summer, rattling off a hat-trick at Newcastle, Thirsk and Newmarket prior to a narrow soft-ground Thirsk defeat towards the end of August.

His handicap mark rose from 64 to 76, but the way he travels through his races suggests the assessor may not have the gelding's measure just yet.

Robero looks a 7f specialist and there will be plenty of opportunities in the north for him in the first part of the turf season.

Big Time Dancer is less exposed and looks the sort to really fulfil his potential in 2017 on the back of just three starts in handicaps.

Winner of both his runs after moving to Ellison, the four-year-old son of Zoffany stormed home by seven lengths at Beverley in August and followed up the following week under a 6lb penalty at Hamilton.

He starts the new year on a mark of 67 and there is ample scope for him to increase that rating by at least 15lb.

The Tony Carroll-trained **Quiet Warrior** is a most interesting runner for both all-weather and turf sprints, particularly when John Egan is engaged to ride.

Rated 85 at one time in his career, Quiet Warrior spent some time in the wilderness, but Carroll has reignited the flame and the six-year-old won back-to-back all-weather handicaps at Wolverhampton and Chelmsford with some authority last summer.

Despite those two victories, he can start his year on a mark of just 61 and it will be a surprise if he isn't rated 75-plus before too much longer.

Although by no means the most straightforward of customers, he clearly goes exceptionally well for Egan and I've a hunch he enjoys a turning 6f more than a straight-track test.

BIG TIME DANCER (left): just the sort to fulfil his potential this season

FORT JEFFERSON (in front): should make his mark in the better handicaps

Quiet Warrior's stablemate **Pour La Victoire** has long been a personal favourite and money-spinner and there is no reason why he cannot win one or two more handicaps at his beloved Brighton or Goodwood this campaign.

He's at his best when coming late off a strong gallop and the race which immediately comes to mind as the natural target is the Brighton Bullet at the Sussex track in August.

Pettochside, who was beaten a length by Pour La Victoire at Goodwood in May – form which worked out well – is a grand old sprinter who always gives his running.

Best suited by a downhill track such as Goodwood or Salisbury when there is significant cut in the ground, John Bridger's eight-year-old maintains his form superbly and can enjoy another profitable year.

The Andrew Balding-trained **Fort Jefferson** routed Class 5 rivals in a Leicester heavy-ground handicap by 11 lengths last June off 62 and followed up at Newbury the following week with a bit more in hand than the narrow winning margin – a short-head – suggests.

His handler does particularly well with this type of late-developing four-year-old and the patient approach can once again pay dividends.

Fort Jefferson starts from a mark of 77 and ought to make his mark in some better handicaps this term.

Brighton is my favourite Flat track for punting, so I am always on the lookout for horses who could excel there.

One who springs to mind is Chris Dwyer's likeable sprint mare **Annie Salts**, who possesses explosive early speed and ought to relish the demands of the south-coast venue.

An all-the-way scorer at Yarmouth last August, the four-year-old Annie Salts returned to peak form when again blazing from the front to win at Wolverhampton in February.

She appeared to have plenty in hand at the finish and ought to rate considerably higher than 61 in due course.

As long as she breaks fluently, it's hard to envisage many sprinters rated in the 60-75 bracket being able to lead her and tracks like Brighton and Epsom should suit her style perfectly.

Happy punting everyone.

Time Test speed figures

Aurelia's return to Ascot will be utterly fascinating

ARM raised in triumph 20 yards from the finish, Frankie Dettori's 54th Royal Ascot winner was probably his easiest. The winning margin was seven lengths, but Dettori was the last back to the winner's enclosure having taken the best part of half a circuit to pull up **Lady Aurelia**.

That performance in the Queen Anne Stakes was the most dazzling to the eye of 2016 and backed up by the clock as it comfortably earned her the highest Time Test mark (85) of any two-year-old last season, a figure bettered by only five older horses.

The question for trainer Wesley Ward is whether she can produce more riches this year, all the while nagged by the fact that stablemate Acapulco did similar in the Queen Mary in 2015 but failed to develop as a three-year-old.

The case for the prosecution can argue the Ascot win was in a Group 2, those behind have not been too busy advertising the form and Lady Aurelia, like Acapulco, was beaten in Group 1 company, in the Cheveley Park, on her final start of the season.

But Lady Aurelia does have a Group 1 success on her CV in the Prix Morny, she had her excuses at Newmarket having broken a blood vessel and that Queen Mary win, which made Acapulco's 12 months earlier look almost ordinary, burnt a deep impression.

The King's Stand back over the same course and distance may well be a wiser plan than the Commonwealth Cup and it will be fascinating to see how she gets on.

As for the Classics, Aidan O'Brien has has usual grip on the 2,000 Guineas market, headed by long-time ante-post Epsom Derby favourite Churchill, but **Caravaggio** has looked more spectacular on the clock.

Unraced since a comfortable success in the Phoenix Stakes, Caravaggio posted a mark of 79 for his Coventry Stakes win the day before Lady Aurelia's blast, form given a solid look by runner-up Mehmas, who went on to land the July Stakes and Richmond Stakes (with a figure of 73) before finishing second to Churchill in the National.

Churchill needed Ryan Moore to stoke him up both there as he recorded a sea-

CLIFFS OF MOHER: clocked a great figure for his Leopardstown maiden win

sonal best speed mark of 74 and it was a similar story in the Dewhurst Stakes, but once the pair got motoring the margin of victory was comfortable so it would be no surprise if he can rate higher in the future.

Much better value for the 2,000 Guineas, however, is stablemate **Cliffs Of Moher**, whose maiden win at Leopardstown at the end of October sailed under the radar a little. Improving massively from his debut at Cork, the first foal out of the speedy Wave showed authority to earn a figure of 74 on only his second start. His potential is vast.

Zip was **Yalta**'s hallmark at Glorious Goodwood where, in earning the same rating of 79 as Caravaggio, he broke the 5f juvenile track record to win the Molecomb Stakes.

He disappointed three times after that, but the Goodwood form looks fairly strong given runner-up The Last Lion (67), also trained by Mark Johnston, went on to land the Middle Park and he should not be dismissed yet.

The Middle Park runner-up was **Blue Point**, who didn't quite look in the same form as when winning the Gimcrack at York in August with a smart Time Test mark of 78. He ran well behind Churchill over a trip that seemed to stretch him in the Dewhurst and should give the likes of Lady Aurelia – and Caravaggio if he heads that way – something to think about in the Commonwealth Cup.

Another meriting respect there will be **Harry Angel** based on his Mill Reef Stakes win, which the clock tells us was as good as anything achieved by Churchill.

Two defeats at odds-on saw **Fair Eva**'s status as ante-post favourite for the 1,000 Guineas evaporate, but her Princess Margaret Stakes win still rates as good anything on the numbers by contenders for that Classic.

Her mark of 76 was matched by both **Queen Kindly** and **Roly Poly** in the Lowther Stakes, a figure that comfortably surpasses the top score of 67 that **Rhododendron**, ante-post favourite for the 1,000 Guineas throughout the winter, notched for her Fillies' Mile triumph.

There was debate last season about whether it was a golden age for sprinters and the big Time Test figures posted by

THE TIN MAN: deserves huge credif for beating progressive Growl and Brando

Mecca's Angel (91), **Limato** (88) and **The Tin Man** (86) suggest it is right to be on the side of the enthusiasts.

August 19 was the day for Mecca's Angel to record the highest figure by any performer in 2016 when she tore off with the Nunthorpe from Limato, whose top number had come the previous month over a furlong further in the July Cup.

The Tin Man, meanwhile, secured the Group 1 prize he had been promising in the Champion Sprint Stakes in a race that looks strong despite the presence of 50-1 shot Growl in second.

Growl's presence was seen as a surprise, but his Time Test ratings had been on the rise all season and a career-high 82 indicates more to come from the Richard Fahey-trained five-year-old.

Similar sentiments apply to **Brando**, who recorded strong figures when runner-up in the Wokingham and in winning the Ayr Gold Cup before his personal best of 81 when third to The Tin Man.

The Prix de l'Arc de Triomphe was a stunner for Aidan O'Brien and the clock rated it sensational as well. The race produced three of the top eight figures of the season, with winner **Found** earning a mark of 88, closely followed by **Highland Reel** (87) and **Order Of St George** (84), an outstanding figure for one with the stamina to win an Ascot Gold Cup.

The Classic generation had no answer, including Harzand, but his Derby win, worthy of a Time Test 85, was the best last

Top two-year-old colts of 2016

	Horse	Speed rating	Distance in furlongs	Going	Track	Date achieved
1	**Lady Aurelia**	**85**	**5**	**SFT**	**Ascot**	**June 15**
2	Fair Eva	76	6	GF	Ascot	July 23
2	Queen Kindly	76	6	GF	York	Aug 18
2	Roly Poly	76	6	GF	York	Aug 18
5	Mrs Danvers	72	5	GF	Newmarket	Oct 7
6	Intricately	68	7	YLD	Curragh	Sept 11
7	Brave Anna	67	6	GF	Newmarket	Sept 24
7	Hydrangea	67	7	YLD	Curragh	Sept 11
7	Rhododendron	67	8	GF	Newmarket	Oct 7
10	Clem Fandango	66	5	GF	Newmarket	Oct 7
10	Sobetsu	66	8	GD	Newmarket	Sept 17

Top two-year-old fillies of 2016

	Horse	Speed rating	Distance in furlongs	Going	Track	Date achieved
1	**Caravaggio**	**79**	**6**	**SFT**	**Ascot**	**June 14**
1	**Yalta**	**79**	**5**	**GD**	**Goodwood**	**July 27**
3	Blue Point	78	6	GD	York	Aug 20
4	Churchill	74	7	YLD	Curragh	Sept 11
4	Cliffs Of Moher	74	7	YLD	Leopardstown	Oct 29
4	Harry Angel	74	6	GS	Newbury	Sept 17
7	Mehmas	73	6	GF	Goodwood	July 28
8	Rivet	72	8	GD	Doncaster	Oct 22
9	Thunder Snow	71	7	SFT	Saint-Cloud	Oct 30
10	Ardad	70	5	SFT	Ascot	June 14
10	Intelligence Cross	69	6	GF	Newmarket	July 7

year's crop of three-year-olds served up and has been underrated, which bodes well for runner-up **US Army Ranger** (80).

While US Army Ranger looks a 1m4f horse, Coolmore have a rock-solid older horse for the top 1m-1m2f races in superstar filly **Minding**, who recorded a figure of 68 or above in all five of her Group 1 wins last year. Her 81-rated Oaks success was top of the heap, but she was only one point shy of that when dropped all the way back to a mile for the QEII, in which runner-up **Ribchester**, conceding 3lb, notched a figure of 80 to cap a hugely progressive campaign.

Another standout performance on Champions Day came from **Journey**, who got to record the Time Test mark she had been threatening when romping off with the British Champions Fillies & Mares from the very useful Speedy Boarding. The John Gosden-trained filly has stayed in training and a figure of 82 may not be the ceiling of her ability.

Group 1 review by Dylan Hill

1 Qipco 2,000 Guineas Stakes (1m) Newmarket April 30 (Good To Soft)

1 **Galileo Gold** 3-9-0 Frankie Dettori
2 **Massaat** 3-9-0 Paul Hanagan
3 **Ribchester** 3-9-0 William Buick
14/1, 9/1, 33/1. 1½l, 2l. 13 ran. 1m 35.91s (Hugo Palmer).

While not the strongest Guineas in terms of strength in depth with the two Group 1-winning juveniles in the field, **Air Force Blue** and **Marcel**, having failed to train on, this still threw up two more top-class colts with **Galileo Gold** able to peak earlier in the season than **Ribchester**. Galileo Gold was always prominent and stayed on really well to see off **Massaat**, while Ribchester, running beyond 6f for the first time, wasn't quite ready for a mile and finished third ahead of **Air Vice Marshal** and 66-1 outsider **Kentuckyconnection**.

2 Qipco 1,000 Guineas Stakes (Fillies) (1m)
Newmarket May 1 (Good)

1 **Minding** 3-9-0 Ryan Moore
2 **Ballydoyle** 3-9-0 Seamie Heffernan
3 **Alice Springs** 3-9-0 Colm O'Donoghue
11/10F, 15/2, 16/1. 3½l, ½l. 16 ran. 1m 36.53s (A P O'Brien).

A middle-distance filly on pedigree with the stamina to follow up in the Oaks, **Minding** still had the speed to absolutely destroy a stellar field in stunning fashion. Always prominent and committed for home early, Minding stormed clear of two top-class stablemates, with **Ballydoyle**, though disappointing later in the season, confirming her quality by holding off triple Group 1 winner **Alice Springs** for second. **Fireglow** was next ahead of Prix de Diane runner-up **Nathra**, who was 2l clear of the rest including Irish 1,000 Guineas heroine **Jet Setting**.

3 Al Shaqab Lockinge Stakes (1m) Newbury May 14 (Good)

1 **Belardo** 4-9-0 Andrea Atzeni
2 **Euro Charline** 5-8-11 Ryan Moore
3 **Endless Drama** 4-9-0 Colin Keane
8/1, 12/1, 8/1. 1l, nk. 12 ran. 1m 38.18s (Roger Varian).

A wide-open contest without a single winner of a Group 1 at the trip, but **Belardo** and **Limato** were the class acts in the field and luck was more in Belardo's favour. Belardo did well to overcome a tardy start as he came home much more strongly than **Euro Charline** and **Endless Drama**, though that might not have been good enough had Limato, whose other attempt at the trip in the Breeders' Cup Mile was similarly inconclusive, not been stopped twice as he tried to make his challenge, eventually finishing fourth. That quartet were clear of **Toormore** and **Gabrial**.

4 Tattersalls Irish 2,000 Guineas (1m) Curragh (IRE) May 21 (Yielding)

1 **Awtaad** 3-9-0 Chris Hayes
2 **Galileo Gold** 3-9-0 Frankie Dettori
3 **Blue De Vega** 3-9-0 Colin Keane
9/2, 5/4F, 7/1. 2½l, 4¼l. 8 ran. 1m 45.26s (Kevin Prendergast).

A minor upset as **Awtaad** turned over **Galileo Gold**, though time would show the Newmarket winner was probably just about the better horse. Awtaad was always going well and stayed on strongly once hitting the front 2f out just as Galileo Gold was short of room on the inside and denied the chance to go with him, the pair both showing their quality by drawing well clear of **Blue De Vega**. **Air Force Blue** was again a bitter disappointment.

5 Tattersalls Irish 1,000 Guineas (Fillies) (1m)
Curragh (IRE) May 22 (Yielding To Soft)

1 **Jet Setting** 3-9-0 Shane Foley
2 **Minding** 3-9-0 Ryan Moore
3 **Now Or Never** 3-9-0 Kieren Fallon
9/1, 4/11F, 13/2. hd, 10l. 10 ran. 1m 42.46s (Adrian Paul Keatley).

A major upset as **Minding** was beaten by **Jet Setting**, but she was easily forgiven having banged her head in the stalls and burst a sinus. It was still a fine effort from Jet Setting, though, as she pulled 10l clear of **Now Or Never** in third and, while her form was very mixed over the rest of the season, a wide-margin Group 3 win underlined her quality on soft ground.

6 Tattersalls Gold Cup (1m2f110y)
Curragh (IRE) May 22 (Yielding To Soft)

1 **Fascinating Rock** 5-9-3 Pat Smullen
2 **Found** 4-9-0 Ryan Moore
3 **Success Days** 4-9-3 Shane Foley
9/4, 8/15F, 8/1. 3¾l, 1½l. 6 ran. 2m 20.72s (D K Weld).

The highlight of what would prove to be an immensely frustrating campaign for **Fascinating Rock**, who missed three big autumn targets due to unsuitably quick ground and was on a summer break at the only time all year conditions were in his favour. This was a fine performance from the 2015 Champion Stakes winner, who proved much too good for **Found**, although the runner-up was nowhere near her Arc form at this stage of the season.

7 Investec Oaks (Fillies) (1m4f10y)
Epsom June 3 (Good To Soft)

1 **Minding** 3-9-0 Ryan Moore
2 **Architecture** 3-9-0 Frankie Dettori
3 **Harlequeen** 3-9-0 Silvestre De Sousa
10/11F, 12/1, 14/1. 1¾l, 8l. 9 ran. 2m 42.66s (A P O'Brien).

A Classic double for **Minding**, who successfully stepped up in trip despite finding every bit of trouble in running, albeit helped by some desperately weak opposition. Minding

BELARDO: the best of a poor bunch of older European milers last season

slipped to the back of the field when short of room turning for home and was then hampered again, but she picked up superbly to cut down **Architecture** and was a most impressive winner. Architecture was 8l clear of **Harlequeen**, whose stamina ebbed away late on off a strong gallop set by the fourth, **Somehow**, with **Seventh Heaven** a big disappointment as she struggled with the undulating track and soft ground.

8 Investec Derby (1m4f10y) Epsom June 4 (Good To Soft)

1 **Harzand** 3-9-0 Pat Smullen
2 **US Army Ranger** 3-9-0 Ryan Moore
3 **Idaho** 3-9-0 Seamie Heffernan
13/2, 7/2F, 14/1. 1½l, 1¼l. 16 ran. 2m 40.09s (D K Weld).

History may well show this crop of middle-distance three-year-olds to be desperately weak after their no-show in the Arc, but that would perhaps be unfair on the three who fought out a thrilling finish as **Harzand** saw off Ballydoyle pair **US Army Ranger** and **Idaho**. Nothing went right for Harzand when he took on his elders later in the season, but he was a worthy Derby winner as he quickened up well and was going away from the runner-up again in the final half-furlong. US Army Ranger was given plenty to do, but this was a race in which it paid to be held up, instead marking up the performance of Idaho, who raced closest to the pace out of the principals and would push Harzand closer at the Curragh. The leading trio were 5l clear of subsequent King George runner-up **Wings Of Desire**, with **Massaat** a non-stayer behind.

9 Queen Elizabeth II Coronation Cup (Sponsored by Investec) (1m4f10y) Epsom June 4 (Good To Soft)

1 **Postponed** 5-9-0 Andrea Atzeni
2 **Found** 4-8-11 Ryan Moore
3 **Roseburg** 5-9-0 Jack Mitchell
8/11F, 3/1, 50/1. 4½l, 1¼l. 8 ran. 2m 43.54s (Roger Varian).

Things couldn't have fallen into place any better for **Postponed**, but he was still really impressive in winning by such a wide margin. Postponed took full advantage of the fine job done by his pacemaker **Roseburg**, who stacked up the field at such a moderate gallop that he was able to stick on into third as the winner scooted clear, showing the speed that would see him later add a 1m2f Group 1 win to his CV. **Found** was given too much to do and could never make any serious inroads in second, while **Simple Verse**, who needed further anyway, was left with no chance by the lack of pace in fourth.

10 Queen Anne Stakes (1m) Ascot June 14 (Soft)

1 **Tepin** 5-8-11 Julien R Leparoux
2 **Belardo** 4-9-0 James Doyle
3 **Lightning Spear** 5-9-0 Oisin Murphy
11/2, 9/2J, 20/1. ½l, 1¼l. 13 ran. 1m 43.98s (Mark Casse).

The lack of an outstanding talent among Europe's older milers meant that American superstar **Tepin** was able to come out on top despite having plenty of factors stacked against her, not least the conditions and her unfamiliarity with the straight mile. That might have played a part in Tepin racing keenly early, but she had enough in hand to hold off Lockinge winner **Belardo**, who was again best of the Europeans in second. **Lightning Spear** ran a stormer on ground softer than ideal to take third ahead of **Toormore** and **Ervedya**.

11 King's Stand Stakes (5f) Ascot June 14 (Soft)

1 **Profitable** 4-9-4 Adam Kirby
2 **Cotai Glory** 4-9-4 George Baker
3 **Goken** 4-9-4 Jamie Spencer
4/1, 33/1, 50/1. nk, 1l. 17 ran. 1m 2.69s (Clive Cox).

The culmination of a wonderful treble for **Profitable**, who became the first horse since Lochsong in 1994 to follow up victories in the Palace House and Temple Stakes. That said, all those wins came narrowly with cut in the ground and conditions were again in Profitable's favour, probably more so than runner-up **Cotai Glory**, while third-placed **Goken** looked unlucky in running. **Mecca's Angel** ran a shocker and there were no three-year-olds – the age group that would later throw up the one-two in the Abbaye – in the race.

12 St James's Palace Stakes (1m) Ascot June 14 (Soft)

1 **Galileo Gold** 3-9-0 Frankie Dettori
2 **The Gurkha** 3-9-0 Ryan Moore
3 **Awtaad** 3-9-0 Chris Hayes
6/1, 4/5F, 5/2. 1¼l, ½l. 7 ran. 1m 44.01s (Hugo Palmer).

A terrific clash between three Guineas winners saw **Galileo Gold** restore his reputation with a fantastic all-the-way win over the potentially unlucky **The Gurkha**. Always in an ideal position just behind the pacemaker, Galileo Gold quickened up well when asked to assert and was always in command,

PROFITABLE: 5f hat-trick came with the ground in his favour every time

whereas The Gurkha was left with too much to do before staying on strongly into second. **Awtaad** could never make an impression on the winner but stuck on well into third, pulling 5l clear of **Cymric** with **Emotionless** behind.

13 Prince of Wales's Stakes (1m2f) Ascot June 15 (Soft)

1 **My Dream Boat** 4-9-0 Adam Kirby
2 **Found** 4-8-11 Ryan Moore
3 **Western Hymn** 5-9-0 Frankie Dettori
16/1, 4/1, 12/1. nk, 3½l. 6 ran. 2m 11.38s (Clive Cox).

A desperately soft Group 1 and **My Dream Boat** took advantage to spring a 16-1 surprise. With Japanese favourite **A Shin Hikari** reportedly unbalanced by coming around the bend, **The Grey Gatsby** and **Tryster** totally unsuited by the ground and **Western Hymn** out of sorts all season, My Dream Boat was effectively left with only **Found** to beat and relished the conditions far more than the subsequent Arc winner, producing a sustained burst to get up close home despite hanging left.

14 Gold Cup (2m4f) Ascot June 16 (Soft)

1 **Order Of St George** 4-9-0 Ryan Moore
2 **Mizzou** 5-9-2 Andrea Atzeni
3 **Sheikhzayedroad** 7-9-2 Martin Harley
10/11F, 10/1, 40/1. 3l, 2¼l. 17 ran. 4m 26.21s (A P O'Brien).

Order Of St George proved himself one of the best stayers of recent times as he managed to show the class that would later see him finish third in the Arc even at the end of this far more gruelling test of stamina. A strong gallop brought out the best in Order Of St George, whose two odds-on defeats later in the season came in far more slowly run affairs, and even with nine ahead of him turning for home he was able to power to a decisive success. **Mizzou** was a fine second ahead of subsequent dual Cup winner **Sheikhzayedroad** and the rest were well strung out, with **Flying Officer** and **Clever Cookie** among those found out.

15 Commonwealth Cup (6f) Ascot June 17 (Good To Soft)

1 **Quiet Reflection** 3-9-0 Dougie Costello
2 **Kachy** 3-9-3 Richard Kingscote
3 **Washington DC** 3-9-3 Ryan Moore
7/4F, 14/1, 8/1. 1l, ½l. 10 ran. 1m 14.50s (K R Burke).

A moderate Group 1, which may become the norm for this race, but it still provided a smart winner in **Quiet Reflection**. Given a patient waiting ride, Quiet Reflection stormed through in the final furlong to win far more cosily than the winning margin suggested, though her task was made easier by the waywardness of **Kachy** as he hung badly left in the closing stages. **Washington DC**, who would do better over 5f, was next ahead of **La Rioja**, with **Donjuan Triumphant** the main disappointment down the field.

16 Coronation Stakes (Fillies) (1m) Ascot June 17 (Good To Soft)

1 **Qemah** 3-9-0 Gregory Benoist
2 **Nemoralia** 3-9-0 Olivier Peslier
3 **Alice Springs** 3-9-0 Ryan Moore
6/1, 4/1, 8/1. 1¾l, shd. 13 ran. 1m 40.56s (J-C Rouget).

A wide-open race with Minding having been stepped up in trip and French filly **Qemah** was the one to take a big step forward, though she might have struggled to see off **Alice Springs** had the latter enjoyed better fortune. Third in the French Guineas behind La Cressonniere, Qemah was always going well and soon put the race to bed when asked to quicken, whereas Alice Springs twice couldn't get a clear run before staying on into third. **Nemoralia** split the pair,

TWILIGHT SON (left): Diamond Jubilee success was as good as it got for him

with **Now Or Never** fourth, while **Jet Setting** came home sick after her tame effort.

17 Diamond Jubilee Stakes (6f) Ascot June 18 (Good To Soft)

1 **Twilight Son** 4-9-3 Ryan Moore
2 **Gold-Fun** 7-9-3 Christophe Soumillon
3 **Signs Of Blessing** 5-9-3 Olivier Peslier
7/2, 7/1, 25/1. nk, shd. 9 ran. 1m 13.84s (Henry Candy).

Beaten only by the mighty Muhaarar in 2015, **Twilight Son** set the form standard and duly secured his second Group 1, though it was desperately hard work and perhaps more of a sign that later-developing opponents were closing the gap. Twilight Son was always in the right place, ridden handily in a slowly run race, which wasn't the case for several key rivals, notably Hong Kong runner-up **Gold-Fun**, the in-form **Magical Memory**, who couldn't quite sustain a sweeping run from last to first and finished a half-length fourth, and **Suedois** in fifth. Subsequent Prix Maurice de Gheest winner **Signs Of Blessing** dictated the gallop and was third, while the ground was too soft for **The Tin Man**.

18 Dubai Duty Free Irish Derby (1m4f) Curragh (IRE) June 25 (Good To Yielding)

1 **Harzand** 3-9-0 Pat Smullen
2 **Idaho** 3-9-0 Ryan Moore
3 **Stellar Mass** 3-9-0 Ronan Whelan
4/6F, 11/4, 33/1. ½l, 3¾l. 9 ran. 2m 38.05s (D K Weld).

A terrific rematch between the Derby first and third saw **Harzand** just about confirm his superiority over **Idaho**. Idaho was ridden behind Harzand this time and all but drew level as the pair duelled from a long way out only for the winner to prove strongest in the final 100 yards. The pair pulled clear of **Stellar Mass**, who was followed by a trio of runners – **Red Verdon**, **Port Douglas** and **Moonlight Magic** – who got closer than at Epsom without seriously threatening.

19 Sea The Stars Pretty Polly Stakes (Fillies & Mares) (1m2f) Curragh (IRE) June 26 (Yielding)

1 **Minding** 3-8-12 Ryan Moore
2 **Bocca Baciata** 4-9-10 Colm O'Donoghue
3 **Lucida** 4-9-10 Kevin Manning
1/5F, 25/1, 14/1. 4½l, 5l. 5 ran. 2m 9.94s (A P O'Brien).

Another breathtaking performance from **Minding**, who blew apart an admittedly moderate field as she burst well clear once asked to assert at the furlong pole. Main rival **Speedy Boarding**, a subsequent dual Group 1 winner in France, was a long way below her best, leaving **Bocca Baciata**, a Group 2 winner next time, to chase home Minding.

20 Coral-Eclipse (1m2f7y) Sandown July 2 (Soft)

1 **Hawkbill** 3-8-10 William Buick
2 **The Gurkha** 3-8-10 Ryan Moore
3 **Time Test** 4-9-7 Pat Smullen
6/1, 4/6F, 6/1. ½l, 1¾l. 7 ran. 2m 10.71s (Charlie Appleby).

Stamina won the day on soft ground as **Hawkbill** wore down **The Gurkha**, who couldn't replicate his outstanding mile form over an extra quarter-mile. The Gurkha was ridden to lead but couldn't sustain his effort in the final furlong and Hawkbill took advantage to bravely complete a six-timer, though three subsequent defeats – two on quicker ground but the other in a weaker German Group 1 on soft – let down the form. **Time Test** was unsuited by the ground but stuck on into third ahead of his pacemaker **Countermeasure**, with the below-par **My Dream Boat** and **Western Hymn** behind.

21 Tattersalls 250th Year Falmouth Stakes (Fillies & Mares) (1m) Newmarket July 8 (Good To Firm)

1 **Alice Springs** 3-8-12 Ryan Moore
2 **Very Special** 4-9-7 James McDonald
3 **Always Smile** 4-9-7 James Doyle
5/2, 16/1, 8/1. 2¼l, nse. 7 ran. 1m 34.42s (A P O'Brien).

Alice Springs confirmed the promise of her Royal Ascot run as she kicked off her outstanding second half of the season. Enjoying the quick ground much more than some of her rivals, Alice Springs was always handy and drew clear of Godolphin pair **Very Special** and **Always Smile**, with **Irish Rookie** back in fourth. **Usherette** looked the best older filly at the trip after Group 2 wins at Newmarket and Royal Ascot but was always in rear and finished a tame sixth.

22 Darley July Cup (6f) Newmarket July 9 (Good To Firm)

1 **Limato** 4-9-6 Harry Bentley
2 **Suedois** 5-9-6 Robert Havlin
3 **Quiet Reflection** 3-8-11 Dougie Costello
9/2F, 25/1, 7/1. 2l, hd. 18 ran. 1m 9.97s (Henry Candy).

By far the best performance at this trip all season as **Limato** stormed to a stunning victory. Back to sprinting after his unlucky fourth in the Lockinge, Limato travelled strongly and quickened well clear of **Suedois** despite going badly right in the final furlong. The ground was perhaps quicker than ideal for **Quiet Reflection**, though she finished an identical distance in front of the fifth, **Washington DC**. **Profitable** split that pair, running well on this step up to 6f, but **Magical Memory** and **Twilight Son** were disappointing.

23 Darley Irish Oaks (Fillies) (1m4f) Curragh (IRE) July 16 (Good)

1 **Seventh Heaven** 3-9-0 Seamie Heffernan
2 **Architecture** 3-9-0 Frankie Dettori
3 **Harlequeen** 3-9-0 Silvestre De Sousa
14/1, 6/1, 14/1. 2¾l, 1¼l. 11 ran. 2m 34.53s (A P O'Brien).

A big transformation from Epsom with **Seventh Heaven** able to easily reverse the form with three fillies who had finished in front of her that day. Best on a flat track and good ground, Seventh Heaven made smooth headway from the rear before staying on strongly to cut down **Architecture** and win going away. **Harlequeen** saw this out much better to finish a clear third ahead of **Turret Rocks** and **Somehow**, with Ribblesdale winner **Even Song** coming up well short.

24 King George VI and Queen Elizabeth Stakes (1m4f) Ascot July 23 (Good To Firm)

1 **Highland Reel** 4-9-7 Ryan Moore
2 **Wings Of Desire** 3-8-9 Frankie Dettori
3 **Dartmouth** 4-9-7 Olivier Peslier
13/8F, 4/1, 9/2. 1¼l, 2¾l. 7 ran. 2m 28.97s (A P O'Brien).

A desperately weak renewal without strong three-year-old representation and Postponed ruled out by injury to join Found and Fascinating Rock on the sidelines, providing easy pickings for the one true class act in Breeders' Cup hero **Highland Reel**. Further helped by a smart front-running ride by Ryan Moore which caught his rivals napping, Highland Reel made all and never looked like getting caught, comfortably holding off **Wings Of Desire**, who upheld the Derby form with a good run in second. **Dartmouth** was given too much to do but stayed on into third past **Sir Isaac Newton** and the disappointing **Erupt**.

25 Qatar Sussex Stakes (1m) Goodwood July 27 (Good To Firm)

1 **The Gurkha** 3-9-0 Ryan Moore
2 **Galileo Gold** 3-9-0 Frankie Dettori
3 **Ribchester** 3-9-0 James Doyle
11/8F, 9/4, 8/1. nk, shd. 10 ran. 1m 37.35s (A P O'Brien).

Confirmation that this was a top-class bunch of three-year-old milers as the Classic generation proved utterly dominant, albeit against a poor older challenge, with **The Gurkha** edging out old rival **Galileo Gold** and a big improver in **Ribchester**. Arguably unlucky in the St James's Palace and the Eclipse, The Gurkha finally claimed a second Group 1 to go with his French Guineas crown as he escaped from a pocket 2f out and produced a smart turn of foot to cut down Galileo Gold, who had the run of the race in front. Ribchester was also short of room at a key time and finished strongly having taken too long to hit top gear, pulling 3l clear of **Toormore**, who was the best of the older horses with **Lightning Spear** below his best. **Awtaad** found the ground too quick as he dropped out quickly.

26 Qatar Nassau Stakes (Fillies & Mares) (1m1f192y)

Goodwood July 30 (Good To Firm)

1 **Minding** 3-8-11 Ryan Moore
2 **Queen's Trust** 3-8-11 James McDonald
3 **Jemayel** 3-8-11 Gregory Benoist
1/5F, 16/1, 16/1. 1¼l, 1¼l. 5 ran. 2m 5.05s (A P O'Brien).

Minding was nowhere near her best but again showed courage to go with her class to come through trying circumstances. Running on good to firm ground for the first time since being beaten as a two-year-old, Minding never looked comfortable but found enough to run out a fairly comfortable winner, with **Queen's Trust**, very much a work in progress and nowhere near her Breeders' Cup form, and **Jemayel** flattered to get so close.

27 Juddmonte International Stakes (1m2f88y)

York August 17 (Good To Firm)

1 **Postponed** 5-9-6 Andrea Atzeni
2 **Highland Reel** 4-9-6 Seamie Heffernan
3 **Mutakayyef** 5-9-6 Paul Hanagan
15/8F, 6/1, 15/2. 1¼l, 1l. 12 ran. 2m 6.58s (Roger Varian).

A terrific race dominated by the two 1m4f Group 1 winners in the field, with the speedier **Postponed** better suited by the shorter trip than **Highland Reel**. The pair ensured it was a true test, with Highland Reel setting the pace and Postponed never far away before quickening into the lead 3f out and staying on strongly. **Mutakayyef** ran a cracker in third and was the only horse to make an impression from further back – he might even have been second had Postponed not drifted across his path – while **Sir Isaac Newton** also stayed on well to pip **Exosphere** (now running in Australia under the name of Exospheric) for fourth. That quartet were 6l clear of **The Grey Gatsby**, with **Wings Of Desire** and **Hawkbill** among those behind.

MECCA'S ANGEL: rarely at her best last year but came good when it mattered

28 Darley Yorkshire Oaks (Fillies & Mares) (1m4f)

York August 18 (Good To Firm)

1 **Seventh Heaven** 3-8-11 C O'Donoghue
2 **Found** 4-9-7 Seamie Heffernan
3 **Queen's Trust** 3-8-11 Andrea Atzeni
100/30, 2/1F, 6/1. 2¾l, 1¼l. 12 ran. 2m 28.50s
(A P O'Brien).

A tremendous win for the rapidly improving **Seventh Heaven**, who came storming through from the rear with a decent field well strung out. Aidan O'Brien had warned that **Found** would need the run on her return from a mid-season break, but even so the form would prove rock-solid with **Queen's Trust** beaten a similar distance in the Fillies and Mares Stakes at Ascot, when unlucky not to finish much closer, and the leading trio 5l clear of **Pretty Perfect**, who set a sensible gallop up front and very nearly won the Park Hill next time.

29 Coolmore Nunthorpe Stakes (5f) York August 19 (Good)

1 **Mecca's Angel** 5-9-8 Paul Mulrennan
2 **Limato** 4-9-11 Harry Bentley
3 **Take Cover** 9-9-11 David Allan
9/2, 15/8F, 25/1. 2l, 2l. 19 ran. 56.24s
(Michael Dods).

Mecca's Angel was rarely at her best in 2016 but came good on the day that mattered most to her connections, storming to a second successive Nunthorpe win with an outstanding display of raw power. **Limato** proved his tremendous versatility with a huge run in second, beating the rest well as **Take Cover** came home next ahead of **Cotai Glory**, who just reversed King's Stand form with **Profitable** on this quicker ground.

30 32Red Sprint Cup Stakes (6f) Haydock September 3 (Soft)

1 **Quiet Reflection** 3-8-12 Dougie Costello
2 **The Tin Man** 4-9-3 Tom Queally
3 **Suedois** 5-9-3 Daniel Tudhope
7/2F, 6/1, 7/1. 1¾l, 2½l. 14 ran. 1m 13.45s
(K R Burke).

Soft ground ruined this race as it went against **The Tin Man** and **Magical Memory** while forcing the non-participation of Limato and Twilight Son, whose trainer Henry Candy read conditions badly wrong, so **Quiet Reflection** was left with very little to beat. That said, the Commonwealth Cup winner was still hugely impressive, quickening up smartly under only minimal assistance from the saddle. The Tin Man managed to come through for second despite the conditions to show the lack of depth to the race, with **Suedois** failing to run to form in third and the rest well strung out, including Magical Memory.

31 Ladbrokes St Leger (1m6f132y) Doncaster September 10 (Good)

1 **Harbour Law** 3-9-1 George Baker
2 **Ventura Storm** 3-9-1 Silvestre De Sousa
3 **Housesofparliament** 3-9-1C O'Donoghue
22/1, 14/1, 7/1. ¾l, shd. 9 ran. 3m 5.48s
(Laura Mongan).

Not a particularly classy Leger, especially with odds-on favourite **Idaho** unseating his rider when travelling strongly in the straight, but stamina came to the fore and **Harbour Law** showed tremendous staying power to come out on top. Harbour Law had been a 2l fourth in the Bahrain Trophy on his previous start behind **Housesofparliament**, who was in turn no match for Idaho in the Great Voltigeur, but he reversed that form over a longer trip and off a stronger gallop, getting on top close home as **Ventura Storm** just held off Housesofparliament for second. It was 10l back to **Muntahaa**, who was too keen.

32 Qipco Irish Champion Stakes (1m2f)

Leopardstown (IRE) September 10 (Yielding)

1 **Almanzor** 3-9-0 Christophe Soumillon
2 **Found** 4-9-4 Frankie Dettori
3 **Minding** 3-8-11 Ryan Moore
7/1, 7/1, 9/4. ¾l, 2¾l. 12 ran. 2m 8.93s
(J-C Rouget).

Probably the race of the season as **Almanzor** proved the best of six previous 2016 Group 1 winners and **Found** took a huge step forward to show the form that would soon see her win the Arc, the pair fighting out a thrilling finish. French Derby winner Almanzor just proved strongest, producing a powerful run down the outside to cut down Found in the final furlong. **Minding** was unlucky not to finish much closer in third, enduring a troubled run down the unfavoured rail, while it was another 1¾l back to **New Bay** and **My Dream Boat**. **Highland Reel** failed to fire in seventh, while **Harzand** was found to have been struck into after managing only eighth but still finished ahead of **Hawkbill**.

33 Coolmore Fastnet Rock Matron Stakes (1m)

Leopardstown (IRE) September 10 (Yielding)

1 **Alice Springs** 3-9-0 Ryan Moore
2 **Persuasive** 3-9-0 Frankie Dettori
3 **Qemah** 3-9-0 Gregory Benoist

5/1, 5/2, 11/8F. 3¼l, 1¼l. 8 ran. 1m 42.08s (A P O'Brien).

Another impressive victory for **Alice Springs**, who ran out a clear winner with main rivals **Qemah** and **Jet Setting** below their best. Still last turning for home, Alice Springs produced a tremendous burst down the outside to win easily from **Persuasive**, who did well on her first crack at Group 1 level having won five out of five previously. However, Qemah failed to settle and could manage only third ahead of **Now Or Never** while Jet Setting was a poor sixth. The only two older horses, both 33-1, filled the last two places.

34 Palmerstown House Estate Irish St. Leger (1m6f)

Curragh (IRE) September 11 (Yielding)

1 **Wicklow Brave** 7-9-11 Frankie Dettori
2 **Order Of St George** 4-9-11 Ryan Moore
3 **Trip To Paris** 5-9-11 Pat Smullen
11/1, 1/7F, 10/1. ½l, 16l. 4 ran. 3m 5.95s (W P Mullins).

A big upset as **Order Of St George** was beaten at 1-7, just failing to peg back **Wicklow Brave** having allowed the former hurdler a soft lead in front. Wicklow Brave did well to hang on as the pair pulled miles clear, but with only four runners, one an 80-1 shot, and the ground too soft for **Trip To Paris**, it may prove wise not to read much into the form.

35 Kingdom Of Bahrain Sun Chariot Stakes (Fillies & Mares) (1m)

Newmarket October 1 (Good To Firm)

1 **Alice Springs** 3-9-0 Ryan Moore
2 **Always Smile** 4-9-3 Andrea Atzeni
3 **Ervedya** 4-9-3 C-P Lemaire
13/8F, 7/1, 4/1. ¾l, 1l. 8 ran. 1m 37.46s (A P O'Brien).

A Group 1 hat-trick for **Alice Springs** and probably the best of the lot as she saw off the best older challenge she had faced, notably French star **Ervedya**. The first three were all ridden fairly prominently and Alice Springs quickened past the much-improved **Always Smile** and Ervedya before the furlong pole before staying on strongly. Another French filly, **Siyoushake**, did best of those held up in fourth ahead of **Irish Rookie**.

36 Qatar Prix de l'Arc de Triomphe (1m4f)

Chantilly (FR) October 2 (Good)

1 **Found** 4-9-2 Ryan Moore
2 **Highland Reel** 4-9-5 Seamie Heffernan
3 **Order Of St George** 4-9-5 Frankie Dettori
6/1, 20/1, 14/1. 1¾l, 1½l. 16 ran. 2m 23.61s (A P O'Brien).

A remarkable achievement for Aidan O'Brien as the Irish maestro sent out the first three, led by **Found**. At her best in the autumn and well suited by stepping up in trip, Found was always well placed just off a steady gallop and had too much speed for stablemates **Highland Reel**, who franked the form by going on to land the Breeders' Cup Turf when Found was below her best in third, and **Order Of St George**. Still, the race took a lot less winning than in most years, with top French three-year-old Almanzor a notable absentee and Derby winner **Harzand** having endured a troubled preparation after his Leopardstown injury – **Savoir Vivre** was the best-placed three-year-old in eighth, meaning no horse from the Classic generation in the first four for the first time since 1975 – while there were two 100-1 shots in the first six, the pair split by the disappointing **Postponed**.

37 Qipco British Champions Sprint Stakes (6f)

Ascot October 15 (Good)

1 **The Tin Man** 4-9-2 Tom Queally
2 **Growl** 4-9-2 Graham Lee
3 **Brando** 4-9-2 Tom Eaves
13/2, 50/1, 14/1. 1l, shd. 13 ran. 1m 12.15s (James Fanshawe).

The Tin Man finally had conditions in his favour and proved himself a Group 1 sprinter as he produced a stunning turn of foot to come through from the rear and win well, although the identity of the placed horses, **Growl** and **Brando**, showed that the gap from handicaps to the top level was perhaps smaller than ever in this division. Growl and Brando had finished first and second in reverse order in the Ayr Gold Cup, Growl reversing that form but with Brando potentially unlucky having done best of the unfavoured group on the stands side, with another progressive handicapper, **Librisa Breeze**, and **Quiet Reflection** next best of those on that side. **Twilight Son** and **Mecca's Angel** were both well below-par on their final runs.

38 Qipco British Champions Fillies & Mares Stakes (1m4f)

Ascot October 15 (Good)

1 **Journey** 4-9-5 Frankie Dettori
2 **Speedy Boarding** 4-9-5 Frederik Tylicki
3 **Queen's Trust** 3-8-12 Andrea Atzeni
4/1, 14/1, 11/1. 4l, nk. 13 ran. 2m 28.41s (John Gosden).

A strange race in which **Journey**'s superiority was exaggerated by trouble behind. Journey still won well as she was always well placed and quickened clear in impressive fashion in the straight. However, despite a solid gallop, several of those behind found all sorts of trouble, most notably the much-improved **Queen's Trust**, who finished strongly in third and would build on such promise when winning the Breeders' Cup Filly & Mare Turf, and the favourite **Seventh Heaven** in fifth. **Speedy Boarding**, a dual Group 1 winner in France, came through late into second, while **Pretty Perfect** and **Architecture** made up the first six before a 9l gap to the rest.

39 Queen Elizabeth II Stakes (1m) Ascot October 15 (Good)

1 **Minding** 3-8-12 Ryan Moore
2 **Ribchester** 3-9-1 William Buick
3 **Lightning Spear** 5-9-4 Oisin Murphy
7/4F, 7/2, 9/1. ½l, 1l. 13 ran. 1m 38.53s (A P O'Brien).

Minding confirmed her legacy with a seventh Group 1 win and first against the boys, justifying connections' decision to bring her back to a mile for the first time since May with a performance to rank alongside her Guineas win as her best. Minding got the better of a terrific duel with Prix Jacques le Marois winner **Ribchester**, who was slower to pick up as Minding quickened past him into a decisive lead before hanging on in the final furlong. The pair were perhaps favoured by being the only pair to track the pacemaker on the far side, with **Lightning Spear** running a stormer in third and pulling 2¼l clear of **Awtaad**. **Galileo Gold** was fifth, well below his best for the second time since the Sussex as his busy first half of the season perhaps took its toll, with **Jet Setting** among the also-rans.

40 Qipco Champion Stakes (1m2f) Ascot October 15 (Good)

1 **Almanzor** 3-9-0 Christophe Soumillon
2 **Found** 4-9-2 Ryan Moore
3 **Jack Hobbs** 4-9-5 William Buick
11/8F, 5/2, 7/1. 2l, 1¾l. 10 ran. 2m 5.94s (J-C Rouget).

A wonderful rematch between **Almanzor** and **Found** that left no doubt about the identity of the European champion, Almanzor proving himself the best around with another superb performance. Almanzor won far more easily this time, ridden closer to a steady gallop and quickening clear in the straight with Found unable to get close despite running on well in second. **Jack Hobbs** and **My Dream Boat** did well against the pace bias to fill the next two places, the latter just pipping **The Grey Gatsby** for fourth, while **US Army Ranger** found this far too sharp.

ALMANZOR: proved himself the best in Europe when winning at Ascot

Group 1 index

All horses placed or commented on in our Group 1 review section, with race numbers

JET SETTING: retired filly was a very different proposition on soft ground

SEVENTH HEAVEN: Yorkshire Oaks winner improved rapidly in the summer

Two-year-old review by Dylan Hill

1 BetVictor Million Pound Goal National Stakes (Listed Race) (5f6y)

Sandown May 26 (Good To Firm)

1 **Global Applause** 2-9-0 Ryan Moore
2 **Mehmas** 2-9-0 Frankie Dettori
3 **Bohemian Flame** 2-9-0 David Probert
9/2, 13/8F, 25/1. 1¼l, 2l. 6 ran. 1m 1.17s (Ed Dunlop).

A good clash between two smart juveniles, with **Mehmas**, who would prove the best of them in time, unlucky not to win. **Global Applause** was soon in front and made virtually all, whereas Mehmas was slowly away from the widest draw and too far back once brought wide to challenge.

2 Coventry Stakes (Group 2) (6f) Ascot June 14 (Soft)

1 **Caravaggio** 2-9-1 Ryan Moore
2 **Mehmas** 2-9-1 Frankie Dettori
3 **Psychedelic Funk** 2-9-1 Colin Keane
13/8F, 8/1, 9/2. 2¼l, 2½l. 18 ran. 1m 16.36s (A P O'Brien).

It's a shame little more was seen of **Caravaggio** over the rest of the season, but this was already enough to stake a strong claim for leading two-year-old honours. Facing a top-class rival in **Mehmas** – a similarly early juvenile and a dual subsequent Group 2 scorer – Caravaggio was also drawn on the wrong side, but he had the class to edge across almost the entire track and still quicken well clear of his rivals. Mehmas also beat the rest comfortably, with **Psychedelic Funk** the best of them, though other fancied runners flopped with **Thunder Snow**, **Yalta** and **Mokarris** struggling on the soft ground.

3 Windsor Castle Stakes (Listed Race) (5f)

Ascot June 14 (Soft)

1 **Ardad** 2-9-3 Robert Havlin
2 **Savannah's Dream** 2-8-12 Phillip Makin
3 **Pedestal** 2-9-3 Ryan Moore
20/1, 100/1, 14/1. 3¼l, nse. 22 ran. 1m 2.56s (John Gosden).

This was a very moderate race – the next three failed to win another race over the rest of the season in seven attempts between them – but **Ardad** still showed he belonged at a higher level by treating them with disdain, quickening up very smartly to win well.

4 Queen Mary Stakes (Group 2) (Fillies) (5f)

Ascot June 15 (Soft)

1 **Lady Aurelia** 2-9-0 Frankie Dettori
2 **Al Johrah** 2-9-0 Gregory Benoist
3 **Clem Fandango** 2-9-0 Phillip Makin
2/1F, 9/2, 16/1. 7l, 2½l. 17 ran. 1m 0.14s (Wesley A Ward).

One of the most astonishing performances seen at Royal Ascot in recent history as **Lady Aurelia** blitzed her rivals with a staggering display of raw speed, winning by 7l even with Frankie Dettori saluting the crowd in the final 100 yards. The opposition weren't slouches either, with smart French filly **Al Johrah** a clear second ahead of **Clem Fandango**, whose subsequent Listed win confirmed her appreciation for some cut in the ground, although Lady Aurelia enjoyed a huge physical advantage over her rivals and it remains to be seen whether that will be the case as a three-year-old. **Roly Poly** was only eighth.

LADY AURELIA: one of the most stunning winners in Royal Ascot history

5 Norfolk Stakes (Group 2) (5f)
Ascot June 16 (Soft)

1 **Prince Of Lir** 2-9-1 Luke Morris
2 **The Last Lion** 2-9-1 Joe Fanning
3 **Silver Line** 2-9-1 James Doyle

8/1, 20/1, 7/2. ½l, nk. 11 ran. 1m 1.17s (Robert Cowell).

A fiercely competitive race with three early-season Listed winners, most notably **Global Applause**, managing no better than fourth behind **Prince Of Lir**, who was much better than he showed subsequently. Perhaps dependent on this soft ground, Prince Of Lir was just too strong for **The Last Lion**, **Silver Line** and **Peace Envoy**, who all finished within little over 1l but would give the form a solid look. Global Applause proved less effective on soft ground in fifth ahead of Woodcote winner **Legendary Lunch**.

6 Albany Stakes (Group 3) (Fillies) (6f)
Ascot June 17 (Good To Soft)

1 **Brave Anna** 2-9-0 Seamie Heffernan
2 **Bletchley** 2-9-0 Oisin Murphy
3 **Queen Kindly** 2-9-0 Jamie Spencer

16/1, 16/1, 13/2. shd, ½l. 16 ran. 1m 15.20s (A P O'Brien).

Favourite **Cuff** sadly fractured a knee in finishing fifth and had to be retired, but Aidan O'Brien had a strong second string to his bow in **Brave Anna**, who ran out a narrow winner over **Bletchley** and **Queen Kindly**. That trio all came from well off the pace, making the most of a good gallop set by **Kilmah**, who would prove much the best of the rest after weakening late into sixth.

7 Chesham Stakes (Listed Race) (7f)
Ascot June 18 (Good To Soft)

1 **Churchill** 2-9-3 Ryan Moore
2 **Isomer** 2-9-3 Jamie Spencer
3 **Cunco** 2-9-3 Robert Havlin

8/11F, 25/1, 7/2. ½l, 1l. 13 ran. 1m 29.57s (A P O'Brien).

Churchill kicked off his winning run without any of the fireworks we would see later in the season. Churchill still did the job with plenty of authority as he was too good for **Isomer**, with his two strongest opponents, **Cunco** and **Frankuus**, both in need of further as they finished third and fifth.

8 GAIN Railway Stakes (Group 2) (6f)
Curragh (IRE) June 25 (Good To Yielding)

1 **Medicine Jack** 2-9-3 Colin Keane
2 **Peace Envoy** 2-9-3 Ryan Moore

ROLY POLY: two Group wins in two weeks but definitely better at Newmarket

3 **Dream Of Dreams** 2-9-3 Pat Smullen
6/1, 7/4J, 7/4J. ½l, 1½l. 8 ran. 1m 13.20s
(G M Lyons).

A gutsy win for **Medicine Jack**, though he probably didn't achieve as much as it looked at the time. Form horse **Peace Envoy**, up in trip after his Norfolk fourth, didn't seem ready for the extra furlong at this stage, wandering in the final 150 yards just as he had headed the winner, while fellow joint-favourite **Dream Of Dreams** would prove a shade disappointing all season. **King Electric** and **Ready To Roc** were next.

9 Grangecon Stud Stakes (Group 3) (Fillies) (6f)

Curragh (IRE) June 26 (Yielding)

1 **Roly Poly** 2-9-0 Ryan Moore
2 **Seafront** 2-9-0 Pat Smullen
3 **Elusive Beauty** 2-9-0 Shane Foley
3/1F, 7/2, 12/1. nk, ¾l. 7 ran. 1m 15.32s
(A P O'Brien).

A good Group 3 which produced three of the first five in the Duchess of Cambridge, although **Roly Poly** was yet to reach her Newmarket level. Roly Poly took her time in shaking off **Seafront**, while **Magical Fire** travelled notably well before fading into fifth in the final furlong.

10 Arqana July Stakes (Group 2) (6f) Newmarket July 7 (Good To Firm)

1 **Mehmas** 2-9-0 Frankie Dettori
2 **Intelligence Cross** 2-9-0 Ryan Moore
3 **Broken Stones** 2-9-0 Jamie Spencer
11/4F, 7/1, 8/1. ½l, 1l. 9 ran. 1m 10.92s
(Richard Hannon).

Deserved compensation for **Mehmas** after his fine second in the Coventry as he saw off a useful field. Mehmas stayed on well and was always holding the more patiently ridden **Intelligence Cross**, while **Broken Stones** just pipped Norfolk third **Silver Line** for third with the leading quartet 2½l clear of **Medici Banchiere**.

11 Duchess of Cambridge Stakes (Group 2) (Fillies) (6f)

Newmarket July 8 (Good To Firm)

1 **Roly Poly** 2-9-0 Ryan Moore
2 **Magical Fire** 2-9-0 Colm O'Donoghue
3 **Nations Alexander** 2-9-0 Pat Dobbs
6/1, 33/1, 16/1. ½l, hd. 10 ran. 1m 10.72s
(A P O'Brien).

Curragh form held the key as **Roly Poly** confirmed her good heart with a quickfire double, improving on quicker ground. This time **Magical Fire** proved her main threat, building on her promising fifth under a far more patient ride, while **Nations Alexander** and **Kilmah** also finished within ¾l before going on to win Group 3 races over further to confirm the form as solid if not spectacular. **Seafront** was 2l back in fifth to underline the progress made by the first two, while **Bletchley** was a disappointing sixth.

12 bet365 Superlative Stakes (Group 2) (7f)

Newmarket July 9 (Good To Firm)

1 **Boynton** 2-9-1 Adam Kirby
2 **War Decree** 2-9-1 Ryan Moore
3 **Mr Scaramanga** 2-9-1 Pat Dobbs
7/1, EvensF, 16/1. ¾l, 5l. 9 ran. 1m 24.86s
(Charlie Appleby).

A tremendous clash between two high-class colts, with **Boynton** getting the better of **War Decree.** Boynton, having quickened into the lead 2f out, was soon headed before knuckling down best in the final furlong, but War Decree looked green in second and would comprehensively reverse the form at Glorious Goodwood. The pair pulled 5l clear of **Mr Scaramanga** and **Cunco**.

13 Jebel Ali Racecourse & Stables Anglesey Stakes (Group 3) (6f63y)

Curragh (IRE) July 16 (Good To Yielding)

1 **Peace Envoy** 2-9-3 Ryan Moore
2 **Psychedelic Funk** 2-9-3 Colin Keane
3 **Mirdif** 2-9-3 Pat Smullen
3/1, 9/10F, 25/1. 1¾l, ½l. 6 ran. 1m 17.13s (A P O'Brien).

Punters expected **Psychedelic Funk** to confirm the strength of the Coventry form, but **Peace Envoy** was improving all the time and won comfortably. Given a more patient ride than when outstayed in the Railway, Peace Envoy quickened up well to come clear of Psychedelic Funk in the final 100 yards. **Mirdif** was third ahead of **Radio Silence** and **Ready To Roc**.

14 Japan Racing Association Tyros Stakes (Group 3) (7f)

Leopardstown (IRE) July 21 (Good To Firm)

1 **Churchill** 2-9-3 Ryan Moore
2 **Alexios Komnenos** 2-9-3 Wayne Lordan
3 **Currency Converter** 2-9-3 Pat Smullen
2/5F, 8/1, 7/1. nk, 2l. 6 ran. 1m 28.37s (A P O'Brien).

The next step up the ladder for **Churchill**, who always looked like landing odds of 2-5 despite the narrow margin. **Alexios Komnenos** ran a fine race and was set to lock horns with the winner again in the National Stakes until meeting a setback, though he was seemingly flattered to get so close with Churchill still green in front and the fourth and fifth, **King Electric** and **Ready To Roc**, both closer than in other races at Group level.

15 Jockey Club Of Turkey Silver Flash Stakes (Group 3) (7f)

Leopardstown (IRE) July 21 (Good To Firm)

1 **Promise To Be True** 2-9-0 Ryan Moore
2 **Take A Deep Breath** 2-9-0 Pat Smullen
3 **Intricately** 2-9-0 Donnacha O'Brien
4/6F, 5/1, 7/1. 1¼l, nse. 6 ran. 1m 28.83s (A P O'Brien).

A really strong race featuring the subsequent Moyglare winner and Marcel Boussac runner-up, although it would have been hard to believe **Promise To Be True** wouldn't be the one to win at the top level on this evidence. Promise To Be True quickened up well to beat **Take A Deep Breath**, with **Intricately** the one to make giant strides to the top after her third, while the fourth, **Drumfad Bay**, would prove a rock-solid yardstick to boost the form further.

16 Princess Margaret Juddmonte Stakes (Group 3) (Fillies) (6f)

Ascot July 23 (Good To Firm)

1 **Fair Eva** 2-9-0 Frankie Dettori
2 **Kilmah** 2-9-0 Joe Fanning
3 **Dainty Dandy** 2-9-0 Olivier Peslier
4/6F, 12/1, 25/1. 4l, ¾l. 12 ran. 1m 12.54s (Roger Charlton).

A spectacular performance from **Fair Eva**, who made smooth progress before storming clear in the final furlong, although two subsequent defeats at a higher level raised justifiable questions over the form. There were two Group 3 winners behind, but runner-up **Kilmah** seemed to improve for an extra furlong when winning at Goodwood and **Madam Dancealot** was well below her best here while there were several seemingly regressive fillies behind, with the next three finishing no better than ninth in four subsequent outings between them over the rest of the summer.

17 Qatar Vintage Stakes (Group 2) (7f)

Goodwood July 26 (Good To Firm)

1 **War Decree** 2-9-1 Ryan Moore
2 **Thunder Snow** 2-9-1 James McDonald
3 **Boynton** 2-9-4 James Doyle
6/4F, 13/2, 2/1. 1¾l, 1l. 9 ran. 1m 25.75s (A P O'Brien).

War Decree won his rematch with **Boynton** in comprehensive fashion as he took a big step forward to win a strong race. War Decree was always going well before forging clear in the final furlong and, while the first and third weren't seen again, the success of runner-up **Thunder Snow** and fourth-placed **Pleaseletmewin** gave the form a serious boost. Boynton ran another good race under his 3lb penalty to split the pair, especially given he had to be switched to find room, though War Decree was far too good.

18 Victoria Racing Club Molecomb Stakes (Group 3) (5f)

Goodwood July 27 (Good)

1 **Yalta** 2-9-1 James Doyle

2 **The Last Lion** 2-9-1 Franny Norton
3 **Global Applause** 2-9-1 Frankie Dettori
8/1, 3/1, 2/1F. 3l, ¾l. 9 ran. 57.14s
(Mark Johnston).

Yalta disappointed far more often than he delivered over the season, but it's hard to find any holes in this devastating victory as he smashed the juvenile course record. Showing great speed on this drop to 5f, Yalta set a blistering gallop and stormed clear of **The Last Lion** and **Global Applause**, who got closer to the runner-up than at Ascot back on quicker ground. **Sportsmanship**, much closer in a Group 3 at the Curragh next time, was next, well clear of **Big Time Baby**, who was too keen and got unbalanced.

19 Qatar Richmond Stakes (Group 2) (6f)

Goodwood July 28 (Good To Firm)

1 **Mehmas** 2-9-3 Frankie Dettori
2 **Blue Point** 2-9-0 James Doyle
3 **Intelligence Cross** 2-9-0 Ryan Moore
7/2, 5/6F, 5/2. nk, 3l. 4 ran. 1m 11.00s
(Richard Hannon).

Mehmas peaked with this tremendous victory as he gave 3lb and a narrow beating to the subsequent Gimcrack winner **Blue Point**. Mehmas showed terrific battling qualities to get the better of a protracted duel with Blue Point, though the runner-up didn't look to handle the track as well as he hung right in the final furlong. **Intelligence Cross** was below his best in third.

20 German-Thoroughbred.com Sweet Solera Stakes (Group 3) (Fillies) (7f)

Newmarket August 6 (Good To Firm)

1 **Nations Alexander** 2-9-0 Pat Dobbs
2 **Grecian Light** 2-9-0 James Doyle
3 **On Her Toes** 2-9-0 Pat Cosgrave
4/1, 9/2, 5/1. 1½l, nk. 9 ran. 1m 26.03s
(Richard Hannon).

An all-the-way win for **Nations Alexander**, who saw out the extra furlong well but probably didn't have to improve on her Duchess of Cambridge third. Nations Alexander comfortably saw off **Grecian Light**, who just took second in a bunch finish behind ahead of Sandown Listed winner **On Her Toes**, **Urban Fox** and **Tiburtina**. **Belle Meade** was very much a work in progress as she finished only seventh.

21 Keeneland Phoenix Stakes (Group 1) (6f)

Curragh (IRE) August 7 (Good To Firm)

1 **Caravaggio** 2-9-3 Seamie Heffernan
2 **Courage Under Fire** 2-9-3 M Hussey
3 **Medicine Jack** 2-9-3 Colin Keane
1/8F, 33/1, 4/1. 4l, 2¾l. 5 ran. 1m 11.79s
(A P O'Brien).

Another win for the brilliant **Caravaggio** but a disappointing non-event with only one of his four rivals priced less than 25-1 and pacemaker **Courage Under Fire**, no better than fifth in two runs at Group 3 level later in the season, staying closest to him as **Medicine Jack** laboured into third.

22 Bathwick Tyres St Hugh's Fillies' Stakes (Listed Race) (5f34y)

Newbury August 12 (Good To Firm)

1 **Mrs Danvers** 2-9-0 Richard Kingscote
2 **Equimou** 2-9-0 Andrea Atzeni
3 **Stormy Clouds** 2-9-0 Pat Dobbs
5/2F, 9/1, 12/1. 2l, 1¼l. 11 ran. 1m 1.30s
(Jonathan Portman).

A strong Listed race in which the unbeaten **Mrs Danvers**, who had been strongly favoured by the weights when winning the Super Sprint, proved she could cut it at a higher level. The flying filly was always going well and quickened clear of **Equimou**, beaten a shade further in the Flying Childers soon after, and **Stormy Clouds**, who went on to win a big sales race at York.

23 Denford Stud Washington Singer Stakes (Listed Race) (7f)

Newbury August 13 (Good To Firm)

1 **Escobar** 2-9-1 Frankie Dettori
2 **Mr Scaramanga** 2-9-1 Sean Levey
3 **Amabilis** 2-8-10 Pat Smullen
EvensF, 6/1, 4/1. 1¼l, 5l. 4 ran. 1m 26.17s
(Hugo Palmer).

An impressive win from **Escobar** but not one to go overboard about on the form book, which was perhaps the case when he was sent off at just 6-5 up in grade next time. Escobar easily saw off **Mr Scaramanga**, though that one didn't seem to step up on his well-beaten Superlative third, while **Frankuus** was well below his best.

24 Tattersalls Acomb Stakes (Group 3) (7f)

York August 17 (Good To Firm)

1 **Syphax** 2-9-1 Jamie Spencer
2 **Best Of Days** 2-9-1 William Buick
3 **Lockheed** 2-9-1 Frankie Dettori
16/1, 10/11F, 7/2. hd, ¾l. 7 ran. 1m 23.46s
(Kevin Ryan).

A good race in which the first three pulled 2¼l clear of the rest, with **Syphax** getting up for a last-gasp success over **Best Of Days** and **Lockheed**. Best Of Days, the subsequent Royal Lodge winner, was perhaps unlucky, travelling like the best horse and reportedly coming back jarred up, although he coped fine with similar ground at Newmarket.

25 Sky Bet Lowther Stakes (Group 2) (Fillies) (6f)

York August 18 (Good To Firm)

1 **Queen Kindly** 2-9-0 Jamie Spencer
2 **Roly Poly** 2-9-3 Seamie Heffernan
3 **Fair Eva** 2-9-0 Pat Smullen
9/2, 15/2, 4/11F. ¾l, ¾l. 8 ran. 1m 9.84s (Richard Fahey).

A big upset as **Fair Eva**'s bubble was burst, with **Queen Kindly**, able to quicken better on this fast ground than when third in the Albany, taking advantage. Queen Kindly was an authoritative winner over **Roly Poly**, who emerged best at the weights under a 3lb penalty, while Fair Eva travelled well on the outside but failed to find a change of gear. That trio were 4½l clear of the rest, but the bare form might be misleading as **Nations Alexander** and **Kilmah** were both better over further, especially in the conditions, while the ground was too quick for **Clem Fandango**.

26 EBF Stallions Stonehenge Stakes (Listed Race) (1m)

Salisbury August 19 (Good)

1 **Montataire** 2-9-1 Franny Norton
2 **Gemina** 2-8-10 Steve Drowne
3 **Sea Fox** 2-9-1 William Twiston-Davies
7/1, 16/1, 20/1. 5l, ¾l. 10 ran. 1m 42.63s (Mark Johnston).

Montataire had progressed rapidly in nurseries and took another big step forward with this excellent victory as he made all at a good enough gallop that it was a whopping 18l back to the fifth. While Montataire was well beaten in two subsequent runs at Newmarket, the fact he finished behind the Salisbury third, **Sea Fox**, in the Royal Lodge underlines how far he was below this form that day.

27 Irish Thoroughbred Marketing Gimcrack Stakes (Group 2) (6f)

York August 20 (Good)

1 **Blue Point** 2-9-0 William Buick
2 **Mokarris** 2-9-0 Paul Hanagan
3 **The Last Lion** 2-9-0 Franny Norton
11/8F, 11/2, 14/1. 3l, 1¾l. 10 ran. 1m 9.00s (Charlie Appleby).

A hugely impressive performance from **Blue Point**, who seemed to appreciate the flat terrain of York much more than Goodwood and perhaps even Newmarket as he stormed to victory over a strong field. Blue Point was always prominent and quickened clear of **Mokarris**, who backed up an easy win in a Listed race at Newbury to prove himself a very useful colt. **The Last Lion**, **Global Applause** and **Grey Britain** were next, with subsequent Middle Park winner The Last Lion not quite seeing out the trip this time on his

BLUE POINT: hugely impressive when running away with the Gimcrack

KILMAH: just held on to win the Prestige Stakes having been gifted a soft lead

first attempt at 6f, while **Medici Banchiere** was beaten 2½l further in sixth than he had been in the July Stakes and both **Ardad** and **Mubtasim** were disappointing.

28 Julia Graves Roses Stakes (Listed Race) (5f)

York August 20 (Good)

1 **Big Time Baby** 2-9-0 Frankie Dettori
2 **Afandem** 2-9-3 Andrea Atzeni
3 **Smokey Lane** 2-9-0 Declan McDonogh
6/1, 7/2, 10/1. hd, 4l. 8 ran. 57.11s
(Tom Dascombe).

Too keen in the Molecomb, **Big Time Baby** settled much better and showed his true form as he held off a very useful rival in **Afandem**, who wasn't beaten far in the Flying Childers soon after and did well to pull 4l clear of **Smokey Lane**.

29 TCA Abu Dhabi Solario Stakes (Group 3) (7f16y)

Sandown August 20 (Good To Soft)

1 **South Seas** 2-9-1 Oisin Murphy
2 **Salouen** 2-9-1 Tom Marquand
3 **Eqtiraan** 2-9-1 Timmy Murphy
9/4F, 16/1, 8/1. 2¼l, 1l. 10 ran. 1m 30.81s
(Andrew Balding).

A really strong Group 3 won in emphatic fashion by **South Seas** as he stayed on strongly to see off the fast-improving **Salouen**, with the pair finishing placed three times between them at Group 1 level later in the year to show the strength of the form. South Seas had won his first two races on soft ground and again appreciated plenty of rain as he stayed on powerfully, suggesting he should be forgiven his Dewhurst flop in quicker conditions. There was plenty of depth to the race with **Apex King**, a Listed winner over the trip at Ascot from **Monticello**, extending his superiority over that horse as they finished fourth and sixth, split by the useful **Majoris**.

30 Jimmy O'Neill Irish Racing Excellence Curragh Stakes (Group 3) (5f)

Curragh (IRE) August 20 (Good)

1 **Hit The Bid** 2-9-3 Leigh Roche
2 **Mur Hiba** 2-9-0 Kevin Manning
3 **Yulong Baobei** 2-9-0 Shane Foley
50/1, 10/1, 9/4. ½l, ½l. 10 ran. 1m 0.04s
(D J Bunyan).

Hit The Bid pulled off a 50-1 shock as he was transformed by a wind operation, though he dropped lucky in a weak race for the grade. Just 2½l covered the first eight, including the filly **Yulong Baobei**, who had won a poor Listed race at Tipperary and seemed to have her limitations exposed, **Velveteen** and **Sportsmanship**.

31 Galileo European Breeders Fund Futurity Stakes (Group 2) (7f)

Curragh (IRE) August 21 (Yielding To Soft)

1 **Churchill** 2-9-3 Seamie Heffernan
2 **Radio Silence** 2-9-3 Kevin Manning
3 **Arcada** 2-9-3 Donnacha O'Brien
1/4F, 5/1, 12/1. 2l, ¾l. 4 ran. 1m 27.36s
(A P O'Brien).

There was little opposition to **Churchill**, who was was sent off just 1-4 to beat an ordinary bunch, but he at least did it more impressively than in previous runs. Having quickened to the front, Churchill was strong at the finish this time as he pulled away from **Radio Silence**, who seemed to improve for the extra furlong after his Anglesey fourth, and subsequent Royal Lodge third **Arcada**.

32 Breast Cancer Research Debutante Stakes (Group 2) (7f)

Curragh (IRE) August 21 (Yielding To Soft)
1 **Rhododendron** 2-9-0 Seamie Heffernan
2 **Hydrangea** 2-9-0 P B Beggy
3 **Intricately** 2-9-0 Donnacha O'Brien
11/8F, 10/1, 14/1. hd, 1¼l. 9 ran. 1m 27.06s
(A P O'Brien).

A fantastic battle between **Rhododendron** and **Hydrangea**, with their subsequent dominance of the Fillies' Mile confirming these were two high-class fillies. Rhododendron looked to have mastered long-time leader Hydrangea at the furlong pole, but the runner-up rallied strongly and went down fighting in a thriller. **Intricately** wasn't beaten far in third, albeit without giving any sign of the shock she would pull off in the Moyglare, while **Rehana** and **Drumfad Bay** were next ahead of the disappointing **Brave Anna**.

33 Darley Prix Morny (Group 1) (6f)

Deauville (FR) August 21 (Good)
1 **Lady Aurelia** 2-8-10 Frankie Dettori
2 **Alrahma** 2-8-10 Aurelien Lemaitre
3 **Peace Envoy** 2-9-0 Colm O'Donoghue
2/7F, 14/1, 12/1. ¾l, hd. 5 ran. 1m 10.61s
(Wesley A Ward).

A rather underwhelming follow-up from **Lady Aurelia**, who didn't need to be anywhere near her best to come out on top with main rival **Peace Envoy** given far too much to do. Lady Aurelia settled nicely in front and was always in command as she saw off fellow fillies **Alrahma** and **Al Johrah**, the Queen Mary runner-up getting a lot closer this time, with that pair split on the line by Peace Envoy, who had been 6l last with little over a furlong out before finishing strongly. British raider **Tis Marvellous**, who had beaten Al Johrah in the Prix Robert Papin, faded tamely to finish last.

34 Prestige Stakes (Group 3) (Fillies) (7f)

Goodwood August 27 (Good To Firm)
1 **Kilmah** 2-9-0 Franny Norton
2 **Promising** 2-9-0 Sean Levey
3 **Urban Fox** 2-9-0 Martin Harley
5/1, 4/1, 6/1. nk, 2¼l. 7 ran. 1m 27.08s
(Mark Johnston).

Kilmah had already proved herself a very useful filly and appreciated this extra furlong, although she was probably flattered slightly as she was gifted a soft lead and managed to make all over **Promising**. Subsequent May Hill winner **Rich Legacy** was the most unlucky having dropped to last when short of room before finishing strongly to split **Urban Fox** and **Tiburtina**, while **Belle Meade** was only sixth and **Grecian Light** last of the septet having failed to settle.

35 Flame Of Tara European Breeders Fund Stakes (Group 3) (Fillies) (1m)

Curragh (IRE) August 28 (Good)
1 **Sea Of Grace** 2-9-0 Declan McDonogh
2 **Eziyra** 2-9-0 Pat Smullen
3 **Butterflies** 2-9-0 Seamie Heffernan
7/2, EvensF, 7/2. nk, 3½l. 7 ran. 1m 37.90s
(John M Oxx).

A good clash between two smart fillies, with **Sea Of Grace**, having travelled best and hit the front early, rallying bravely when headed to get the better of **Eziyra**. The pair pulled well clear of the rest and the form proved strong with Eziyra and the fourth, **Legitimus**, running to the pound when first and third in another Group 3 at the track the following month.

36 Round Tower Stakes (Group 3) (6f)

Curragh (IRE) August 28 (Good)
1 **Intelligence Cross** 2-9-3 S Heffernan
2 **Holy Cat** 2-9-0 Colin Keane
3 **De Boss Man** 2-9-3 Colm O'Donoghue
11/8F, 2/1, 10/1. 4¼l, nk. 9 ran. 1m 12.06s
(A P O'Brien).

Disappointing in the Richmond, **Intelligence Cross** got back on track with a tremendous victory as he proved different class on this drop in grade. Intelligence Cross coasted clear of **Holy Cat** and **De Boss Man**, who in turn had daylight to the rest including **Velveteen** and **Sportsmanship**.

37 Longines Irish Champions Weekend EBF Ripon Champion 2YO Trophy (Listed Race) (6f)

Ripon August 29 (Good To Soft)
1 **Alicante Dawn** 2-9-3 Connor Beasley
2 **Private Matter** 2-9-3 Paul Hanagan
3 **Grand Coalition** 2-9-3 Daniel Tudhope
7/2, 9/1, 7/1. 2¼l, 1¾l. 6 ran. 1m 12.81s
(Bryan Smart).

While there may not have been much to beat – disappointing favourite **Kodiline** was odds-on despite being well beaten already in this grade by Mokarris – this was still mightily impressive from **Alicante Dawn**, who made all the running and kept on strongly for a comfortable win. **Private Matter** was a clear second and would later win at this level at Maisons-Laffitte.

38 Bathwick Tyres Dick Poole Fillies' Stakes (Group 3) (6f)

Salisbury September 1 (Good)
1 **Madam Dancealot** 2-9-0 Tom Queally
2 **Mystic Dawn** 2-9-0 F M Berry
3 **Pellucid** 2-9-0 Jamie Spencer
10/1, 4/1, 5/1. 1¼l, 1l. 9 ran. 1m 14.49s
(Joseph Tuite).

Moderate form with the first four all well beaten several times in similar grade, but **Madam Dancealot** at least proved much better than a tame effort in the Princess Margaret as she made most of the running and galloped her rivals into submission. Favourite **Perfect Angel** would prove just about the best filly in the race but was a below-par fifth.

39 totequadpot Sirenia Stakes (Group 3) (6f)

Kempton (AW) September 3 (Standard To Slow)
1 **The Last Lion** 2-9-1 Joe Fanning
2 **Koropick** 2-9-1 Jim Crowley
3 **Unabated** 2-9-1 James Doyle
11/8, 11/10F, 10/1. 4l, ½l. 7 ran. 1m 12.70s
(Mark Johnston).

An overdue breakthrough at Group level for **The Last Lion**, who showed he was still progressing with a commanding victory. Always prominent, The Last Lion only needed to be shaken up to storm clear of **Koropick**, while **Smokey Lane** failed to handle the bend.

40 32Red Casino Stakes (registered as the Ascendant Stakes) (Listed Race) (1m)

Haydock September 3 (Soft)
1 **Frankuus** 2-9-2 Franny Norton
2 **Star Of Rory** 2-9-2 Richard Kingscote
3 **Cunco** 2-9-2 Frankie Dettori
5/1, 7/1, 9/4F. ¾l, ½l. 6 ran. 1m 47.97s
(Mark Johnston).

An interesting race for bringing back together Frankel colts **Frankuus** and **Cunco**, who had disappointed since maiden wins saw them go off well fancied for the Chesham, but a stiffer stamina test saw both improve, with Frankuus coming out on top before landing a Group 3 at Chantilly when stepped up to 1m1f. **Star Of Rory** did well to split the pair. with **Contrast** also beaten just 2l.

41 Weatherbys Hamilton £300,000 2YO Stakes (6f110y)

Doncaster September 8 (Good)
1 **Mubtasim** 2-8-9 Pat Cosgrave
2 **Mazyoun** 2-8-9 William Buick
3 **Firefright** 2-8-12 Jamie Spencer
4/1, 12/1, 16/1. 1¾l, ¾l. 19 ran. 1m 19.58s
(William Haggas).

This looked a good race on paper, much better than the numerous other valuable sales races over the season, though a significant pace bias worked in **Mubtasim**'s favour. Mubtasim came through strongly from the rear for a decisive success, but he flopped either side of it in the Gimcrack and Middle Park while the third, fourth and fifth also disappointed after benefiting from hold-up rides. **Mazyoun** did much the best of those ridden prominently before a half-length third behind Wick Powell in the Two-Year-Old Trophy at Redcar, while York sales winner **Stormy Clouds** faded late into seventh and **Global Applause** got no luck in running.

42 Clugston Construction May Hill Stakes (Group 2) (1m)

Doncaster September 8 (Good)
1 **Rich Legacy** 2-9-0 Oisin Murphy
2 **Grecian Light** 2-9-0 William Buick
3 **Urban Fox** 2-9-0 Martin Harley
3/1, 8/1, 11/1. ¾l, 2¼l. 9 ran. 1m 41.24s
(Ralph Beckett).

Probably not a vintage renewal with none of the Irish or French fillies who would go on to dominate similar races in Britain, but **Rich Legacy** at least showed her true colours as she built on her promising run at Goodwood. In front 2f out, Rich Legacy showed her staying power as she rallied strongly once headed by **Grecian Light**, who bounced back to form in second. **Urban Fox**, briefly short of room but well held in the end, finished third ahead of **Reachforthestars**, while **Tiburtina** raced much too keenly, favourite **Blending**, an impressive maiden winner at Newbury, was only sixth and **Kilmah** blew out after boiling over in the stalls.

ARDAD: back to his best as he returned to the minimum trip at Doncaster

43 Pepsi Max Flying Childers Stakes (Group 2) (5f)

Doncaster September 9 (Good)

1 **Ardad** 2-9-1 Frankie Dettori
2 **Legendary Lunch** 2-9-1 Ryan Moore
2 **The Last Lion** 2-9-1 Joe Fanning
5/1, 25/1, 11/2. ¾l, dht. 11 ran. 59.19s (John Gosden).

Ardad put a couple of disappointments over 6f behind him as he won well on his first run at the minimum trip since his Windsor Castle success from a solid bunch of sprinters. Ardad travelled strongly in rear and stuck on well to see off dead-heaters **Legendary Lunch**, running by far his best race, and **The Last Lion**, who may have just found the return to 5f or quick turnaround from Kempton against him. **Afandem** was next ahead of **Rainbow Mist** and **Equimou**, while **Prince Of Lir**, **Tis Marvellous**, **Yalta** and **Hit The Bid** were all behind.

44 Weatherbys Stallion Book Flying Scotsman Stakes (Listed Race) (7f)

Doncaster September 9 (Good)

1 **Rodaini** 2-9-0 Silvestre De Sousa
2 **Salsabeel** 2-9-0 William Buick
3 **Larchmont Lad** 2-9-0 Sean Levey
6/1, 7/2, 6/1. shd, nse. 7 ran. 1m 27.49s (Simon Crisford).

A really good Listed race on paper, with five of the seven runners unbeaten and the form working out really well courtesy of the third, **Larchmont Lad**, who couldn't quite match **Rodaini** and **Salsabeel**. Most of the field pulled hard off a slow pace, but Rodaini was one of the most keen yet still managed to sweep to a narrow victory and can be forgiven two subsequent disappointments, having nothing go right in the Autumn Stakes before being forced very wide at the Breeders' Cup. The first three also did well to pull 3½l clear of **Majoris**, who had been beaten only a shade further by South Seas in the Solario.

45 At The Races Champagne Stakes (Group 2) (7f)

Doncaster September 10 (Good)

1 **Rivet** 2-9-0 Andrea Atzeni
2 **Thunder Snow** 2-9-0 James Doyle
3 **D'bai** 2-9-0 William Buick
7/4F, 2/1, 8/1. hd, 5l. 6 ran. 1m 26.63s (William Haggas).

A terrific clash between two subsequent Group 1 winners, with **Rivet** too good for **Thunder Snow**. Rivet took a long time to get on top, but that was understandable off a slow pace for a colt who would thrive over a mile later in the season. The pair were much better than the rest, with **D'bai**, good enough to win a soft Listed race at Pontefract later, edging out **Majeste** for a distant third ahead of Gimcrack fourth **Grey Britain**, who didn't seem to stay the extra furlong.

46 Willis Towers Watson Champions Juvenile Stakes (Group 3) (1m)

Leopardstown (IRE) September 10 (Good)

1 **Landfall** 2-9-3 Shane Foley
2 **Firey Speech** 2-9-3 Pat Smullen
3 **Douglas Macarthur** 2-9-3 Ryan Moore
9/1, 7/1, 8/13F. 2¼l, hd. 5 ran. 1m 43.49s (K J Condon).

A clearcut win for **Landfall**, who mastered odds-on favourite **Douglas Macarthur** early in the straight and stayed on far too strongly for **Firey Speech**. There was little strength in depth, with Douglas Macarthur having his limitations exposed again in the Royal Lodge and **Radio Silence**, next best in the market, also below his best in fifth, but fourth-placed **Percy** would finish much closer in the Eyrefield to give the form a pretty solid look.

47 Goffs Vincent O'Brien National Stakes (Group 1) (7f)

Curragh (IRE) September 11 (Yielding)

1 **Churchill** 2-9-3 Ryan Moore
2 **Mehmas** 2-9-3 Frankie Dettori
3 **Lockheed** 2-9-3 Pat Smullen
4/5F, 9/4, 11/1. 4¼l, nk. 7 ran. 1m 28.28s (A P O'Brien).

This was probably **Churchill**'s toughest test of the season and he passed it with flying colours, thrashing **Mehmas** in comprehensive fashion to put himself right up there with stablemate Caravaggio for champion two-year-old honours. Churchill had to show plenty of speed to match Mehmas, especially when slightly impeded, but he had comfortably taken the British raider's measure before stamina became an issue, with Mehmas only just holding on to second. **Lockheed** ran on well to finish a good third with the rest well strung out, **Son Of Rest** taking fourth ahead of **Lancaster Bomber**, who was sacrificed as a pacemaker, and the disappointing **Psychedelic Funk**.

48 Moyglare Stud Stakes (Group 1) (Fillies) (7f)

Curragh (IRE) September 11 (Yielding)

1 **Intricately** 2-9-0 Donnacha O'Brien
2 **Hydrangea** 2-9-0 P B Beggy
3 **Rhododendron** 2-9-0 Frankie Dettori
25/1, 7/1, 5/2. shd, 1¾l. 7 ran. 1m 28.50s (Joseph Patrick O'Brien).

A major upset as **Intricately** turned around the Debutante form with **Hydrangea** and **Rhododendron**. While Rhododendron was certainly below her best in third, Hydrangea seemed to run her race – especially as **Rehana** was beaten an identical distance in fourth in both races – and was simply beaten by a fast-improving filly as Intricately kept pulling out more under pressure and held on in a desperately tight finish. **Promise To Be True** failed to pick up in fifth, perhaps finding softer ground against her, while **Brave Anna** flopped for the second time over 7f to prompt her return to sprinting.

49 Shadwell Stud/EBF Stallions Harry Rosebery Stakes (Listed Race) (5f)

Ayr September 16 (Good To Soft)

1 **Clem Fandango** 2-8-12 Phillip Makin
2 **Angel Meadow** 2-8-12 P J McDonald
3 **Smokey Lane** 2-9-3 Graham Gibbons
11/4F, 40/1, 9/1. 3¾l, ½l. 11 ran. 1m 0.72s (Keith Dalgleish).

Clem Fandango was back on softer ground for the first time since the Queen Mary and stormed to a hugely impressive victory.

INTRICATELY (right): no fluke about her Moyglare win despite 25-1 odds

The speedy filly was always going well and stormed clear of **Angel Meadow**, who ran a long way above the rest of her form, and **Smokey Lane**.

50 Dubai Duty Free Mill Reef Stakes (Group 2) (6f8y)

Newbury September 17 (Good To Soft)

1 **Harry Angel** 2-9-1 Adam Kirby
2 **Perfect Angel** 2-8-12 Martin Dwyer
3 **Global Applause** 2-9-1 George Baker
2/1F, 7/1, 3/1. 2½l, nk. 7 ran. 1m 13.18s (Clive Cox).

A modest Group 2 but a hugely authoritative win from **Harry Angel**, who was always in command on only his second start and pushed out to a clearcut success. **Perfect Angel** ran possibly her best race in second, though she only just saw off **Global Applause** even with soft ground against that one, while **Grey Britain** again seemed below his Gimcrack form just a week after running in the Champagne.

51 William Hill Firth Of Clyde Stakes (Group 3) (6f)

Ayr September 17 (Good To Soft)

1 **Delectation** 2-9-0 Paul Mulrennan
2 **Rosebride** 2-9-0 Tony Hamilton
3 **Belle Meade** 2-9-0 Jack Garritty
11/1, 12/1, 20/1. 2¾l, 1¼l. 12 ran. 1m 14.27s (Bryan Smart).

A decent Group 3 won in terrific fashion by **Delectation**, now with Andreas Wohler, who came from last to first with a fine turn of foot despite an unfavourable high draw. **Drumfad Bay** was a fascinating challenger from Ireland given the strength of the Irish form yet could get little closer in fourth than she had managed in the Debutante Stakes, finishing behind **Rosebride** and apparent improver **Belle Meade**, who was a big eyecatcher as she stayed on well on this drop in trip having been outpaced. That leading quartet pulled clear of the rest, who included disappointing favourite **Bletchley** and **Stormy Clouds**.

52 Tattersalls Stakes (Group 3) (7f)

Newmarket September 22 (Good To Firm)

1 **Larchmont Lad** 2-9-0 Sean Levey
2 **Whitecliffsofdover** 2-9-0 Ryan Moore
3 **Sir Dancealot** 2-9-0 Jim Crowley
8/1, 9/2, 9/1. ¾l, shd. 8 ran. 1m 24.81s (Richard Hannon).

There was very little between the first four but the form looks good with **Larchmont Lad**, building on his close third at Doncaster and perhaps better suited by a stronger gallop, holding off a trio of smart colts. **Whitecliffsofdover** was second ahead of **Sir Dancealot** and the unlucky **Best Solution**, who would have gone close but for being stopped in his run and proved the point by winning the Autumn Stakes next time, with a 2l gap back to **Law And Order** in fifth. **Escobar** scoped badly after finishing seventh.

53 Shadwell Rockfel Stakes (Group 2) (Fillies) (7f)

Newmarket September 23 (Good To Firm)

1 **Spain Burg** 2-9-0 Frankie Dettori
2 **Fair Eva** 2-9-0 Pat Smullen
3 **Miss Infinity** 2-9-0 Joe Fanning
14/1, 4/9F, 25/1. 1¼l, nk. 8 ran. 1m 24.92s (X Thomas-Demeaulte).

A hugely impressive performance from US-bound **Spain Burg**, who had far too much speed for **Fair Eva** as she came from almost last to first even though a steadily increasing gallop favoured those ridden prominently with the next three all to the fore throughout. Fair Eva saw out the extra furlong well and probably stepped up on her previous form in holding off **Miss Infinity** and subsequent Oh So Sharp runner-up **Glitter Girl**, with **Nations Alexander** next in fifth.

54 Connolly's Red Mills Cheveley Park Stakes (Group 1) (Fillies) (6f)

Newmarket September 24 (Good To Firm)

1 **Brave Anna** 2-9-0 Seamie Heffernan
2 **Roly Poly** 2-9-0 Ryan Moore
3 **Lady Aurelia** 2-9-0 Frankie Dettori
25/1, 11/2, 4/6F. shd, 2l. 6 ran. 1m 11.92s (A P O'Brien).

A dramatic contest which saw **Lady Aurelia** look set to win comfortably before stopping suddenly in the final 100 yards, meaning it rather fell into Brave Anna's lap. The Albany winner was clearly much better back over 6f, but Lady Aurelia's late collapse and **Queen Kindly**'s no-show in a distant fourth meant she was left with only **Roly Poly** to beat, doing so by a short-head. Lady Aurelia looked a patent non-stayer, although she was later found to have broken blood vessels. **Pellucid** and **Holy Cat** were outclassed behind.

55 Juddmonte Middle Park Stakes (Group 1) (6f)

Newmarket September 24 (Good To Firm)

1 **The Last Lion** 2-9-0 Joe Fanning
2 **Blue Point** 2-9-0 William Buick
3 **Mehmas** 2-9-0 Frankie Dettori
25/1, 11/10F, 6/1. ¾l, 2¼l. 10 ran. 1m 12.13s (Mark Johnston).

A major upset as **The Last Lion**, on the go since the Brocklesby and beaten in four of his five previous Group races, made all the running. The Last Lion had at least kept on improving, especially since stepped up to 6f, but even so his victory was more due to the jockeys behind giving him far too much rope in front as he allowed to dictate a steady gallop and couldn't be caught once quickening smartly. It was certainly an opportunity missed for **Blue Point**, who got much the closest in second, though **Mehmas** and **Intelligence Cross** had even less chance as they ran on to finish next, while **Mokarris** was another who did well from the rear in sixth. Mokarris split **Koropick** and **Medicine Jack**, who were perhaps flattered to finish among better horses having been ridden more prominently, while **Peace Envoy** was reported to have lost his action, **Mubtasim** disappointed and **Silver Line** was well below his best on his return from a long absence.

56 Juddmonte Royal Lodge Stakes (Group 2) (1m)

Newmarket September 24 (Good To Firm)

1 **Best Of Days** 2-9-0 James Doyle
2 **The Anvil** 2-9-0 Seamie Heffernan
3 **Arcada** 2-9-0 Donnacha O'Brien
6/5F, 25/1, 12/1. nk, ¾l. 8 ran. 1m 38.98s (Hugo Palmer).

Moderate form on paper with some exposed runners finishing close, but the first two were better than that as the cream rose to the top with **Best Of Days**, who travelled strongly and was always in command once hitting the front, leading the way. **The Anvil** was much less fancied but ran a stormer given he lost his action in the Dip before staying on again ahead of dead-heaters **Arcada** and **Sea Fox** as well as **Douglas Macarthur**. **Montataire** was nowhere near his Salisbury form, not helped by making the running into a strong headwind, finishing sixth ahead of **Kings Gift**.

57 Juddmonte Beresford Stakes (Group 2) (1m)

Curragh (IRE) September 25 (Heavy)

1 **Capri** 2-9-3 Ryan Moore
2 **Yucatan** 2-9-3 Donnacha O'Brien
3 **Exemplar** 2-9-3 Seamie Heffernan
8/11F, 10/1, 3/1. ¾l, ¾l. 6 ran. 1m 45.05s (A P O'Brien).

A good race in which **Capri**, the Derby favourite at the time after a Listed win at Tipperary, was pushed hard by stablemate **Yucatan**, though the pair may well have been overrated with both beaten at short prices at Group 1 level subsequently. Capri battled past the front-running **Exemplar** and was always holding Yucatan as that one came through strongly late, with the Aidan O'Brien trio 16l clear of some very weak opposition.

58 C.L. & M.F. Weld Park Stakes (Group 3) (7f)

Curragh (IRE) September 25 (Heavy)

1 **Eziyra** 2-9-0 Pat Smullen
2 **Grecian Light** 2-9-0 William Buick
3 **Legitimus** 2-9-0 Ronan Whelan
5/4F, 5/1, 16/1. 2l, 4¼l. 10 ran. 1m 30.36s (D K Weld).

Having bumped into a good one when second to Sea Of Grace previously, **Eziyra** deservedly got off the mark at Pattern level as she proved much too good for British raider **Grecian Light**. The pair made good progress to dispute the lead approaching the furlong pole, but Eziyra pulled nicely clear after that with a bigger gap back to the staying-on **Legitimus** in third.

59 Blenheim Stakes (Listed) (6f)

Fairyhouse (IRE) September 27 (Soft To Heavy)

1 **Moonlit Show** 2-8-12 Billy Lee
2 **Born To Be** 2-9-3 Declan McDonogh
3 **Istan** 2-9-3 Seamie Heffernan
6/1, 5/2F, 9/2. 1¾l, 1¼l. 6 ran. 1m 18.45s (Charlie Fellowes).

This was a soft win for **Moonlit Show** in a very weak Listed race, so it was little surprise when she was thumped in a higher grade at Maisons-Laffitte, as was runner-up **Born To Be** in the Killavullan. Moonlit Show was gifted an easy lead and never looked in danger once kicking clear off the home turn, though **Istan** would have got close given a clear run.

60 Total Prix Marcel Boussac (Group 1) (1m)

Chantilly (FR) October 2 (Good)

1 **Wuheida** 2-8-11 William Buick
2 **Promise To Be True** 2-8-11 Ryan Moore
3 **Dabyah** 2-8-11 Frankie Dettori
10/1, 7/2, 3/1F. ¾l, snk. 11 ran. 1m 35.85s (Charlie Appleby).

A one-two-three for British and Irish fillies, led by Godolphin's once-raced maiden winner **Wuheida**, though it may not prove wise to read a lot into that given the trio were strongly favoured by a stop-start gallop. Wuheida and the back-to-form **Promise To Be True** still did well to battle past the front-running **Dabyah** in the final furlong, both relishing the mile, though those ridden further back never stood

EZIYRA: underlined the superiority of the Irish fillies when beating Grecian Light

a chance. **Senga** did much the best of them in a clear fourth while leading French fancy **Toulifaut** had a particularly poor passage.

61 Qatar Prix Jean-Luc Lagardere (Group 1) (1m)

Chantilly (FR) October 2 (Good)

1 **National Defense** 2-9-0 P-C Boudot
2 **Salouen** 2-9-0 Maxime Guyon
3 **Whitecliffsofdover** 2-9-0 Ryan Moore
5/1, 8/1, 2/1F. 4½l, snk. 7 ran. 1m 35.53s (Mme C Head-Maarek).

A moderate Group 1, with **Whitecliffsofdover** favourite despite his Newmarket defeat and leading French fancy **Kontrastat** given far too much to do, but **National Defense** could hardly have won more easily as he beat runner-up **Salouen** by a lot further than the likes of South Seas and Rivet either side of this. National Defense made all the running and quickened away in the straight as Whitecliffsofdover, who was virtually upsides before the furlong pole, was left behind, perhaps failing to see out the extra furlong as he lost second to the staying-on Salouen. Kontrastat ran on into a never-threatening fourth.

62 Dubai Fillies' Mile (Group 1) (1m) Newmarket October 7 (Good To Firm)

1 **Rhododendron** 2-9-0 Ryan Moore
2 **Hydrangea** 2-9-0 Seamie Heffernan
3 **Urban Fox** 2-9-0 Martin Harley
5/2J, 4/1, 40/1. 2¼l, 6l. 8 ran. 1m 37.73s (A P O'Brien).

A remarkable display of power from Aidan O'Brien as favourite **Rhododendron** bounced back to form to see off **Hydrangea** with no other horse within 8l of her, confirming the clear superiority of the Irish form in the juvenile fillies' division. Rhododendron seemed to improve for this quicker ground and stiffer test of stamina, always travelling well before storming clear of Hydrangea, who ran another solid race to finish second. **Urban Fox** stayed on to take third, beaten more than 5l further than when filling the same spot in the May Hill, as Doncaster winner **Rich Legacy** paid the price for going too fast early. So, too, did **Spatial**, with joint-favourite **Sobetsu** only fifth as she failed to fulfil her promise at a lower level.

63 Newmarket Academy Godolphin Beacon Project Cornwallis Stakes (Group 3) (5f)

Newmarket October 7 (Good To Firm)

1 **Mrs Danvers** 2-8-12 Richard Kingscote
2 **Clem Fandango** 2-8-12 Phillip Makin
3 **Battaash** 2-9-1 Paul Hanagan
2/1F, 15/2, 9/1. 1½l, ½l. 9 ran. 58.69s (Jonathan Portman).

Mrs Danvers didn't even have to run to her Newbury form as she maintained her unbeaten record in a modest renewal. Always going

MRS DANVERS: stepped up again but main rivals failed to handle the track

well, Mrs Danvers handled the track far better than placed horses **Clem Fandango**, who lost her action at one stage, and **Battaash**, who hung right, that pair still managing to finish just in front of the penalised **Afandem**. **Nuclear Power** ran a cracker in fifth, staying on strongly from the rear despite being impeded, but **Yalta** and **Courage Under Fire** were below-par.

64 visionsport.com Oh So Sharp Stakes (Group 3) (Fillies) (7f)

Newmarket October 7 (Good To Firm)

1 **Poet's Vanity** 2-9-0 Oisin Murphy
2 **Glitter Girl** 2-9-0 Ryan Moore
3 **Unforgetable Filly** 2-9-0 Jim Crowley
13/2, 8/1, 10/1. 1l, 1l. 12 ran. 1m 25.47s (Andrew Balding).

Poet's Vanity had bolted up by 10l in a Salisbury maiden on her previous start and took the step up in class very much in her stride as she beat Rockfel fourth **Glitter Girl** in decisive fashion. Three of their main rivals were below their best, though, with French favourite **Double Lady** given too much to do before staying on nicely into fifth, **Miss Infinity** failing to run to her Rockfel form in seventh and **Grecian Light** finishing tailed off.

65 Irish Stallion Farms European Breeders Fund Star Appeal Stakes (Listed Race) (7f)

Dundalk (AW) (IRE) October 7 (Standard)

1 **Ambassadorial** 2-9-3 Shane Foley
2 **Executive Force** 2-9-3 Pat Cosgrave
3 **Leo Minor** 2-9-3 Donnacha O'Brien
4/1, 2/1F, 7/2. 1½l, 3l. 9 ran. 1m 23.70s (M Halford).

A desperately weak race – the first six had run seven times between them at Group or Listed level, managing no better than an 8l fourth, and three subsequent runs over the season produced nothing better than a ninth in a nursery – but **Ambassadorial** at least won easily. Ambassadorial showed a good turn of foot to ease clear of British raider **Executive Force**, with the rest looking decidedly one-paced.

66 Dubai Dewhurst Stakes (Group 1) (7f)

Newmarket October 8 (Good)

1 **Churchill** 2-9-1 Ryan Moore
2 **Lancaster Bomber** 2-9-1 C O'Donoghue
3 **Blue Point** 2-9-1 William Buick
8/11F, 66/1, 8/1. 1¼l, ½l. 7 ran. 1m 23.80s (A P O'Brien).

A slightly disappointing race with the British challengers all fluffing their lines, but it was still another tremendous performance from **Churchill**, who had to be switched to make his challenge yet picked up well once in the clear and swept to a comfortable victory. The proximity of **Lancaster Bomber**, seemingly in the race as a pacemaker yet able to get back up for second once headed, could have been used to crab the form initially, but a fine second in the Breeders' Cup Juvenile Turf showed that he was improving fast. Even so, **Blue Point** failed to run up to his best over this extra furlong, his stamina ebbing away close home, and **Thunder Snow** also seemed below-par despite reversing Champagne form with **Rivet**, who struggled on the undulations. **South Seas** failed to reproduce his best form on quicker ground and **Seven Heavens** was far too keen.

67 Dubai 100 Autumn Stakes (Group 3) (1m)

Newmarket October 8 (Good)

1 **Best Solution** 2-9-1 William Carson
2 **Zainhom** 2-9-1 Paul Hanagan
3 **The Anvil** 2-9-1 Ryan Moore
12/1, 16/1, 11/4F. 2l, 2l. 10 ran. 1m 37.15s (Saeed bin Suroor).

A strong Group 3 with plenty of decent horses well strung out behind subsequent Group 1 runner-up **Best Solution**, though several weren't quite at their best. Best Solution was always travelling well and quickened to a decisive success over **Zainhom**, who also finished well despite still looking green. **The Anvil** and **Montataire** finished much closer than in the Royal Lodge, the latter doing much better and losing second only in the final 100 yards as The Anvil, who didn't look in the same form, also stayed on past him. **Lockheed** was next, seemingly not at his best on the track, ahead of **Sea Fox**, **Pleaseletmewin** and **Law And Order**, who was slowly away and hampered. **Rodaini** never stood a chance as he lost ground at the start and later stumbled badly when short of room.

68 Godolphin Flying Start Zetland Stakes (Listed Race) (1m2f)

Newmarket October 8 (Good)

1 **Coronet** 2-8-11 Frankie Dettori
2 **Cunco** 2-9-2 Robert Havlin
3 **Permian** 2-9-2 Joe Fanning
3/1F, 11/1, 20/1. nk, ½l. 12 ran. 2m 2.89s (John Gosden).

This may well turn out to be a good race – the second and fourth were both regarded highly enough by strong connections to run in a Group 1 next time, although both were well beaten – and **Coronet** did really well to win with a surging run from the rear. **Cunco** again showed himself to be a strong stayer in second having always been prominent, as was **Permian**, and the first three were 3¾l clear of **Wings Of Eagles**, who didn't get a clear run.

69 coral.co.uk Rockingham Stakes (Listed Race) (6f)

York October 8 (Good)

1 **Sir Dancealot** 2-9-1 Shane Kelly
2 **Dream Of Dreams** 2-9-1 Kevin Stott
3 **Perfect Angel** 2-8-10 Martin Dwyer
6/1, 8/1, 9/2F. ¾l, ½l. 12 ran. 1m 12.15s (David Elsworth).

A decent Listed race and an impressive win for **Sir Dancealot**, who had to pick his way through from the rear after a slow start and did it much more cosily than the winning margin suggests. Sir Dancealot cut down **Dream Of Dreams** and **Perfect Angel** as the leading trio pulled clear of **De Boss Man** and **Silver Line**, who was again below his early-season form with the trip seemingly too short. **Smokey Lane** was beaten a shade further than in two other Listed races but probably not in the same form.

70 Staffordstown Stud Stakes (Listed Race) (Fillies) (1m)

Curragh (IRE) October 9 (Good)

1 **Calare** 2-9-0 James Doyle
2 **Bound** 2-9-0 Colm O'Donoghue
3 **Queen Anne's Lace** 2-9-0 Pat Smullen
8/1, 8/1, 11/8F. ¾l, ¾l. 7 ran. 1m 44.95s (Charlie Appleby).

Calare had twice finished second in modest races at this level but seemed to improve for the extra furlong as she stayed on stoutly to edge past **Bound** close home despite not getting a clear run. **Queen Anne's Lace** travelled best but finished weakly in third, that trio pulling clear of **Kazimiera** and the below-par **Butterflies**.

71 Racing Post Trophy (Group 1) (1m)

Doncaster October 22 (Good)

1 **Rivet** 2-9-1 Andrea Atzeni
2 **Yucatan** 2-9-1 Ryan Moore
3 **Salouen** 2-9-1 Tom Marquand
11/4, 11/8F, 16/1. 1¾l, nk. 10 ran. 1m 37.08s (William Haggas).

Rivet put his disappointing effort in the Dew-hurst behind him to win a Group 1 that probably took a lot less winning, indeed little more than his previous Champagne Stakes victory at the track. Rivet set a steady gallop and quickened well to comfortably hold off favourite **Yucatan**, who edged out **Salouen** and **Raheem House** for second. **Brutal** was next ahead of **Sir Dancealot**, who travelled smoothly but failed to stay the mile, while **The Anvil** was well below his best and trailed home last.

72 Scott Dobson 30th Birthday Memorial Doncaster Stakes (Listed Race) (6f)

Doncaster October 22 (Good)

1 **Rosie Briar** 2-8-10 Rob Hornby
2 **Tomily** 2-9-1 Jim Crowley
3 **Nuclear Power** 2-9-1 Martin Dwyer
20/1, 8/1, 6/1. ½l, nk. 11 ran. 1m 11.53s (Andrew Balding).

No more than an ordinary race for the grade, especially as **Rosie Briar** benefited from a significant pace bias in which the first three were allowed to dictate a moderate gallop and held those positions throughout. Rosie Briar held off **Tomily**, with Cornwallis eye-catcher **Nuclear Power** third despite racing too keenly.

73 **Worthington's Alzheimers Society Stakes (registered as the Horris Hill) (Group 3) (7f)**
Newbury October 22 (Good To Soft)

1 **Pleaseletmewin** 2-9-0 F M Berry
2 **Kings Gift** 2-9-0 Paul Mulrennan
3 **Law And Order** 2-9-0 Martin Harley
16/1, 20/1, 16/1. 2¼l, hd. 13 ran. 1m 27.48s
(Ralph Beckett).

Pleaseletmewin was much better suited by this shorter trip than when well beaten in the Autumn Stakes, albeit in a weaker race, as he was driven out to a comfortable win. **Kings Gift** was second ahead of **Law And Order** and **Sea Fox**, while **Silver Line** was fifth despite doing everything wrong, racing too keenly and hanging badly, and **Executive Force** was among several to flop behind.

74 **JLT Stakes (registered as the Radley Stakes) (Listed Race) (Fillies) (7f)**
Newbury October 22 (Good To Soft)

1 **Cristal Fizz** 2-9-0 Frankie Dettori
2 **Glitter Girl** 2-9-0 Pat Cosgrave
3 **Pichola Dance** 2-9-0 Harry Bentley
4/1, 6/4F, 25/1. nk, 2¼l. 11 ran. 1m 27.42s
(William Haggas).

Glitter Girl set a clear form standard on her Oh So Sharp second but couldn't run to her best on softer ground, a busy period perhaps also taking its toll, as **Cristal Fizz** ran out a cosy winner, taking the favourite's measure in the final furlong. The pair still pulled nicely clear of **Pichola Dance** and **Castleacre** with another gap back to the rest.

75 **Killavullan Stakes (Group 3) (7f)**
Leopardstown (IRE) October 23 (Yielding)

1 **Making Light** 2-9-0 Pat Smullen
2 **Spirit Of Valor** 2-9-3 Donnacha O'Brien
3 **Taj Mahal** 2-9-3 Seamie Heffernan
3/1J, 7/2, 7/1. 1l, nk. 7 ran. 1m 31.15s
(D K Weld).

An impressive win for sole filly **Making Light**, though her task was made a lot easier by the below-par performance of **Holistic Approach**, who was later found to be coughing, in a race that already lacked much Group/Listed form. Making Light was always handy and asserted in the final 100 yards to see off **Spirit Of Valor** and **Taj Mahal**, who were progressive but had still won just once each from eight previous starts at a modest level between them. **Born To Be** was a poor sixth.

76 **Irish Stallion Farms "Bosra Sham" EBF Fillies' Stakes (Listed Race) (6f)**
Newmarket October 28 (Good)

1 **Spiritual Lady** 2-9-0 Frankie Dettori
2 **Spy Ring** 2-9-0 Oisin Murphy
3 **Mystic Dawn** 2-9-0 Dane O'Neill
3/1F, 16/1, 7/1. 1½l, 1l. 10 ran. 1m 11.08s
(Philip McBride).

A hugely impressive win for **Spiritual Lady**, who had been rated just 78 when winning a nursery on her previous start but showed she was improving fast as she cruised into the lead and won eased down. Irish raider **Spy Ring** was second ahead of **Mystic Dawn**, who ran to form with the sixth, **Pellucid**, on their runs behind Madam Dancealot in a Group 3 at Salisbury with both beaten further by a much better winner. **Perfect Angel** didn't seem quite at her best in fourth.

77 **British Stallion Studs EBF Montrose Fillies' Stakes (Listed) (1m)**
Newmarket October 29 (Good To Firm)

1 **Really Special** 2-9-0 Jim Crowley
2 **Kazimiera** 2-9-0 William Buick
3 **Island Vision** 2-9-0 Martin Harley
3 Tansholpan 2-9-0 Andrea Atzeni
2/1F, 9/2, 6/1. 2¾l, ½l, dht. 10 ran. 1m 37.39s
(Saeed bin Suroor).

Really Special had little to beat but couldn't have done it much better, making all the running and drawing well clear in the final furlong. **Kazimiera** stuck on for second, though she had been well beaten at this level at the Curragh and 90-rated **Teofonic**, who finished just behind dead-heaters **Island Vision** and **Tansholpan** in fifth, was the highest-rated filly in the field.

78 **TheTote.com Eyrefield Stakes (Listed Race) (1m1f)**
Leopardstown (IRE) October 29 (Yielding)

1 **Dubai Sand** 2-9-3 Kevin Manning
2 **Diodorus** 2-9-3 Michael Hussey
3 **Youarewonder** 2-9-3 David Nolan
7/1, 20/1, 25/1. ½l, 1½l. 11 ran. 1m 56.81s
(J S Bolger).

The first three had remarkably won just one out of 13 previous races between them and **Dubai Sand,** beaten in his two maidens, seemingly got lucky in a desperate race. **Per-**

cy perhaps set the standard, getting much closer in fourth than when well beaten by Landfall previously, as **Butterflies** was given far too much to do and **Queen Anne's Lace** was a patent non-stayer having traded at an in-running low of 1.5. **Bound** was a disappointing seventh.

79 Criterium International (Group 1) (7f)

Saint-Cloud (FR) October 30 (Soft)

1 **Thunder Snow** 2-9-0 C Soumillon
2 **South Seas** 2-9-0 Oisin Murphy
3 **Promise To Be True** 2-8-10 S Heffernan
3/1, 11/4, 15/8F. 5l, 1¾l. 9 ran. 1m 28.20s (Saeed bin Suroor).

Perhaps not the most reliable form coming so late in the season on soft ground, but this certainly looked a remarkable effort from **Thunder Snow** as he drew clear of a couple of high-class rivals in **South Seas** and **Promise To Be True**. Relishing the conditions, Thunder Snow stormed home off a strong gallop for a comfortable win. South Seas and Promise To Be True may not have coped with a second Group 1 in a short space of time as well as the winner, although they were in turn clear of a disappointing French defence.

80 Criterium de Saint-Cloud (Group 1) (1m2f)

Saint-Cloud (FR) October 30 (Soft)

1 **Waldgeist** 2-9-0 Pierre-Charles Boudot
2 **Best Solution** 2-9-0 Christophe Soumillon
3 **Capri** 2-9-0 Seamie Heffernan
10/1, 17/2, 10/11F. 1l, ½l. 13 ran. 2m 12.73s (A Fabre).

Waldgeist was one of only two French runners in a field of 13 but came out on top ahead of **Best Solution**, who looked likely to follow up his Autumn Stakes win for much of the straight but was treading water in the final furlong as Waldgeist reeled him in. **Capri** stayed on into third having lost his place and wasn't beaten far, but that was still a shade disappointing with the bare form not up to much, his stablemates **Douglas Macarthur** and **Taj Mahal**, albeit both possibly better for the step up in trip, close behind him in fourth and fifth. **Cunco** and, in particular, **Frankuus** seemed below their best as **Wings Of Eagles**, always likely to get closer to the former after his unlucky Zetland run, did so despite being unfavoured by coming from a long way back off a steady gallop, with **D'bai** and **Rich Legacy** always behind.

MAKING LIGHT: the sole filly in the Killavullan but the boys weren't up to much

Two-year-old index

All horses placed or commented on in our two-year-old review section, with race numbers

SALOUEN: second twice at the top level and a credit to Sylvester Kirk

Trainer Statistics

Richard Fahey

Fahey fell just two short of a second double-century and, while it's hard to find fault, it's worth considering he had far more runners than before but a much worse strike-rate and incurred a huge level-stakes loss for his followers.

By month - 2016

	Overall			Two-year-olds			Three-year-olds			Older horses		
	W-R	%	£1	W-R	%	£1	W-R	%	£1	W-R	%	£1
January	7-48	15	+0.25	0-0	-	+0.00	1-16	6	-9.50	6-32	19	+9.75
February	6-42	14	-13.25	0-0	-	+0.00	3-17	18	+0.50	3-25	12	-13.75
March	6-45	13	-13.30	0-1	-	-1.00	2-20	10	-12.39	4-24	17	+0.08
April	22-130	17	-13.13	3-11	27	+12.23	12-49	24	+2.89	7-70	10	-28.25
May	18-211	9	-67.50	5-38	13	+34.25	5-70	7	-40.13	8-103	8	-61.63
June	35-220	16	+25.23	6-51	12	-19.85	15-84	18	+10.08	14-85	16	+35.00
July	27-278	10	-84.00	10-91	11	-40.63	9-79	11	+7.75	8-108	7	-51.13
August	27-240	11	-46.73	11-90	12	-20.83	11-62	18	+16.60	5-88	6	-42.50
September	19-200	10	-77.85	9-66	14	-14.72	6-50	12	-6.75	4-84	5	-56.39
October	18-171	11	-62.80	10-61	16	-12.80	5-49	10	-8.00	3-61	5	-42.00
November	9-89	10	-28.75	4-30	13	-1.75	3-24	13	-3.00	2-35	6	-24.00
December	4-65	6	-16.00	0-17	-	-17.00	3-24	13	-1.00	1-24	4	+2.00

By month - 2015

	Overall			Two-year-olds			Three-year-olds			Older horses		
	W-R	%	£1	W-R	%	£1	W-R	%	£1	W-R	%	£1
January	5-52	10	-22.50	0-0	-	+0.00	2-19	11	-6.50	3-33	9	-16.00
February	10-38	26	+27.63	0-0	-	+0.00	3-15	20	+5.50	7-23	30	+22.13
March	10-43	23	+16.98	0-1	-	-1.00	2-13	15	-4.40	8-29	28	+22.38
April	23-106	22	+16.43	5-14	36	+9.88	12-50	24	+4.81	6-42	14	+1.75
May	30-209	14	-24.30	7-45	16	-9.34	11-73	15	-4.96	12-91	13	-10.00
June	24-215	11	-97.29	2-45	4	-34.38	15-88	17	-17.79	7-82	9	-45.13
July	23-228	10	-86.11	6-66	9	-15.51	11-91	12	-45.35	6-71	8	-25.25
August	43-249	17	+42.52	19-78	24	+44.19	13-81	16	+16.60	11-90	12	-18.27
September	30-218	14	-3.83	13-86	15	-12.08	8-55	15	+3.25	9-77	12	+5.00
October	21-181	12	-67.99	12-65	18	+2.00	2-50	4	-43.97	7-66	11	-26.02
November	9-86	10	-11.72	3-38	8	-26.25	2-20	10	+14.00	4-28	14	+0.53
December	7-66	11	-17.50	1-28	4	-17.00	2-19	11	-5.00	4-19	21	+4.50

By month - 2014

	Overall			Two-year-olds			Three-year-olds			Older horses		
	W-R	%	£1	W-R	%	£1	W-R	%	£1	W-R	%	£1
January	8-46	17	+10.30	0-0	-	+0.00	2-14	14	-10.20	6-32	19	+20.50
February	3-23	13	-15.00	0-0	-	+0.00	2-11	18	-5.88	1-12	8	-9.13
March	4-34	12	-3.75	0-0	-	+0.00	1-14	7	-10.75	3-20	15	+7.00
April	16-120	13	-16.77	4-18	22	-4.27	6-53	11	-24.75	6-49	12	+12.25
May	27-205	13	-42.00	10-48	21	-7.28	11-80	14	+4.78	6-77	8	-39.50
June	32-218	15	+40.43	8-61	13	-3.27	14-84	17	+36.83	10-73	14	+6.88
July	20-187	11	-56.34	8-77	10	-32.59	8-62	13	-14.25	4-48	8	-9.50
August	34-206	17	-13.92	12-77	16	-13.63	11-60	18	+0.88	11-69	16	-1.17
September	16-208	8	-77.25	11-94	12	-13.50	2-44	5	-29.25	3-70	4	-34.50
October	19-160	12	+11.21	8-64	13	-3.13	6-38	16	+28.00	5-58	9	-13.67
November	11-57	19	+7.85	5-21	24	-2.40	2-14	14	+2.50	4-22	18	+7.75
December	2-38	5	+36.00	2-13	15	+61.00	0-8	-	-8.00	0-17	-	-17.00

By race type - 2016

	Overall			Two-year-olds			Three-year-olds			Older horses		
	W-R	%	£1	W-R	%	£1	W-R	%	£1	W-R	%	£1
Handicap	125-1241	10	-334.48	17-137	12	-27.29	56-446	13	-42.03	52-658	8	-265.17
Group	2-51	4	-37.50	1-13	8	-7.50	1-16	6	-8.00	0-22	-	-22.00
Maiden	33-237	14	-84.87	21-177	12	-77.37	11-56	20	-8.00	1-4	25	+0.50

By race type - 2015

	Overall			Two-year-olds			Three-year-olds			Older horses		
	W-R	%	£1	W-R	%	£1	W-R	%	£1	W-R	%	£1
Handicap	147-1152	13	-104.08	16-103	16	+15.38	60-462	13	-53.33	71-587	12	-66.13
Group	3-28	11	-11.88	2-10	20	+0.63	0-3	-	-3.00	1-15	7	-9.50
Maiden	62-371	17	-96.66	41-290	14	-87.55	20-78	26	-10.61	1-3	33	+1.50

By race type - 2014

	Overall			Two-year-olds			Three-year-olds			Older horses		
	W-R	%	£1	W-R	%	£1	W-R	%	£1	W-R	%	£1
Handicap	130-991	13	-7.28	21-115	18	+33.88	54-376	14	+17.51	55-500	11	-58.67
Group	1-30	3	-25.50	0-9	-	-9.00	1-7	14	-2.50	0-14	-	-14.00
Maiden	42-371	11	-98.80	34-284	12	-55.96	8-82	10	-37.84	0-5	-	-5.00

By jockey - 2016

	Overall			Two-year-olds			Three-year-olds			Older horses		
	W-R	%	£1	W-R	%	£1	W-R	%	£1	W-R	%	£1
Tony Hamilton	66-528	13	-151.07	31-195	16	-21.97	21-175	12	-37.29	14-158	9	-91.80
A McNamara	33-247	13	-61.28	6-32	19	+7.38	11-68	16	-14.53	16-147	11	-54.13
David Nolan	20-143	14	+0.17	3-38	8	-5.50	13-54	24	+30.17	4-51	8	-24.50
P Mathers	14-117	12	+15.25	5-36	14	+0.25	5-47	11	-10.50	4-34	12	+25.50
G Chaloner	14-137	10	-23.78	3-42	7	-20.00	6-30	20	+31.10	5-65	8	-34.88
Paul Hanagan	10-89	11	-4.50	3-24	13	-6.00	2-17	12	-6.00	5-48	10	+7.50
Sammy Jo Bell	7-57	12	-18.89	0-1	-	-1.00	1-17	6	-15.39	6-39	15	-2.50
Jack Garritty	7-117	6	-52.88	2-36	6	+0.88	4-37	11	-15.25	1-44	2	-38.50
Jamie Spencer	6-29	21	-2.04	3-9	33	-1.04	3-13	23	+6.00	0-7	-	-7.00
N Hambling	3-37	8	-21.25	0-2	-	-2.00	0-10	-	-10.00	3-25	12	-9.25
Graham Lee	2-14	14	-9.09	1-4	25	-2.09	0-2	-	-2.00	1-8	13	-5.00
Barry McHugh	2-46	4	-35.00	0-14	-	-14.00	2-18	11	-7.00	0-14	-	-14.00

By jockey - 2015

	Overall			Two-year-olds			Three-year-olds			Older horses		
	W-R	%	£1	W-R	%	£1	W-R	%	£1	W-R	%	£1
Tony Hamilton	82-555	15	-136.59	26-194	13	-56.01	29-187	16	-46.69	27-174	16	-33.89
Jack Garritty	41-256	16	-30.81	14-74	19	-17.57	12-80	15	-26.99	15-102	15	+13.75
Paul Hanagan	24-140	17	+6.76	7-25	28	+11.83	9-52	17	-11.83	8-63	13	+6.75
Sammy Jo Bell	23-148	16	+0.10	0-17	-	-17.00	10-56	18	-6.28	13-75	17	+23.38
P Mathers	14-116	12	+37.03	4-30	13	+30.00	8-51	16	+25.03	2-35	6	-18.00
David Nolan	13-112	12	-42.93	4-38	11	-16.63	6-28	21	+1.95	3-46	7	-28.25
G Chaloner	11-125	9	-28.75	2-27	7	-13.50	4-41	10	+0.00	5-57	9	-15.25
N Hambling	5-24	21	+12.50	0-1	-	-1.00	1-9	11	-1.00	4-14	29	+14.50
Tom Eaves	3-11	27	+3.75	3-7	43	+7.75	0-1	-	-1.00	0-3	-	-3.00

By jockey - 2014

	Overall			Two-year-olds			Three-year-olds			Older horses		
	W-R	%	£1	W-R	%	£1	W-R	%	£1	W-R	%	£1
Tony Hamilton	56-408	14	-121.06	25-183	14	-74.38	20-131	15	-26.55	11-94	12	-20.13
G Chaloner	36-259	14	-9.79	7-69	10	-9.63	10-82	12	-33.38	19-108	18	+33.21
Paul Hanagan	21-94	22	+48.05	10-29	34	+20.55	5-28	18	+3.25	6-37	16	+24.25
Jack Garritty	18-105	17	+30.56	8-36	22	+13.23	8-35	23	+39.50	2-34	6	-22.17
David Nolan	16-125	13	+28.43	5-33	15	+48.60	3-35	9	-20.92	8-57	14	+0.75
P Mathers	8-83	10	+18.50	4-29	14	+18.50	3-33	9	+4.00	1-21	5	-4.00
Sammy Jo Bell	6-99	6	-36.17	0-14	-	-14.00	2-23	9	-11.67	4-62	6	-10.50
Graham Lee	4-13	31	+19.25	0-3	-	-3.00	3-6	50	+15.25	1-4	25	+7.00
Ryan Moore	4-60	7	-48.94	2-21	10	-17.44	1-15	7	-11.25	1-24	4	-20.25

By course - 2012-2016

	Overall			Two-year-olds			Three-year-olds			Older horses		
	W-R	%	£1	W-R	%	£1	W-R	%	£1	W-R	%	£1
Ascot	7-166	4	-104.50	0-25	-	-25.00	3-41	7	-14.00	4-100	4	-65.50
Ayr	38-393	10	-94.88	11-99	11	-16.26	10-112	9	-28.00	17-182	9	-50.63
Bath	2-9	22	+3.00	0-0	-	+0.00	2-6	33	+6.00	0-3	-	-3.00
Beverley	43-305	14	-87.45	20-114	18	-15.03	16-110	15	-40.92	7-81	9	-31.50
Brighton	0-5	-	-5.00	0-2	-	-2.00	0-3	-	-3.00	0-0	-	+0.00
Carlisle	21-217	10	-122.43	6-78	8	-57.71	10-81	12	-36.72	5-58	9	-28.00
Catterick	42-180	23	+27.30	24-72	33	+17.40	8-47	17	+1.83	10-61	16	+8.06
Chelms (AW)	8-75	11	-27.08	3-12	25	-1.25	1-28	4	-26.33	4-35	11	+0.50
Chepstow	0-5	-	-5.00	0-3	-	-3.00	0-2	-	-2.00	0-0	-	+0.00
Chester	57-449	13	-78.51	16-83	19	+7.12	13-137	9	-40.75	28-229	12	-44.88
Doncaster	50-448	11	-21.91	14-113	12	-8.47	10-131	8	-36.03	26-204	13	+22.58
Epsom	14-100	14	+14.88	3-15	20	-1.50	2-24	8	-14.50	9-61	15	+30.88
Goodwood	11-163	7	-46.75	3-36	8	-9.00	5-34	15	+4.25	3-93	3	-42.00
Hamilton	33-248	13	-80.55	6-70	9	-24.25	19-93	20	-3.79	8-85	9	-52.51
Haydock	37-379	10	-153.92	11-101	11	-30.00	19-117	16	+0.21	7-161	4	-124.13
Kempton (AW)	4-123	3	-98.00	1-35	3	-29.00	2-38	5	-26.00	1-50	2	-43.00
Leicester	28-135	21	+103.78	9-48	19	+53.63	11-55	20	+26.91	8-32	25	+23.25
Lingfield	0-6	-	-6.00	0-4	-	-4.00	0-2	-	-2.00	0-0	-	+0.00
Lingfield (AW)	25-207	12	-32.69	2-17	12	-6.75	8-72	11	-30.04	15-118	13	+4.10
Musselburgh	46-231	20	+40.94	15-63	24	-9.65	18-86	21	+53.98	13-82	16	-3.39
Newbury	10-92	11	-1.38	6-41	15	+18.13	1-22	5	-14.00	3-29	10	-5.50
Newcastle	32-210	15	+11.40	15-67	22	-11.43	6-58	10	+1.00	11-85	13	+21.83
N'castle (AW)	12-114	11	-29.63	7-45	16	-0.13	5-36	14	+3.50	0-33	-	-33.00
Newmarket	15-179	8	-70.70	3-44	7	-28.70	7-71	10	-19.00	5-64	8	-23.00
Newmarket (J)	26-162	16	+45.38	6-38	16	+8.75	11-65	17	+8.13	9-59	15	+28.50
Nottingham	29-173	17	+13.80	11-44	25	+2.00	15-85	18	+30.30	3-44	7	-18.50
Pontefract	50-252	20	+43.47	19-75	25	+58.98	19-92	21	-0.51	12-85	14	-15.00
Redcar	41-260	16	-17.07	16-107	15	-20.55	13-81	16	-14.68	12-72	17	+18.16
Ripon	40-299	13	-79.05	15-87	17	-0.17	16-99	16	-19.04	9-113	8	-59.84
Salisbury	1-8	13	-3.50	0-4	-	-4.00	0-3	-	-3.00	1-1	100	+3.50
Sandown	5-44	11	-28.63	1-9	11	-6.75	1-19	5	-15.50	3-16	19	-6.38
S'well (AW)	24-185	13	-82.09	6-39	15	-11.49	11-68	16	-25.10	7-78	9	-45.50
Thirsk	40-272	15	-6.34	13-94	14	-15.85	15-92	16	+18.27	12-86	14	-8.75
Warwick	4-28	14	-5.83	2-11	18	-5.33	2-9	22	+7.50	0-8	-	-8.00
Wetherby	1-11	9	-2.00	0-3	-	-3.00	1-3	33	+6.00	0-5	-	-5.00
Windsor	8-37	22	+29.50	1-6	17	+11.00	4-19	21	+11.00	3-12	25	+7.50
Wolves (AW)	74-575	13	-64.36	13-144	9	-9.65	21-167	13	-44.00	40-264	15	-10.71
Yarmouth	10-46	22	+2.93	2-13	15	-6.94	5-21	24	+9.13	3-12	25	+0.75
York	40-643	6	-215.46	18-196	9	-12.54	7-134	5	-61.00	15-313	5	-141.92

Ten-year summary

	Wins	Runs	%	Win prize-money	Total prize-money	£1
2016	198	1739	11	£1,555,029.70	£3,162,107.98	-397.84
2015	235	1691	14	£2,394,305.99	£3,846,973.63	-227.69
2014	192	1502	13	£1,882,767.02	£2,882,652.01	-119.24
2013	164	1287	13	£1,588,826.54	£2,455,584.17	-236.90
2012	142	1294	11	£1,213,826.13	£1,982,267.62	-294.66
2011	151	1224	12	£980,328.63	£1,650,127.14	-260.88
2010	181	1356	13	£1,325,389.94	£2,075,925.44	-273.54
2009	165	1106	15	£1,123,057.39	£1,657,128.68	+25.22
2008	113	971	12	£753,492.30	£1,247,043.13	-285.77
2007	85	926	9	£643,994.08	£1,132,827.97	-327.77

IMSHIVALLA: typically busy Richard Fahey charge, winning twice in 13 runs

Mark Johnston

No double century either for Johnston for the first time since 2011 but still much to smile about. His strike-rate was still decent and four Group wins in Britain included The Last Lion's Middle Park.

By month - 2016

	Overall			Two-year-olds			Three-year-olds			Older horses		
	W-R	%	£1	W-R	%	£1	W-R	%	£1	W-R	%	£1
January	5-34	15	-13.70	0-0	-	+0.00	5-23	22	-2.70	0-11	-	-11.00
February	4-23	17	-12.40	0-0	-	+0.00	4-15	27	-4.40	0-8	-	-8.00
March	11-49	22	-10.64	3-3	100	+4.82	4-28	14	-18.45	4-18	22	+3.00
April	12-117	10	-75.76	3-24	13	-15.76	7-68	10	-41.88	2-25	8	-18.13
May	21-168	13	-62.71	11-52	21	+0.25	7-75	9	-38.79	3-41	7	-24.17
June	35-204	17	-33.23	23-74	31	+17.31	8-96	8	-48.04	4-34	12	-2.50
July	38-233	16	+24.03	15-84	18	-28.05	16-109	15	+42.58	7-40	18	+9.50
August	23-178	13	-98.89	12-82	15	-43.36	8-62	13	-36.94	3-34	9	-18.59
September	19-149	13	-4.29	10-67	15	+17.46	7-62	11	-10.00	2-20	10	-11.75
October	14-140	10	+10.41	10-82	12	+28.91	2-43	5	-17.00	2-15	13	-1.50
November	7-64	11	-32.53	5-41	12	-25.03	0-16	-	-16.00	2-7	29	+8.50
December	6-54	11	-7.25	2-31	6	-13.00	3-17	18	-3.25	1-6	17	+9.00

By month - 2015

	Overall			Two-year-olds			Three-year-olds			Older horses		
	W-R	%	£1	W-R	%	£1	W-R	%	£1	W-R	%	£1
January	0-7	-	-7.00	0-0	-	+0.00	0-4	-	-4.00	0-3	-	-3.00
February	2-18	11	+9.91	0-0	-	+0.00	2-11	18	+16.91	0-7	-	-7.00
March	11-41	27	-1.75	3-3	100	+9.75	6-25	24	-2.80	2-13	15	-8.70
April	11-100	11	-29.30	3-22	14	-14.22	5-55	9	-2.50	3-23	13	-12.58
May	30-141	21	+58.48	11-49	22	-1.04	13-66	20	+49.05	6-26	23	+10.48
June	35-183	19	-24.16	18-72	25	-10.29	11-88	13	-35.88	6-23	26	+22.00
July	47-213	22	+36.10	19-88	22	-9.69	22-96	23	+20.29	6-29	21	+25.50
August	24-172	14	-38.65	14-80	18	-18.06	10-70	14	+1.41	0-22	-	-22.00
September	23-148	16	-54.91	12-77	16	-40.32	10-51	20	+2.53	1-20	5	-17.13
October	12-135	9	-68.32	5-87	6	-65.25	4-36	11	-7.73	3-12	25	+4.66
November	5-36	14	-7.47	4-26	15	-2.47	0-6	-	-6.00	1-4	25	+1.00
December	4-14	29	+15.25	3-8	38	+13.25	1-6	17	+2.00	0-0	-	+0.00

By month - 2014

	Overall			Two-year-olds			Three-year-olds			Older horses		
	W-R	%	£1	W-R	%	£1	W-R	%	£1	W-R	%	£1
January	16-45	36	+6.61	0-0	-	+0.00	9-19	47	+14.78	7-26	27	-8.17
February	9-49	18	-16.27	0-0	-	+0.00	5-26	19	-8.38	4-23	17	-7.90
March	21-72	29	+1.84	0-0	-	+0.00	12-36	33	-5.76	9-36	25	+7.60
April	19-127	15	-42.45	1-7	14	-0.50	9-63	14	-20.26	9-57	16	-21.69
May	19-166	11	-26.55	3-21	14	+5.10	11-91	12	-5.65	5-54	9	-26.00
June	32-192	17	+5.71	13-40	33	+32.13	14-99	14	-7.92	5-53	9	-18.50
July	40-203	20	+25.44	7-53	13	-27.89	26-116	22	+5.34	7-34	21	+48.00
August	21-177	12	-70.38	7-49	14	-16.33	14-101	14	-27.04	0-27	-	-27.00
September	25-165	15	-40.78	9-64	14	-42.77	14-85	16	-3.34	2-16	13	+5.33
October	3-102	3	-90.00	1-43	2	-37.50	2-44	5	-37.50	0-15	-	-15.00
November	1-38	3	-32.00	1-23	4	-17.00	0-14	-	-14.00	0-1	-	-1.00
December	1-8	13	-4.25	1-3	33	+0.75	0-4	-	-4.00	0-1	-	-1.00

By race type - 2016

	Overall			Two-year-olds			Three-year-olds			Older horses		
	W-R	%	£1	W-R	%	£1	W-R	%	£1	W-R	%	£1
Handicap	101-854	12	-153.82	19-142	13	+21.22	55-485	11	-123.41	27-227	12	-51.63
Group	4-51	8	-7.63	4-31	13	+12.38	0-15	-	-15.00	0-5	-	-5.00
Maiden	41-277	15	-124.77	30-192	16	-78.22	11-83	13	-44.55	0-2	-	-2.00

By race type - 2015

	Overall			Two-year-olds			Three-year-olds			Older horses		
	W-R	%	£1	W-R	%	£1	W-R	%	£1	W-R	%	£1
Handicap	117-721	16	-34.31	21-132	16	-58.47	71-426	17	+25.69	25-163	15	-1.52
Group	2-43	5	-31.67	2-35	6	-23.67	0-4	-	-4.00	0-4	-	-4.00
Maiden	67-358	19	-19.03	54-277	19	-41.15	13-77	17	+26.11	0-4	-	-4.00

By race type - 2014

	Overall			Two-year-olds			Three-year-olds			Older horses		
	W-R	%	£1	W-R	%	£1	W-R	%	£1	W-R	%	£1
Handicap	146-919	16	-140.43	9-68	13	-28.17	96-549	17	-62.61	41-302	14	-49.66
Group	3-40	8	-23.25	1-20	5	-12.00	2-16	13	-7.25	0-4	-	-4.00
Maiden	45-295	15	-101.22	28-182	15	-57.85	13-99	13	-38.87	4-14	29	-4.50

By jockey - 2016

	Overall			Two-year-olds			Three-year-olds			Older horses		
	W-R	%	£1	W-R	%	£1	W-R	%	£1	W-R	%	£1
Joe Fanning	73-491	15	-100.76	27-176	15	-19.01	34-221	15	-55.12	12-94	13	-26.63
Franny Norton	46-253	18	-3.72	23-103	22	-11.88	18-110	16	+15.92	5-40	13	-7.75
S De Sousa	15-91	16	-37.96	6-32	19	-8.65	6-35	17	-16.07	3-24	13	-13.25
James Doyle	12-67	18	-22.43	10-30	33	+10.43	1-33	3	-32.36	1-4	25	-0.50
P J McDonald	10-61	16	+21.25	7-32	22	+21.25	1-19	5	-15.00	2-10	20	+15.00
William Buick	8-57	14	-25.66	6-27	22	-9.66	2-27	7	-13.00	0-3	-	-3.00
Paul Mulrennan	5-61	8	-29.00	4-28	14	-9.00	1-27	4	-14.00	0-6	-	-6.00
R Kingscote	4-36	11	-8.00	2-12	17	+5.00	1-16	6	-12.50	1-8	13	-0.50
Andrew Mullen	3-34	9	+0.50	3-24	13	+10.50	0-8	-	-8.00	0-2	-	-2.00
George Baker	2-10	20	+1.50	0-5	-	-5.00	0-0	-	+0.00	2-5	40	+6.50
J McDonald	2-13	15	+22.00	1-5	20	+4.00	1-5	20	+21.00	0-3	-	-3.00
Jason Hart	2-14	14	+3.00	0-7	-	-7.00	2-5	40	+12.00	0-2	-	-2.00

By jockey - 2015

	Overall			Two-year-olds			Three-year-olds			Older horses		
	W-R	%	£1	W-R	%	£1	W-R	%	£1	W-R	%	£1
Joe Fanning	70-397	18	-49.98	29-148	20	-35.13	30-177	17	-4.94	11-72	15	-9.92
S De Sousa	41-182	23	+17.21	19-74	26	-5.32	18-83	22	+14.53	4-25	16	+8.00
Franny Norton	38-279	14	-92.43	14-121	12	-70.68	19-114	17	-6.17	5-44	11	-15.58
William Buick	13-51	25	+22.87	10-36	28	-2.13	2-11	18	+8.00	1-4	25	+17.00
Paul Mulrennan	10-46	22	+0.43	6-21	29	+8.93	3-13	23	-4.00	1-12	8	-4.50
James Doyle	6-33	18	+15.13	5-26	19	+3.13	1-7	14	+12.00	0-0	-	+0.00
Adam Kirby	5-16	31	+14.75	3-9	33	+13.50	0-3	-	-3.00	2-4	50	+4.25
Adrian Nicholls	4-37	11	+13.75	1-15	7	-11.75	3-20	15	+27.50	0-2	-	-2.00
Nicky Mackay	3-9	33	+11.00	0-1	-	-1.00	3-7	43	+13.00	0-1	-	-1.00

By jockey - 2014

	Overall			Two-year-olds			Three-year-olds			Older horses		
	W-R	%	£1	W-R	%	£1	W-R	%	£1	W-R	%	£1
Joe Fanning	110-601	18	-62.24	21-132	16	-40.39	60-300	20	-9.83	29-169	17	-12.02
Franny Norton	26-254	10	-117.42	8-69	12	-43.88	11-134	8	-62.38	7-51	14	-11.17
S De Sousa	18-125	14	-41.87	1-21	5	-15.50	13-74	18	-17.98	4-30	13	-8.39
Dane O'Neill	11-27	41	+37.00	5-13	38	+15.00	6-12	50	+24.00	0-2	-	-2.00
Adrian Nicholls	9-54	17	-1.35	4-16	25	+6.90	4-25	16	-6.25	1-13	8	-2.00
M J M Murphy	9-74	12	-22.07	1-6	17	+7.00	4-38	11	-18.32	4-30	13	-10.75
Adam Kirby	5-26	19	-14.60	0-1	-	-1.00	5-14	36	-2.60	0-11	-	-11.00
Paul Mulrennan	4-6	67	+14.25	1-1	100	+2.75	3-5	60	+11.50	0-0	-	+0.00
Paul Hanagan	4-24	17	-1.50	1-12	8	-5.00	3-12	25	+3.50	0-0	-	+0.00

By course - 2012-2016

	Overall			Two-year-olds			Three-year-olds			Older horses		
	W-R	%	£1	W-R	%	£1	W-R	%	£1	W-R	%	£1
Ascot	25-274	9	-63.47	5-66	8	-45.88	14-147	10	-56.09	6-61	10	+38.50
Ayr	18-158	11	-90.00	9-69	13	-45.43	7-63	11	-35.90	2-26	8	-8.67
Bath	14-63	22	-0.67	3-17	18	-7.17	9-36	25	+10.50	2-10	20	-4.00
Beverley	65-282	23	+15.27	13-79	16	-33.81	41-161	25	+33.71	11-42	26	+15.37
Brighton	12-81	15	-23.52	3-29	10	-21.61	8-43	19	-0.92	1-9	11	-1.00
Carlisle	23-138	17	-8.93	7-41	17	+3.58	11-67	16	-11.59	5-30	17	-0.92
Catterick	29-143	20	-35.96	11-64	17	-35.61	16-63	25	+5.65	2-16	13	-6.00
Chelms (AW)	25-163	15	-41.80	12-60	20	+6.70	7-71	10	-38.92	6-32	19	-9.58
Chepstow	7-37	19	-3.90	0-9	-	-9.00	7-24	29	+9.10	0-4	-	-4.00
Chester	40-276	14	-29.72	15-78	19	-13.55	19-140	14	-10.67	6-58	10	-5.50
Doncaster	19-207	9	-106.16	9-81	11	-25.74	9-97	9	-54.92	1-29	3	-25.50
Epsom	16-141	11	-59.25	6-30	20	-10.75	7-74	9	-33.00	3-37	8	-15.50
Ffos Las	1-19	5	-16.13	1-6	17	-3.13	0-10	-	-10.00	0-3	-	-3.00
Folkestone	3-7	43	+2.41	0-0	-	+0.00	3-7	43	+2.41	0-0	-	+0.00
Goodwood	46-280	16	+116.12	16-81	20	+7.49	19-135	14	+43.75	11-64	17	+64.88
Hamilton	51-224	23	-12.37	17-65	26	+15.11	29-131	22	-20.97	5-28	18	-6.50
Haydock	34-268	13	-34.42	10-86	12	-50.13	19-126	15	+30.70	5-56	9	-15.00
Kempton (AW)	42-360	12	-139.56	13-99	13	-43.35	24-186	13	-57.21	5-75	7	-39.00
Leicester	18-144	13	-53.22	8-61	13	-16.34	7-62	11	-24.63	3-21	14	-12.25
Lingfield	3-37	8	-20.75	1-11	9	-4.00	1-19	5	-16.75	1-7	14	+0.00
Lingfield (AW)	60-417	14	-143.21	8-54	15	+2.00	38-251	15	-91.14	14-112	13	-54.06
Musselburgh	55-268	21	+1.15	19-77	25	+15.96	29-138	21	-3.09	7-53	13	-11.72
Newbury	13-97	13	-10.63	7-39	18	-5.13	2-39	5	-18.50	4-19	21	+13.00
Newcastle	12-85	14	-25.13	5-33	15	-5.75	7-32	22	+0.63	0-20	-	-20.00
N'castle (AW)	8-64	13	-27.64	5-41	12	-24.64	2-18	11	-10.00	1-5	20	+7.00
Newmarket	32-257	12	+25.21	15-95	16	-8.27	10-110	9	-20.87	7-52	13	+54.35
Newmarket (J)	45-235	19	+49.14	10-68	15	-33.29	28-133	21	+68.68	7-34	21	+13.75
Nottingham	16-137	12	-54.29	10-63	16	-4.79	6-61	10	-36.50	0-13	-	-13.00
Pontefract	32-193	17	-65.21	9-59	15	-33.98	17-102	17	-26.99	6-32	19	-4.24
Redcar	16-109	15	-19.77	4-39	10	-25.30	8-50	16	-11.97	4-20	20	+17.50
Ripon	35-201	17	+8.83	11-50	22	-9.02	20-110	18	+44.04	4-41	10	-26.19
Salisbury	3-28	11	-11.00	3-12	25	+5.00	0-13	-	-13.00	0-3	-	-3.00
Sandown	9-108	8	-71.79	5-31	16	-13.59	4-60	7	-41.20	0-17	-	-17.00
S'well (AW)	48-201	24	+1.35	8-35	23	-15.11	23-99	23	+23.66	17-67	25	-7.21
Thirsk	9-112	8	-62.85	4-36	11	-21.35	3-52	6	-25.50	2-24	8	-16.00
Warwick	3-19	16	-7.63	2-4	50	+2.38	1-11	9	-6.00	0-4	-	-4.00
Wetherby	2-5	40	+8.10	1-2	50	+0.10	1-2	50	+9.00	0-1	-	-1.00
Windsor	8-63	13	-23.28	3-16	19	-2.40	3-30	10	-18.88	2-17	12	-2.00
Wolves (AW)	103-555	19	-126.66	13-118	11	-72.72	60-319	19	-74.16	30-118	25	+20.22
Yarmouth	15-83	18	+51.05	4-19	21	+59.73	8-49	16	-12.51	3-15	20	+3.83
York	14-258	5	-131.40	6-102	6	-62.90	5-91	5	-30.50	3-65	5	-38.00

Ten-year summary

	Wins	Runs	%	Win prize-money	Total prize-money	£1
2016	195	1413	14	£1,553,727.94	£2,724,680.66	-316.95
2015	204	1208	17	£1,806,254.46	£2,748,949.40	-111.80
2014	207	1344	15	£1,985,940.54	£2,992,111.82	-283.07
2013	216	1557	14	£1,826,629.78	£2,743,581.49	-396.21
2012	215	1344	16	£1,545,130.29	£2,284,275.76	-148.88
2011	179	1311	14	£927,711.46	£1,550,631.62	-270.93
2010	211	1458	14	£1,657,512.68	£2,419,718.15	-377.04
2009	216	1227	18	£1,747,013.96	£2,843,943.25	-139.14
2008	164	1145	14	£1,345,669.48	£2,070,937.14	-200.11
2007	161	998	16	£1,188,791.46	£1,651,628.48	-122.33

THE LAST LION: a Group 1 winner for Mark Johnston before being retired

Richard Hannon

Are these worrying times for this powerhouse stable? Hannon Jr's three seasons have seen winners, strike-rate and prize-money fall every time and 173 winners was the lowest tally for the yard since 2007.

By month - 2016

	Overall			Two-year-olds			Three-year-olds			Older horses		
	W-R	%	£1	W-R	%	£1	W-R	%	£1	W-R	%	£1
January	8-28	29	+13.82	0-0	-	+0.00	7-23	30	+13.82	1-5	20	+0.00
February	2-18	11	-7.00	0-0	-	+0.00	2-17	12	-6.00	0-1	-	-1.00
March	2-19	11	-11.63	0-1	-	-1.00	1-12	8	-9.13	1-6	17	-1.50
April	13-110	12	-41.26	4-18	22	-9.31	8-73	11	-17.46	1-19	5	-14.50
May	36-196	18	+68.61	15-56	27	+17.08	20-118	17	+60.53	1-22	5	-9.00
June	20-191	10	-71.97	9-75	12	-28.63	11-97	11	-24.34	0-19	-	-19.00
July	31-223	14	-9.35	15-103	15	-13.50	15-91	16	+31.15	1-29	3	-27.00
August	24-170	14	-47.07	19-102	19	-4.40	5-56	9	-30.67	0-12	-	-12.00
September	9-178	5	-119.92	7-112	6	-64.25	2-50	4	-39.67	0-16	-	-16.00
October	17-145	12	+3.75	10-101	10	+0.00	6-34	18	+9.25	1-10	10	-5.50
November	7-44	16	+26.00	4-31	13	+16.00	3-10	30	+13.00	0-3	-	-3.00
December	4-35	11	-7.92	4-23	17	+4.08	0-12	-	-12.00	0-0	-	+0.00

By month - 2015

	Overall			Two-year-olds			Three-year-olds			Older horses		
	W-R	%	£1	W-R	%	£1	W-R	%	£1	W-R	%	£1
January	1-18	6	-15.75	0-0	-	+0.00	1-10	10	-7.75	0-8	-	-8.00
February	1-13	8	-10.50	0-0	-	+0.00	1-6	17	-3.50	0-7	-	-7.00
March	8-28	29	+17.50	0-1	-	-1.00	6-19	32	+16.13	2-8	25	+2.38
April	15-100	15	-0.75	4-14	29	+0.62	9-71	13	-16.87	2-15	13	+15.50
May	33-177	19	-16.72	10-47	21	-10.37	20-105	19	+9.24	3-25	12	-15.59
June	32-198	16	-42.14	17-81	21	-26.39	14-103	14	-13.75	1-14	7	-2.00
July	34-234	15	-52.13	21-127	17	-22.13	12-93	13	-19.25	1-14	7	-10.75
August	30-209	14	-57.38	23-124	19	-10.13	6-67	9	-32.50	1-18	6	-14.75
September	18-200	9	-111.04	16-138	12	-69.04	1-48	2	-40.00	1-14	7	-2.00
October	11-126	9	-52.17	10-83	12	-14.67	1-33	3	-27.50	0-10	-	-10.00
November	6-37	16	+5.00	4-24	17	+7.50	2-13	15	-2.50	0-0	-	+0.00
December	5-42	12	-15.80	3-36	8	-19.90	2-6	33	+4.10	0-0	-	+0.00

By month - 2014

	Overall			Two-year-olds			Three-year-olds			Older horses		
	W-R	%	£1	W-R	%	£1	W-R	%	£1	W-R	%	£1
January	2-19	11	-12.00	0-0	-	+0.00	2-15	13	-8.00	0-4	-	-4.00
February	0-6	-	-6.00	0-0	-	+0.00	0-5	-	-5.00	0-1	-	-1.00
March	5-18	28	-2.64	1-2	50	-0.39	4-10	40	+3.75	0-6	-	-6.00
April	18-98	18	-7.51	5-16	31	+2.54	10-67	15	-13.05	3-15	20	+3.00
May	31-180	17	+40.64	16-48	33	+18.77	13-105	12	+43.75	2-27	7	-21.88
June	39-218	18	-36.14	21-83	25	-16.50	14-108	13	-23.44	4-27	15	+3.80
July	28-213	13	-118.97	18-105	17	-53.09	9-87	10	-47.51	1-21	5	-18.38
August	32-234	14	-79.77	24-125	19	-24.12	6-84	7	-38.25	2-25	8	-17.40
September	27-183	15	-47.65	18-115	16	-22.35	7-54	13	-19.04	2-14	14	-6.25
October	15-151	10	-64.25	11-100	11	-41.50	3-38	8	-13.00	1-13	8	-9.75
November	2-48	4	-34.50	0-27	-	-27.00	0-12	-	-12.00	2-9	22	+4.50
December	7-36	19	+2.38	5-17	29	+2.88	2-10	20	+8.50	0-9	-	-9.00

By race type - 2016

	Overall			Two-year-olds			Three-year-olds			Older horses		
	W-R	%	£1	W-R	%	£1	W-R	%	£1	W-R	%	£1
Handicap	66-636	10	-116.18	13-140	9	-41.00	51-408	13	-4.68	2-88	2	-70.50
Group	6-74	8	-43.75	4-29	14	-6.75	1-26	4	-22.50	1-19	5	-14.50
Maiden	52-381	14	-40.77	40-275	15	+6.68	12-106	11	-47.45	0-0	-	+0.00

By race type - 2015

	Overall			Two-year-olds			Three-year-olds			Older horses		
	W-R	%	£1	W-R	%	£1	W-R	%	£1	W-R	%	£1
Handicap	62-549	11	-91.19	22-138	16	+0.40	36-337	11	-62.59	4-74	5	-29.00
Group	8-113	7	-63.50	3-41	7	-30.50	2-38	5	-18.00	3-34	9	-15.00
Maiden	93-541	17	-139.93	68-412	17	-105.34	25-129	19	-34.60	0-0	-	+0.00

By race type - 2014

	Overall			Two-year-olds			Three-year-olds			Older horses		
	W-R	%	£1	W-R	%	£1	W-R	%	£1	W-R	%	£1
Handicap	66-604	11	-225.55	19-119	16	-15.84	38-394	10	-164.46	9-91	10	-45.25
Group	17-122	14	-12.17	11-46	24	+11.31	2-35	6	+8.00	4-41	10	-31.48
Maiden	84-475	18	-155.71	65-382	17	-134.13	19-91	21	-19.58	0-2	-	-2.00

By jockey - 2016

	Overall			Two-year-olds			Three-year-olds			Older horses		
	W-R	%	£1	W-R	%	£1	W-R	%	£1	W-R	%	£1
Sean Levey	44-371	12	-96.99	21-185	11	-44.76	22-154	14	-25.23	1-32	3	-27.00
Tom Marquand	26-209	12	+11.53	15-100	15	+27.28	10-95	11	-14.75	1-14	7	-1.00
Pat Dobbs	20-233	9	-91.95	14-109	13	-39.95	6-95	6	-23.00	0-29	-	-29.00
Kieran O'Neill	18-152	12	-34.22	6-62	10	-16.00	11-69	16	-1.72	1-21	5	-16.50
Hollie Doyle	10-60	17	+2.50	3-19	16	+3.00	7-35	20	+5.50	0-6	-	-6.00
Frankie Dettori	9-43	21	-2.67	6-24	25	+3.58	3-14	21	-1.25	0-5	-	-5.00
Timmy Murphy	7-22	32	+16.67	5-15	33	+6.83	2-7	29	+9.83	0-0	-	+0.00
Megan Nicholls	5-23	22	+39.50	1-3	33	+10.00	4-19	21	+30.50	0-1	-	-1.00
Gary Mahon	5-31	16	-15.19	3-12	25	-2.60	2-13	15	-6.59	0-6	-	-6.00
Dane O'Neill	4-18	22	-4.08	3-11	27	-1.58	0-6	-	-6.00	1-1	100	+3.50
Paul Hanagan	4-26	15	-12.63	3-14	21	-4.63	1-11	9	-7.00	0-1	-	-1.00
Ryan Moore	4-34	12	-16.63	2-18	11	-7.00	2-13	15	-6.63	0-3	-	-3.00

By jockey - 2015

	Overall			Two-year-olds			Three-year-olds			Older horses		
	W-R	%	£1	W-R	%	£1	W-R	%	£1	W-R	%	£1
Sean Levey	42-277	15	-29.62	26-142	18	-2.79	14-112	13	-14.21	2-23	9	-12.63
R Hughes	38-185	21	-21.50	16-75	21	-21.72	19-95	20	+5.06	3-15	20	-4.84
Pat Dobbs	29-253	11	-124.38	24-141	17	-51.63	3-88	3	-64.00	2-24	8	-8.75
Cam Hardie	17-121	14	-10.09	6-48	13	+10.00	11-66	17	-13.09	0-7	-	-7.00
Kieran O'Neill	12-86	14	-1.80	7-49	14	-7.40	4-31	13	-14.40	1-6	17	+20.00
Frankie Dettori	11-57	19	-13.62	3-21	14	-15.60	8-35	23	+2.98	0-1	-	-1.00
Tom Marquand	11-122	9	-35.13	6-55	11	-14.00	4-49	8	-15.13	1-18	6	-6.00
Ryan Moore	7-32	22	+2.50	4-18	22	+1.13	3-10	30	+5.38	0-4	-	-4.00
Paul Hanagan	6-26	23	+3.38	4-16	25	+2.13	2-10	20	+1.25	0-0	-	+0.00

By jockey - 2014

	Overall			Two-year-olds			Three-year-olds			Older horses		
	W-R	%	£1	W-R	%	£1	W-R	%	£1	W-R	%	£1
R Hughes	80-433	18	-93.07	53-205	26	-15.01	23-166	14	-28.71	4-62	6	-49.35
Sean Levey	24-213	11	-104.30	13-101	13	-56.52	8-88	9	-38.15	3-24	13	-9.63
Pat Dobbs	19-162	12	-16.93	9-80	11	-31.76	8-64	13	+10.58	2-18	11	+4.25
Frankie Dettori	17-65	26	+7.86	12-48	25	+2.78	4-16	25	+3.70	1-1	100	+1.38
Ryan Moore	12-76	16	-35.33	3-24	13	-16.73	6-37	16	-19.60	3-15	20	+1.00
Paul Hanagan	11-37	30	-9.32	7-18	39	-1.30	4-19	21	-8.03	0-0	-	+0.00
Cam Hardie	10-138	7	-91.26	5-44	11	-28.26	2-79	3	-63.50	3-15	20	+0.50
Kieran O'Neill	7-64	11	-21.09	1-23	4	-14.00	6-36	17	-2.09	0-5	-	-5.00
James Doyle	5-10	50	+30.00	5-8	63	+32.00	0-1	-	-1.00	0-1	-	-1.00

By course - 2012-2016

	Overall			Two-year-olds			Three-year-olds			Older horses		
	W-R	%	£1	W-R	%	£1	W-R	%	£1	W-R	%	£1
Ascot	20-242	8	-121.95	13-81	16	-1.00	5-99	5	-64.00	2-62	3	-56.95
Ayr	2-19	11	-4.00	1-13	8	-6.00	1-4	25	+4.00	0-2	-	-2.00
Bath	16-110	15	-44.87	9-55	16	-20.85	7-52	13	-21.02	0-3	-	-3.00
Beverley	2-3	67	+2.17	2-3	67	+2.17	0-0	-	+0.00	0-0	-	+0.00
Brighton	18-83	22	-17.09	12-44	27	-6.37	6-39	15	-10.72	0-0	-	+0.00
Carlisle	0-1	-	-1.00	0-0	-	+0.00	0-1	-	-1.00	0-0	-	+0.00
Chelms (AW)	18-121	15	-20.08	8-60	13	-16.03	10-53	19	+3.95	0-8	-	-8.00
Chepstow	21-95	22	-11.83	12-38	32	-1.08	7-49	14	-20.25	2-8	25	+9.50
Chester	9-60	15	-11.86	8-29	28	+6.14	1-25	4	-12.00	0-6	-	-6.00
Doncaster	23-173	13	-15.50	11-88	13	-27.35	10-60	17	+29.98	2-25	8	-18.13
Epsom	10-57	18	-11.04	5-19	26	-0.13	4-31	13	-15.92	1-7	14	+5.00
Ffos Las	5-25	20	-2.25	4-15	27	-0.25	1-9	11	-1.00	0-1	-	-1.00
Goodwood	35-277	13	-76.76	17-115	15	-45.86	15-115	13	+8.00	3-47	6	-38.90
Hamilton	1-2	50	+7.00	0-1	-	-1.00	1-1	100	+8.00	0-0	-	+0.00
Haydock	19-151	13	-20.40	8-68	12	-11.02	8-58	14	-16.75	3-25	12	+7.38
Kempton (AW)	40-346	12	-138.84	21-184	11	-69.54	15-134	11	-66.55	4-28	14	-2.75
Leicester	18-123	15	-29.25	11-65	17	-10.50	6-45	13	-10.25	1-13	8	-8.50
Lingfield	11-71	15	-10.45	6-35	17	-10.95	5-32	16	+4.50	0-4	-	-4.00
Lingfield (AW)	41-238	17	-16.44	15-66	23	-9.43	24-134	18	+20.50	2-38	5	-27.50
Musselburgh	0-1	-	-1.00	0-0	-	+0.00	0-1	-	-1.00	0-0	-	+0.00
Newbury	33-319	10	-120.47	18-172	10	-92.35	13-113	12	-0.25	2-34	6	-27.88
N'castle (AW)	1-4	25	-2.67	1-4	25	-2.67	0-0	-	+0.00	0-0	-	+0.00
Newmarket	28-217	13	-1.46	9-92	10	-49.46	18-98	18	+70.50	1-27	4	-22.50
Newmarket (J)	34-256	13	-53.58	26-140	19	+10.08	8-106	8	-53.67	0-10	-	-10.00
Nottingham	15-105	14	-32.16	9-51	18	+0.19	5-49	10	-32.85	1-5	20	+0.50
Pontefract	2-13	15	-7.50	1-7	14	-4.38	1-4	25	-1.13	0-2	-	-2.00
Redcar	4-13	31	+5.58	2-6	33	+1.58	2-6	33	+5.00	0-1	-	-1.00
Ripon	0-6	-	-6.00	0-3	-	-3.00	0-1	-	-1.00	0-2	-	-2.00
Salisbury	40-256	16	-25.91	28-126	22	+4.59	10-113	9	-35.75	2-17	12	+5.25
Sandown	22-180	12	-33.91	13-74	18	+0.89	7-85	8	-24.29	2-21	10	-10.50
S'well (AW)	7-25	28	+8.88	2-10	20	+0.50	4-12	33	+6.38	1-3	33	+2.00
Thirsk	3-5	60	+4.88	1-2	50	+3.50	1-2	50	+0.38	1-1	100	+1.00
Warwick	1-8	13	-6.20	1-3	33	-1.20	0-5	-	-5.00	0-0	-	+0.00
Wetherby	0-2	-	-2.00	0-0	-	+0.00	0-2	-	-2.00	0-0	-	+0.00
Windsor	34-263	13	-92.55	20-117	17	-60.63	12-120	10	-13.83	2-26	8	-18.09
Wolves (AW)	23-123	19	-17.06	10-60	17	+9.25	13-57	23	-20.31	0-6	-	-6.00
Yarmouth	2-5	40	+0.91	0-3	-	-3.00	1-1	100	+0.91	1-1	100	+3.00
York	8-91	9	-11.13	4-49	8	-19.13	3-30	10	+7.00	1-12	8	+1.00

Ten-year summary

	Wins	Runs	%	Win prize-money	Total prize-money	£1
2016	173	1357	13	£1,602,588.35	£2,847,607.05	-203.92
2015	194	1382	14	£2,027,558.78	£3,593,428.97	-351.88
2014	206	1404	15	£2,729,648.95	£4,749,469.60	-366.41
2013*	235	1412	17	£3,137,720.00	£4,532,464.69	-306.32
2012*	218	1367	16	£1,767,369.39	£2,821,469.49	-165.90
2011*	218	1408	15	£2,283,589.58	£3,726,396.80	-46.12
2010*	210	1341	16	£2,054,058.90	£3,218,574.92	-203.61
2009*	188	1371	14	£1,751,642.04	£2,814,384.49	-193.61
2008*	189	1406	13	£1,884,767.33	£2,982,090.39	-283.60
2007*	148	1075	14	£1,192,346.67	£2,083,975.15	-178.24

OH THIS IS US: five-time winner boosted the Hannons' lowest tally since 2007

John Gosden

Another stellar season for Gosden, whose total of 141 winners means he has improved his best tally in four of the last five campaigns. No Golden Horn this time but still a 23 per cent strike-rate and 12 Group winners.

By month - 2016

	Overall			Two-year-olds			Three-year-olds			Older horses		
	W-R	%	£1	W-R	%	£1	W-R	%	£1	W-R	%	£1
January	5-17	29	-3.99	0-0	-	+0.00	4-14	29	-3.09	1-3	33	-0.90
February	1-11	9	-6.00	0-0	-	+0.00	0-6	-	-6.00	1-5	20	+0.00
March	2-8	25	-1.80	0-0	-	+0.00	2-6	33	+0.20	0-2	-	-2.00
April	16-61	26	-3.01	0-0	-	+0.00	14-53	26	-2.84	2-8	25	-0.17
May	14-79	18	-18.66	1-8	13	-3.50	11-56	20	-19.16	2-15	13	+4.00
June	12-89	13	-32.10	4-21	19	+8.42	8-56	14	-28.52	0-12	-	-12.00
July	18-75	24	+22.09	6-21	29	-1.52	10-39	26	+23.61	2-15	13	+0.00
August	16-45	36	+21.59	3-12	25	-5.70	12-29	41	+19.29	1-4	25	+8.00
September	14-69	20	-1.50	7-32	22	-5.90	5-24	21	-1.97	2-13	15	+6.38
October	26-93	28	+34.64	17-53	32	+40.42	8-26	31	+3.22	1-14	7	-9.00
November	11-49	22	-10.38	9-39	23	-5.13	1-5	20	-2.50	1-5	20	-2.75
December	6-17	35	+1.25	6-17	35	+1.25	0-0	-	+0.00	0-0	-	+0.00

By month - 2015

	Overall			Two-year-olds			Three-year-olds			Older horses		
	W-R	%	£1	W-R	%	£1	W-R	%	£1	W-R	%	£1
January	7-20	35	+1.89	0-0	-	+0.00	5-15	33	+1.81	2-5	40	+0.08
February	2-11	18	-2.50	0-0	-	+0.00	1-8	13	-6.00	1-3	33	+3.50
March	4-12	33	-3.61	0-0	-	+0.00	1-6	17	-4.67	3-6	50	+1.06
April	18-60	30	+13.03	0-0	-	+0.00	15-49	31	-1.47	3-11	27	+14.50
May	15-88	17	-20.67	1-6	17	-0.50	11-67	16	-17.67	3-15	20	-2.50
June	13-75	17	-29.46	1-11	9	-5.50	10-54	19	-25.71	2-10	20	+1.75
July	13-53	25	+2.78	3-14	21	+6.88	10-30	33	+4.91	0-9	-	-9.00
August	10-52	19	+22.31	2-14	14	-9.99	8-28	29	+42.30	0-10	-	-10.00
September	23-67	34	+7.75	12-34	35	+3.31	8-27	30	-0.45	3-6	50	+4.89
October	13-77	17	-22.36	10-50	20	-9.97	2-19	11	-11.39	1-8	13	-1.00
November	11-41	27	+19.41	11-33	33	+27.41	0-7	-	-7.00	0-1	-	-1.00
December	4-21	19	-6.10	3-18	17	-4.50	1-3	33	-1.60	0-0	-	+0.00

By month - 2014

	Overall			Two-year-olds			Three-year-olds			Older horses		
	W-R	%	£1	W-R	%	£1	W-R	%	£1	W-R	%	£1
January	2-11	18	-5.05	0-0	-	+0.00	2-10	20	-4.05	0-1	-	-1.00
February	1-8	13	-4.50	0-0	-	+0.00	1-7	14	-3.50	0-1	-	-1.00
March	2-12	17	-1.50	0-0	-	+0.00	2-8	25	+2.50	0-4	-	-4.00
April	20-64	31	+7.20	1-1	100	+10.00	17-56	30	-1.38	2-7	29	-1.42
May	12-81	15	+8.52	0-5	-	-5.00	7-59	12	+1.45	5-17	29	+12.07
June	16-80	20	-9.54	1-4	25	+7.00	12-63	19	-18.29	3-13	23	+1.75
July	12-70	17	-23.83	1-13	8	-11.09	10-49	20	-13.74	1-8	13	+1.00
August	19-65	29	+23.05	3-16	19	-5.25	12-40	30	+9.50	4-9	44	+18.80
September	17-73	23	+33.67	9-32	28	+19.67	6-30	20	+8.50	2-11	18	+5.50
October	11-76	14	-38.77	7-44	16	-22.52	4-25	16	-9.25	0-7	-	-7.00
November	8-41	20	-13.14	5-31	16	-10.19	3-8	38	-0.95	0-2	-	-2.00
December	12-32	38	-0.73	10-25	40	+3.13	2-7	29	-3.86	0-0	-	+0.00

By race type - 2016

	Overall			Two-year-olds			Three-year-olds			Older horses		
	W-R	%	£1	W-R	%	£1	W-R	%	£1	W-R	%	£1
Handicap	28-126	22	+35.44	3-14	21	-4.09	23-98	23	+27.03	2-14	14	+12.50
Group	12-84	14	-18.87	1-8	13	-2.00	6-28	21	+2.30	5-48	10	-19.17
Maiden	83-302	27	+10.64	41-148	28	+30.01	39-149	26	-38.47	3-5	60	+19.10

By race type - 2015

	Overall			Two-year-olds			Three-year-olds			Older horses		
	W-R	%	£1	W-R	%	£1	W-R	%	£1	W-R	%	£1
Handicap	24-98	24	-5.60	2-8	25	-2.63	15-71	21	-17.72	7-19	37	+14.75
Group	17-81	21	-11.09	5-10	50	+16.13	8-35	23	-11.46	4-36	11	-15.75
Maiden	66-306	22	-49.39	31-147	21	-4.31	34-156	22	-43.42	1-3	33	-1.67

By race type - 2014

	Overall			Two-year-olds			Three-year-olds			Older horses		
	W-R	%	£1	W-R	%	£1	W-R	%	£1	W-R	%	£1
Handicap	30-173	17	-33.96	4-15	27	-0.50	21-136	15	-50.29	5-22	23	+16.83
Group	13-63	21	+14.50	0-3	-	-3.00	8-34	24	+5.00	5-26	19	+12.50
Maiden	73-296	25	+14.44	28-140	20	-17.95	43-150	29	+31.59	2-6	33	+0.80

By jockey - 2016

	Overall			Two-year-olds			Three-year-olds			Older horses		
	W-R	%	£1	W-R	%	£1	W-R	%	£1	W-R	%	£1
Robert Havlin	55-211	26	+48.38	22-71	31	+14.40	25-105	24	-1.38	8-35	23	+35.35
Frankie Dettori	38-144	26	-2.57	13-43	30	+8.60	22-76	29	+4.46	3-25	12	-15.63
Nicky Mackay	13-63	21	-9.68	3-24	13	-13.02	10-36	28	+6.35	0-3	-	-3.00
James Doyle	11-42	26	+1.45	8-20	40	+5.36	3-19	16	-0.91	0-3	-	-3.00
Paul Hanagan	7-32	22	-12.56	1-6	17	-2.25	5-15	33	-3.65	1-11	9	-6.67
Tom Queally	5-11	45	+6.41	0-0	-	+0.00	5-11	45	+6.41	0-0	-	+0.00
Robert Tart	3-22	14	+12.75	3-12	25	+22.75	0-8	-	-8.00	0-2	-	-2.00
Graham Lee	2-7	29	-2.29	0-3	-	-3.00	2-3	67	+1.71	0-1	-	-1.00
William Buick	2-36	6	-28.75	0-9	-	-9.00	2-21	10	-13.75	0-6	-	-6.00
C O'Donoghue	1-1	100	+10.00	0-0	-	+0.00	1-1	100	+10.00	0-0	-	+0.00
Jim Crowley	1-2	50	+4.00	1-1	100	+5.00	0-1	-	-1.00	0-0	-	+0.00
R Kingscote	1-3	33	+7.00	1-2	50	+8.00	0-1	-	-1.00	0-0	-	+0.00

By jockey - 2015

	Overall			Two-year-olds			Three-year-olds			Older horses		
	W-R	%	£1	W-R	%	£1	W-R	%	£1	W-R	%	£1
Robert Havlin	40-175	23	+32.19	12-62	19	+5.60	22-88	25	+19.84	6-25	24	+6.75
Frankie Dettori	36-134	27	-12.71	13-39	33	+3.48	19-71	27	-12.85	4-24	17	-3.33
Paul Hanagan	13-31	42	+14.72	4-6	67	+2.14	6-21	29	+6.08	3-4	75	+6.50
William Buick	12-52	23	-6.22	3-12	25	-1.67	8-31	26	-0.55	1-9	11	-4.00
Nicky Mackay	12-74	16	-19.51	3-25	12	-5.50	8-44	18	-10.63	1-5	20	-3.39
James Doyle	7-35	20	-10.17	4-11	36	+0.58	2-20	10	-10.50	1-4	25	-0.25
Dane O'Neill	4-15	27	-2.00	0-2	-	-2.00	4-12	33	+1.00	0-1	-	-1.00
Ryan Moore	3-10	30	+3.08	1-2	50	+0.25	1-7	14	-5.17	1-1	100	+8.00
Jimmy Fortune	3-13	23	+11.25	2-6	33	+14.75	1-5	20	-1.50	0-2	-	-2.00

By jockey - 2014

	Overall			Two-year-olds			Three-year-olds			Older horses		
	W-R	%	£1	W-R	%	£1	W-R	%	£1	W-R	%	£1
William Buick	56-291	19	-55.62	9-61	15	-20.47	36-182	20	-46.45	11-48	23	+11.30
Robert Havlin	29-148	20	-27.21	14-60	23	+1.69	15-80	19	-20.89	0-8	-	-8.00
Paul Hanagan	15-38	39	+14.50	3-8	38	-0.48	12-25	48	+19.98	0-5	-	-5.00
Nicky Mackay	13-53	25	+6.03	4-16	25	-2.50	7-32	22	-12.47	2-5	40	+21.00
James Doyle	8-27	30	-5.91	2-7	29	-1.50	5-13	38	+0.75	1-7	14	-5.17
Dane O'Neill	5-20	25	+12.00	4-10	40	+14.00	1-10	10	-2.00	0-0	-	+0.00
Frankie Dettori	3-12	25	-1.43	1-2	50	+2.00	0-5	-	-5.00	2-5	40	+1.57
Ted Durcan	1-1	100	+40.00	0-0	-	+0.00	1-1	100	+40.00	0-0	-	+0.00
Graham Lee	1-3	33	+6.00	0-0	-	+0.00	0-1	-	-1.00	1-2	50	+7.00

By course - 2012-2016

	Overall			Two-year-olds			Three-year-olds			Older horses		
	W-R	%	£1	W-R	%	£1	W-R	%	£1	W-R	%	£1
Ascot	35-208	17	+14.82	5-24	21	+28.00	15-100	15	-19.83	15-84	18	+6.65
Ayr	0-2	-	-2.00	0-1	-	-1.00	0-0	-	+0.00	0-1	-	-1.00
Bath	2-12	17	-3.50	0-1	-	-1.00	2-10	20	-1.50	0-1	-	-1.00
Beverley	0-4	-	-4.00	0-0	-	+0.00	0-4	-	-4.00	0-0	-	+0.00
Brighton	1-6	17	-4.83	1-3	33	-1.83	0-3	-	-3.00	0-0	-	+0.00
Carlisle	0-4	-	-4.00	0-1	-	-1.00	0-2	-	-2.00	0-1	-	-1.00
Catterick	2-3	67	+1.58	1-1	100	+1.75	1-2	50	-0.17	0-0	-	+0.00
Chelms (AW)	19-61	31	-5.44	3-14	21	-3.88	13-43	30	-9.51	3-4	75	+7.94
Chepstow	3-7	43	-0.70	1-1	100	+0.80	2-6	33	-1.50	0-0	-	+0.00
Chester	7-37	19	-9.04	1-3	33	-0.13	5-24	21	-3.92	1-10	10	-5.00
Doncaster	35-168	21	-31.28	9-35	26	-1.74	23-98	23	-13.04	3-35	9	-16.50
Epsom	11-45	24	-6.96	1-2	50	-0.33	7-30	23	-5.21	3-13	23	-1.42
Folkestone	0-2	-	-2.00	0-0	-	+0.00	0-2	-	-2.00	0-0	-	+0.00
Goodwood	21-113	19	-11.53	7-26	27	+2.84	10-51	20	+2.56	4-36	11	-16.93
Hamilton	1-2	50	-0.86	0-0	-	+0.00	1-2	50	-0.86	0-0	-	+0.00
Haydock	27-89	30	+34.82	11-29	38	+12.25	10-34	29	+8.90	6-26	23	+13.67
Kempton (AW)	71-332	21	-25.89	26-146	18	-8.28	38-153	25	-8.70	7-33	21	-8.91
Leicester	13-61	21	-4.47	5-24	21	-6.24	7-34	21	-12.23	1-3	33	+14.00
Lingfield	6-27	22	-4.75	2-8	25	-1.50	4-18	22	-2.25	0-1	-	-1.00
Lingfield (AW)	56-281	20	-57.53	11-74	15	-18.30	38-173	22	-34.43	7-34	21	-4.80
Newbury	34-188	18	-10.81	9-48	19	-3.44	21-104	20	+3.63	4-36	11	-11.00
Newcastle	1-18	6	-13.67	0-5	-	-5.00	1-9	11	-4.67	0-4	-	-4.00
N'castle (AW)	5-14	36	+3.80	5-13	38	+4.80	0-1	-	-1.00	0-0	-	+0.00
Newmarket	52-287	18	-23.26	17-93	18	-8.51	23-143	16	-43.24	12-51	24	+28.49
Newmarket (J)	45-215	21	+69.67	14-73	19	+10.66	24-115	21	+18.39	7-27	26	+40.63
Nottingham	22-117	19	+3.84	9-42	21	+8.81	11-63	17	-13.73	2-12	17	+8.75
Pontefract	2-20	10	-10.75	0-2	-	-2.00	1-13	8	-6.50	1-5	20	-2.25
Redcar	0-7	-	-7.00	0-4	-	-4.00	0-2	-	-2.00	0-1	-	-1.00
Ripon	0-3	-	-3.00	0-0	-	+0.00	0-3	-	-3.00	0-0	-	+0.00
Salisbury	13-53	25	+22.14	3-12	25	+2.00	6-33	18	+14.67	4-8	50	+5.48
Sandown	32-148	22	-9.57	8-31	26	+3.62	15-88	17	-29.15	9-29	31	+15.96
S'well (AW)	9-21	43	-1.24	2-3	67	+2.44	4-13	31	-5.25	3-5	60	+1.56
Thirsk	0-4	-	-4.00	0-1	-	-1.00	0-3	-	-3.00	0-0	-	+0.00
Warwick	0-2	-	-2.00	0-1	-	-1.00	0-0	-	+0.00	0-1	-	-1.00
Wetherby	1-1	100	+6.00	0-0	-	+0.00	1-1	100	+6.00	0-0	-	+0.00
Windsor	15-83	18	-24.17	3-11	27	+3.38	12-59	20	-14.54	0-13	-	-13.00
Wolves (AW)	52-138	38	+9.34	18-47	38	+6.93	30-82	37	+3.36	4-9	44	-0.95
Yarmouth	16-61	26	-4.80	6-20	30	-0.21	8-36	22	-4.39	2-5	40	-0.20
York	17-80	21	+12.59	0-5	-	-5.00	12-41	29	+23.84	5-34	15	-6.25

Ten-year summary

	Wins	Runs	%	Win prize-money	Total prize-money	£1
2016	141	613	23	£1,957,729.28	£3,462,783.77	+2.14
2015	133	577	23	£3,094,711.38	£5,277,650.54	-17.52
2014	132	613	22	£2,876,012.06	£4,241,990.89	-24.63
2013	108	525	21	£1,263,914.58	£2,033,077.64	-24.83
2012	119	629	19	£2,150,284.26	£3,739,407.23	-60.64
2011	99	553	18	£1,828,265.33	£2,529,369.21	-14.31
2010	105	518	20	£1,101,277.72	£1,714,237.43	-28.71
2009	88	516	17	£1,447,841.46	£2,308,709.36	-97.55
2008	95	498	19	£1,843,697.13	£2,596,896.00	+19.30
2007	68	401	17	£1,055,409.41	£1,644,331.67	-75.22

JOURNEY: the highest earner during another stellar season for John Gosden

William Haggas

Haggas has long been known for maintaining a remarkable strike-rate and now seems to be getting long-overdue ammunition. The result was 137 winners, a big step up on his previous best of 113.

By month - 2016

	Overall			*Two-year-olds*			*Three-year-olds*			*Older horses*		
	W-R	*%*	*£1*	*W-R*	*%*	*£1*	*W-R*	*%*	*£1*	*W-R*	*%*	*£1*
January	3-15	20	+0.20	0-0	-	+0.00	1-12	8	-10.80	2-3	67	+11.00
February	0-3	-	-3.00	0-0	-	+0.00	0-0	-	+0.00	0-3	-	-3.00
March	4-8	50	+8.25	0-0	-	+0.00	2-5	40	+0.50	2-3	67	+7.75
April	7-30	23	-10.36	0-0	-	+0.00	6-25	24	-10.36	1-5	20	+0.00
May	10-60	17	-15.97	0-4	-	-4.00	9-44	20	-11.97	1-12	8	+0.00
June	15-71	21	-15.72	2-11	18	-3.75	11-51	22	-10.72	2-9	22	-1.25
July	21-102	21	-25.32	6-25	24	-9.89	13-62	21	-21.93	2-15	13	+6.50
August	20-86	23	-30.63	6-28	21	-10.22	14-48	29	-10.41	0-10	-	-10.00
September	36-104	35	+42.88	12-39	31	+18.95	21-54	39	+18.43	3-11	27	+5.50
October	13-80	16	-25.40	8-47	17	-20.65	2-21	10	-10.50	3-12	25	+5.75
November	6-24	25	-0.33	4-19	21	-2.00	2-4	50	+2.67	0-1	-	-1.00
December	2-13	15	-7.89	2-10	20	-4.89	0-1	-	-1.00	0-2	-	-2.00

By month - 2015

	Overall			*Two-year-olds*			*Three-year-olds*			*Older horses*		
	W-R	*%*	*£1*	*W-R*	*%*	*£1*	*W-R*	*%*	*£1*	*W-R*	*%*	*£1*
January	0-5	-	-5.00	0-0	-	+0.00	0-4	-	-4.00	0-1	-	-1.00
February	1-5	20	-1.25	0-0	-	+0.00	0-3	-	-3.00	1-2	50	+1.75
March	0-4	-	-4.00	0-0	-	+0.00	0-2	-	-2.00	0-2	-	-2.00
April	3-20	15	-9.88	0-0	-	+0.00	3-20	15	-9.88	0-0	-	+0.00
May	12-48	25	+7.70	3-6	50	+10.30	9-33	27	+6.40	0-9	-	-9.00
June	14-63	22	-21.25	3-16	19	-11.87	11-39	28	-1.38	0-8	-	-8.00
July	24-82	29	-14.14	10-24	42	+5.05	11-44	25	-16.77	3-14	21	-2.42
August	20-85	24	-0.73	9-33	27	+4.03	10-38	26	+3.24	1-14	7	-8.00
September	15-87	17	-42.48	7-43	16	-20.13	6-33	18	-17.23	2-11	18	-5.13
October	10-77	13	-36.17	7-44	16	-15.38	3-28	11	-15.79	0-5	-	-5.00
November	6-35	17	-12.02	5-21	24	+0.25	1-11	9	-9.27	0-3	-	-3.00
December	8-22	36	+12.10	4-13	31	+0.48	2-5	40	+9.00	2-4	50	+2.63

By month - 2014

	Overall			*Two-year-olds*			*Three-year-olds*			*Older horses*		
	W-R	*%*	*£1*	*W-R*	*%*	*£1*	*W-R*	*%*	*£1*	*W-R*	*%*	*£1*
January	2-10	20	-5.50	0-0	-	+0.00	2-6	33	-1.50	0-4	-	-4.00
February	0-3	-	-3.00	0-0	-	+0.00	0-1	-	-1.00	0-2	-	-2.00
March	2-4	50	+2.75	0-0	-	+0.00	1-1	100	+1.25	1-3	33	+1.50
April	10-29	34	+12.91	0-1	-	-1.00	9-24	38	+15.16	1-4	25	-1.25
May	16-66	24	-2.01	1-11	9	-7.00	14-45	31	+10.49	1-10	10	-5.50
June	24-83	29	+18.29	6-16	38	+5.86	16-50	32	+17.68	2-17	12	-5.25
July	17-65	26	+19.57	3-16	19	-7.33	11-40	28	+13.40	3-9	33	+13.50
August	19-74	26	+33.96	6-20	30	+16.36	9-40	23	+9.09	4-14	29	+8.50
September	15-78	19	+5.97	7-45	16	+3.25	7-27	26	+4.72	1-6	17	-2.00
October	6-78	8	-43.38	2-46	4	-31.50	2-24	8	-17.88	2-8	25	+6.00
November	2-19	11	-11.50	1-9	11	-6.50	0-6	-	-6.00	1-4	25	+1.00
December	0-11	-	-11.00	0-6	-	-6.00	0-4	-	-4.00	0-1	-	-1.00

By race type - 2016

	Overall			Two-year-olds			Three-year-olds			Older horses		
	W-R	%	£1	W-R	%	£1	W-R	%	£1	W-R	%	£1
Handicap	54-241	22	-16.18	4-30	13	-15.59	41-158	26	-6.09	9-53	17	+5.50
Group	6-45	13	-16.93	2-12	17	-5.50	1-16	6	-14.43	3-17	18	+3.00
Maiden	63-244	26	-45.34	26-118	22	-19.52	37-126	29	-25.82	0-0	-	+0.00

By race type - 2015

	Overall			Two-year-olds			Three-year-olds			Older horses		
	W-R	%	£1	W-R	%	£1	W-R	%	£1	W-R	%	£1
Handicap	29-201	14	-70.99	4-28	14	-1.47	21-137	15	-49.73	4-36	11	-19.79
Group	8-52	15	-12.38	4-20	20	-3.88	3-16	19	+3.50	1-16	6	-12.00
Maiden	58-222	26	-45.78	31-136	23	-29.09	27-84	32	-14.70	0-2	-	-2.00

By race type - 2014

	Overall			Two-year-olds			Three-year-olds			Older horses		
	W-R	%	£1	W-R	%	£1	W-R	%	£1	W-R	%	£1
Handicap	51-211	24	+9.22	5-28	18	-13.14	35-137	26	+5.35	11-46	24	+17.00
Group	1-38	3	-23.00	0-8	-	-8.00	0-16	-	-16.00	1-14	7	+1.00
Maiden	46-199	23	+4.11	18-118	15	-14.31	27-77	35	+20.91	1-4	25	-2.50

By jockey - 2016

	Overall			Two-year-olds			Three-year-olds			Older horses		
	W-R	%	£1	W-R	%	£1	W-R	%	£1	W-R	%	£1
Pat Cosgrave	57-218	26	+20.37	17-75	23	-0.07	30-107	28	+2.19	10-36	28	+18.25
Ben Curtis	13-32	41	+14.23	7-16	44	+2.78	5-13	38	+2.45	1-3	33	+9.00
Frankie Dettori	12-28	43	+7.72	5-8	63	+7.91	6-15	40	-1.69	1-5	20	+1.50
G Gibbons	7-30	23	-6.26	0-4	-	-4.00	7-25	28	-1.26	0-1	-	-1.00
Ryan Moore	7-32	22	-10.29	3-9	33	+1.13	4-17	24	-5.42	0-6	-	-6.00
Georgia Cox	7-37	19	-11.26	0-8	-	-8.00	6-22	27	-3.26	1-7	14	+0.00
Paul Hanagan	6-43	14	-30.00	1-14	7	-12.39	5-20	25	-8.61	0-9	-	-9.00
Jim Crowley	4-18	22	-5.63	0-6	-	-6.00	4-12	33	+0.38	0-0	-	+0.00
Dane O'Neill	3-17	18	+7.50	0-5	-	-5.00	1-8	13	-5.00	2-4	50	+17.50
Andrea Atzeni	3-22	14	-11.75	2-6	33	+0.50	1-14	7	-10.25	0-2	-	-2.00
Oisin Murphy	2-7	29	-3.60	0-0	-	+0.00	2-6	33	-2.60	0-1	-	-1.00
Joe Fanning	2-10	20	-5.93	0-1	-	-1.00	2-6	33	-1.93	0-3	-	-3.00

By jockey - 2015

	Overall			Two-year-olds			Three-year-olds			Older horses		
	W-R	%	£1	W-R	%	£1	W-R	%	£1	W-R	%	£1
Pat Cosgrave	39-201	19	-65.97	17-94	18	-36.71	19-81	23	-16.26	3-26	12	-13.00
Paul Hanagan	14-51	27	+0.40	4-12	33	-1.34	7-29	24	+0.16	3-10	30	+1.58
Joe Fanning	8-18	44	+15.05	4-6	67	+9.75	4-12	33	+5.30	0-0	-	+0.00
G Gibbons	8-24	33	+3.99	6-14	43	+8.64	2-8	25	-2.65	0-2	-	-2.00
Harry Bentley	7-31	23	+0.33	2-8	25	+0.13	5-19	26	+4.20	0-4	-	-4.00
Frankie Dettori	4-10	40	+1.62	1-4	25	+1.00	3-5	60	+1.62	0-1	-	-1.00
Seb Sanders	4-10	40	+4.32	0-1	-	-1.00	3-6	50	+4.57	1-3	33	+0.75
Tom Queally	4-13	31	+14.00	3-9	33	+14.00	1-1	100	+3.00	0-3	-	-3.00
Graham Lee	4-14	29	-4.56	2-2	100	+2.29	2-8	25	-2.85	0-4	-	-4.00

By jockey - 2014

	Overall			Two-year-olds			Three-year-olds			Older horses		
	W-R	%	£1	W-R	%	£1	W-R	%	£1	W-R	%	£1
Ryan Moore	15-68	22	-11.48	2-19	11	-14.02	11-34	32	+6.79	2-15	13	-4.25
Paul Hanagan	14-55	25	+15.03	2-14	14	-8.17	9-32	28	+4.20	3-9	33	+19.00
Seb Sanders	12-41	29	-0.59	2-11	18	-7.39	8-19	42	+9.30	2-11	18	-2.50
Liam Jones	11-67	16	+5.10	4-28	14	+1.25	7-38	18	+4.85	0-1	-	-1.00
G Gibbons	7-19	37	+9.64	3-10	30	+1.94	3-8	38	+5.95	1-1	100	+1.75
S De Sousa	7-23	30	+9.15	2-8	25	+8.75	5-14	36	+1.40	0-1	-	-1.00
Nathan Alison	6-19	32	+13.96	0-2	-	-2.00	6-15	40	+17.96	0-2	-	-2.00
Andrea Atzeni	6-21	29	+21.16	3-9	33	+8.25	3-11	27	+13.91	0-1	-	-1.00
Graham Lee	6-22	27	-0.76	2-10	20	-4.09	1-8	13	-3.67	3-4	75	+7.00

By course - 2012-2016

	Overall			Two-year-olds			Three-year-olds			Older horses		
	W-R	%	£1	W-R	%	£1	W-R	%	£1	W-R	%	£1
Ascot	16-176	9	-83.63	4-35	11	-2.88	10-90	11	-39.75	2-51	4	-41.00
Ayr	2-12	17	+1.00	2-7	29	+6.00	0-2	-	-2.00	0-3	-	-3.00
Bath	12-33	36	-0.27	4-7	57	+4.03	7-24	29	-6.80	1-2	50	+2.50
Beverley	8-32	25	-5.40	3-9	33	+6.00	5-21	24	-9.40	0-2	-	-2.00
Brighton	7-28	25	-6.43	2-13	15	-8.14	5-15	33	+1.71	0-0	-	+0.00
Carlisle	7-16	44	+6.95	1-3	33	+0.75	6-13	46	+6.20	0-0	-	+0.00
Catterick	5-10	50	-1.11	3-8	38	-2.93	2-2	100	+1.82	0-0	-	+0.00
Chelms (AW)	11-57	19	-11.48	4-19	21	-0.50	5-31	16	-14.86	2-7	29	+3.88
Chepstow	9-28	32	-1.60	1-10	10	-8.47	7-17	41	+3.86	1-1	100	+3.00
Chester	11-42	26	-7.90	5-8	63	+9.12	5-26	19	-14.02	1-8	13	-3.00
Doncaster	20-112	18	-20.90	9-32	28	+14.28	6-60	10	-46.19	5-20	25	+11.00
Epsom	2-31	6	-13.50	0-4	-	-4.00	2-19	11	-1.50	0-8	-	-8.00
Ffos Las	3-8	38	-1.93	1-2	50	-0.39	1-4	25	-2.17	1-2	50	+0.63
Folkestone	0-3	-	-3.00	0-0	-	+0.00	0-3	-	-3.00	0-0	-	+0.00
Goodwood	19-76	25	+12.21	3-13	23	+0.50	10-43	23	-9.54	6-20	30	+21.25
Hamilton	3-11	27	-3.49	0-0	-	+0.00	2-10	20	-6.99	1-1	100	+3.50
Haydock	29-98	30	+21.51	8-24	33	+9.71	16-49	33	+7.30	5-25	20	+4.50
Kempton (AW)	26-158	16	-28.12	6-56	11	-29.16	15-78	19	-3.62	5-24	21	+4.66
Leicester	10-56	18	-16.28	4-26	15	-3.86	6-28	21	-10.43	0-2	-	-2.00
Lingfield	13-38	34	+7.80	4-15	27	-0.45	9-21	43	+10.25	0-2	-	-2.00
Lingfield (AW)	43-167	26	-3.93	10-53	19	-4.45	23-87	26	-9.65	10-27	37	+10.17
Musselburgh	9-18	50	+20.07	5-6	83	+3.48	4-10	40	+18.58	0-2	-	-2.00
Newbury	30-148	20	+1.79	9-58	16	-13.49	16-69	23	+18.08	5-21	24	-2.80
Newcastle	8-27	30	-3.52	1-2	50	-0.80	7-18	39	+4.28	0-7	-	-7.00
N'castle (AW)	6-17	35	+2.28	4-10	40	+3.62	2-7	29	-1.33	0-0	-	+0.00
Newmarket	20-194	10	-33.90	7-83	8	+10.00	11-84	13	-32.40	2-27	7	-11.50
Newmarket (J)	19-149	13	-57.29	4-39	10	-20.13	13-84	15	-31.41	2-26	8	-5.75
Nottingham	9-65	14	-27.55	1-22	5	-20.64	6-35	17	-10.67	2-8	25	+3.75
Pontefract	12-45	27	-4.68	3-16	19	-7.34	9-26	35	+5.66	0-3	-	-3.00
Redcar	11-24	46	+8.25	2-5	40	+0.60	8-17	47	+4.65	1-2	50	+3.00
Ripon	18-49	37	-1.21	5-14	36	-0.02	11-33	33	-3.43	2-2	100	+2.25
Salisbury	9-41	22	-8.53	2-14	14	-3.75	6-24	25	-6.78	1-3	33	+2.00
Sandown	16-68	24	+2.88	4-16	25	-2.58	8-33	24	-2.38	4-19	21	+7.83
S'well (AW)	4-11	36	-0.44	1-3	33	-1.64	3-7	43	+2.20	0-1	-	-1.00
Thirsk	8-33	24	+13.20	4-11	36	+10.50	4-19	21	+5.70	0-3	-	-3.00
Warwick	3-17	18	+9.25	2-9	22	+14.75	1-7	14	-4.50	0-1	-	-1.00
Wetherby	1-3	33	-1.33	0-0	-	+0.00	1-3	33	-1.33	0-0	-	+0.00
Windsor	19-74	26	-10.97	5-24	21	-9.72	10-39	26	-2.00	4-11	36	+0.75
Wolves (AW)	22-129	17	-64.07	7-43	16	-25.73	13-75	17	-37.10	2-11	18	-1.25
Yarmouth	34-109	31	+14.56	9-42	21	-5.13	22-57	39	+14.81	3-10	30	+4.88
York	34-164	21	+36.12	12-48	25	+10.34	11-58	19	+15.75	11-58	19	+10.03

Ten-year summary

	Wins	Runs	%	Win prize-money	Total prize-money	£1
2016	137	596	23	£1,423,781.23	£2,126,782.18	-83.29
2015	113	533	21	£1,583,672.69	£2,364,888.31	-127.11
2014	113	520	22	£1,478,038.78	£2,281,869.22	+17.06
2013	107	503	21	£1,133,364.77	£1,896,067.18	-12.27
2012	83	448	19	£748,501.35	£1,257,840.26	-65.35
2011	76	423	18	£848,955.18	£1,228,089.25	-96.35
2010	59	361	16	£942,548.43	£1,181,417.91	-91.16
2009	69	346	20	£793,312.00	£1,320,567.05	-53.39
2008	86	425	20	£793,358.07	£1,056,524.73	+93.92
2007	66	376	18	£546,929.84	£763,916.97	+34.50

DAL HARRAILD: a big contributor to William Haggas's best ever year

Michael Stoute

A resurgent campaign for Stoute, who roared back to the big time with his first century of winners since 2007 including 12 Group winners in Britain. There was also Breeders' Cup success with Queen's Trust.

By month - 2016

	Overall			Two-year-olds			Three-year-olds			Older horses		
	W-R	%	£1	W-R	%	£1	W-R	%	£1	W-R	%	£1
January	0-0	-	+0.00	0-0	-	+0.00	0-0	-	+0.00	0-0	-	+0.00
February	0-0	-	+0.00	0-0	-	+0.00	0-0	-	+0.00	0-0	-	+0.00
March	0-0	-	+0.00	0-0	-	+0.00	0-0	-	+0.00	0-0	-	+0.00
April	13-57	23	+1.26	0-0	-	+0.00	9-46	20	-6.49	4-11	36	+7.75
May	17-73	23	-15.09	0-0	-	+0.00	15-61	25	-8.84	2-12	17	-6.25
June	18-73	25	+39.48	1-5	20	+0.00	14-56	25	+32.23	3-12	25	+7.25
July	15-68	22	-19.14	0-5	-	-5.00	13-50	26	-6.48	2-13	15	-7.67
August	21-73	29	-7.67	5-14	36	+7.04	15-48	31	-5.72	1-11	9	-9.00
September	16-82	20	-5.36	5-34	15	-0.08	10-44	23	-3.38	1-4	25	-1.90
October	9-59	15	-27.95	7-26	27	-6.45	2-28	7	-16.50	0-5	-	-5.00
November	2-16	13	+13.00	2-13	15	+16.00	0-3	-	-3.00	0-0	-	+0.00
December	0-4	-	-4.00	0-3	-	-3.00	0-1	-	-1.00	0-0	-	+0.00

By month - 2015

	Overall			Two-year-olds			Three-year-olds			Older horses		
	W-R	%	£1	W-R	%	£1	W-R	%	£1	W-R	%	£1
January	0-0	-	+0.00	0-0	-	+0.00	0-0	-	+0.00	0-0	-	+0.00
February	0-0	-	+0.00	0-0	-	+0.00	0-0	-	+0.00	0-0	-	+0.00
March	0-0	-	+0.00	0-0	-	+0.00	0-0	-	+0.00	0-0	-	+0.00
April	5-51	10	-27.55	0-0	-	+0.00	3-45	7	-26.60	2-6	33	-0.95
May	15-67	22	+6.32	0-1	-	-1.00	12-50	24	+12.70	3-16	19	-5.39
June	17-66	26	+7.39	1-3	33	+3.00	14-51	27	+1.39	2-12	17	+3.00
July	11-65	17	+2.00	0-11	-	-11.00	10-42	24	+10.00	1-12	8	+3.00
August	14-79	18	-19.93	3-27	11	-4.75	11-44	25	-7.18	0-8	-	-8.00
September	8-70	11	-31.28	4-35	11	-16.88	4-28	14	-7.40	0-7	-	-7.00
October	7-44	16	+3.76	6-29	21	+9.76	1-11	9	-2.00	0-4	-	-4.00
November	2-12	17	-8.72	2-10	20	-6.72	0-2	-	-2.00	0-0	-	+0.00
December	0-1	-	-1.00	0-1	-	-1.00	0-0	-	+0.00	0-0	-	+0.00

By month - 2014

	Overall			Two-year-olds			Three-year-olds			Older horses		
	W-R	%	£1	W-R	%	£1	W-R	%	£1	W-R	%	£1
January	0-0	-	+0.00	0-0	-	+0.00	0-0	-	+0.00	0-0	-	+0.00
February	0-0	-	+0.00	0-0	-	+0.00	0-0	-	+0.00	0-0	-	+0.00
March	1-2	50	-0.33	0-0	-	+0.00	0-0	-	+0.00	1-2	50	-0.33
April	6-44	14	-30.75	0-0	-	+0.00	3-32	9	-24.25	3-12	25	-6.50
May	13-64	20	-2.75	0-4	-	-4.00	8-43	19	-2.13	5-17	29	+3.38
June	11-54	20	-18.77	1-6	17	-4.20	6-33	18	-12.83	4-15	27	-1.75
July	15-73	21	-22.46	2-16	13	-12.23	12-39	31	+4.89	1-18	6	-15.13
August	8-76	11	-50.92	2-21	10	-15.25	6-44	14	-24.67	0-11	-	-11.00
September	15-79	19	-12.22	7-38	18	-6.08	5-34	15	-13.76	3-7	43	+7.63
October	11-55	20	+16.43	9-35	26	+14.93	1-14	7	+3.00	1-6	17	-1.50
November	1-12	8	-7.50	0-9	-	-9.00	1-3	33	+1.50	0-0	-	+0.00
December	0-2	-	-2.00	0-1	-	-1.00	0-1	-	-1.00	0-0	-	+0.00

By race type - 2016

	Overall			Two-year-olds			Three-year-olds			Older horses		
	W-R	%	£1	W-R	%	£1	W-R	%	£1	W-R	%	£1
Handicap	40-202	20	-23.75	1-5	20	+16.00	35-166	21	-22.25	4-31	13	-17.50
Group	12-59	20	-2.67	0-5	-	-5.00	4-28	14	-9.52	8-26	31	+11.85
Maiden	48-200	24	+6.98	17-84	20	-4.12	31-112	28	+15.10	0-4	-	-4.00

By race type - 2015

	Overall			Two-year-olds			Three-year-olds			Older horses		
	W-R	%	£1	W-R	%	£1	W-R	%	£1	W-R	%	£1
Handicap	28-175	16	-33.38	0-6	-	-6.00	27-141	19	-14.38	1-28	4	-13.00
Group	4-40	10	-14.25	0-3	-	-3.00	0-10	-	-10.00	4-27	15	-1.25
Maiden	43-210	20	-5.50	16-104	15	-15.58	26-105	25	+9.79	1-1	100	+0.30

By race type - 2014

	Overall			Two-year-olds			Three-year-olds			Older horses		
	W-R	%	£1	W-R	%	£1	W-R	%	£1	W-R	%	£1
Handicap	31-183	17	-46.37	2-14	14	-6.75	22-126	17	-23.24	7-43	16	-16.38
Group	10-46	22	-6.75	0-2	-	-2.00	2-11	18	-2.75	8-33	24	-2.00
Maiden	38-203	19	-58.16	19-110	17	-24.08	16-89	18	-35.25	3-4	75	+1.17

By jockey - 2016

	Overall			Two-year-olds			Three-year-olds			Older horses		
	W-R	%	£1	W-R	%	£1	W-R	%	£1	W-R	%	£1
Ryan Moore	32-129	25	-17.19	5-30	17	-11.58	18-73	25	-13.19	9-26	35	+7.58
Ted Durcan	25-130	19	-35.85	6-22	27	+5.64	18-92	20	-29.99	1-16	6	-11.50
Andrea Atzeni	8-28	29	-3.24	1-5	20	-2.25	7-19	37	+3.01	0-4	-	-4.00
G Gibbons	8-30	27	+29.88	2-10	20	+19.00	6-20	30	+10.88	0-0	-	+0.00
Paul Hanagan	6-28	21	-7.84	2-11	18	+0.50	4-12	33	-3.34	0-5	-	-5.00
Jim Crowley	4-10	40	+4.30	1-2	50	-0.43	2-6	33	+4.63	1-2	50	+0.10
William Buick	3-5	60	+16.00	0-1	-	-1.00	3-4	75	+17.00	0-0	-	+0.00
Dane O'Neill	3-12	25	+7.91	0-2	-	-2.00	3-7	43	+12.91	0-3	-	-3.00
R Kingscote	3-14	21	-7.04	0-3	-	-3.00	3-11	27	-4.04	0-0	-	+0.00
Pat Smullen	3-16	19	+1.00	2-4	50	+11.00	0-6	-	-6.00	1-6	17	-4.00
Frankie Dettori	3-19	16	-5.70	0-1	-	-1.00	3-18	17	-4.70	0-0	-	+0.00
Daniel Tudhope	2-3	67	+5.33	0-0	-	+0.00	2-3	67	+5.33	0-0	-	+0.00

By jockey - 2015

	Overall			Two-year-olds			Three-year-olds			Older horses		
	W-R	%	£1	W-R	%	£1	W-R	%	£1	W-R	%	£1
Ted Durcan	26-153	17	+3.47	8-53	15	-8.96	17-86	20	+11.43	1-14	7	+1.00
Ryan Moore	22-105	21	-33.38	3-15	20	-7.74	14-60	23	-12.01	5-30	17	-13.64
Paul Hanagan	8-21	38	+13.07	2-5	40	+13.62	6-13	46	+2.45	0-3	-	-3.00
Stevie Donohoe	8-44	18	+22.41	3-19	16	-0.50	5-25	20	+22.91	0-0	-	+0.00
Graham Gibbons	3-16	19	-1.25	0-4	-	-4.00	3-12	25	+2.75	0-0	-	+0.00
Dane O'Neill	2-16	13	-12.90	0-1	-	-1.00	1-12	8	-10.20	1-3	33	-1.70
Hayley Turner	1-1	100	+1.10	0-0	-	+0.00	1-1	100	+1.10	0-0	-	+0.00
Tom Eaves	1-1	100	+0.36	0-0	-	+0.00	1-1	100	+0.36	0-0	-	+0.00
Graham Lee	1-2	50	-0.78	0-0	-	+0.00	1-2	50	-0.78	0-0	-	+0.00

By jockey - 2014

	Overall			Two-year-olds			Three-year-olds			Older horses		
	W-R	%	£1	W-R	%	£1	W-R	%	£1	W-R	%	£1
Ryan Moore	41-197	21	-24.31	9-48	19	-8.98	17-89	19	-11.13	15-60	25	-4.21
James Doyle	18-75	24	-26.40	3-12	25	-6.42	12-46	26	-9.98	3-17	18	-10.00
Shane Kelly	6-79	8	-49.68	3-34	9	-17.43	3-42	7	-29.25	0-3	-	-3.00
Graham Lee	4-9	44	+7.69	3-4	75	+11.25	1-5	20	-3.56	0-0	-	+0.00
Ted Durcan	4-19	21	-5.45	0-7	-	-7.00	4-12	33	+1.55	0-0	-	+0.00
Joe Fanning	2-5	40	+1.75	0-2	-	-2.00	2-3	67	+3.75	0-0	-	+0.00
Graham Gibbons	2-7	29	+7.50	2-5	40	+9.50	0-2	-	-2.00	0-0	-	+0.00
Phillip Makin	1-1	100	+1.25	1-1	100	+1.25	0-0	-	+0.00	0-0	-	+0.00
Jim Crowley	1-4	25	+2.00	0-3	-	-3.00	1-1	100	+5.00	0-0	-	+0.00

By course - 2012-2016

	Overall			Two-year-olds			Three-year-olds			Older horses		
	W-R	%	£1	W-R	%	£1	W-R	%	£1	W-R	%	£1
Ascot	22-154	14	-8.13	1-7	14	+1.00	11-81	14	-12.38	10-66	15	+3.25
Ayr	0-6	-	-6.00	0-1	-	-1.00	0-3	-	-3.00	0-2	-	-2.00
Bath	5-23	22	-5.54	0-1	-	-1.00	5-22	23	-4.54	0-0	-	+0.00
Beverley	5-21	24	-2.88	3-5	60	+8.80	2-16	13	-11.68	0-0	-	+0.00
Brighton	2-13	15	-6.88	0-3	-	-3.00	2-10	20	-3.88	0-0	-	+0.00
Carlisle	5-6	83	+1.85	1-1	100	+1.38	4-5	80	+0.48	0-0	-	+0.00
Catterick	4-9	44	-2.82	0-0	-	+0.00	4-9	44	-2.82	0-0	-	+0.00
Chelms (AW)	12-58	21	+8.98	3-16	19	+19.25	6-37	16	-14.53	3-5	60	+4.25
Chepstow	4-5	80	+4.04	1-1	100	+0.83	3-4	75	+3.21	0-0	-	+0.00
Chester	10-46	22	-14.87	1-4	25	-1.38	5-29	17	-15.08	4-13	31	+1.58
Doncaster	19-76	25	+14.42	4-16	25	+0.63	11-51	22	+7.42	4-9	44	+6.38
Epsom	4-27	15	-9.00	0-1	-	-1.00	2-16	13	-7.50	2-10	20	-0.50
Ffos Las	3-4	75	+17.29	0-0	-	+0.00	3-4	75	+17.29	0-0	-	+0.00
Folkestone	1-2	50	+0.20	0-1	-	-1.00	1-1	100	+1.20	0-0	-	+0.00
Goodwood	24-114	21	-19.30	2-11	18	-5.58	16-75	21	-2.75	6-28	21	-10.96
Hamilton	2-3	67	+1.86	0-0	-	+0.00	2-3	67	+1.86	0-0	-	+0.00
Haydock	10-60	17	-17.13	1-7	14	-3.00	9-37	24	+1.88	0-16	-	-16.00
Kempton (AW)	40-207	19	-47.55	16-87	18	-30.36	21-107	20	-9.21	3-13	23	-7.98
Leicester	21-76	28	-8.72	6-32	19	-14.53	15-41	37	+8.81	0-3	-	-3.00
Lingfield	6-30	20	+2.90	1-11	9	-8.90	5-16	31	+14.80	0-3	-	-3.00
Lingfield (AW)	30-87	34	+62.28	9-20	45	+35.46	20-64	31	+25.83	1-3	33	+1.00
Musselburgh	0-3	-	-3.00	0-0	-	+0.00	0-3	-	-3.00	0-0	-	+0.00
Newbury	13-98	13	-31.15	3-19	16	+14.00	6-60	10	-37.26	4-19	21	-7.89
Newcastle	7-11	64	+16.85	3-4	75	+13.25	4-7	57	+3.60	0-0	-	+0.00
N'castle (AW)	4-10	40	+19.98	2-2	100	+20.73	1-5	20	-2.25	1-3	33	+1.50
Newmarket	17-156	11	-59.76	3-47	6	-26.89	8-80	10	-39.13	6-29	21	+6.25
Newmarket (J)	18-133	14	-62.08	4-45	9	-30.08	9-64	14	-25.75	5-24	21	-6.25
Nottingham	11-82	13	-21.17	1-21	5	-19.47	10-61	16	-1.70	0-0	-	+0.00
Pontefract	11-50	22	-13.57	0-4	-	-4.00	10-37	27	-2.40	1-9	11	-7.17
Redcar	1-5	20	-3.43	1-3	33	-1.43	0-1	-	-1.00	0-1	-	-1.00
Ripon	2-14	14	-1.00	0-1	-	-1.00	2-13	15	+0.00	0-0	-	+0.00
Salisbury	15-88	17	-7.29	2-27	7	-18.50	13-58	22	+14.21	0-3	-	-3.00
Sandown	30-140	21	-9.56	2-21	10	-15.13	25-98	26	+3.91	3-21	14	+1.66
S'well (AW)	0-2	-	-2.00	0-0	-	+0.00	0-2	-	-2.00	0-0	-	+0.00
Thirsk	7-19	37	+2.91	1-3	33	-0.75	6-15	40	+4.66	0-1	-	-1.00
Warwick	3-7	43	+4.38	1-1	100	+4.50	2-6	33	-0.13	0-0	-	+0.00
Wetherby	0-1	-	-1.00	0-0	-	+0.00	0-1	-	-1.00	0-0	-	+0.00
Windsor	17-102	17	-28.04	2-9	22	-0.75	14-87	16	-27.29	1-6	17	+0.00
Wolves (AW)	12-77	16	-44.29	2-24	8	-15.33	9-52	17	-29.26	1-1	100	+0.30
Yarmouth	12-68	18	-33.42	4-25	16	-12.15	7-41	17	-21.52	1-2	50	+0.25
York	17-82	21	-16.00	2-3	67	+8.00	10-44	23	-5.13	5-35	14	-18.88

Ten-year summary

	Wins	Runs	%	Win prize-money	Total prize-money	£1
2016	111	505	22	£1,491,547.82	£2,525,773.73	-25.48
2015	79	455	17	£988,868.57	£1,696,525.96	-69.01
2014	81	461	18	£1,293,230.34	£2,211,794.30	-131.27
2013	87	398	22	£1,167,720.87	£1,687,826.91	-69.86
2012	69	363	19	£609,776.18	£1,022,421.28	-30.99
2011	53	366	14	£596,991.20	£1,554,607.39	-130.34
2010	73	465	16	£2,245,094.20	£3,027,131.17	-141.94
2009	99	429	23	£2,077,608.50	£3,421,892.26	-64.76
2008	88	467	19	£1,511,579.51	£2,760,173.51	-100.52
2007	113	498	23	£1,691,390.12	£2,555,461.62	-24.92

QUEEN'S TRUST: capped Sir Michael Stoute's resurgent season

Andrew Balding

Balding has now passed the 90-winner mark in each of the last five seasons and last year brought a second century in that time. His partnership with Eddy Greatrex has been particularly profitable for two years now.

By month - 2016

	Overall			Two-year-olds			Three-year-olds			Older horses		
	W-R	%	£1	W-R	%	£1	W-R	%	£1	W-R	%	£1
January	4-35	11	-18.25	0-0	-	+0.00	1-6	17	-1.50	3-29	10	-16.75
February	1-20	5	-15.00	0-0	-	+0.00	0-7	-	-7.00	1-13	8	-8.00
March	7-33	21	-7.38	0-0	-	+0.00	3-11	27	-2.25	4-22	18	-5.13
April	5-50	10	-25.50	0-0	-	+0.00	2-28	7	-18.00	3-22	14	-7.50
May	9-104	9	-42.00	2-12	17	+14.00	5-60	8	-35.00	2-32	6	-21.00
June	21-109	19	+4.98	2-14	14	-4.25	14-57	25	+18.32	5-38	13	-9.09
July	21-119	18	+5.53	6-30	20	-0.10	15-66	23	+28.63	0-23	-	-23.00
August	13-79	16	-1.50	6-18	33	+8.25	7-38	18	+13.25	0-23	-	-23.00
September	14-85	16	-18.75	6-27	22	+1.75	7-42	17	-7.25	1-16	6	-13.25
October	8-65	12	+29.38	4-27	15	+12.38	2-20	10	-9.00	2-18	11	+26.00
November	4-24	17	-6.25	2-10	20	+0.75	1-6	17	-2.75	1-8	13	-4.25
December	0-8	-	-8.00	0-4	-	-4.00	0-3	-	-3.00	0-1	-	-1.00

By month - 2015

	Overall			Two-year-olds			Three-year-olds			Older horses		
	W-R	%	£1	W-R	%	£1	W-R	%	£1	W-R	%	£1
January	2-17	12	-10.93	0-0	-	+0.00	1-5	20	-3.43	1-12	8	-7.50
February	4-19	21	+10.75	0-0	-	+0.00	2-6	33	+0.25	2-13	15	+10.50
March	5-22	23	-3.30	0-0	-	+0.00	2-9	22	-3.00	3-13	23	-0.30
April	9-54	17	-10.24	0-0	-	+0.00	3-27	11	-5.59	6-27	22	-4.65
May	8-93	9	-50.67	0-1	-	-1.00	3-46	7	-28.75	5-46	11	-20.92
June	13-98	13	-40.30	0-6	-	-6.00	8-53	15	-25.50	5-39	13	-8.80
July	20-103	19	+12.33	2-18	11	+13.00	11-47	23	+0.75	7-38	18	-1.42
August	10-101	10	-58.42	3-26	12	-8.05	3-41	7	-33.37	4-34	12	-17.00
September	11-95	12	-44.94	3-28	11	-10.50	8-41	20	-8.44	0-26	-	-26.00
October	3-63	5	-38.75	1-24	4	-16.00	1-19	5	-15.75	1-20	5	-7.00
November	7-50	14	-13.97	2-19	11	-10.20	3-17	18	-5.52	2-14	14	+1.75
December	3-40	8	-24.50	0-13	-	-13.00	3-14	21	+1.50	0-13	-	-13.00

By month - 2014

	Overall			Two-year-olds			Three-year-olds			Older horses		
	W-R	%	£1	W-R	%	£1	W-R	%	£1	W-R	%	£1
January	2-14	14	-9.81	0-0	-	+0.00	2-4	50	+0.19	0-10	-	-10.00
February	4-18	22	-8.40	0-0	-	+0.00	4-10	40	-0.40	0-8	-	-8.00
March	11-32	34	-5.47	0-0	-	+0.00	9-21	43	-0.72	2-11	18	-4.75
April	10-53	19	+3.95	0-0	-	+0.00	6-35	17	+8.10	4-18	22	-4.15
May	15-83	18	-23.88	0-2	-	-2.00	7-47	15	-23.13	8-34	24	+1.25
June	8-78	10	-30.25	0-5	-	-5.00	5-43	12	-8.25	3-30	10	-17.00
July	11-63	17	+24.25	2-7	29	+4.50	5-33	15	+11.50	4-23	17	+8.25
August	12-78	15	+2.50	3-15	20	-7.38	7-36	19	+18.88	2-27	7	-9.00
September	12-86	14	-17.13	4-22	18	-6.75	7-45	16	+5.75	1-19	5	-16.13
October	16-87	18	+30.42	5-26	19	+11.09	6-38	16	-0.17	5-23	22	+19.50
November	6-36	17	-13.23	2-12	17	-6.89	2-12	17	-4.09	2-12	17	-2.25
December	12-31	39	+11.42	1-7	14	+6.00	9-16	56	+7.42	2-8	25	-2.00

By race type - 2016

	Overall			Two-year-olds			Three-year-olds			Older horses		
	W-R	%	£1	W-R	%	£1	W-R	%	£1	W-R	%	£1
Handicap	59-410	14	-82.87	0-13	-	-13.00	43-205	21	+29.85	16-192	8	-99.72
Group	4-28	14	+7.25	2-9	22	+1.75	0-5	-	-5.00	2-14	14	+10.50
Maiden	34-204	17	-21.58	20-81	25	+17.83	14-120	12	-36.40	0-3	-	-3.00

By race type - 2015

	Overall			Two-year-olds			Three-year-olds			Older horses		
	W-R	%	£1	W-R	%	£1	W-R	%	£1	W-R	%	£1
Handicap	52-429	12	-154.05	1-13	8	-6.00	20-192	10	-99.00	31-224	14	-49.05
Group	2-31	6	-7.00	0-2	-	-2.00	1-6	17	+7.00	1-23	4	-12.00
Maiden	33-222	15	-77.42	10-108	9	-31.75	22-111	20	-45.17	1-3	33	-0.50

By race type - 2014

	Overall			Two-year-olds			Three-year-olds			Older horses		
	W-R	%	£1	W-R	%	£1	W-R	%	£1	W-R	%	£1
Handicap	73-380	19	+10.83	3-12	25	+0.75	45-207	22	+40.73	25-161	16	-30.65
Group	4-35	11	-14.13	2-4	50	+2.38	0-6	-	-6.00	2-25	8	-10.50
Maiden	30-172	17	-37.05	10-73	14	-9.17	20-98	20	-26.88	0-1	-	-1.00

By jockey - 2016

	Overall			Two-year-olds			Three-year-olds			Older horses		
	W-R	%	£1	W-R	%	£1	W-R	%	£1	W-R	%	£1
Oisin Murphy	31-201	15	-40.33	12-49	24	+27.08	12-86	14	-36.65	7-66	11	-30.75
David Probert	28-191	15	-57.45	7-38	18	+2.45	18-102	18	-25.90	3-51	6	-34.00
Rob Hornby	17-74	23	+16.75	6-11	55	+28.25	9-37	24	+5.50	2-26	8	-17.00
E Greatrex	9-57	16	+27.00	0-6	-	-6.00	8-32	25	+43.00	1-19	5	-10.00
Liam Keniry	7-51	14	+11.41	1-15	7	-10.50	3-22	14	+7.25	3-14	21	+14.66
Jimmy Quinn	5-14	36	+25.75	0-0	-	+0.00	5-12	42	+27.75	0-2	-	-2.00
Jim Crowley	4-15	27	+5.38	1-1	100	+7.00	1-3	33	+1.50	2-11	18	-3.13
Graham Lee	2-3	67	+20.75	0-0	-	+0.00	0-0	-	+0.00	2-3	67	+20.75
Luke Morris	1-1	100	+1.00	0-0	-	+0.00	1-1	100	+1.00	0-0	-	+0.00
P J McDonald	1-2	50	+0.50	1-2	50	+0.50	0-0	-	+0.00	0-0	-	+0.00
Cathy Gannon	1-7	14	-2.00	0-0	-	+0.00	0-2	-	-2.00	1-5	20	+0.00
Jimmy Fortune	1-9	11	-5.50	0-0	-	+0.00	0-1	-	-1.00	1-8	13	-4.50

By jockey - 2015

	Overall			Two-year-olds			Three-year-olds			Older horses		
	W-R	%	£1	W-R	%	£1	W-R	%	£1	W-R	%	£1
David Probert	40-317	13	-127.91	5-61	8	-34.75	26-152	17	-36.34	9-104	9	-56.82
Oisin Murphy	15-117	13	-65.24	3-32	9	-19.20	8-47	17	-18.07	4-38	11	-27.97
E Greatrex	12-51	24	+39.81	2-4	50	+27.20	3-21	14	-9.38	7-26	27	+21.99
Rob Hornby	6-47	13	-6.00	0-7	-	-7.00	1-12	8	-4.00	5-28	18	+5.00
Liam Keniry	6-60	10	-25.03	1-12	8	+1.00	2-32	6	-22.00	3-16	19	-4.03
Andrea Atzeni	3-14	21	-4.68	0-2	-	-2.00	3-11	27	-1.68	0-1	-	-1.00
Jim Crowley	3-29	10	-20.64	0-4	-	-4.00	3-12	25	-3.64	0-13	-	-13.00
Mr H Hunt	2-5	40	+0.50	0-0	-	+0.00	0-0	-	+0.00	2-5	40	+0.50
Cathy Gannon	2-15	13	-5.00	0-3	-	-3.00	1-10	10	-6.50	1-2	50	+4.50

By jockey - 2014

	Overall			Two-year-olds			Three-year-olds			Older horses		
	W-R	%	£1	W-R	%	£1	W-R	%	£1	W-R	%	£1
David Probert	59-278	21	-11.84	7-47	15	-17.58	43-163	26	+30.49	9-68	13	-24.75
Oisin Murphy	26-132	20	+17.35	2-17	12	-7.50	11-61	18	+4.75	13-54	24	+20.10
Liam Keniry	6-46	13	+5.25	2-10	20	+19.50	2-20	10	-7.25	2-16	13	-7.00
Jimmy Fortune	5-22	23	+3.12	2-4	50	+2.12	1-5	20	+3.00	2-13	15	-2.00
Jim Crowley	5-26	19	+11.98	0-3	-	-3.00	4-20	20	+8.98	1-3	33	+6.00
Thomas Brown	4-33	12	-16.38	1-5	20	+2.00	1-12	8	-8.00	2-16	13	-10.38
Andrea Atzeni	3-4	75	+4.04	3-4	75	+4.04	0-0	-	+0.00	0-0	-	+0.00
Rob Hornby	3-20	15	+11.50	0-0	-	+0.00	2-8	25	+18.00	1-12	8	-6.50
Mr H Hunt	2-8	25	+3.00	0-0	-	+0.00	1-4	25	+2.00	1-4	25	+1.00

By course - 2012-2016

	Overall			Two-year-olds			Three-year-olds			Older horses		
	W-R	%	£1	W-R	%	£1	W-R	%	£1	W-R	%	£1
Ascot	13-197	7	-107.75	0-20	-	-20.00	7-66	11	-24.25	6-111	5	-63.50
Ayr	4-14	29	+17.11	1-2	50	+1.00	1-2	50	+3.50	2-10	20	+12.61
Bath	19-122	16	-23.29	2-15	13	+13.50	9-74	12	-32.70	8-33	24	-4.09
Beverley	1-8	13	-4.50	0-2	-	-2.00	1-5	20	-1.50	0-1	-	-1.00
Brighton	11-64	17	-6.60	3-12	25	+1.12	6-32	19	+3.03	2-20	10	-10.75
Carlisle	4-10	40	+2.00	1-1	100	+1.75	3-7	43	+2.25	0-2	-	-2.00
Catterick	0-2	-	-2.00	0-0	-	+0.00	0-2	-	-2.00	0-0	-	+0.00
Chelms (AW)	12-81	15	-30.14	0-6	-	-6.00	7-30	23	+1.25	5-45	11	-25.39
Chepstow	22-112	20	-12.84	2-14	14	-7.30	11-69	16	-10.88	9-29	31	+5.35
Chester	34-154	22	+33.96	4-24	17	+0.50	22-81	27	+36.38	8-49	16	-2.92
Doncaster	14-91	15	+53.00	6-13	46	+55.13	3-29	10	-8.00	5-49	10	+5.88
Epsom	20-133	15	+1.74	7-25	28	+30.66	3-52	6	-34.25	10-56	18	+5.33
Ffos Las	15-49	31	+42.18	3-11	27	+6.00	8-27	30	+29.60	4-11	36	+6.58
Folkestone	1-8	13	-4.25	0-1	-	-1.00	1-5	20	-1.25	0-2	-	-2.00
Goodwood	14-157	9	-70.38	3-33	9	-14.75	7-62	11	-24.64	4-62	6	-31.00
Hamilton	1-8	13	-5.50	1-1	100	+1.50	0-5	-	-5.00	0-2	-	-2.00
Haydock	13-84	15	-20.73	4-13	31	+0.20	5-37	14	-7.06	4-34	12	-13.88
Kempton (AW)	60-454	13	-83.12	7-83	8	-56.29	37-228	16	+21.60	16-143	11	-48.44
Leicester	8-67	12	-13.93	1-9	11	-7.43	6-39	15	-8.50	1-19	5	+2.00
Lingfield	9-44	20	-9.93	1-6	17	+0.00	5-23	22	-11.18	3-15	20	+1.25
Lingfield (AW)	49-304	16	-39.37	9-41	22	+44.02	24-156	15	-62.95	16-107	15	-20.44
Musselburgh	1-4	25	+0.50	0-0	-	+0.00	1-4	25	+0.50	0-0	-	+0.00
Newbury	21-163	13	-37.22	4-52	8	-27.25	15-75	20	-7.97	2-36	6	-2.00
Newcastle	0-1	-	-1.00	0-0	-	+0.00	0-0	-	+0.00	0-1	-	-1.00
N'castle (AW)	0-3	-	-3.00	0-1	-	-1.00	0-0	-	+0.00	0-2	-	-2.00
Newmarket	14-165	8	-37.63	2-49	4	-37.75	6-53	11	-6.13	6-63	10	+6.25
Newmarket (J)	11-105	10	-12.25	1-25	4	-16.50	4-40	10	+3.50	6-40	15	+0.75
Nottingham	9-62	15	-1.38	3-23	13	-6.13	4-28	14	+2.75	2-11	18	+2.00
Pontefract	1-18	6	-7.00	0-2	-	-2.00	0-9	-	-9.00	1-7	14	+4.00
Redcar	0-2	-	-2.00	0-1	-	-1.00	0-1	-	-1.00	0-0	-	+0.00
Ripon	1-5	20	-2.50	0-0	-	+0.00	1-2	50	+0.50	0-3	-	-3.00
Salisbury	27-180	15	-56.15	9-49	18	+3.32	9-81	11	-46.70	9-50	18	-12.77
Sandown	24-185	13	-25.74	5-43	12	-21.31	12-94	13	+0.07	7-48	15	-4.50
S'well (AW)	18-57	32	+8.50	2-4	50	+12.50	11-29	38	+0.68	5-24	21	-4.68
Thirsk	1-4	25	+13.00	0-0	-	+0.00	1-4	25	+13.00	0-0	-	+0.00
Warwick	2-15	13	-8.00	0-4	-	-4.00	1-9	11	-5.25	1-2	50	+1.25
Wetherby	1-4	25	-2.50	0-0	-	+0.00	1-1	100	+0.50	0-3	-	-3.00
Windsor	28-164	17	-10.10	9-26	35	+9.47	14-93	15	-1.45	5-45	11	-18.13
Wolves (AW)	18-141	13	-54.99	2-24	8	-21.29	12-67	18	-9.80	4-50	8	-23.90
Yarmouth	3-24	13	-12.50	0-2	-	-2.00	2-13	15	-5.25	1-9	11	-5.25
York	7-84	8	-29.89	2-16	13	-8.50	1-23	4	-19.00	4-45	9	-2.38

Ten-year summary

	Wins	Runs	%	Win prize-money	Total prize-money	£1
2016	107	731	15	£1,038,999.35	£1,672,623.97	-102.74
2015	95	755	13	£837,267.45	£1,539,900.15	-272.93
2014	119	659	18	£1,335,198.23	£2,035,497.26	-35.60
2013	99	713	14	£873,940.78	£1,356,742.43	-13.36
2012	93	712	13	£779,847.73	£1,365,377.42	-155.54
2011	70	543	13	£620,393.39	£971,676.62	-59.07
2010	78	511	15	£707,996.22	£1,116,809.38	-11.81
2009	68	498	14	£460,056.19	£783,172.54	-38.44
2008	67	436	15	£510,631.82	£865,416.84	+12.56
2007	39	410	10	£525,039.35	£711,375.94	-114.90

TALENT: Andrew Balding's young riders including Eddy Greatrex (second left)

David O'Meara

Few trainers have had such a rapid ascent as O'Meara, but last year was tricky. Though he scraped to a century, it came at his lowest strike-rate since his first full season in 2011 without a British Group success.

By month - 2016

	Overall			Two-year-olds			Three-year-olds			Older horses		
	W-R	%	£1	W-R	%	£1	W-R	%	£1	W-R	%	£1
January	2-17	12	-2.00	0-0	-	+0.00	0-3	-	-3.00	2-14	14	+1.00
February	0-10	-	-10.00	0-0	-	+0.00	0-2	-	-2.00	0-8	-	-8.00
March	1-10	10	-7.63	0-0	-	+0.00	0-2	-	-2.00	1-8	13	-5.63
April	7-77	9	-24.13	2-3	67	+4.88	0-13	-	-13.00	5-61	8	-16.00
May	15-125	12	-20.42	2-9	22	-2.13	3-20	15	+6.13	10-96	10	-24.42
June	12-151	8	-68.50	3-21	14	+9.75	3-28	11	-15.00	6-102	6	-63.25
July	14-141	10	-65.71	3-22	14	-10.46	2-23	9	-11.00	9-96	9	-44.25
August	14-125	11	-33.17	2-15	13	-3.50	2-26	8	-12.50	10-84	12	-17.17
September	8-125	6	-76.38	0-19	-	-19.00	3-22	14	-4.63	5-84	6	-52.75
October	16-114	14	-22.18	0-13	-	-13.00	5-23	22	+9.00	11-78	14	-18.18
November	7-53	13	-7.02	0-5	-	-5.00	2-16	13	+1.00	5-32	16	-3.02
December	7-27	26	+0.50	0-3	-	-3.00	2-9	22	+0.00	5-15	33	+3.50

By month - 2015

	Overall			Two-year-olds			Three-year-olds			Older horses		
	W-R	%	£1	W-R	%	£1	W-R	%	£1	W-R	%	£1
January	4-22	18	-7.65	0-0	-	+0.00	0-3	-	-3.00	4-19	21	-4.65
February	1-18	6	-14.00	0-0	-	+0.00	1-6	17	-2.00	0-12	-	-12.00
March	5-41	12	-15.25	0-1	-	-1.00	2-16	13	-7.25	3-24	13	-7.00
April	14-71	20	+7.77	0-5	-	-5.00	0-18	-	-18.00	14-48	29	+30.77
May	16-125	13	-10.88	2-7	29	+6.00	3-33	9	-20.13	11-85	13	+3.25
June	18-127	14	+20.84	0-6	-	-6.00	5-40	13	+13.06	13-81	16	+13.78
July	21-135	16	-31.07	2-10	20	+0.00	4-46	9	-33.87	15-79	19	+2.80
August	18-135	13	-44.88	1-11	9	-8.75	11-44	25	+11.63	6-80	8	-47.75
September	7-113	6	-59.17	0-13	-	-13.00	3-34	9	-12.17	4-66	6	-34.00
October	8-81	10	-28.88	0-8	-	-8.00	4-29	14	-11.38	4-44	9	-9.50
November	4-34	12	-15.25	0-10	-	-10.00	3-10	30	+4.75	1-14	7	-10.00
December	6-29	21	+22.10	0-5	-	-5.00	4-11	36	+31.00	2-13	15	-3.90

By month - 2014

	Overall			Two-year-olds			Three-year-olds			Older horses		
	W-R	%	£1	W-R	%	£1	W-R	%	£1	W-R	%	£1
January	3-20	15	-8.25	0-0	-	+0.00	0-3	-	-3.00	3-17	18	-5.25
February	3-20	15	+1.75	0-0	-	+0.00	0-7	-	-7.00	3-13	23	+8.75
March	3-27	11	-12.25	0-0	-	+0.00	1-8	13	-1.00	2-19	11	-11.25
April	11-56	20	+10.38	0-0	-	+0.00	4-18	22	-4.00	7-38	18	+14.38
May	15-108	14	-18.40	0-5	-	-5.00	6-28	21	-11.23	9-75	12	-2.17
June	19-119	16	+7.92	0-8	-	-8.00	5-29	17	-2.80	14-82	17	+18.73
July	11-110	10	-43.17	1-16	6	-8.00	2-25	8	-16.67	8-69	12	-18.50
August	21-117	18	-6.50	4-21	19	-4.25	5-37	14	-7.50	12-59	20	+5.25
September	16-102	16	+24.86	3-17	18	-3.40	4-29	14	+1.23	9-56	16	+27.03
October	3-84	4	-56.00	0-12	-	-12.00	1-21	5	-12.00	2-51	4	-32.00
November	4-36	11	+7.50	1-6	17	-1.50	0-5	-	-5.00	3-25	12	+14.00
December	3-31	10	-10.00	0-7	-	-7.00	2-10	20	+5.50	1-14	7	-8.50

By race type - 2016

	Overall			Two-year-olds			Three-year-olds			Older horses		
	W-R	%	£1	W-R	%	£1	W-R	%	£1	W-R	%	£1
Handicap	74-749	10	-230.79	2-25	8	-10.00	14-139	10	-26.50	58-585	10	-194.29
Group	0-37	-	-37.00	0-2	-	-2.00	0-0	-	+0.00	0-35	-	-35.00
Maiden	11-88	13	-47.33	2-39	5	-31.83	6-41	15	-20.50	3-8	38	+5.00

By race type - 2015

	Overall			Two-year-olds			Three-year-olds			Older horses		
	W-R	%	£1	W-R	%	£1	W-R	%	£1	W-R	%	£1
Handicap	91-728	13	-131.73	0-24	-	-24.00	32-229	14	-21.63	59-475	12	-86.11
Group	5-32	16	+17.00	0-0	-	+0.00	0-2	-	-2.00	5-30	17	+19.00
Maiden	13-103	13	-42.47	5-46	11	-20.75	8-49	16	-13.72	0-8	-	-8.00

By race type - 2014

	Overall			Two-year-olds			Three-year-olds			Older horses		
	W-R	%	£1	W-R	%	£1	W-R	%	£1	W-R	%	£1
Handicap	84-625	13	-63.48	3-24	13	-9.00	20-156	13	-42.54	61-445	14	-11.94
Group	4-22	18	+39.00	0-1	-	-1.00	1-6	17	+6.00	3-15	20	+34.00
Maiden	14-103	14	-45.68	4-53	8	-32.90	8-36	22	-7.03	2-14	14	-5.75

By jockey - 2016

	Overall			Two-year-olds			Three-year-olds			Older horses		
	W-R	%	£1	W-R	%	£1	W-R	%	£1	W-R	%	£1
D Tudhope	47-343	14	-85.09	5-39	13	-18.58	11-62	18	+13.88	31-242	13	-80.38
Josh Doyle	9-119	8	-68.52	1-8	13	-4.00	2-21	10	-8.00	6-90	7	-56.52
Phillip Makin	8-79	10	-24.13	1-15	7	-12.13	1-17	6	-13.50	6-47	13	+1.50
G Gibbons	7-44	16	-5.25	1-5	20	-1.50	3-16	19	+7.00	3-23	13	-10.75
Shelley Birkett	7-57	12	+14.25	0-2	-	-2.00	0-9	-	-9.00	7-46	15	+25.25
David Nolan	5-77	6	-38.38	0-2	-	-2.00	1-7	14	-4.38	4-68	6	-32.00
Sam James	4-83	5	-50.25	3-21	14	+1.75	0-19	-	-19.00	1-43	2	-33.00
Martin Harley	3-9	33	+3.00	0-0	-	+0.00	0-0	-	+0.00	3-9	33	+3.00
Harry Bentley	3-14	21	+19.00	1-4	25	+11.00	0-3	-	-3.00	2-7	29	+11.00
Jim Crowley	3-15	20	-5.75	0-1	-	-1.00	1-4	25	+0.00	2-10	20	-4.75
Patrick Vaughan	2-22	9	-5.00	0-0	-	+0.00	1-7	14	+6.00	1-15	7	-11.00
Frankie Dettori	1-1	100	+8.00	0-0	-	+0.00	0-0	-	+0.00	1-1	100	+8.00

By jockey - 2015

	Overall			Two-year-olds			Three-year-olds			Older horses		
	W-R	%	£1	W-R	%	£1	W-R	%	£1	W-R	%	£1
D Tudhope	49-301	16	-53.32	3-25	12	-9.75	19-97	20	-14.92	27-179	15	-28.65
Sam James	19-181	10	-62.38	1-18	6	-15.00	5-60	8	-17.25	13-103	13	-30.13
David Nolan	15-97	15	-10.51	0-6	-	-6.00	5-33	15	-4.78	10-58	17	+0.28
Josh Doyle	14-122	11	-30.00	0-9	-	-9.00	7-38	18	+11.00	7-75	9	-32.00
Phillip Makin	8-45	18	+9.23	0-4	-	-4.00	1-8	13	-6.27	7-33	21	+19.50
Miss R H'stall	3-6	50	+5.50	0-0	-	+0.00	0-1	-	-1.00	3-5	60	+6.50
G Gibbons	3-22	14	+2.75	0-3	-	-3.00	1-9	11	+6.00	2-10	20	-0.25
Shelley Birkett	3-33	9	+20.00	0-3	-	-3.00	1-11	9	+10.00	2-19	11	+13.00
James Doyle	2-7	29	+28.50	0-0	-	+0.00	0-2	-	-2.00	2-5	40	+30.50

By jockey - 2014

	Overall			Two-year-olds			Three-year-olds			Older horses		
	W-R	%	£1	W-R	%	£1	W-R	%	£1	W-R	%	£1
D Tudhope	65-398	16	-65.84	4-35	11	-11.90	18-108	17	-35.70	43-255	17	-18.24
Sam James	20-177	11	-21.17	5-33	15	-13.25	6-51	12	-10.50	9-93	10	+2.58
David Nolan	9-65	14	-4.50	0-6	-	-6.00	2-14	14	-2.00	7-45	16	+3.50
Josh Doyle	4-43	9	-9.00	0-1	-	-1.00	1-12	8	-3.50	3-30	10	-4.50
S De Sousa	3-12	25	+38.00	0-0	-	+0.00	0-3	-	-3.00	3-9	33	+41.00
Julie Burke	2-37	5	-17.50	0-5	-	-5.00	0-18	-	-18.00	2-14	14	+5.50
James Doyle	1-1	100	+10.00	0-0	-	+0.00	0-0	-	+0.00	1-1	100	+10.00
Oisin Murphy	1-2	50	+15.00	0-0	-	+0.00	1-1	100	+16.00	0-1	-	-1.00
Pat Dobbs	1-2	50	+3.00	0-1	-	-1.00	0-0	-	+0.00	1-1	100	+4.00

By course - 2012-2016

	Overall			Two-year-olds			Three-year-olds			Older horses		
	W-R	%	£1	W-R	%	£1	W-R	%	£1	W-R	%	£1
Ascot	5-119	4	-26.50	0-5	-	-5.00	1-12	8	-7.50	4-102	4	-14.00
Ayr	31-182	17	-10.08	1-17	6	+0.00	4-27	15	-11.04	26-138	19	+0.96
Bath	0-1	-	-1.00	0-0	-	+0.00	0-0	-	+0.00	0-1	-	-1.00
Beverley	40-209	19	+34.07	1-32	3	-25.00	16-78	21	+14.64	23-99	23	+44.43
Carlisle	10-88	11	-20.00	2-11	18	-0.50	3-27	11	-9.00	5-50	10	-10.50
Catterick	25-198	13	-59.91	4-25	16	-5.63	9-63	14	-15.41	12-110	11	-38.88
Chelms (AW)	4-52	8	-32.30	0-5	-	-5.00	1-10	10	-4.00	3-37	8	-23.30
Chester	4-63	6	-24.50	0-5	-	-5.00	0-7	-	-7.00	4-51	8	-12.50
Doncaster	25-256	10	-65.59	4-14	29	+10.13	3-35	9	-21.38	18-207	9	-54.34
Epsom	3-24	13	-11.15	0-0	-	+0.00	1-6	17	-3.90	2-18	11	-7.25
Goodwood	1-31	3	-27.50	0-0	-	+0.00	0-5	-	-5.00	1-26	4	-22.50
Hamilton	21-112	19	-26.03	1-16	6	-5.00	9-43	21	-16.60	11-53	21	-4.43
Haydock	29-217	13	+6.76	0-11	-	-11.00	6-25	24	+26.00	23-181	13	-8.24
Kempton (AW)	6-47	13	+14.75	1-2	50	+2.50	1-17	6	+0.00	4-28	14	+12.25
Leicester	12-57	21	-4.45	0-3	-	-3.00	5-20	25	+6.75	7-34	21	-8.20
Lingfield	3-7	43	+6.25	0-2	-	-2.00	0-2	-	-2.00	3-3	100	+10.25
Lingfield (AW)	5-33	15	-9.95	0-2	-	-2.00	3-12	25	-2.95	2-19	11	-5.00
Musselburgh	24-147	16	-26.01	2-29	7	-18.00	7-36	19	+0.00	15-82	18	-8.01
Newbury	0-17	-	-17.00	0-2	-	-2.00	0-4	-	-4.00	0-11	-	-11.00
Newcastle	20-151	13	-33.26	5-19	26	+4.10	11-60	18	-9.86	4-72	6	-27.50
N'castle (AW)	10-77	13	-17.00	0-7	-	-7.00	3-26	12	-11.38	7-44	16	+1.38
Newmarket	5-72	7	-31.00	0-1	-	-1.00	1-10	10	-6.00	4-61	7	-24.00
Newmarket (J)	4-34	12	-10.38	0-1	-	-1.00	1-6	17	+0.50	3-27	11	-9.88
Nottingham	3-54	6	-35.25	0-6	-	-6.00	0-16	-	-16.00	3-32	9	-13.25
Pontefract	8-133	6	-62.75	0-13	-	-13.00	1-28	4	-13.00	7-92	8	-36.75
Redcar	39-245	16	-4.44	8-50	16	+3.38	11-78	14	-7.25	20-117	17	-0.57
Ripon	44-264	17	+1.28	4-36	11	-10.63	11-58	19	-13.27	29-170	17	+25.17
Salisbury	0-3	-	-3.00	0-0	-	+0.00	0-0	-	+0.00	0-3	-	-3.00
Sandown	4-24	17	-5.25	0-1	-	-1.00	1-10	10	-5.50	3-13	23	+1.25
S'well (AW)	28-196	14	-63.91	2-18	11	+0.57	9-58	16	-14.30	17-120	14	-50.19
Thirsk	28-227	12	-28.30	7-30	23	+22.42	6-55	11	-8.04	15-142	11	-42.68
Warwick	0-1	-	-1.00	0-0	-	+0.00	0-0	-	+0.00	0-1	-	-1.00
Wetherby	2-12	17	+1.50	0-2	-	-2.00	0-4	-	-4.00	2-6	33	+7.50
Windsor	1-7	14	+2.00	0-0	-	+0.00	0-1	-	-1.00	1-6	17	+3.00
Wolves (AW)	44-376	12	-135.89	1-44	2	-42.75	13-125	10	-36.50	30-207	14	-56.64
Yarmouth	1-2	50	+7.00	0-0	-	+0.00	0-0	-	+0.00	1-2	50	+7.00
York	42-396	11	-54.75	1-26	4	-22.00	8-58	14	-9.50	33-312	11	-23.25

Ten-year summary

	Wins	Runs	%	Win prize-money	Total prize-money	£1
2016	103	975	11	£767,371.55	£1,679,545.29	-336.62
2015	122	931	13	£1,024,052.53	£1,580,568.78	-176.30
2014	112	830	13	£1,257,328.64	£1,772,806.65	-102.16
2013	136	905	15	£777,659.87	£1,159,386.21	-121.29
2012	69	542	13	£517,175.66	£709,691.68	-34.43
2011	48	423	11	£297,865.68	£479,370.95	-149.06
2010	25	153	16	£87,754.32	£122,742.04	-29.60

TAWDEEA: one of the highlights of David O'Meara's more difficult season

Ralph Beckett

Beckett managed a first century of winners last season and, typically, it came at a level-stakes profit had you backed all of them. That's eight of the last 13 years and three of the last four, an astonishing record.

By month - 2016

	Overall			Two-year-olds			Three-year-olds			Older horses		
	W-R	%	£1	W-R	%	£1	W-R	%	£1	W-R	%	£1
January	3-15	20	-3.84	0-0	-	+0.00	2-7	29	+0.91	1-8	13	-4.75
February	2-10	20	-5.99	0-0	-	+0.00	1-6	17	-4.09	1-4	25	-1.90
March	4-9	44	+1.90	0-0	-	+0.00	2-5	40	+1.50	2-4	50	+0.40
April	8-40	20	-1.00	0-2	-	-2.00	6-23	26	+6.75	2-15	13	-5.75
May	11-57	19	-12.97	3-10	30	+0.00	5-34	15	-17.80	3-13	23	+4.83
June	17-69	25	+59.83	3-8	38	+36.00	9-43	21	-1.18	5-18	28	+25.00
July	20-74	27	+23.26	5-18	28	-0.15	11-39	28	+7.06	4-17	24	+16.36
August	9-65	14	-25.19	4-24	17	+1.41	5-28	18	-13.60	0-13	-	-13.00
September	11-67	16	-17.62	6-31	19	-10.12	3-24	13	-7.00	2-12	17	-0.50
October	6-60	10	-14.42	6-33	18	+12.58	0-17	-	-17.00	0-10	-	-10.00
November	5-22	23	+1.50	2-15	13	-1.50	2-2	100	+2.50	1-5	20	+0.50
December	5-18	28	+2.38	5-14	36	+6.38	0-1	-	-1.00	0-3	-	-3.00

By month - 2015

	Overall			Two-year-olds			Three-year-olds			Older horses		
	W-R	%	£1	W-R	%	£1	W-R	%	£1	W-R	%	£1
January	2-22	9	-13.50	0-0	-	+0.00	1-14	7	-8.00	1-8	13	-5.50
February	2-14	14	+5.00	0-0	-	+0.00	1-11	9	-9.00	1-3	33	+14.00
March	4-12	33	+0.34	0-0	-	+0.00	4-11	36	+1.34	0-1	-	-1.00
April	6-33	18	-1.45	0-3	-	-3.00	6-26	23	+5.55	0-4	-	-4.00
May	12-59	20	-8.71	2-4	50	+3.50	6-38	16	-8.96	4-17	24	-3.25
June	10-51	20	+4.25	2-9	22	+5.50	7-33	21	+5.38	1-9	11	-6.63
July	9-60	15	-21.22	0-15	-	-15.00	8-35	23	+1.53	1-10	10	-7.75
August	7-57	12	-20.32	2-17	12	-2.50	4-28	14	-9.82	1-12	8	-8.00
September	10-57	18	+7.38	7-30	23	+0.38	2-20	10	-3.00	1-7	14	+10.00
October	14-67	21	+2.16	4-27	15	-14.38	8-29	28	+15.03	2-11	18	+1.50
November	3-24	13	+12.00	2-16	13	+9.00	0-5	-	-5.00	1-3	33	+8.00
December	1-18	6	-13.00	0-13	-	-13.00	0-4	-	-4.00	1-1	100	+4.00

By month - 2014

	Overall			Two-year-olds			Three-year-olds			Older horses		
	W-R	%	£1	W-R	%	£1	W-R	%	£1	W-R	%	£1
January	1-7	14	-5.00	0-0	-	+0.00	1-5	20	-3.00	0-2	-	-2.00
February	4-11	36	-1.07	0-0	-	+0.00	4-9	44	+0.93	0-2	-	-2.00
March	2-7	29	+16.50	0-0	-	+0.00	2-7	29	+16.50	0-0	-	+0.00
April	10-42	24	+28.88	0-3	-	-3.00	8-32	25	+24.38	2-7	29	+7.50
May	12-67	18	+2.50	2-7	29	+5.00	6-47	13	-14.50	4-13	31	+12.00
June	8-48	17	-21.69	0-8	-	-8.00	7-33	21	-8.26	1-7	14	-5.43
July	4-51	8	-29.17	0-13	-	-13.00	2-27	7	-14.00	2-11	18	-2.17
August	14-59	24	+29.92	2-17	12	-4.00	11-35	31	+37.92	1-7	14	-4.00
September	8-56	14	+5.25	3-26	12	+9.88	4-24	17	-4.13	1-6	17	-0.50
October	8-62	13	-27.15	6-35	17	-16.15	2-21	10	-5.00	0-6	-	-6.00
November	7-30	23	+6.74	6-19	32	+14.87	0-5	-	-5.00	1-6	17	-3.13
December	2-13	15	-3.75	2-10	20	-0.75	0-1	-	-1.00	0-2	-	-2.00

By race type - 2016

	Overall			Two-year-olds			Three-year-olds			Older horses		
	W-R	%	£1	W-R	%	£1	W-R	%	£1	W-R	%	£1
Handicap	47-250	19	-10.86	8-27	30	+17.33	26-136	19	-26.64	13-87	15	-1.55
Group	3-30	10	-5.00	2-9	22	+12.00	0-8	-	-8.00	1-13	8	-9.00
Maiden	40-173	23	+3.96	20-99	20	+8.76	17-67	25	-4.72	3-7	43	-0.08

By race type - 2015

	Overall			Two-year-olds			Three-year-olds			Older horses		
	W-R	%	£1	W-R	%	£1	W-R	%	£1	W-R	%	£1
Handicap	40-232	17	+0.09	1-20	5	-17.25	28-150	19	+3.72	11-62	18	+13.63
Group	5-20	25	+24.50	0-3	-	-3.00	4-8	50	+32.00	1-9	11	-4.50
Maiden	30-182	16	-49.04	15-97	15	-5.38	15-78	19	-36.67	0-7	-	-7.00

By race type - 2014

	Overall			Two-year-olds			Three-year-olds			Older horses		
	W-R	%	£1	W-R	%	£1	W-R	%	£1	W-R	%	£1
Handicap	34-213	16	-20.62	1-22	5	-13.00	25-144	17	-7.21	8-47	17	-0.42
Group	1-21	5	-13.00	0-2	-	-2.00	0-7	-	-7.00	1-12	8	-4.00
Maiden	39-188	21	+35.86	19-105	18	+7.56	19-77	25	+32.05	1-6	17	-3.75

By jockey - 2016

	Overall			Two-year-olds			Three-year-olds			Older horses		
	W-R	%	£1	W-R	%	£1	W-R	%	£1	W-R	%	£1
F M Berry	26-156	17	-14.38	13-51	25	+23.71	8-77	10	-33.63	5-28	18	-4.47
R Kingscote	14-50	28	+5.57	6-17	35	+10.63	8-20	40	+7.95	0-13	-	-13.00
Oisin Murphy	14-70	20	+24.48	5-30	17	+12.63	3-20	15	-6.50	6-20	30	+18.36
Jim Crowley	8-19	42	+29.29	1-2	50	-0.78	4-11	36	+3.37	3-6	50	+26.70
P O'Donnell	8-31	26	+18.10	0-0	-	+0.00	4-17	24	+11.75	4-14	29	+6.35
G Gibbons	7-22	32	-2.94	1-2	50	-0.09	5-11	45	+2.90	1-9	11	-5.75
S De Sousa	5-13	38	-1.85	2-4	50	+2.25	3-8	38	-3.10	0-1	-	-1.00
Hector Crouch	3-12	25	+5.75	2-6	33	+6.25	0-1	-	-1.00	1-5	20	+0.50
Harry Bentley	2-5	40	+4.20	0-0	-	+0.00	2-5	40	+4.20	0-0	-	+0.00
Pat Dobbs	2-20	10	-9.75	0-5	-	-5.00	1-12	8	-8.25	1-3	33	+3.50
Kevin Stott	1-1	100	+1.63	0-0	-	+0.00	1-1	100	+1.63	0-0	-	+0.00
Georgia Cox	1-2	50	+2.50	0-0	-	+0.00	1-2	50	+2.50	0-0	-	+0.00

By jockey - 2015

	Overall			Two-year-olds			Three-year-olds			Older horses		
	W-R	%	£1	W-R	%	£1	W-R	%	£1	W-R	%	£1
Harry Bentley	11-58	19	+6.25	2-29	7	-15.13	7-18	39	+12.87	2-11	18	+8.50
R Kingscote	11-84	13	-39.39	3-28	11	-11.88	7-41	17	-14.76	1-15	7	-12.75
P O'Donnell	9-46	20	+0.63	1-4	25	-1.25	8-31	26	+12.88	0-11	-	-11.00
Andrea Atzeni	8-27	30	+9.25	2-6	33	+3.25	5-19	26	+3.50	1-2	50	+2.50
Pat Dobbs	8-66	12	-21.13	3-12	25	+4.00	3-41	7	-18.50	2-13	15	-6.63
G Gibbons	6-17	35	+17.30	1-6	17	-2.50	4-9	44	+4.80	1-2	50	+15.00
Oisin Murphy	6-21	29	+21.23	2-9	22	+8.00	4-11	36	+14.23	0-1	-	-1.00
Martin Lane	4-29	14	+1.00	3-16	19	+3.00	1-10	10	+1.00	0-3	-	-3.00
S De Sousa	3-7	43	+9.75	1-1	100	+2.00	1-5	20	+6.00	1-1	100	+1.75

By jockey - 2014

	Overall			Two-year-olds			Three-year-olds			Older horses		
	W-R	%	£1	W-R	%	£1	W-R	%	£1	W-R	%	£1
Jim Crowley	27-135	20	+11.12	2-19	11	-10.50	19-90	21	+9.53	6-26	23	+12.08
R Kingscote	9-50	18	-4.50	2-17	12	-9.00	6-28	21	+1.50	1-5	20	+3.00
S De Sousa	8-46	17	-20.56	2-21	10	-14.38	6-21	29	-2.18	0-4	-	-4.00
Pat Dobbs	5-14	36	+5.28	3-8	38	+6.16	2-6	33	-0.88	0-0	-	+0.00
Andrea Atzeni	5-17	29	+16.25	0-5	-	-5.00	5-10	50	+23.25	0-2	-	-2.00
Seb Sanders	5-23	22	+33.94	5-14	36	+42.94	0-7	-	-7.00	0-2	-	-2.00
Jamie Spencer	3-7	43	-0.39	2-3	67	+2.04	0-1	-	-1.00	1-3	33	-1.43
Oisin Murphy	3-14	21	+1.50	1-7	14	+0.00	0-4	-	-4.00	2-3	67	+5.50
G Gibbons	3-18	17	-3.75	1-9	11	-5.00	1-6	17	+2.00	1-3	33	-0.75

By course - 2012-2016

	Overall			Two-year-olds			Three-year-olds			Older horses		
	W-R	%	£1	W-R	%	£1	W-R	%	£1	W-R	%	£1
Ascot	7-80	9	-31.25	1-17	6	-12.50	3-35	9	-11.00	3-28	11	-7.75
Ayr	2-13	15	-3.27	0-4	-	-4.00	1-4	25	-2.27	1-5	20	+3.00
Bath	4-32	13	-16.51	1-6	17	-2.75	3-23	13	-10.76	0-3	-	-3.00
Beverley	2-15	13	-11.03	1-4	25	-3.28	1-9	11	-5.75	0-2	-	-2.00
Brighton	2-14	14	-7.88	1-5	20	-1.25	1-7	14	-4.63	0-2	-	-2.00
Carlisle	3-4	75	+5.33	0-1	-	-1.00	3-3	100	+6.33	0-0	-	+0.00
Catterick	0-2	-	-2.00	0-0	-	+0.00	0-2	-	-2.00	0-0	-	+0.00
Chelms (AW)	7-34	21	+7.50	1-5	20	+7.00	5-21	24	+4.50	1-8	13	-4.00
Chepstow	16-59	27	-11.41	2-17	12	-13.00	11-32	34	+1.84	3-10	30	-0.25
Chester	6-37	16	-16.04	1-5	20	-1.00	5-24	21	-7.04	0-8	-	-8.00
Doncaster	13-103	13	-39.37	3-32	9	-22.88	8-50	16	-12.49	2-21	10	-4.00
Epsom	12-53	23	+19.32	3-7	43	+4.50	7-36	19	+3.32	2-10	20	+11.50
Ffos Las	6-22	27	+9.24	1-6	17	-4.09	3-11	27	-2.17	2-5	40	+15.50
Folkestone	0-1	-	-1.00	0-0	-	+0.00	0-0	-	+0.00	0-1	-	-1.00
Goodwood	7-76	9	-17.50	1-20	5	-11.00	5-29	17	+14.00	1-27	4	-20.50
Hamilton	1-3	33	+0.50	0-0	-	+0.00	1-3	33	+0.50	0-0	-	+0.00
Haydock	4-41	10	-20.25	1-5	20	-1.00	3-23	13	-6.25	0-13	-	-13.00
Kempton (AW)	62-321	19	+9.13	29-130	22	+23.01	24-144	17	-10.73	9-47	19	-3.15
Leicester	9-48	19	+33.08	5-19	26	+15.75	4-29	14	+17.33	0-0	-	+0.00
Lingfield	9-39	23	+7.61	2-16	13	+2.00	6-20	30	+7.04	1-3	33	-1.43
Lingfield (AW)	35-160	22	-6.91	6-31	19	-9.79	16-94	17	-25.32	13-35	37	+28.20
Musselburgh	0-3	-	-3.00	0-0	-	+0.00	0-3	-	-3.00	0-0	-	+0.00
Newbury	18-125	14	-9.09	4-43	9	-14.13	7-62	11	-16.75	7-20	35	+21.79
Newcastle	3-5	60	+8.38	1-1	100	+1.75	2-2	100	+8.63	0-2	-	-2.00
N'castle (AW)	1-5	20	+4.00	0-1	-	-1.00	0-1	-	-1.00	1-3	33	+6.00
Newmarket	13-109	12	-0.13	3-31	10	-14.50	3-48	6	-14.00	7-30	23	+28.38
Newmarket (J)	16-101	16	-22.97	2-31	6	-19.00	11-53	21	-4.22	3-17	18	+0.25
Nottingham	13-82	16	-6.98	2-30	7	-0.50	7-40	18	-12.90	4-12	33	+6.42
Pontefract	6-14	43	+6.44	3-3	100	+6.21	3-9	33	+2.23	0-2	-	-2.00
Redcar	0-2	-	-2.00	0-1	-	-1.00	0-1	-	-1.00	0-0	-	+0.00
Ripon	3-15	20	-7.00	1-3	33	-0.50	2-9	22	-3.50	0-3	-	-3.00
Salisbury	27-154	18	+1.14	7-58	12	-14.75	15-76	20	+13.81	5-20	25	+2.08
Sandown	10-73	14	-11.80	1-16	6	-13.00	9-42	21	+16.20	0-15	-	-15.00
S'well (AW)	4-23	17	+4.18	0-2	-	-2.00	3-9	33	+1.17	1-12	8	+5.00
Thirsk	4-8	50	+5.66	3-5	60	+6.41	0-2	-	-2.00	1-1	100	+1.25
Warwick	4-13	31	+8.25	2-5	40	+5.25	1-3	33	+2.50	1-5	20	+0.50
Wetherby	0-1	-	-1.00	0-0	-	+0.00	0-1	-	-1.00	0-0	-	+0.00
Windsor	28-137	20	-1.94	6-43	14	-20.87	19-81	23	+17.33	3-13	23	+1.60
Wolves (AW)	25-108	23	+32.19	9-32	28	+30.19	13-61	21	-0.21	3-15	20	+2.20
Yarmouth	1-6	17	+2.00	1-1	100	+7.00	0-1	-	-1.00	0-4	-	-4.00
York	7-64	11	-6.83	2-10	20	+2.83	1-26	4	-21.00	4-28	14	+11.33

Ten-year summary

	Wins	Runs	%	Win prize-money	Total prize-money	£1
2016	101	506	20	£834,319.54	£1,300,688.65	+7.83
2015	80	474	17	£1,290,761.62	£1,559,241.27	-47.07
2014	80	453	18	£514,051.36	£839,361.71	+1.97
2013	73	418	17	£645,013.20	£1,117,771.73	+6.61
2012	64	381	17	£350,313.64	£582,999.26	-53.17
2011	56	369	15	£199,901.73	£358,540.98	-48.96
2010	69	400	17	£394,285.66	£541,891.28	+107.15
2009	58	394	15	£845,576.81	£1,061,281.59	+84.44
2008	42	334	13	£380,168.56	£553,888.98	-3.52
2007	41	321	13	£197,813.44	£330,349.54	+109.32

PLEASELETMEWIN (right): profitable to follow, like so many of Ralph Beckett's

Roger Varian

Varian's year was hit by a bug in the middle of summer that, at its peak, saw him out send out just 21 runners in August. Still, he recovered strongly to come within three of a second successive century and surely it's onwards and upwards.

By month - 2016

	Overall			Two-year-olds			Three-year-olds			Older horses		
	W-R	%	£1	W-R	%	£1	W-R	%	£1	W-R	%	£1
January	3-11	27	-3.44	0-0	-	+0.00	3-5	60	+2.56	0-6	-	-6.00
February	6-15	40	-4.11	0-0	-	+0.00	3-6	50	-0.04	3-9	33	-4.07
March	2-10	20	+3.50	0-0	-	+0.00	1-6	17	+3.00	1-4	25	+0.50
April	7-41	17	-22.64	0-0	-	+0.00	5-30	17	-15.08	2-11	18	-7.55
May	15-99	15	-37.00	1-6	17	-4.43	7-62	11	-32.92	7-31	23	+0.35
June	17-93	18	-20.22	2-11	18	-3.83	11-58	19	-1.85	4-24	17	-14.54
July	7-42	17	-16.13	1-9	11	-5.25	5-18	28	+0.62	1-15	7	-11.50
August	5-21	24	+2.38	0-0	-	+0.00	1-10	10	-8.00	4-11	36	+10.38
September	17-78	22	+10.29	7-26	27	+16.93	6-36	17	-18.51	4-16	25	+11.88
October	11-98	11	-44.97	4-57	7	-31.20	7-33	21	-5.77	0-8	-	-8.00
November	5-32	16	+0.63	3-20	15	+6.88	2-10	20	-4.25	0-2	-	-2.00
December	2-14	14	-9.63	0-6	-	-6.00	2-7	29	-2.63	0-1	-	-1.00

By month - 2015

	Overall			Two-year-olds			Three-year-olds			Older horses		
	W-R	%	£1	W-R	%	£1	W-R	%	£1	W-R	%	£1
January	3-12	25	+2.48	0-0	-	+0.00	2-9	22	+1.73	1-3	33	+0.75
February	3-8	38	+6.60	0-0	-	+0.00	1-6	17	-1.50	2-2	100	+8.10
March	1-4	25	+1.00	0-0	-	+0.00	0-2	-	-2.00	1-2	50	+3.00
April	5-38	13	-18.00	0-1	-	-1.00	3-29	10	-16.25	2-8	25	-0.75
May	6-51	12	-27.59	0-10	-	-10.00	3-26	12	-13.59	3-15	20	-4.00
June	14-62	23	-12.29	2-10	20	-6.52	10-38	26	+2.61	2-14	14	-8.38
July	27-76	36	+27.44	5-15	33	+2.50	19-46	41	+26.03	3-15	20	-1.09
August	11-68	16	-22.08	1-14	7	-10.50	10-43	23	-0.58	0-11	-	-11.00
September	16-69	23	+27.18	5-25	20	-8.70	7-33	21	+21.38	4-11	36	+14.50
October	4-51	8	-14.00	2-29	7	-4.00	2-19	11	-7.00	0-3	-	-3.00
November	6-21	29	+8.38	0-8	-	-8.00	3-7	43	+6.38	3-6	50	+10.00
December	4-14	29	-0.70	3-6	50	+1.30	0-4	-	-4.00	1-4	25	+2.00

By month - 2014

	Overall			Two-year-olds			Three-year-olds			Older horses		
	W-R	%	£1	W-R	%	£1	W-R	%	£1	W-R	%	£1
January	0-4	-	-4.00	0-0	-	+0.00	0-1	-	-1.00	0-3	-	-3.00
February	3-7	43	+5.30	0-0	-	+0.00	3-5	60	+7.30	0-2	-	-2.00
March	4-12	33	-4.35	0-0	-	+0.00	4-9	44	-1.35	0-3	-	-3.00
April	10-52	19	-3.97	0-1	-	-1.00	6-34	18	+0.91	4-17	24	-3.88
May	10-62	16	-0.08	2-8	25	-2.59	6-35	17	+9.02	2-19	11	-6.50
June	17-93	18	+1.93	3-15	20	+3.34	10-51	20	-9.16	4-27	15	+7.75
July	10-56	18	-4.27	1-13	8	-11.27	7-29	24	+11.75	2-14	14	-4.75
August	6-48	13	-23.78	2-12	17	-1.75	2-22	9	-15.63	2-14	14	-6.40
September	10-69	14	-27.24	5-41	12	-21.63	5-21	24	+1.38	0-7	-	-7.00
October	7-41	17	-1.75	6-24	25	+7.25	1-13	8	-5.00	0-4	-	-4.00
November	1-20	5	-11.50	0-13	-	-13.00	1-3	33	+5.50	0-4	-	-4.00
December	0-7	-	-7.00	0-4	-	-4.00	0-2	-	-2.00	0-1	-	-1.00

By race type - 2016

	Overall			Two-year-olds			Three-year-olds			Older horses		
	W-R	%	£1	W-R	%	£1	W-R	%	£1	W-R	%	£1
Handicap	37-228	16	-75.33	2-11	18	+7.75	21-131	16	-56.04	14-86	16	-27.04
Group	4-34	12	-5.40	0-3	-	-3.00	0-7	-	-7.00	4-24	17	+4.60
Maiden	41-229	18	-42.23	13-102	13	-21.40	25-123	20	-24.59	3-4	75	+3.77

By race type - 2015

	Overall			Two-year-olds			Three-year-olds			Older horses		
	W-R	%	£1	W-R	%	£1	W-R	%	£1	W-R	%	£1
Handicap	51-223	23	+28.06	3-21	14	+9.50	31-139	22	-0.17	17-63	27	+18.73
Group	3-28	11	+3.83	0-4	-	-4.00	2-11	18	+16.33	1-13	8	-8.50
Maiden	39-188	21	-56.40	15-88	17	-45.42	24-100	24	-10.98	0-0	-	+0.00

By race type - 2014

	Overall			Two-year-olds			Three-year-olds			Older horses		
	W-R	%	£1	W-R	%	£1	W-R	%	£1	W-R	%	£1
Handicap	30-187	16	-19.38	3-10	30	+2.50	19-109	17	+7.24	8-68	12	-29.13
Group	4-42	10	-7.25	2-6	33	+20.00	1-11	9	-7.75	1-25	4	-19.50
Maiden	35-195	18	-72.12	13-106	12	-60.40	21-86	24	-10.98	1-3	33	-0.75

By jockey - 2016

	Overall			Two-year-olds			Three-year-olds			Older horses		
	W-R	%	£1	W-R	%	£1	W-R	%	£1	W-R	%	£1
Andrea Atzeni	52-242	21	-5.88	12-70	17	+4.75	21-107	20	-29.29	19-65	29	+18.66
Harry Bentley	16-95	17	-22.07	1-12	8	+3.00	13-64	20	-11.40	2-19	11	-13.67
Jack Mitchell	16-103	16	-41.93	3-24	13	-12.46	11-53	21	-15.97	2-26	8	-13.50
Paul Hanagan	3-25	12	-10.25	1-6	17	-0.50	2-13	15	-3.75	0-6	-	-6.00
Joe Fanning	2-4	50	+0.71	0-1	-	-1.00	2-3	67	+1.71	0-0	-	+0.00
Frederik Tylicki	2-10	20	+1.50	0-2	-	-2.00	2-8	25	+3.50	0-0	-	+0.00
Dane O'Neill	2-14	14	-9.20	1-5	20	-3.70	1-7	14	-3.50	0-2	-	-2.00
William Buick	1-3	33	-1.17	0-1	-	-1.00	1-1	100	+0.83	0-1	-	-1.00
Jim Crowley	1-5	20	-3.50	0-2	-	-2.00	0-1	-	-1.00	1-2	50	-0.50
James Doyle	1-7	14	-5.39	0-1	-	-1.00	0-1	-	-1.00	1-5	20	-3.39
Paul Mulrennan	1-8	13	-6.17	0-2	-	-2.00	0-2	-	-2.00	1-4	25	-2.17
Andrew Mullen	0-1	-	-1.00	0-0	-	+0.00	0-0	-	+0.00	0-1	-	-1.00

By jockey - 2015

	Overall			Two-year-olds			Three-year-olds			Older horses		
	W-R	%	£1	W-R	%	£1	W-R	%	£1	W-R	%	£1
Jack Mitchell	20-69	29	+49.83	6-24	25	+7.80	13-41	32	+40.03	1-4	25	+2.00
Andrea Atzeni	15-81	19	-25.51	3-23	13	-15.45	9-46	20	-5.59	3-12	25	-4.47
Frederik Tylicki	13-78	17	-12.65	0-18	-	-18.00	8-44	18	-0.25	5-16	31	+5.60
Paul Hanagan	11-45	24	+0.15	4-17	24	-3.68	7-26	27	+5.83	0-2	-	-2.00
Graham Lee	9-45	20	-15.65	1-5	20	-1.00	4-22	18	-13.15	4-18	22	-1.50
Jim Crowley	7-22	32	+9.91	1-4	25	-2.00	3-9	33	+3.91	3-9	33	+8.00
William Buick	5-22	23	-6.79	0-5	-	-5.00	3-10	30	-2.29	2-7	29	+0.50
James Doyle	4-14	29	-1.75	1-4	25	-1.50	3-9	33	+0.75	0-1	-	-1.00
Joe Fanning	3-5	60	+21.00	1-2	50	+8.00	1-2	50	+7.00	1-1	100	+6.00

By jockey - 2014

	Overall			Two-year-olds			Three-year-olds			Older horses		
	W-R	%	£1	W-R	%	£1	W-R	%	£1	W-R	%	£1
Andrea Atzeni	29-156	19	+0.92	8-46	17	-1.76	12-69	17	-9.30	9-41	22	+11.98
Paul Hanagan	8-37	22	-0.26	0-4	-	-4.00	8-24	33	+12.74	0-9	-	-9.00
Frederik Tylicki	8-49	16	-23.36	2-17	12	-13.27	6-24	25	-2.09	0-8	-	-8.00
Jack Mitchell	7-52	13	-20.85	2-21	10	-9.00	4-26	15	-9.10	1-5	20	-2.75
Graham Lee	6-16	38	+11.78	1-4	25	-1.50	5-11	45	+14.28	0-1	-	-1.00
Ryan Moore	4-6	67	+6.09	2-3	67	+1.98	1-1	100	+0.62	1-2	50	+3.50
Kieren Fallon	3-11	27	+3.33	0-0	-	+0.00	2-5	40	+2.33	1-6	17	+1.00
James Doyle	2-5	40	+7.00	0-1	-	-1.00	2-4	50	+8.00	0-0	-	+0.00
Martin Dwyer	2-6	33	+14.00	1-4	25	+4.00	1-2	50	+10.00	0-0	-	+0.00

By course - 2012-2016

	Overall			Two-year-olds			Three-year-olds			Older horses		
	W-R	%	£1	W-R	%	£1	W-R	%	£1	W-R	%	£1
Ascot	15-108	14	+18.50	3-17	18	+26.00	6-41	15	+0.75	6-50	12	-8.25
Ayr	3-6	50	+1.74	0-0	-	+0.00	2-2	100	+3.91	1-4	25	-2.17
Bath	4-18	22	-3.78	1-6	17	-0.50	2-9	22	-4.28	1-3	33	+1.00
Beverley	7-25	28	+6.00	4-8	50	+12.50	3-12	25	-1.50	0-5	-	-5.00
Brighton	6-38	16	+3.25	0-7	-	-7.00	5-24	21	+14.00	1-7	14	-3.75
Carlisle	1-6	17	-3.75	0-2	-	-2.00	1-4	25	-1.75	0-0	-	+0.00
Catterick	2-6	33	-1.29	0-1	-	-1.00	2-5	40	-0.29	0-0	-	+0.00
Chelms (AW)	13-64	20	-10.14	1-12	8	-2.00	10-37	27	+1.76	2-15	13	-9.90
Chepstow	2-14	14	-9.95	0-5	-	-5.00	2-7	29	-2.95	0-2	-	-2.00
Chester	10-43	23	+6.41	1-3	33	-1.09	8-28	29	+16.00	1-12	8	-8.50
Doncaster	30-128	23	+33.20	4-29	14	-17.22	14-57	25	+20.95	12-42	29	+29.47
Epsom	9-42	21	-3.77	0-5	-	-5.00	5-22	23	-2.25	4-15	27	+3.48
Ffos Las	3-9	33	-2.95	1-2	50	-0.70	1-5	20	-3.50	1-2	50	+1.25
Folkestone	3-8	38	+2.54	0-1	-	-1.00	3-6	50	+4.54	0-1	-	-1.00
Goodwood	6-72	8	-50.38	2-8	25	-2.88	1-32	3	-27.50	3-32	9	-20.00
Hamilton	2-7	29	+1.40	0-0	-	+0.00	1-3	33	-1.60	1-4	25	+3.00
Haydock	26-114	23	-3.30	5-28	18	-15.07	14-58	24	+4.12	7-28	25	+7.65
Kempton (AW)	36-202	18	-24.48	14-84	17	-14.82	17-88	19	+3.43	5-30	17	-13.10
Leicester	15-73	21	-11.98	3-28	11	-14.55	9-35	26	+1.95	3-10	30	+0.63
Lingfield	11-39	28	+2.81	3-8	38	+3.35	7-27	26	+0.21	1-4	25	-0.75
Lingfield (AW)	25-144	17	-48.16	5-31	16	-20.01	15-84	18	-23.01	5-29	17	-5.14
Musselburgh	2-8	25	+0.00	0-0	-	+0.00	1-5	20	-1.00	1-3	33	+1.00
Newbury	12-89	13	-13.75	4-29	14	-2.75	6-41	15	-5.50	2-19	11	-5.50
Newcastle	3-13	23	-0.80	2-4	50	+6.00	1-6	17	-3.80	0-3	-	-3.00
N'castle (AW)	6-33	18	-14.40	1-11	9	-8.13	5-18	28	-2.27	0-4	-	-4.00
Newmarket	18-157	11	-34.42	8-58	14	-0.50	8-74	11	-24.92	2-25	8	-9.00
Newmarket (J)	8-89	9	-55.84	1-23	4	-19.50	3-46	7	-28.50	4-20	20	-7.84
Nottingham	14-82	17	+4.08	3-28	11	-1.50	6-38	16	+3.08	5-16	31	+2.50
Pontefract	2-27	7	-13.00	0-1	-	-1.00	2-21	10	-7.00	0-5	-	-5.00
Redcar	5-20	25	+1.70	2-6	33	+4.50	2-8	25	-0.80	1-6	17	-2.00
Ripon	5-30	17	-14.13	0-6	-	-6.00	5-19	26	-3.14	0-5	-	-5.00
Salisbury	11-53	21	+11.33	1-10	10	-6.50	10-39	26	+21.83	0-4	-	-4.00
Sandown	12-79	15	-37.98	2-13	15	-8.89	9-50	18	-15.47	1-16	6	-13.63
S'well (AW)	7-21	33	-5.90	1-2	50	-0.33	6-15	40	-1.57	0-4	-	-4.00
Thirsk	6-25	24	-2.88	0-2	-	-2.00	5-18	28	-0.88	1-5	20	+0.00
Warwick	2-11	18	-3.00	0-2	-	-2.00	2-7	29	+1.00	0-2	-	-2.00
Wetherby	0-2	-	-2.00	0-0	-	+0.00	0-2	-	-2.00	0-0	-	+0.00
Windsor	29-99	29	+19.46	2-12	17	-7.67	22-69	32	+10.69	5-18	28	+16.43
Wolves (AW)	37-132	28	+18.94	5-30	17	-5.68	24-83	29	+13.44	8-19	42	+11.18
Yarmouth	16-71	23	-6.20	7-28	25	-6.04	7-30	23	+5.83	2-13	15	-6.00
York	9-73	12	-21.52	2-15	13	-6.77	0-18	-	-18.00	7-40	18	+3.25

Ten-year summary

	Wins	Runs	%	Win prize-money	Total prize-money	£1
2016	97	554	18	£1,788,831.62	£2,393,914.99	-141.34
2015	100	474	21	£887,554.86	£1,541,464.56	-21.60
2014	78	471	17	£1,374,851.71	£2,252,219.09	-80.70
2013	89	402	22	£921,239.74	£1,332,296.98	+19.63
2012	72	398	18	£532,154.46	£877,983.27	-55.48
2011	53	272	19	£387,237.31	£702,386.72	+56.94

POSTPONED: led the way in stunning fashion for Roger Varian last season

Top trainers by winners (Turf)

All runs				*First time out*			*Horses*		
Won	*Ran*	*%*	*Trainer*	*Won*	*Ran*	*%*	*Won*	*Ran*	*%*
156	1346	12	**Richard Fahey**	38	285	13	136	285	48
138	992	14	**Mark Johnston**	33	228	14	115	228	50
119	1014	12	**Richard Hannon**	34	288	12	117	288	41
103	456	23	**William Haggas**	27	154	18	87	154	56
90	443	20	**John Gosden**	44	196	22	100	196	51
87	398	22	**Sir Michael Stoute**	22	138	16	73	138	53
77	534	14	**Andrew Balding**	13	159	8	73	159	46
74	746	10	**David O'Meara**	13	157	8	60	157	38
73	733	10	**Tim Easterby**	6	115	5	50	115	43
71	592	12	**Kevin Ryan**	17	127	13	61	127	48
68	360	19	**Ralph Beckett**	22	129	17	66	129	51
65	477	14	**Keith Dalgleish**	16	105	15	50	105	48
64	381	17	**Roger Varian**	29	162	18	66	162	41
59	285	21	**Charlie Appleby**	26	116	22	52	116	45
58	536	11	**Mick Channon**	9	94	10	46	94	49
54	410	13	**Charles Hills**	14	129	11	50	129	39
53	345	15	**Clive Cox**	12	95	13	43	95	45
52	440	12	**K R Burke**	15	119	13	50	119	42
47	235	20	**Hugo Palmer**	19	95	20	46	95	48
46	393	12	**Tom Dascombe**	14	105	13	47	105	45
46	332	14	**John Quinn**	7	71	10	39	71	55
46	334	14	**Brian Ellison**	14	96	15	39	96	41
44	245	18	**David Simcock**	22	108	20	51	108	47
44	412	11	**Michael Dods**	7	83	8	36	83	43
39	223	17	**Saeed bin Suroor**	27	117	23	49	117	42
36	185	19	**Roger Charlton**	7	68	10	29	68	43
36	338	11	**Ruth Carr**	0	43	—	24	43	56
33	234	14	**Eve Johnson Houghton**	3	54	6	24	54	44
33	376	9	**Michael Appleby**	19	130	15	50	130	38
32	239	13	**Ed Dunlop**	9	84	11	30	84	36
31	221	14	**Hughie Morrison**	3	69	4	26	69	38
31	400	8	**David Evans**	8	97	8	40	97	41
30	303	10	**Michael Easterby**	3	64	5	29	64	45
28	133	21	**A P O'Brien**	11	66	17	20	66	30
27	150	18	**James Tate**	12	74	16	34	74	46
27	181	15	**Iain Jardine**	3	40	8	20	40	50
26	216	12	**Michael Bell**	7	72	10	25	72	35
25	276	9	**Tony Carroll**	3	93	3	35	93	38
24	248	10	**Paul Midgley**	0	38	—	15	38	39
24	191	13	**David Loughnane**	2	32	6	14	32	44
23	135	17	**Sir Mark Prescott**	9	61	15	29	61	48
23	202	11	**Brian Meehan**	3	63	5	21	63	33
23	216	11	**George Baker**	4	54	7	20	54	37
23	130	18	**Paul Cole**	6	43	14	16	43	37
23	187	12	**Richard Hughes**	4	65	6	23	65	35
22	140	16	**James Fanshawe**	10	61	16	24	61	39
22	190	12	**Luca Cumani**	12	69	17	26	69	38

Top trainers by prize-money (Turf)

Total prize-money	Trainer	Win prize-money	Wins	Class 1-3 Won	Class 1-3 Ran	Class 1-3 %	Class 4-6 Won	Class 4-6 Ran	Class 4-6 %
£8,130,756	**A P O'Brien**	£5,059,170	28	28	132	21	0	1	—
£3,131,054	**John Gosden**	£1,719,241	90	43	220	20	47	223	21
£2,725,169	**Richard Fahey**	£1,260,570	156	40	545	7	116	801	14
£2,472,498	**Richard Hannon**	£1,355,329	119	35	387	9	84	627	13
£2,275,848	**Sir Michael Stoute**	£1,288,102	87	39	204	19	48	194	25
£2,149,522	**Mark Johnston**	£1,197,404	138	46	474	10	92	518	18
£2,076,106	**Roger Varian**	£1,563,700	64	26	167	16	38	214	18
£1,910,572	**Hugo Palmer**	£1,148,231	47	21	116	18	26	119	22
£1,790,116	**William Haggas**	£1,189,167	103	27	179	15	76	277	27
£1,760,778	**Charlie Appleby**	£1,164,515	59	27	172	16	32	113	28
£1,452,705	**Clive Cox**	£1,132,860	53	20	102	20	33	243	14
£1,426,050	**Andrew Balding**	£901,792	77	28	217	13	49	317	15
£1,394,461	**David O'Meara**	£586,634	74	20	336	6	54	410	13
£1,341,499	**David Simcock**	£765,931	44	19	123	15	25	122	20
£1,264,663	**Kevin Ryan**	£626,078	71	20	204	10	51	388	13
£1,080,102	**Saeed bin Suroor**	£516,963	39	18	148	12	21	75	28
£1,071,670	**J-C Rouget**	£964,070	2	2	5	40	0	0	—
£1,054,024	**Charles Hills**	£594,928	54	12	144	8	42	266	16
£1,034,617	**K R Burke**	£788,019	52	16	160	10	36	280	13
£1,023,344	**Roger Charlton**	£611,503	36	9	65	14	27	120	23
£1,012,407	**Ralph Beckett**	£603,513	68	18	144	13	50	216	23
£1,007,777	**Henry Candy**	£781,614	20	8	66	12	12	131	9
£914,572	**Mick Channon**	£524,850	58	15	190	8	43	346	12
£889,715	**D K Weld**	£876,170	1	1	8	13	0	0	—
£827,568	**James Fanshawe**	£543,440	22	9	70	13	13	70	19
£753,071	**Tim Easterby**	£456,820	73	15	207	7	58	526	11
£726,853	**Michael Dods**	£504,734	44	10	101	10	34	311	11
£634,755	**Tom Dascombe**	£395,818	46	19	121	16	27	272	10
£619,052	**Keith Dalgleish**	£418,949	65	13	90	14	52	387	13
£610,012	**Michael Bell**	£481,484	26	7	48	15	19	168	11
£545,779	**Hughie Morrison**	£394,284	31	9	79	11	22	142	15
£516,758	**Ed Dunlop**	£292,551	32	12	82	15	20	157	13
£467,260	**Sir Mark Prescott**	£227,387	23	8	42	19	15	93	16
£466,131	**Luca Cumani**	£165,716	22	6	78	8	16	112	14
£457,024	**Eve Johnson Houghton**	£332,440	33	5	62	8	28	172	16
£440,530	**Laura Mongan**	£412,010	5	1	5	20	4	39	10
£430,263	**Dean Ivory**	£329,092	14	5	61	8	9	98	9
£390,881	**Michael Easterby**	£268,358	30	8	68	12	22	235	9
£370,383	**Brian Meehan**	£265,952	23	7	73	10	16	129	12
£367,521	**David Evans**	£136,896	31	3	114	3	28	286	10
£367,468	**John Quinn**	£233,807	46	7	79	9	39	253	15
£365,139	**Marco Botti**	£187,130	14	6	77	8	8	87	9
£364,487	**David Barron**	£226,133	22	4	122	3	18	137	13
£360,018	**Robert Cowell**	£266,617	18	7	90	8	11	125	9
£347,767	**Brian Ellison**	£228,635	46	7	80	9	39	254	15
£345,179	**Alan King**	£199,428	19	5	45	11	14	101	14
£344,207	**Bryan Smart**	£267,067	21	10	42	24	11	129	9

Top trainers by winners (AW)

All runs				First time out			Horses		
Won	Ran	%	Trainer	Won	Ran	%	Won	Ran	%
57	421	14	**Mark Johnston**	33	237	14	120	237	51
54	343	16	**Richard Hannon**	36	297	12	125	297	42
51	170	30	**John Gosden**	49	211	23	111	211	53
42	393	11	**Richard Fahey**	38	294	13	142	294	48
41	212	19	**David Simcock**	23	114	20	55	114	48
39	320	12	**David Evans**	10	108	9	47	108	44
37	233	16	**Marco Botti**	11	106	10	38	106	36
37	411	9	**Michael Appleby**	19	138	14	52	138	38
36	205	18	**Stuart Williams**	11	63	17	28	63	44
34	140	24	**William Haggas**	27	156	17	91	156	58
33	173	19	**Roger Varian**	29	167	17	68	167	41
33	146	23	**Ralph Beckett**	22	133	17	71	133	53
32	143	22	**Sir Mark Prescott**	9	61	15	30	61	49
32	276	12	**Daniel Mark Loughnane**	3	65	5	24	65	37
31	173	18	**Michael Easterby**	4	68	6	33	68	49
30	197	15	**Andrew Balding**	13	160	8	75	160	47
29	96	30	**Saeed bin Suroor**	27	123	22	51	123	41
29	229	13	**David O'Meara**	13	164	8	66	164	40
29	337	9	**Tony Carroll**	3	102	3	39	102	38
29	176	16	**Tom Dascombe**	14	105	13	49	105	47
27	232	12	**Jamie Osborne**	5	73	7	32	73	44
27	152	18	**James Tate**	12	77	16	34	77	44
25	130	19	**Chris Dwyer**	6	28	21	17	28	61
24	107	22	**Sir Michael Stoute**	22	140	16	75	140	54
24	109	22	**Hugo Palmer**	20	102	20	49	102	48
23	141	16	**Kevin Ryan**	17	127	13	63	127	50
22	133	17	**Charles Hills**	14	133	11	50	133	38
21	159	13	**Dean Ivory**	5	50	10	19	50	38
21	103	20	**James Fanshawe**	10	63	16	26	63	41
20	172	12	**Phil McEntee**	3	37	8	13	37	35
19	203	9	**Derek Shaw**	4	42	10	12	42	29
19	107	18	**Amanda Perrett**	5	52	10	22	52	42
19	146	13	**Ed Dunlop**	9	86	10	32	86	37
19	174	11	**Gary Moore**	7	78	9	22	78	28
19	143	13	**Sylvester Kirk**	5	53	9	28	53	53
18	102	18	**Ian Williams**	7	56	13	25	56	45
17	87	20	**Simon Crisford**	12	67	18	23	67	34
17	189	9	**Conor Dore**	4	26	15	11	26	42
17	163	10	**Michael Attwater**	4	39	10	12	39	31
16	95	17	**David Barron**	10	67	15	26	67	39
16	147	11	**K R Burke**	16	126	13	52	126	41
16	187	9	**Keith Dalgleish**	16	108	15	50	108	46
16	125	13	**Robert Cowell**	13	79	16	26	79	33
16	65	25	**Luca Cumani**	13	72	18	29	72	40
15	78	19	**David Elsworth**	3	38	8	15	38	39
14	126	11	**Gay Kelleway**	5	37	14	17	37	46
14	137	10	**Brian Ellison**	16	105	15	41	105	39

Top trainers by prize-money (AW)

Total prize-money	Trainer	Win prize-money	Wins	Class 1-3 Won	Class 1-3 Ran	Class 1-3 %	Class 4-6 Won	Class 4-6 Ran	Class 4-6 %
£575,158	Mark Johnston	£356,324	57	16	86	19	41	333	12
£530,589	Marco Botti	£393,387	37	8	54	15	29	179	16
£436,939	Richard Fahey	£294,460	42	7	84	8	35	309	11
£375,109	Richard Hannon	£247,259	54	6	38	16	48	304	16
£359,716	Stuart Williams	£282,255	36	11	51	22	25	153	16
£336,666	William Haggas	£234,614	34	7	31	23	27	109	25
£331,729	John Gosden	£238,488	51	5	24	21	46	146	32
£317,809	Roger Varian	£225,132	33	8	24	33	25	149	17
£313,104	Michael Appleby	£200,073	37	10	69	14	27	337	8
£305,546	Saeed bin Suroor	£203,181	29	10	37	27	19	59	32
£304,520	David Simcock	£189,422	41	5	59	8	35	152	23
£288,282	Ralph Beckett	£230,807	33	4	26	15	29	120	24
£285,084	David O'Meara	£180,738	29	8	55	15	21	174	12
£253,834	David Evans	£150,556	39	6	51	12	33	269	12
£249,925	Sir Michael Stoute	£203,446	24	6	17	35	18	90	20
£246,574	Andrew Balding	£137,207	30	4	47	9	26	147	18
£228,692	Jamie Osborne	£139,026	27	4	38	11	22	191	12
£227,413	Michael Easterby	£158,596	31	6	30	20	25	140	18
£218,508	Charlie Appleby	£142,959	11	4	19	21	7	27	26
£218,477	Mick Channon	£170,184	13	4	18	22	9	69	13
£213,052	David Elsworth	£189,398	15	6	21	29	9	57	16
£194,564	David Barron	£156,884	16	2	25	8	14	70	20
£192,906	Kevin Ryan	£143,325	23	4	22	18	19	119	16
£189,193	Dean Ivory	£111,635	21	4	24	17	16	129	12
£188,622	Sir Mark Prescott	£139,871	32	4	20	20	28	123	23
£183,134	James Tate	£122,027	27	1	15	7	26	137	19
£181,026	Hugo Palmer	£129,077	24	3	11	27	21	98	21
£179,469	Tony Carroll	£118,062	29	2	14	14	25	294	9
£171,779	Chris Dwyer	£93,251	25	0	21	—	24	108	22
£161,799	K R Burke	£95,208	16	3	43	7	13	104	13
£161,762	Tom Dascombe	£110,102	29	1	31	3	28	145	19
£150,793	Derek Shaw	£101,849	19	2	31	6	17	168	10
£146,812	James Fanshawe	£97,018	21	3	19	16	18	84	21
£143,030	Simon Crisford	£106,326	17	3	13	23	14	74	19
£138,259	Jeremy Noseda	£114,330	12	4	15	27	8	40	20
£135,973	Daniel Mark Loughnane	£89,958	32	0	1	—	30	273	11
£134,198	Amanda Perrett	£86,746	19	4	24	17	15	83	18
£130,246	Phil McEntee	£88,202	20	2	14	14	18	149	12
£123,725	Gay Kelleway	£79,697	14	2	26	8	12	96	13
£123,465	Keith Dalgleish	£77,248	16	2	24	8	14	162	9
£119,482	Ed Dunlop	£74,202	19	0	12	—	19	134	14
£118,049	Charles Hills	£75,655	22	0	11	—	22	122	18
£117,025	Robert Cowell	£75,889	16	3	19	16	13	103	13
£114,784	Brian Ellison	£49,456	14	0	17	—	14	120	12
£114,369	Roger Charlton	£71,687	12	3	10	30	9	55	16
£112,628	David Nicholls	£42,655	7	1	13	8	6	57	11
£108,356	Luca Cumani	£86,890	16	2	8	25	14	57	25

Top jockeys (Turf)

Won	Ran	%	Jockey	Best Trainer	Won	Ran
108	651	17	**Silvestre De Sousa**	Mick Channon	19	148
107	607	18	**Jim Crowley**	Hugo Palmer	20	80
84	404	21	**Ryan Moore**	Sir Michael Stoute	32	129
83	485	17	**Andrea Atzeni**	Roger Varian	52	242
79	451	18	**James Doyle**	Saeed bin Suroor	23	128
77	638	12	**Paul Mulrennan**	Michael Dods	23	233
76	349	22	**Frankie Dettori**	John Gosden	38	144
76	596	13	**Oisin Murphy**	Andrew Balding	31	201
76	612	12	**Joe Fanning**	Mark Johnston	67	466
69	454	15	**Adam Kirby**	Clive Cox	40	180
69	387	18	**Pat Cosgrave**	William Haggas	53	205
68	361	19	**William Buick**	Charlie Appleby	35	160
68	416	16	**Jamie Spencer**	David Simcock	30	122
65	505	13	**Tony Hamilton**	Richard Fahey	64	487
64	441	15	**Daniel Tudhope**	David O'Meara	41	328
62	401	15	**Richard Kingscote**	Tom Dascombe	49	317
60	587	10	**P J McDonald**	Ann Duffield	18	178
57	480	12	**David Allan**	Tim Easterby	27	294
57	368	15	**Franny Norton**	Mark Johnston	46	253
56	423	13	**Paul Hanagan**	Richard Fahey	10	89
53	347	15	**George Baker**	David Lanigan	12	54
52	387	13	**Phillip Makin**	Keith Dalgleish	35	218
50	364	14	**Ben Curtis**	Brian Ellison	27	174
47	520	9	**James Sullivan**	Ruth Carr	34	306
46	481	10	**Luke Morris**	Sir Mark Prescott Bt	43	189
45	418	11	**Graham Gibbons**	David Barron	21	167
44	338	13	**Adam McNamara**	Richard Fahey	33	247
43	473	9	**Graham Lee**	Mick Channon	8	45
43	395	11	**Connor Beasley**	Michael Dods	16	125
43	426	10	**Tom Marquand**	Richard Hannon	25	198
43	349	12	**Josephine Gordon**	Hugo Palmer	9	31
42	508	8	**Tom Eaves**	Kevin Ryan	17	148
42	319	13	**David Probert**	Andrew Balding	28	185
37	239	15	**Harry Bentley**	Roger Varian	16	95
37	272	14	**Robert Havlin**	John Gosden	49	193
37	340	11	**Sean Levey**	Richard Hannon	40	346
37	342	11	**Shane Kelly**	Richard Hughes	24	210
35	304	12	**Martin Harley**	James Tate	15	73
32	247	13	**Ted Durcan**	Sir Michael Stoute	25	130
32	285	11	**F M Berry**	Ralph Beckett	26	156
32	231	14	**Dane O'Neill**	Henry Candy	8	43
32	361	9	**Jason Hart**	Keith Dalgleish	8	83
31	312	10	**Martin Dwyer**	William Muir	16	142
31	402	8	**Andrew Mullen**	Michael Appleby	25	301
30	286	10	**Nathan Evans**	Michael Easterby	29	221
29	285	10	**Frederik Tylicki**	Rod Millman	9	86
27	344	8	**Pat Dobbs**	Richard Hannon	20	233
27	167	16	**Kevin Stott**	Kevin Ryan	24	112

Top jockeys (AW)

Won	Ran	%	Jockey	Best Trainer	Won	Ran
113	910	12	**Luke Morris**	Sir Mark Prescott	45	199
83	478	17	**Adam Kirby**	Clive Cox	42	191
82	410	20	**Jim Crowley**	Hugo Palmer	20	82
61	336	18	**George Baker**	David Lanigan	12	54
57	277	21	**Silvestre De Sousa**	Mick Channon	19	148
53	413	13	**Joe Fanning**	Mark Johnston	73	491
51	347	15	**Pat Cosgrave**	William Haggas	57	218
51	302	17	**Richard Kingscote**	Tom Dascombe	56	337
48	239	20	**Graham Gibbons**	David Barron	22	178
44	285	15	**Robert Havlin**	John Gosden	55	211
44	485	9	**Josephine Gordon**	Hugo Palmer	11	41
41	298	14	**Martin Harley**	James Tate	15	78
38	273	14	**Oisin Murphy**	Andrew Balding	31	201
38	298	13	**J F Egan**	David Evans	15	123
37	229	16	**Robert Winston**	Dean Ivory	27	174
33	133	25	**Andrea Atzeni**	Roger Varian	52	242
33	370	9	**William Carson**	Jamie Osborne	14	154
32	350	9	**Liam Keniry**	Neil Mulholland	12	59
30	179	17	**Sean Levey**	Richard Hannon	44	371
29	329	9	**Tom Eaves**	Kevin Ryan	18	153
29	294	10	**Paul Mulrennan**	Michael Dods	26	237
28	181	15	**Jamie Spencer**	David Simcock	30	132
26	162	16	**Jack Mitchell**	Roger Varian	16	103
26	269	10	**Andrew Mullen**	Michael Appleby	26	312
26	154	17	**Daniel Tudhope**	David O'Meara	47	343
26	330	8	**Kieran O'Neill**	Richard Hannon	18	152
25	264	9	**Stevie Donohoe**	Charlie Fellowes	15	92
25	216	12	**Kieren Fox**	John Best	16	169
24	256	9	**Ben Curtis**	Brian Ellison	29	186
24	248	10	**Tony Hamilton**	Richard Fahey	66	528
24	199	12	**Callum Shepherd**	Brian Ellison	11	78
23	171	13	**Martin Dwyer**	William Muir	19	157
23	248	9	**Tom Queally**	James Fanshawe	15	89
23	182	13	**George Downing**	Tony Carroll	23	206
22	329	7	**Shane Kelly**	Richard Hughes	26	238
22	105	21	**Harry Bentley**	Roger Varian	16	95
21	221	10	**Martin Lane**	Jeremy Gask	7	51
21	221	10	**Timmy Murphy**	Richard Hannon	7	22
20	90	22	**James Doyle**	Saeed bin Suroor	23	128
20	237	8	**Tom Marquand**	Richard Hannon	26	209
19	58	33	**Ryan Moore**	Sir Michael Stoute	32	129
19	165	12	**Nathan Evans**	Michael Easterby	34	249
19	225	8	**P J McDonald**	Ann Duffield	18	178
19	207	9	**Rob Hornby**	Andrew Balding	17	74
18	208	9	**Connor Beasley**	Michael Dods	16	128
18	141	13	**Daniel Muscutt**	Marco Botti	12	81
18	149	12	**David Probert**	Andrew Balding	28	191
18	258	7	**Adam Beschizza**	Julia Feilden	7	80

Group 1 records

Year	Winner	Age (if appropriate)	Trainer	Jockey	SP	draw/ran

2,000 Guineas (1m) Newmarket

Year	Winner	Age	Trainer	Jockey	SP	draw/ran
2007	**Cockney Rebel**		G Huffer	O Peslier	25-1	8/24
2008	**Henrythenavigator**		A O'Brien	J Murtagh	11-1	6/15
2009	**Sea The Stars**		J Oxx	M Kinane	8-1	15/15
2010	**Makfi**		M Delzangles	C-P Lemaire	33-1	5/19
2011	**Frankel**		Sir H Cecil	T Queally	1-2f	1/13
2012	**Camelot**		A O'Brien	J O'Brien	15-8f	12/18
2013	**Dawn Approach**		J Bolger	K Manning	11-8f	6/13
2014	**Night Of Thunder**		R Hannon	K Fallon	40-1	3/14
2015	**Gleneagles**		A O'Brien	R Moore	4-1f	16/18
2016	**Galileo Gold**		H Palmer	L Dettori	14-1	1/13

THIS IS a specialist miler's race rather than a stepping stone to the Derby despite the recent success of Camelot and Sea The Stars – prior to the latter there had been a 20-year wait for a horse to do the double. Most winners had proved themselves at two, with 16 of the last 25 having won a Group race including 11 at the highest level. Six of those (Dawn Approach, Frankel, Rock Of Gibraltar, Pennekamp, Zafonic and Rodrigo De Triano) had won the Dewhurst, which tends to be a far better guide than the Racing Post Trophy, with Camelot the only horse to complete that double since High Top in 1973. Favourites had a desperate record until four of the last six winners hit back for punters. There have been just four British-trained winners in 12 years, with only Frankel and Haafhd following up victory in one of the domestic trials since Mystiko in 1991.

1,000 Guineas (1m) Newmarket

Year	Winner	Age	Trainer	Jockey	SP	draw/ran
2007	**Finsceal Beo**		J Bolger	K Manning	5-4f	14/21
2008	**Natagora**		P Bary	C Lemaire	11-4f	3/15
2009	**Ghanaati**		B Hills	R Hills	20-1	7/14
2010	**Special Duty**		C Head-Maarek	S Pasquier	9-2f	18/17
2011	**Blue Bunting**		M Al Zarooni	L Dettori	16-1	16/18
2012	**Homecoming Queen**		A O'Brien	R Moore	25-1	16/17
2013	**Sky Lantern**		R Hannon Sr	R Hughes	9-1	7/15
2014	**Miss France**		A Fabre	M Guyon	7-1	4/17
2015	**Legatissimo**		D Wachman	R Moore	13-2	13/13
2016	**Minding**		A O'Brien	R Moore	11-10f	8/16

COURSE FORM is the key factor in this race and is likely to become even more vital with the Fillies' Mile run at Newmarket for the first time in 2011. Last year's winner Minding followed up victory in that race, while five of the last 15 winners came via the Rockfel; four of the last 14 had been first or second in the Cheveley Park; 2006 winner Speciosa won the Nell Gwyn, in which Sky Lantern was second; Miss France landed the Oh So Sharp Stakes; and Blue Bunting won a Listed race over course and distance the previous October. Punters have hit back a little in recent years, but still ten of the last 19 winners have been priced in double figures. French fillies have a good record, with seven winners since 1993, and Miss France was the first of those not to have Group 1 form as a juvenile.

Lockinge Stakes (1m) Newbury

2007	**Red Evie**	4	M Bell	J Spencer	8-1	7/8
2008	**Creachadoir**	4	S bin Suroor	L Dettori	3-1f	7/11
2009	**Virtual**	4	J Gosden	J Fortune	6-1	10/11
2010	**Paco Boy**	5	R Hannon Sr	R Hughes	8-11f	3/9
2011	**Canford Cliffs**	4	R Hannon Sr	R Hughes	4-5f	4/7
2012	**Frankel**	4	Sir H Cecil	T Queally	2-7f	6/6
2013	**Farhh**	5	S bin Suroor	S de Sousa	10-3	5/12
2014	**Olympic Glory**	4	R Hannon	F Dettori	11-8f	3/8
2015	**Night Of Thunder**	4	R Hannon	J Doyle	11-4jf	3/16
2016	**Belardo**	4	R Varian	A Atzeni	8-1	6/12

IT'S ESSENTIAL to look for horses who have already shown themselves to be Group 1 milers as 18 of the last 22 winners had won at the top level, all but one over the trip, and three of the exceptions had been second. Consequently it has been straightforward to identify the winner as ten of the last 14 favourites have obliged and two of the exceptions were second in the market. Four-year-olds have by far the strongest record, accounting for 21 of the last 30 winners, and fillies can also do well with three winners in the last 12 years. The Sandown Mile is a popular prep race yet Belardo was only the second horse to do the double with 20 other Sandown winners failing.

Coronation Cup (1m4f) Epsom

2007	**Scorpion**	5	A O'Brien	M Kinane	8-1	2/7
2008	**Soldier Of Fortune**	4	A O'Brien	J Murtagh	9-4	7/11
2009	**Ask**	6	Sir M Stoute	R Moore	5-1	8/8
2010	**Fame And Glory**	4	A O'Brien	J Murtagh	5-6f	8/9
2011	**St Nicholas Abbey**	4	A O'Brien	R Moore	Evsf	1/5
2012	**St Nicholas Abbey**	5	A O'Brien	J O'Brien	8-11f	4/6
2013	**St Nicholas Abbey**	6	A O'Brien	J O'Brien	3-10f	3/5
2014	**Cirrus Des Aigles**	8	C Barande-Barbe	C Soumillon	10-11f	7/7
2015	**Pether's Moon**	5	R Hannon	P Dobbs	11-1	5/4
2016	**Postponed**	5	R Varian	A Atzeni	8-11f	3/8

AIDAN O'BRIEN has trained seven of the last 12 winners, led by St Nicholas Abbey's hat-trick. That horse was favourite on every occasion, as were Fame And Glory, Cirrus Des Aigles and Postponed in the last seven years, although history shows that the traditionally small fields for this race can produce plenty of upsets, which was the case again in 2015 with Pether's Moon. The key is to oppose four-year-olds as youngsters are often well fancied yet none have won since 2011, making it just four in 14 years overall.

The Oaks (1m4f) Epsom

2007	**Light Shift**	H Cecil	T Durcan	13-2	11/14
2008	**Look Here**	R Beckett	S Sanders	33-1	13/16
2009	**Sariska**	M Bell	J Spencer	9-4f	5/10
2010	**Snow Fairy**	E Dunlop	R Moore	9-1	15/15
2011	**Dancing Rain**	W Haggas	J Murtagh	20-1	7/13
2012	**Was**	A O'Brien	S Heffernan	20-1	10/12
2013	**Talent**	R Beckett	R Hughes	20-1	3/11
2014	**Taghrooda**	J Gosden	P Hanagan	5-1	9/17
2015	**Qualify**	A O'Brien	C O'Donoghue	50-1	2/11
2016	**Minding**	A O'Brien	R Moore	10-11f	4/9

GUARANTEED STAMINA is more important than proven top-class form for this race, which can make things tricky for punters with four of the last eight winners priced at least 20-1. Aidan O'Brien has won the last two runnings with horses who came via the Guineas, but they were the first winners not to have been tried beyond a mile since Casual Look in 2003. It therefore follows that the 1,000 Guineas has become a weaker guide than was once the case, with Minding the first winner to follow up since Kazzia in 2002 and four failures in between. Prior to Qualify none of the last eight winners had been tried in a Group 1 and six of them had triumphed over at least 1m2f, although none of the trials stands above any other and too much is often made of the Musidora winner, with three beaten favourites since 2008 and Sariska the only one to double up since Reams Of Verse in 1997.

TAGHROODA: had a more typical profile for an Oaks winner than Aidan O'Brien's two subsequent winners, who had both never run beyond a mile

HARZAND: the 12th successive Derby winner from the first three in the betting

The Derby (1m4f) Epsom

2007	**Authorized**	P Chapple-Hyam	L Dettori	5-4f	14/17
2008	**New Approach**	J Bolger	K Manning	5-1	3/16
2009	**Sea The Stars**	J Oxx	M Kinane	11-4	4/12
2010	**Workforce**	Sir M Stoute	R Moore	6-1	8/12
2011	**Pour Moi**	A Fabre	M Barzalona	4-1	7/13
2012	**Camelot**	A O'Brien	J O'Brien	8-13f	5/9
2013	**Ruler Of The World**	A O'Brien	R Moore	7-1	10/12
2014	**Australia**	A O'Brien	J O'Brien	11-8f	12/16
2015	**Golden Horn**	J Gosden	L Dettori	13-8f	8/12
2016	**Harzand**	D Weld	P Smullen	13-2	9/16

MANY HIGH-CLASS colts are beaten here due to lack of stamina and it's important to have a top-class staying sire (12 of the last 14 winners had one with a stamina index of at least 1m1f) plus more stamina on the dam's side. Australia, Camelot and Sea The Stars came via the 2,000 Guineas, but they all had middle-distance pedigrees and 14 of the last 20 winners warmed up in one of the recognised trials with five Dante winners (Golden Horn, Authorized, Motivator, North Light and Benny The Dip) and a runner-up (Workforce), four Leopardstown winners (Harzand, High Chaparral, Galileo and Sinndar), three Chester winners (Ruler Of The World, Kris Kin and Oath) and one Lingfield winner (High-Rise). This is a race for fancied runners, with the last 12 winners coming from the first three in the betting, including three of the last five favourites, and 20-1 hero High-Rise in 1998 the biggest-priced winner in more than 40 years.

Queen Anne Stakes (1m) Royal Ascot

2007	**Ramonti**	5	S bin Suroor	L Dettori	5-1	7/8
2008	**Haradasun**	5	A O'Brien	J Murtagh	5-1	2/11
2009	**Paco Boy**	4	R Hannon Sr	R Hughes	10-3	7/9
2010	**Goldikova**	5	F Head	O Peslier	11-8f	10/10
2011	**Canford Cliffs**	4	R Hannon Sr	R Hughes	11-8	6/7

2012	**Frankel**	4	Sir H Cecil	T Queally	1-10f	8/11
2013	**Declaration Of War**	4	A O'Brien	J O'Brien	15-2	6/13
2014	**Toronado**	4	R Hannon	R Hughes	4-5f	8/10
2015	**Solow**	5	F Head	M Guyon	11-8f	4/8
2016	**Tepin**	5	M Casse	J Leparoux	11-2	12/13

FOUR-YEAR-OLDS once considered Classic contenders fit the bill and this age group has taken 21 of the last 28 runnings. No horse older than five has triumphed since 1976 with Goldikova among some top-class ones to fail when defending her crown in 2010. Six of the last ten winners ran in the Lockinge at Newbury, which is obviously the key trial, and while only Canford Cliffs and Frankel have done the double since Medicean in 2001, 12 of the last 13 winners had previously won a Group 1 at some stage. Toronado was the first horse to ever win the race first time out.

St James's Palace Stakes (1m) Royal Ascot

2007	**Excellent Art**	A O'Brien	J Spencer	8-1	8/8
2008	**Henrythenavigator**	A O'Brien	J Murtagh	4-7f	3/8
2009	**Mastercraftsman**	A O'Brien	J Murtagh	5-6f	3/10
2010	**Canford Cliffs**	R Hannon Sr	R Hughes	11-4j	4/9
2011	**Frankel**	Sir H Cecil	T Queally	3-10f	5/9
2012	**Most Improved**	B Meehan	K Fallon	9-1	15/16
2013	**Dawn Approach**	J Bolger	K Manning	5-4f	5/9
2014	**Kingman**	J Gosden	J Doyle	8-11f	7/7
2015	**Gleneagles**	A O'Brien	R Moore	8-15f	5/5
2016	**Galileo Gold**	H Palmer	L Dettori	6-1	7/7

GUINEAS FORM holds the key to this prize and ten of the last 12 winners had come out on top in one of the Classics. The Curragh is just about the best guide as six Irish 2,000 Guineas winners have followed up in that time compared to five from Newmarket and one from Longchamp (Gleneagles and Henrythenavigator had won at Newmarket and the Curragh) and it's also worth bearing in mind that Frankel is the only Newmarket winner to follow up without a run in between since Bolkonski in 1975. Most Improved is the only winner to have skipped the Classics altogether since Dr Fong in 1998 and the last winner not to have previously run in a Group 1 at all was Shavian in 1990.

Prince of Wales's Stakes (1m2f) Royal Ascot

2007	**Manduro**	5	A Fabre	S Pasquier	15-8f	3/6
2008	**Duke Of Marmalade**	4	A O'Brien	J Murtagh	Evsf	1/12
2009	**Vision D'Etat**	4	E Libaud	O Peslier	4-1	2/8
2010	**Byword**	4	A Fabre	M Guyon	5-2f	5/12
2011	**Rewilding**	4	M Al Zarooni	L Dettori	17-2	6/7
2012	**So You Think**	6	A O'Brien	J O'Brien	4-5f	7/11
2013	**Al Kazeem**	5	R Charlton	J Doyle	11-4	9/11
2014	**The Fugue**	5	J Gosden	W Buick	11-2	7/8
2015	**Free Eagle**	4	D Weld	P Smullen	5-2f	4/9
2016	**My Dream Boat**	4	C Cox	A Kirby	16-1	3/6

A RACE that has altered hugely since gaining Group 1 status in 2000, when Dubai Millennium provided one of the outstanding moments in Royal Ascot history. The race now attracts an international field and 11 of the last 17 winners had won a Group 1 outside Britain and Ireland. That also shows the quality required as three of the six exceptions had won a Group 1 at home, with only My Dream Boat, Free Eagle and Byword not successful at the highest level. Only four of the last 12 winners were trained in Britain as traditional trials such as the Brigadier Gerard Stakes and the Gordon Richards Stakes have waned in influence, although My Dream Boat followed up victory in the latter last year. The Tattersalls Gold Cup is the best pointer with four of the last six horses to try it managing to complete the double.

Gold Cup (2m4f) Royal Ascot

2007	**Yeats**	6	A O'Brien	M Kinane	8-13f	13/14
2008	**Yeats**	7	A O'Brien	J Murtagh	11-8f	7/10
2009	**Yeats**	8	A O'Brien	J Murtagh	6-4f	4/9
2010	**Rite Of Passage**	6	D Weld	P Smullen	20-1	1/12
2011	**Fame And Glory**	5	A O'Brien	J Spencer	11-8f	3/15
2012	**Colour Vision**	4	S Bin Suroor	L Dettori	6-1	5/9
2013	**Estimate**	4	Sir M Stoute	R Moore	7-2f	5/14
2014	**Leading Light**	4	A O'Brien	J O'Brien	10-11f	14/13
2015	**Trip To Paris**	4	E Dunlop	G Lee	12-1	13/12
2016	**Order Of St George**	4	A O'Brien	R Moore	10-11f	10/17

THREE-QUARTERS of a mile longer than any other British or Irish Group 1, this race understandably attracts plenty of real specialists, with Royal Rebel, Kayf Tara, Drum Taps and Sadeem all dual winners since 1988 before Yeats became the first ever four-time winner in 2009. His trainer Aidan O'Brien remains the trainer to follow as he has since won with Order Of St George, Leading Light and Fame And Glory, as well as finishing second with Age Of Aquarius and Kingfisher, and five of his last six winners started their year in the Vintage Crop Stakes at Navan. The other strong trials are the Sagaro Stakes, which has come back into vogue with Estimate and Colour Vision winning both races to match Celeric, Double Trigger, Sadeem, Longboat and Gildoran since the mid-1980s, and the Henry II Stakes, the route taken by eight of the 13 winners prior to Yeats's reign plus the 2015 winner Trip To Paris. Wherever it's been, 14 of the last 17 winners had been successful over 2m. Four-year-olds have won the last five renewals and any older horse has to have proved themselves at the top level already as eight of the last ten older winners had previously landed a Group 1.

Coronation Stakes (1m) Royal Ascot

2007	**Indian Ink**	R Hannon Sr	R Hughes	8-1	12/13
2008	**Lush Lashes**	J Bolger	K Manning	5-1	9/11
2009	**Ghanaati**	B Hills	R Hills	2-1f	5/10
2010	**Lillie Langtry**	A O'Brien	J Murtagh	7-2f	3/13
2011	**Immortal Verse**	R Collet	G Mosse	8-1	11/12
2012	**Fallen For You**	J Gosden	W Buick	12-1	11/10
2013	**Sky Lantern**	R Hannon Sr	R Hughes	9-2jf	16/17
2014	**Rizeena**	C Brittain	R Moore	11-2	7/12
2015	**Ervedya**	J-C Rouget	C Soumillon	3-1	7/9
2016	**Qemah**	J-C Rouget	G Benoist	6-1	11/13

A CHAMPIONSHIP race for three-year-old fillies. The 1,000 Guineas at Newmarket is much the best guide as nine of the last 14 winners had run on the Rowley Mile, with eight achieving a top-seven finish including four fillies who did the double (Sky Lantern, Ghanaati, Attraction and Russian Rhythm). It's generally best to have been off the track since then, though, as just two of the last 23 winners ran in the Newmarket Classic and the

Irish 1,000 Guineas at the Curragh, which often counts against many in the field. The last two winners, both trained by Jean-Claude Rouget, had been first and third in the French Guineas. Any horse who has been stepped up in trip can be opposed as Lush Lashes is the only winner in the last 23 years to have raced over further.

Diamond Jubilee Stakes (6f) Royal Ascot

2007	**Soldier's Tale**	6	J Noseda	J Murtagh	9-1	11/21
2008	**Kingsgate Native**	3	J Best	S Sanders	33-1	15/17
2009	**Art Connoisseur**	3	M Bell	T Queally	20-1	11/14
2010	**Starspangledbanner**	4	A O'Brien	J Murtagh	13-2j	21/24
2011	**Society Rock**	4	J Fanshawe	P Cosgrave	25-1	3/16
2012	**Black Caviar**	5	P Moody	L Nolen	1-6f	15/14
2013	**Lethal Force**	4	C Cox	A Kirby	11-1	15/18
2014	**Slade Power**	5	E Lynam	W Lordan	7-2f	4/14
2015	**Undrafted**	5	W Ward	L Dettori	14-1	6/15
2016	**Twilight Son**	4	H Candy	R Moore	7-2	3/9

A RACE whose whose profile has been steadily on the rise and reached fever pitch with its inauguration into the Global Sprint Challenge alongside the King's Stand Stakes, attracting the best sprinters from around the world, most notably the legendary Black Caviar in 2012. Yet despite Black Caviar and the American winner Undrafted last year, the percentage call is to side with domestic talent as they are the only winners trained outside Britain and Ireland since Cape Of Good Hope in 2005, during which time several fancied foreign raiders – Takeover Target (twice), J J The Jet Plane, Sacred Kingdom, Star Witness and Brazen Beau – have been beaten at 4-1 or shorter. In contrast course form remains critical because, of the last 17 winners at Ascot, eight had already been successful at the course and nine had managed a top-four finish at Royal Ascot. The race throws up more than its share of shocks, with four winners priced 20-1 or bigger in the last nine years, but two of those were among a host of unfancied three-year-olds to run well from very few representatives - including five places at 40-1 or bigger since 2003 – and that age group is now barred from running because of the Commonwealth Cup.

Coral-Eclipse (1m2f) Sandown

2007	**Notnowcato**	5	Sir M Stoute	R Moore	7-1	8/8
2008	**Mount Nelson**	4	A O'Brien	J Murtagh	7-2	8/8
2009	**Sea The Stars**	3	J Oxx	M Kinane	4-7f	6/10
2010	**Twice Over**	5	H Cecil	T Queally	13-8f	1/5
2011	**So You Think**	5	A O'Brien	S Heffernan	4-6f	3/5
2012	**Nathaniel**	4	J Gosden	W Buick	7-2	4/9
2013	**Al Kazeem**	5	R Charlton	J Doyle	15-8f	2/7
2014	**Mukhadram**	5	W Haggas	P Hanagan	14-1	10/9
2015	**Golden Horn**	3	J Gosden	L Dettori	4-9f	1/5
2016	**Hawkbill**	3	C Appleby	W Buick	6-1	3/7

TRADITIONALLY THE first clash of the generations, though in recent times it has suffered from a lack of three-year-old representation. Perhaps the victories of Hawkbill and Golden Horn will make a difference in that respect, especially as the latter became the second Derby winner to succeed following Sea The Stars in 2009 after the previous four to take their chance – Authorized, Motivator, Benny The Dip and Erhaab – were all beaten. Fillies are to be avoided as Pebbles in 1985 is the only one to succeed since the 19th century, since when Bosra Sham and Ouija Board were beaten favourites. Royal

Ascot form is the key, particularly the Prince of Wales's Stakes, although Al Kazeem was the first to do the double since Mtoto 26 years earlier with many horses beaten at Ascot - most recently Mukhadram, So You Think, Twice Over and David Junior - improving on that form.

July Cup (6f) Newmarket

2007	**Sakhee's Secret**	3	H Morrison	S Drowne	9-2	3/18
2008	**Marchand d'Or**	5	F Head	D Bonilla	5-2f	5/13
2009	**Fleeting Spirit**	4	J Noseda	T Queally	12-1	5/13
2010	**Starspangledbanner**	4	A O'Brien	J Murtagh	2-1f	4/14
2011	**Dream Ahead**	3	D Simcock	H Turner	7-1	2/16
2012	**Mayson**	4	R Fahey	P Hanagan	20-1	11/12
2013	**Lethal Force**	4	C Cox	A Kirby	9-2	4/11
2014	**Slade Power**	5	E Lynam	W Lordan	7-4f	13/13
2015	**Muhaarar**	3	C Hills	P Hanagan	2-1jf	7/14
2016	**Limato**	4	H Candy	H Bentley	9-2f	16/18

FIVE OF the last 11 winners were following up victories over the same trip at Royal Ascot – four in the Diamond Jubilee Stakes before Muhaarar from the inaugural Commonwealth Cup – but surprisingly it pays to ignore Group 1 form in other races as nine of the other 11 winners since 2001 were scoring for the first time at the top level. Indeed, this is a race in which stars are often born with 40 of the 49 winners being aged three or four. Often that's because horses are dropping into sprints having been tried over further as stamina is an important asset on this stiff uphill finish. Greats like Ajdal and Soviet Song are memorable for that many years ago and more recently the likes of Limato, Muhaarar and Dream Ahead had run over a mile earlier in the season.

King George VI and Queen Elizabeth Stakes (1m4f) Ascot

2007	**Dylan Thomas**	4	A O'Brien	J Murtagh	5-4f	3/7
2008	**Duke Of Marmalade**	4	A O'Brien	J Murtagh	4-6f	5/8
2009	**Conduit**	4	Sir M Stoute	R Moore	13-8f	8/9

HIGHLAND REEL: the 11th four-year-old to win the King George in 13 years as, unlike in the Coronation Cup, they tend to have improved past their elders

2010	**Harbinger**	4	Sir M Stoute	O Peslier	4-1	1/6
2011	**Nathaniel**	3	J Gosden	W Buick	11-2	3/5
2012	**Danedream**	4	P Schiergen	A Starke	9-1	4/10
2013	**Novellist**	4	A Wohler	J Murtagh	13-2	3/8
2014	**Taghrooda**	3	J Gosden	P Hanagan	7-2	7/8
2015	**Postponed**	4	L Cumani	A Atzeni	6-1	9/7
2016	**Highland Reel**	4	A O'Brien	R Moore	13-8f	3/7

THIS RACE has suffered from a lack of three-year-old representation in recent years, with Taghrooda, Nathaniel, Alamshar and Galileo the only horses of that age to come out on top since Lammtarra in 1995. Taghrooda was an even bigger trends-buster in another way as she became the first British-trained three-year-old filly to win any Group 1 over this trip against older males in the worldwide history of the sport. It generally pays to look for a four-year-old (the age of 11 of the last 13 winners) proven at the top level and the trip because since Belmez in 1990 just four winners hadn't previously landed a Group 1 and just five hadn't been first or second in a Group 1 over 1m4f. The Coronation Cup is a poor guide, though, with only Opera House and Daylami doing the double in more than 40 years.

Sussex Stakes (1m) Goodwood

2007	**Ramonti**	5	Sir M Stoute	L Dettori	9-2	1/8
2008	**Henrythenavigator**	3	A O'Brien	J Murtagh	4-11f	4/6
2009	**Rip Van Winkle**	3	A O'Brien	J Murtagh	6-4f	7/8
2010	**Canford Cliffs**	3	R Hannon Sr	R Hughes	4-6f	7/7
2011	**Frankel**	3	Sir H Cecil	T Queally	8-13f	3/4
2012	**Frankel**	4	Sir H Cecil	T Queally	1-20f	3/4
2013	**Toronado**	3	R Hannon Sr	R Hughes	11-4	7/7
2014	**Kingman**	3	J Gosden	J Doyle	2-5f	4/4
2015	**Solow**	5	F Head	M Guyon	2-5f	5/8
2016	**The Gurkha**	3	A O'Brien	R Moore	11-8f	1/10

THIS IS a great race for glamorous three-year-olds as that age group has provided 29 of the 42 winners since it was opened to all ages in 1975. Nine of the last 12 triumphant three-year-olds were favourites and 11 of the last 13 had been first or second in the St James's Palace Stakes, which is the key trial. Seven of the last nine successful older horses had contested the Queen Anne Stakes, the last three having won it. With Royal Ascot form holding up so well, it's perhaps little wonder that eight of the last nine favourites have obliged, six of them at odds-on.

Nassau Stakes (1m1f192yds) Goodwood

2007	**Peeping Fawn**	3	A O'Brien	J Murtagh	2-1f	5/8
2008	**Halfway To Heaven**	3	A O'Brien	J Murtagh	5-1	6/9
2009	**Midday**	3	H Cecil	T Queally	11-2	10/10
2010	**Midday**	4	H Cecil	T Queally	15-8f	6/7
2011	**Midday**	5	Sir H Cecil	T Queally	6-4f	6/6
2012	**The Fugue**	3	J Gosden	R Hughes	11-4	7/8
2013	**Winsili**	3	J Gosden	W Buick	20-1	15/14
2014	**Sultanina**	4	J Gosden	W Buick	11-2	2/6
2015	**Legatissimo**	3	D Wachman	W Lordan	2-1f	8/9
2016	**Minding**	3	A O'Brien	R Moore	1-5f	1/5

THIS IS another fantastic race for punters as 21 of the last 23 winners emerged from the top three in the market including 14 favourites. The key is to side with a top-class three-year-old as the Classic generation have provided 32 of the 42 winners since the race was opened to older fillies in 1975, despite Midday's best efforts in racking up a hat-trick. Preferably they should be dropping down in trip rather than stepping up as Halfway To Heaven is the only winner to have had her previous run over a mile since 2004, during which time Minding has followed up victory in the Oaks while Legatissimo, The Fugue, Midday and Peeping Fawn all improved on placed efforts at Epsom.

Juddmonte International Stakes (1m2f85yds) York

2007	**Authorized**	3	P Chapple-Hyam	L Dettori	6-4f	1/7
2008	**Duke Of Marmalade**	4	A O'Brien	J Murtagh	4-6f	4/9*
2009	**Sea The Stars**	3	J Oxx	M Kinane	1-4f	3/4
2010	**Rip Van Winkle**	4	A O'Brien	J Murtagh	7-4f	7/9
2011	**Twice Over**	6	Sir H Cecil	I Mongan	11-2	4/5
2012	**Frankel**	4	Sir H Cecil	T Queally	1-10f	7/9
2013	**Declaration Of War**	4	A O'Brien	J O'Brien	7-1	2/6
2014	**Australia**	3	A O'Brien	J O'Brien	8-13f	6/6
2015	**Arabian Queen**	3	D Elsworth	S De Sousa	50-1	5/7
2016	**Postponed**	5	R Varian	A Atzeni	15-8f	6/12

**Note – this race and following two York races all run at Newmarket in 2008*

FAMOUS FOR its many upsets since Brigadier Gerard suffered his only defeat to Roberto in 1972, this race rediscovered its teeth in 2015 when 50-1 shot Arabian Queen stunned the mighty Golden Horn. Otherwise, though, it has turned in punters' favour in recent times with no other winner returned bigger than 8-1 since Ezzoud in 1993 and seven of the last ten favourites winning. Older horses have dominated the three-year-olds with just six younger horses triumphing since 1984, all of whom were recent Group 1 winners apart from Arabian Queen with the previous three being Derby winners. The best trial is the Coral-Eclipse, which has provided nine of the last 23 winners, including six who did the double.

Yorkshire Oaks (1m3f195yds) York

2007	**Peeping Fawn**	3	A O'Brien	J Murtagh	4-9f	8/8
2008	**Lush Lashes**	3	J Bolger	K Manning	Evsf	2/6*
2009	**Dar Re Mi**	4	J Gosden	J Fortune	11-2	4/6
2010	**Midday**	4	H Cecil	T Queally	11-4	6/8
2011	**Blue Bunting**	3	M Al Zarooni	L Dettori	11-4f	6/8
2012	**Shareta**	4	A de Royer-Dupre	C Lemaire	2-1	7/6
2013	**The Fugue**	4	J Gosden	W Buick	2-1f	6/7
2014	**Tapestry**	3	A O'Brien	R Moore	8-1	6/7
2015	**Pleascach**	3	J Bolger	K Manning	8-1	8/11
2016	**Seventh Heaven**	3	A O'Brien	C O'Donoghue	10-3	10/12

ALWAYS A top-class race, this has been won by the Classic generation 11 times in the last 17 years, although older horses have had fewer representatives. However, the last four Oaks heroines to run – Taghrooda, Was, Snow Fairy and Sariska – were all beaten, three of them when favourite, and the last Epsom winner to follow up, Alexandrova, had significantly won the Irish Oaks in between because that has been a better guide. The last six Curragh winners to take their chance have finished 122121, while 2014 heroine Tapestry had finished second in Ireland.

SOLE POWER: the first since 2000 to do the King's Stand/Nunthorpe double

Nunthorpe Stakes (5f) York

2007	**Kingsgate Native**	2	J Best	J Quinn	12-1	13/16
2008	**Borderlescott**	6	R Bastiman	P Cosgrave	12-1	12/14
2009	**Borderlescott**	7	R Bastiman	N Callan	9-1	2/16
2010	**Sole Power**	3	E Lynam	W Lordan	100-1	11/12
2011	**Margot Did**	3	M Bell	H Turner	20-1	11/15
2012	**Ortensia**	7	P Messara	W Buick	7-2jf	8/19
2013	**Jwala**	4	R Cowell	S Drowne	40-1	8/17
2014	**Sole Power**	7	E Lynam	R Hughes	11-4f	10/13
2015	**Mecca's Angel**	4	M Dods	P Mulrennan	15-2	10/19
2016	**Mecca's Angel**	5	M Dods	P Mulrennan	9-2	7/19

THIS HAS become a real race for upsets, none bigger than Sole Power at 100-1 in 2010, and there have also been 20-1 and 40-1 winners since then. The main reason is that the race is rarely won by a proven top-level sprinter, with eight of the last 15 winners never having previously landed a Group race, let alone a Group 1 race, and the King's Stand is less influential than many might think as only Sole Power has done the double since 2000. It's therefore little wonder that progressive younger horses have tended to hold sway, although all six winners older than five since 1945 have come in the last 20 years.

Sprint Cup (6f) Haydock

2007	**Red Clubs**	4	B Hills	M Hills	33-1	4/18
2008	**African Rose**	3	Mme C Head	S Pasquier	7-2f	12/15
2009	**Regal Parade**	5	D Nicholls	A Nicholls	14-1	13/14
2010	**Markab**	7	H Candy	P Cosgrave	12-1	14/13
2011	**Dream Ahead**	3	D Simcock	W Buick	4-1f	9/16

2012	**Society Rock**	5	J Fanshawe	K Fallon	10-1	3/13
2013	**Gordon Lord Byron**	5	T Hogan	J Murtagh	7-2	2/13
2014	**G Force**	3	D O'Meara	D Tudhope	11-1	10/17
2015	**Twilight Son**	3	H Candy	F Sweeney	10-1	5/15
2016	**Quiet Reflection**	3	K Burke	D Costello	7-2f	4/14

THIS CAN often be run on ground with plenty of give, so there have been a string of upsets as midsummer form proves misleading. Of the last 15 winners, just five had previously won a Group 1 and ten were returned in double figures, including 33-1 Red Clubs in 2007. There have been just three winning favourites this century, including Dream Ahead, who was the first July Cup winner to follow up at Haydock since Ajdal in 1987 with Lethal Force, Starspangledbanner and Fleeting Spirit the latest to be beaten jollies in the last seven years.

St Leger (1m6f132yds) Doncaster

2007	**Lucarno**	J Gosden	J Fortune	11-8f	11/11
2008	**Conduit**	Sir M Stoute	L Dettori	8-1	5/14
2009	**Mastery**	S bin Suroor	T Durcan	14-1	7/8
2010	**Arctic Cosmos**	J Gosden	W Buick	12-1	8/10
2011	**Masked Marvel**	J Gosden	W Buick	15-2	3/9
2012	**Encke**	M Al Zarooni	M Barzalona	25-1	1/9
2013	**Leading Light**	A O'Brien	J O'Brien	7-2f	7/11
2014	**Kingston Hill**	R Varian	A Atzeni	9-4f	4/12
2015	**Simple Verse**	R Beckett	A Atzeni	8-1	1/7
2016	**Harbour Law**	L Mongan	G Baker	22-1	9/9

TOP-CLASS horses are increasingly being kept to shorter trips and Kingston Hill is the only winner in more than 25 years to have had his prep run over just 1m2f, though during that time only Leading Light warmed up beyond the Leger distance. Sixteen of the last 19 winners had previously landed a Group race so it's rare for a real dark horse to emerge, though their progress tends to have been steady rather than spectacular – four of the seven winners to come via the Derby since 1997 finished outside the places at Epsom and three of the eight to have warmed up in the Great Voltigeur in that time were beaten there. In the same period Gordon Stakes winners have had more success, with four doing the double, though none since Conduit in 2008. Simple Verse was the first filly to prevail since User Friendly in 1992.

Prix de l'Arc de Triomphe (1m4f) Longchamp

2007	**Dylan Thomas**	4	A O'Brien	K Fallon	11-2	6/12
2008	**Zarkava**	3	A de Royer-Dupre	C Soumillon	13-8f	1/16
2009	**Sea The Stars**	3	J Oxx	M Kinane	4-6f	6/19
2010	**Workforce**	3	Sir M Stoute	R Moore	6-1	8/19
2011	**Danedream**	3	P Schiergen	A Starke	20-1	2/16
2012	**Solemia**	4	C Laffon-Parias	O Peslier	33-1	6/18
2013	**Treve**	3	C Head-Maarek	T Jarnet	9-2	15/17
2014	**Treve**	4	C Head-Maarek	T Jarnet	11-1	3/20
2015	**Golden Horn**	3	J Gosden	L Dettori	9-2	14/17
2016	**Found**	4	A O'Brien	R Moore	6-1	12/16

THE PREMIER middle-distance championship of Europe is generally one for the French, with 17 of the last 27 winners trained at home, although the tide is turning. There hasn't been a successful French-trained colt since Rail Link in 2006 and six of the subsequent ten winners came from abroad, while three of the last seven runners-up were Japanese and it's surely a matter of time before they break their duck. Part of the reason is the poor record of the big domestic trials, with the Prix Niel, having thrown up ten winners in 13 years up to 2006, drawing a blank since then and the Prix Foy enduring an even worse run, with no winner since Subotica in 1992. Fillies are enjoying a remarkable period, with six of the last nine renewals going to the girls. Only four horses older than four have won since the Second World War, with the losers including two recent favourites in Orfevre and Treve.

Queen Elizabeth II Stakes (1m) Ascot

2007	**Ramonti**	5	S bin Suroor	L Dettori	5-1	1/7
2008	**Raven's Pass**	3	J Gosden	J Fortune	3-1	7/7
2009	**Rip Van Winkle**	3	A O'Brien	J Murtagh	8-13f	4/4
2010	**Poet's Voice**	3	S Bin Suroor	L Dettori	9-2	7/8
2011	**Frankel**	3	Sir H Cecil	T Queally	4-11f	2/8
2012	**Excelebration**	4	A O'Brien	J O'Brien	10-11f	6/8
2013	**Olympic Glory**	3	R Hannon Sr	R Hughes	11-2	7/12
2014	**Charm Spirit**	3	F Head	O Peslier	5-1	7/11
2015	**Solow**	5	F Head	M Guyon	11-10f	2/9
2016	**Minding**	3	A O'Brien	R Moore	7-4f	8/13

THE MILE championship of Europe in which the Classic generation has held sway with 22 of the last 32 winners, although Minding was the first filly to win since Milligram in 1987. That has made the St James's Palace Stakes the key trial as seven of the last 15 winning three-year-olds ran there, although Frankel was the first to do the double since Bahri in 1995, while Frankel and George Washington followed up 2,000 Guineas victories. Twelve of the last 14 winners had already won a Group 1 and the last six older winners all contested a Group 1 at Royal Ascot.

Champion Stakes (1m2f) Ascot

2007	**Literato**	3	J-C Rouget	C Lemaire	7-2	8/12
2008	**New Approach**	3	J Bolger	K Manning	6-5f	2/11
2009	**Twice Over**	4	H Cecil	T Queally	14-1	6/14
2010	**Twice Over**	5	H Cecil	T Queally	7-2	4/10
2011	**Cirrus Des Aigles**	5	C Barande-Barbe	C Soumillon	12-1	1/12
2012	**Frankel**	4	Sir H Cecil	T Queally	2-11f	6/8
2013	**Farhh**	5	S Bin Suroor	S de Sousa	11-4	5/10
2014	**Noble Mission**	5	Lady Cecil	J Doyle	7-1	5/9
2015	**Fascinating Rock**	4	D Weld	P Smullen	10-1	7/13
2016	**Almanzor**	3	J-C Rouget	C Soumillon	11-8f	1/10

Run at Newmarket until 2011.

THE SUBJECT of a big-money makeover when switched to Ascot in 2011. Older horses have increasingly come to the fore, accounting for seven of the last eight winners including four five-year-olds. While Almanzor stopped the rot last year, that's a trend likely to grow stronger because, among the 17 successful three-year-olds since 1980, mile form has proved a lot more influential than form over further – 12 of those 17 had won a Classic with New Approach the only one since Time Charter in 1982 to have done it over 1m4f – yet top milers now have the option of the QEII on the same day. There have been just three successful market leaders in 15 years, with seven winners in that time priced in double figures, while this has been the best British Group 1 for French horses, with four winners in the last 11 years extending a long tradition of success.

Big handicap records

Lincoln (1m) Doncaster

Year	Winner	Age	Weight	Trainer	Jockey	SP	Draw/ran
2007	**Very Wise**	5	8-11	W Haggas	J Fanning	9-1	16/20
2008	**Smokey Oakey**	4	8-9	M Tompkins	J Quinn	10-1	12/21
2009	**Expresso Star**	4	8-12	J Gosden	J Fortune	10-3f	9/20
2010	**Penitent**	4	9-2	W Haggas	J Murtagh	3-1f	1/21
2011	**Sweet Lightning**	6	9-4	M Dods	J Murtagh	16-1	16/21*
2012	**Brae Hill**	6	9-1	R Fahey	T Hamilton	25-1	12/22
2013	**Levitate**	5	8-7	J Quinn	D Egan (3)	20-1	3/22
2014	**Ocean Tempest**	5	9-3	J Ryan	A Kirby	20-1	3/17
2015	**Gabrial**	6	9-0	R Fahey	T Hamilton	12-1	15/22
2016	**Secret Brief**	4	9-4	C Appleby	W Buick	12-1	22/22

**Run at Newcastle*

AS WITH all big handicaps, the rating required to get a run gets higher and higher, so long-standing trends about siding with a progressive horse on a low weight have been rendered obsolete. Even so, a big weight is still a huge disadvantage as the last winner to carry more than 9st 4lb was Babodana in 2004. Older horses have come to the fore and the switch hasn't been good news for punters, with Secret Brief the first winning four-year-old since Expresso Star and Penitent made it nine in 16 years for that age group and every winner has been at least 12-1 since those huge gambles. It's common for runners to come via the all-weather or Dubai, but 11 of the last 15 winners were having their first run of the season and it's wise to side with trainers who have a proven track record of getting one ready as four of the last eight winning trainers – Richard Fahey, John Quinn, William Haggas and Mark Tompkins – had also won the race within the previous seven years. A high draw is a concern as nine of the last ten winners at Doncaster came from a stall no higher than 16.

Royal Hunt Cup (1m) Royal Ascot

2007	**Royal Oath**	4	9-0	J Gosden	J Fortune	9-1	13/26
2008	**Mr Aviator**	4	9-5	R Hannon Sr	R Hughes	25-1	26/29
2009	**Forgotten Voice**	4	9-1	J Noseda	J Murtagh	4-1f	25/25
2010	**Invisible Man**	4	8-9	S Bin Suroor	L Dettori	28-1	7/29
2011	**Julienas**	4	8-8	W Swinburn	E Ahern	12-1	24/28
2012	**Prince Of Johanne**	6	9-3	T Tate	J Fahy	16-1	33/30
2013	**Belgian Bill**	5	8-11	G Baker	J Doyle	33-1	6/28
2014	**Field Of Dream**	7	9-1	J Osborne	A Kirby	20-1	33/28
2015	**GM Hopkins**	4	9-3	J Gosden	R Moore	8-1	11/30

2016	**Portage**	4	9-5	M Halford	J Doyle	10-1	4/28

A REAL puzzle for punters with Forgotten Voice in 2009 the only winning favourite in the last 20 years. A common mistake is to side with a lightly raced improver because experience is in fact a vital commodity – 17 of the last 19 winners had run at least eight times, which is more than many of the beaten favourites. The weights had changed markedly even before the further condensing of the handicap caused by the demise of the Buckingham Palace Stakes, with fewer runners getting in below the 9st barrier, so it's telling that Portage (with just 9st 5lb) was the first to carry more than 9st 3lb since 2008, making it three in 28 years to have defied a greater burden. A high draw is generally essential, with only three of the last 14 winners at Ascot overcoming a single-figure berth.

Wokingham (6f) Royal Ascot

2007	**Dark Missile**	4	8-6	A Balding	W Buick	22-1	2/26
2008	**Big Timer**	4	9-2	Miss L Perrett	T Eaves	20-1	1/27
2009	**High Standing**	4	8-12	W Haggas	R Moore	6-1	4/26
2010	**Laddies Poker Two**	5	8-11	J Noseda	J Murtagh	9-2f	26/27
2011	**Deacon Blues**	4	8-13	J Fanshawe	J Murtagh	15-2	11/25
2012	**Dandy Boy**	6	9-8	D Marnane	P Dobbs	33-1	15/28
2013	**York Glory**	5	9-2	K Ryan	J Spencer	14-1	22/26
2014	**Baccarat**	5	9-5	R Fahey	G Chaloner (3)	9-1	27/28
2015	**Interception**	5	9-3	D Lanigan	G Baker	10-1	21/25
2016	**Outback Traveller**	5	9-1	R Cowell	M Harley	10-1	28/28

THIS RACE is run at such a furious gallop that stamina comes to the fore and, while 12 of the last 13 winners had already triumphed over the big-race trip, the exception had done his winning over further – in all nine of those 13 had a 7f victory to their name and 2015 winner Interception had been placed four times at 7f, including in a Listed race. Therefore the Victoria Cup, run over 7f at the same track in May, is one of the key trials, along with the 6f handicaps at Newmarket's Guineas meeting and York's Dante meeting. Fresh horses are preferred, with 11 of the last 15 winners having run no more than twice

PORTAGE: the third Hunt Cup winner in 28 years to carry more than 9st 3lb

ANTIQUARIUM: the fourth successive Plate winner out of lowest four stalls

that year, which is remarkable for a sprint handicap in June. There's nothing to fear about a big weight, but only two winners have been older than five since 1999.

Northumberland Plate (2m) Newcastle

2007	**Juniper Girl**	4	8-11	M Bell	L Morris	5-1f	13/20
2008	**Arc Bleu**	7	8-2	A Martin	A Nicholls	14-1	6/18
2009	**Som Tala**	6	8-8	M Channon	T Culhane	16-1	4/17
2010	**Overturn**	6	8-7	D McCain	E Ahern	14-1	21/19
2011	**Tominator**	4	8-8	R Hollinshead	P Pickard (3)	25-1	14/19
2012	**Ile De Re**	6	9-3	D McCain	J Crowley	5-2f	9/16
2013	**Tominator**	6	9-10	J O'Neill	G Lee	8-1	4/18
2014	**Angel Gabrial**	5	9-1	R Fahey	G Chaloner (3)	4-1f	1/19
2015	**Quest For More**	5	9-4	R Charlton	G Baker	15-2	3/19
2016	**Antiquarium**	4	9-5	C Appleby	J McDonald	16-1	3/20

WITH SO much of the season revolving around Royal Ascot and Newcastle's biggest day of the summer generally coming just a week later, this provides a good opportunity for horses laid out for the race rather than coming here as an afterthought. Just two of the last 14 winners had run at Royal Ascot despite several fancied runners, including four beaten favourites, coming from the royal meeting. Older horses have increasingly come to the fore, with five of the last nine winners aged at least six and two eight-year-olds among the previous eight to triumph. The first bend comes shortly after the start, so those drawn high can be disadvantaged, with 12 of the last 18 winners drawn seven or lower, and Overturn used controversial tactics to overcome that in 2010. The Chester Cup is traditionally a strong guide and that has been reinforced recently with Ile De Re doing the double before Tominator and Angel Gabrial stepped up on placed efforts at Chester. Nine of the last 14 winners were opening their account for the season.

Bunbury Cup (7f) Newmarket

2007	**Giganticus**	4	8-8	B Hills	P Robinson	16-1	16/18
2008	**Little White Lie**	4	9-0	J Jenkins	D Holland	14-1	1/18
2009	**Plum Pudding**	6	9-10	R Hannon Sr	R Moore	12-1	15/19
2010	**St Moritz**	4	9-1	M Johnston	L Dettori	4-1f	4/19
2011	**Brae Hill**	5	9-1	R Fahey	B McHugh	11-1	2/20
2012	**Bonnie Brae**	5	9-9	D Elsworth	R Moore	13-2	12/15
2013	**Field Of Dream**	6	9-7	J Osborne	A Kirby	14-1	20/19
2014	**Heaven's Guest**	4	9-3	R Fahey	T Hamilton	12-1	9/13
2015	**Rene Mathis**	5	9-1	R Fahey	P Hanagan	16-1	10/17
2016	**Golden Steps**	5	9-0	M Botti	L Dettori	7-1jf	14/16

IT'S REMARKABLE how often this race is won by a horse carrying a big weight. Mine, a three-time winner between 2002 and 2006, twice defied a burden of at least 9st 9lb and has been emulated by Bonnie Brae and Plum Pudding since then. Despite that only one of the last 23 winners had won more than once that year – 16 hadn't won at all, including each of the last seven – so the key is clearly to find a horse slipping down the weights but classy enough to still be near the top of the handicap. This is run over a specialist trip and Golden Steps is the only winner not to have already won a handicap over the distance since 2002.

John Smith's Cup (1m2f85yds) York

2007	**Charlie Tokyo**	4	8-12	R Fahey	J Moriarty (3)	11-1	4/17
2008	**Flying Clarets**	5	8-12	R Fahey	F Tylicki (7)	12-1	12/16
2009	**Sirvino**	4	8-8	T Brown	N Brown (3)	16-1	16/18
2010	**Wigmore Hall**	3	8-5	M Bell	M Lane (3)	5-1	13/19
2011	**Green Destiny**	4	8-13	W Haggas	A Beschizza (3)	6-1	17-19
2012	**King's Warrior**	5	8-9	P Chapple-Hyam	R Havlin	33-1	19/18
2013	**Danchai**	4	8-11	W Haggas	A Atzeni	10-1	16/19
2014	**Farraaj**	5	9-11	R Varian	A Atzeni	6-1	22/16
2015	**Master Carpenter**	4	9-4	R Millman	P Makin	14-1	1/17
2016	**Educate**	7	9-8	I Mohammed	T Brown	18-1	14/19

YOUTH SEEMS to be the key to this race, with Educate the only winner older than five – and just three of that age successful – since Vintage Premium in 2002 despite three-year-olds struggling desperately to get a run. Indeed, subsequent Grade 1 winner Wigmore Hall was the only three-year-old when successful in 2010 and none have made the field since. Like the Northumberland Plate, this is another handicap in which missing Royal Ascot is vital, in keeping with ten of the last 14 winners, whereas 13 of the last 15 beaten favourites registered a top-four finish at the royal meeting. This is run on one of the best Saturdays of the summer and, with many top jockeys engaged elsewhere, it provides an opportunity for some younger riders as six of the last 11 winners were partnered by an apprentice.

Stewards' Cup (6f) Goodwood

2007	**Zidane**	5	9-1	J Fanshawe	J Spencer	6-1f	17/27
2008	**Conquest**	4	8-9	W Haggas	D O'Neill	40-1	13/26
2009	**Genki**	5	9-1	R Charlton	S Drowne	14-1	17/26
2010	**Evens And Odds**	6	9-1	D Nicholls	B Cray (5)	20-1	11/28
2011	**Hoof It**	4	10-0	M Easterby	K Fallon	13-2jf	18/27
2012	**Hawkeyethenoo**	6	9-9	J Goldie	G Lee	9-1	4/27

2013	**Rex Imperator**	4	9-4	W Haggas	N Callan	12-1	26/27
2014	**Intrinsic**	4	8-11	R Cowell	R Hughes	6-1	22/24
2015	**Magical Memory**	3	8-12	C Hills	L Dettori	6-1f	1/27
2016	**Dancing Star**	3	8-12	A Balding	D Probert	9-2f	4/27

THIS IS a major betting heat with a strong ante-post market and the betting has become a good guide as nine winners at single-figure odds in 14 years, plus three more not a lot bigger, is a fine record given the size of the field. This is a race for established sprint handicappers and even the two three-year-old winners in the last two years had landed the big 6f handicap for that age group at Newmarket's July meeting. Fourteen of the last 19 older winners came via the Wokingham, though none of them had won at Royal Ascot and all but one had another run in between. That run tends to have been a good one as nine of the last 14 winners finished first or second in their prep race, which is amazing given the competitiveness of sprint handicaps. Only two winners since 1984 carried more than 9st 7lb, while the last winner to have warmed up in Pattern company was Crews Hill in 1981.

Ebor (1m6f) York

2007	**Purple Moon**	4	9-4	L Cumani	J Spencer	7-2f	14/19
2008	**All The Good**	5	9-0	S Bin Suroor	D O'Neill	25-1	7/20*
2009	**Sesenta**	5	8-8	W Mullins	G Carroll (5)	25-1	16/19
2010	**Dirar**	5	9-1	G Elliott	J Spencer	14-1	22/20
2011	**Moyenne Corniche**	6	8-13	B Ellison	D Swift (3)	25-1	10/20
2012	**Willing Foe**	5	9-2	S Bin Suroor	L Dettori	12-1	16/19
2013	**Tiger Cliff**	4	9-0	Lady Cecil	T Queally	5-1	18/14
2014	**Mutual Regard**	5	9-9	J Murtagh	L Steward (5)	20-1	16/19
2015	**Litigant**	7	9-1	J Tuite	O Murphy	33-1	6/19
2016	**Heartbreak City**	6	9-6	T Martin	A McNamara (5)	15-2	15/20

**Run at Newbury as the Newburgh Handicap*

ONE OF the oldest and most famous handicaps, first run in 1847, this has an extremely strong ante-post market and was moved to a Saturday in 2011 to boost its profile further. Sea Pigeon brought the house down when lumping top-weight home in 1979, but low weights are massively favoured and, once taking into account jockeys' claims, just three winners have carried more than 9st 2lb since 1998 and none more than 9st 4lb despite the handicap becoming more and more condensed. Watch out for three-year-olds as they had a tremendous record around the turn of the century and have simply found it increasingly tough to get a run since then, with two of the four to run since 2006, Honolulu and Changingoftheguard, finishing second. Indeed, progressive horses are always preferred with just four winners older than five since Sea Pigeon and ten of the last 14 having raced no more than nine times on the Flat in Britain or Ireland.

Ayr Gold Cup (6f) Ayr

2007	**Advanced**	4	9-9	K Ryan	J Spencer	20-1	22/28
2008	**Regal Parade**	4	8-10	D Nicholls	W Carson (5)	18-1	20/27
2009	**Jimmy Styles**	5	9-2	C Cox	L Dettori	14-1	15/26
2010	**Redford**	5	9-2	D Nicholls	L Dettori	14-1	17/26
2011	**Our Jonathan**	4	9-6	K Ryan	F Norton	11-1	12/26
2012	**Captain Ramius**	6	9-0	K Ryan	P Smullen	16-1	8/26
2013	**Highland Colori**	5	9-4	A Balding	O Murphy (5)	20-1	19/26
2014	**Louis The Pious**	6	9-4	D O'Meara	J Doyle	10-1	19/27
2015	**Don't Touch**	3	9-1	R Fahey	T Hamilton	6-1f	8/25

DANCING STAR: the second successive three-year-old to win the Stewards' Cup – but tellingly both were already proven in a big-field sprint handicap

2016	**Brando**	4	9-10	K Ryan	T Eaves	11-1	8/23

A HISTORIC race first run in 1804, but punters are still struggling to get to grips with it – Don't Touch is the only successful favourite in the last 20 years with no other winner priced in single figures. The key is to ignore winning form as that can mean too much weight, with eight of the last 14 winners having not won in any of their four most recent outings. Nine of the last 11 runnings have gone to major northern yards, with Kevin Ryan leading the way with four victories. The effect of the draw can be gleaned from the consolation races – the Bronze Cup was run for the first time in 2009 and is now on the Friday of the meeting, with the Silver Cup preceding the big one.

Cambridgeshire (1m1f) Newmarket

2007	**Pipedreamer**	3	8-12	J Gosden	J Fortune	5-1f	24/34
2008	**Tazeez**	4	9-2	J Gosden	R Hills	25-1	8/28
2009	**Supaseus**	6	9-1	H Morrison	T Block	16-1	7/32
2010	**Credit Swap**	5	8-7	M Wigham	J Crowley	14-1	3/35
2011	**Prince Of Johanne**	5	8-12	T Tate	J Fahy (3)	40-1	31/32
2012	**Bronze Angel**	3	8-8	M Tregoning	W Buick	9-1	21/33
2013	**Educate**	4	9-9	I Mohammed	J Murtagh	8-1f	4/33
2014	**Bronze Angel**	5	8-13	M Tregoning	L Steward (5)	14-1	11/31
2015	**Third Time Lucky**	3	8-4	R Fahey	A Beschizza	14-1	7/34
2016	**Spark Plug**	5	9-4	B Meehan	J Fortune	12-1	28/31

THE FIRST leg of the Autumn Double. Because of its unusual distance and its straight course, this has thrown up a number of specialists down the years, with dual winner Bronze Angel being the most obvious recent example, so consider horses who have run well in the race before. Many of the runners are milers racing over an extra furlong, but stronger stayers often come to the fore and ten of the last 15 winners had triumphed over 1m2f while Spark Plug had been second in a Listed race at the trip. Handicap experience is vital and 12 of the last 13 winners had won a race of at least 13 runners, 11 of them in a handicap. Big weights spell trouble as Educate is the only horse to carry more than 9st 4lb to victory since Beauchamp Pilot in 2002.

Cesarewitch (2m2f) Newmarket

2007	**Leg Spinner**	6	8-11	A Martin	J Murtagh	14-1	11/33
2008	**Caracciola**	11	9-6	N Henderson	E Ahern	50-1	22/32
2009	**Darley Sun**	3	8-6	D Simcock	A Atzeni (3)	9-2f	8/32
2010	**Aaim To Prosper**	7	8-2	B Meehan	L-P Beuzelin (3)	16-1	3/32
2011	**Never Can Tell**	4	8-11	J Osborne	L Dettori	25-1	36/33
2012	**Aaim To Prosper**	8	9-10	B Meehan	K Fallon	66-1	1/34
2013	**Scatter Dice**	4	8-8	M Johnston	S de Sousa	66-1	18/33
2014	**Big Easy**	7	8-7	P Hobbs	T Queally	10-1	2/33
2015	**Grumeti**	7	8-2	A King	A Beschizza	50-1	15/34
2016	**Sweet Selection**	4	8-8	H Morrison	S de Sousa	7-1	23/33

THE SECOND leg of the Autumn Double. This is another race in which the draw is far more important than you would think from the trip, with only three winners drawn higher than 18 since 1997. Generally punters are too swayed by a young improver as Darley Sun is one of only two winning three-year-olds in 23 years and he was the only favourite to win in the last ten years during a spell that has seen winners returned twice at 66-1 and twice at 50-1 - St Michel was the latest losing favourite from the Classic generation last year. One of the big-priced winners, Aaim To Prosper, reinforced the significance of previous form in the race as he followed up his victory two years earlier. Scatter Dice is the only winner since 1995 not to have already been successful over at least 2m and the success of jumps yards reinforces the importance of proven stamina as just four of the last 21 runnings didn't have a recognised hurdler in the first two. The Northumberland Plate is the best trial having thrown up nine of the last 22 winners.

November Handicap (1m4f) Doncaster

2007	**Malt Or Mash**	3	8-10	R Hannon Sr	R Moore	5-1	13/21
2008	**Tropical Strait**	5	8-13	D Arbuthnot	M Dwyer	20-1	22/21
2009	**Charm School**	4	8-12	J Gosden	J Fortune	17-2	14/23
2010	**Times Up**	4	8-13	J Dunlop	D O'Neill	14-1	9/22
2011	**Zuider Zee**	4	8-13	J Gosden	R Havlin	8-1	20/23
2012	**Art Scholar**	5	8-7	M Appleby	F Norton	20-1	9/23
2013	**Conduct**	6	9-2	W Haggas	S Sanders	8-1	21/23
2014	**Open Eagle**	5	8-12	D O'Meara	D Tudhope	15-2f	18/23
2015	**Litigant**	7	9-10	J Tuite	G Baker	10-1	12/22
2016	**Prize Money**	3	9-1	S bin Suroor	G Wood (5)	4-1	12/15

THE LAST big betting heat of the season and one that has changed in recent years due to the lack of three-year-olds able to get a run. When Malt Or Mash won in 2007 that age group had won 14 of the last 24 renewals and three-year-olds still have to be feared if getting in, as Prize Money proved last year – bear in mind he had run just once as a two-year-old and four of the previous eight had been unraced so all were therefore late developers. However, four of the last five winners were at least five, a massive change given just five of the previous 32 had been older than four. A big weight remains a drawback as eight of the last ten winners carried less than 9st once taking into account jockeys' claims. Eleven of the last 17 winners were returned at double-figure odds and favourites have a desperate record, with Open Eagle the only one to oblige since 1995.

Big-Race Dates, Fixtures and Track Facts

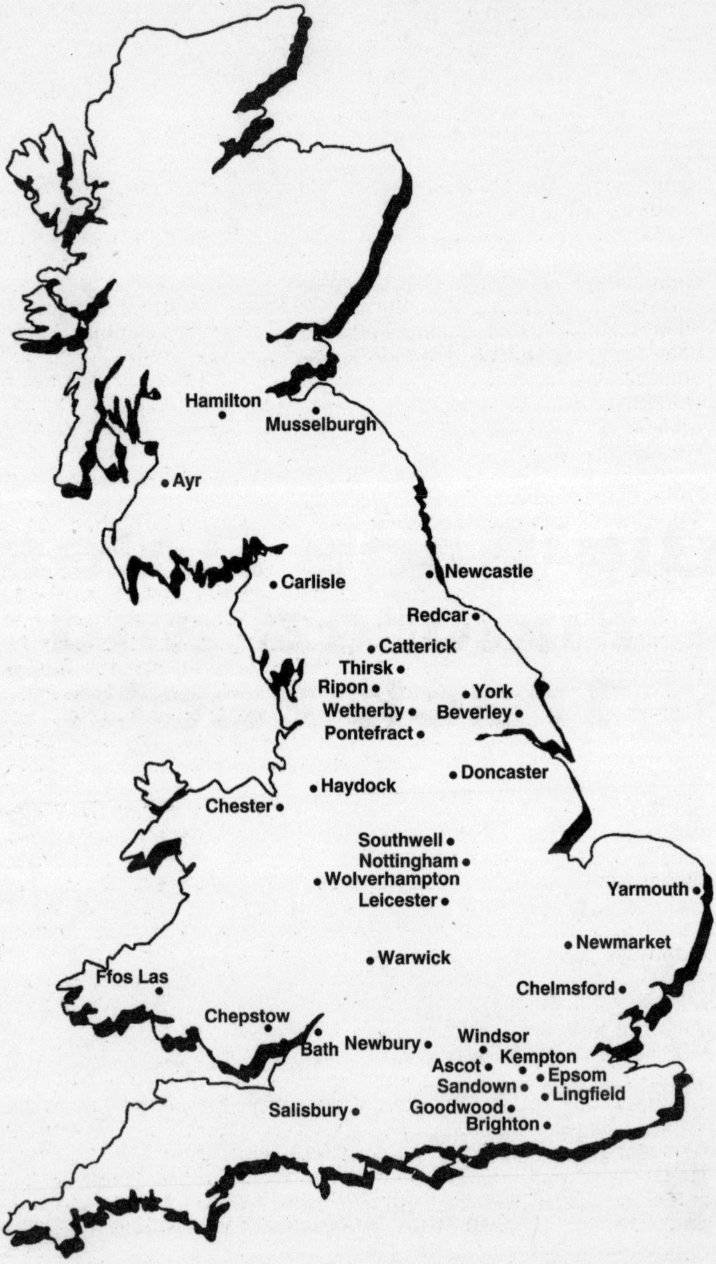
Hamilton
Musselburgh
Ayr
Carlisle
Newcastle
Redcar
Catterick
Thirsk
Ripon
York
Wetherby
Beverley
Pontefract
Doncaster
Haydock
Chester
Southwell
Nottingham
Wolverhampton
Leicester
Yarmouth
Newmarket
Warwick
Ffos Las
Chelmsford
Chepstow
Bath
Newbury
Windsor
Kempton
Ascot
Epsom
Sandown
Lingfield
Salisbury
Goodwood
Brighton

Fixtures

Key - Flat, **Jumps**

April

1 Saturday .... Doncaster, Kempton, **Stratford**, **Uttoxeter**, Chelmsford City
2 Sunday .... **Ascot**, Doncaster
3 Monday .... **Huntingdon**, **Kelso**, **Ludlow**
4 Tuesday .... **Kempton**, **Newton Abbot**, Southwell
5 Wednesday .... **Carlisle**, **Wincanton**, Wolverhampton, Kempton
6 Thursday .... **Aintree**, Southwell, **Taunton**, Chelmsford City
7 Friday .... **Aintree**, Leicester, **Sedgefield**, Kempton
8 Saturday .... **Aintree**, **Chepstow**, Lingfield, **Newcastle**, Wolverhampton
9 Sunday .... **Ffos Las**, **Market Rasen**
10 Monday .... **Kelso**, Redcar, Windsor
11 Tuesday .... **Exeter**, Lingfield, Pontefract
12 Wednesday .... Catterick, **Fontwell**, Nottingham, Kempton
13 Thursday .... Chelmsford City, **Towcester**, **Wetherby**
14 Friday .... Bath, Lingfield, Newcastle
15 Saturday ......**Carlisle**, **Haydock**, Kempton, Musselburgh, **Newton Abbot**,
.... Brighton, **Stratford**
16 Sunday .... **Ffos Las**, **Plumpton**, Southwell
17 Monday .... **Chepstow**, **Fakenham**, **Huntingdon**, **Market Rasen**,
.... **Plumpton**, Redcar, Wolverhampton
18 Tuesday .... **Kempton**, Newmarket, Southwell, **Exeter**, **Ludlow**
19 Wednesday .... Beverley, **Cheltenham**, Newmarket, **Sedgefield**,
.... Wolverhampton
20 Thursday .... **Cheltenham**, Newmarket, Ripon, Lingfield, **Taunton**
21 Friday .... **Ayr**, **Fontwell**, Newbury, Bath, **Southwell**
22 Saturday .... **Ayr**, **Bangor**, Newbury, Thirsk, Nottingham,
.... Wolverhampton
23 Sunday .... **Stratford**, **Wetherby**, **Wincanton**
24 Monday .... Kempton, Pontefract, **Warwick**, Lingfield, Windsor
25 Tuesday .... **Hexham**, **Ludlow**, Yarmouth, Brighton, Wolverhampton
26 Wednesday .... Catterick, Epsom, **Perth**, **Exeter**, Lingfield
27 Thursday .... Beverley, **Perth**, **Taunton**, Chelmsford City, **Market Rasen**
28 Friday .... Doncaster, **Perth**, Sandown, **Chepstow**, **Huntingdon**
29 Saturday .... Haydock, Leicester, Ripon, **Sandown**, Doncaster,
.... Wolverhampton
30 Sunday .... Salisbury, Thirsk

May

1 Monday .... Bath, Beverley, **Kempton**, **Warwick**, Windsor
2 Tuesday .... Brighton, Nottingham, Yarmouth, Chelmsford City,
.... Wolverhampton
3 Wednesday .... Ascot, Pontefract, Wolverhampton, Brighton, Yarmouth
4 Thursday .... Lingfield, Redcar, **Towcester**, Musselburgh, **Sedgefield**
5 Friday .... Chepstow, Lingfield, Musselburgh, **Cheltenham**, **Fontwell**
6 Saturday .... Goodwood, Newmarket, Thirsk, **Uttoxeter**, Doncaster,
.... **Hexham**

7 Sunday....Hamilton, Newmarket
8 Monday....Ayr, Southwell, **Stratford**, Chelmsford City, Windsor
9 Tuesday.... Ayr, **Fakenham**, **Ffos Las**, **Exeter**, Leicester
10 Wednesday.... Chester, **Kelso**, **Newton Abbot**, Bath, Chelmsford City
11 Thursday....Catterick, Chester, **Worcester**, **Carlisle**, **Wincanton**
12 Friday....Chester, Lingfield, **Market Rasen**, Ascot, Nottingham, Ripon
13 Saturday .... Ascot, Haydock, **Hexham**, Lingfield, Nottingham, Thirsk, **Warwick**
14 Sunday.... **Ludlow**, **Plumpton**
15 Monday....Brighton, **Kempton**, Wetherby, **Towcester**, Windsor
16 Tuesday....Beverley, **Sedgefield**, **Wincanton**, Chepstow, **Southwell**
17 Wednesday....**Worcester**, Yarmouth, York, Bath, **Perth**
18 Thursday.... **Perth**, Salisbury, York, **Fontwell**, Newmarket
19 Friday....Newbury, Newmarket, York, **Aintree**, Hamilton, Newcastle
20 Saturday ....**Bangor**, Newbury, Newmarket, Thirsk, Doncaster, **Uttoxeter**
21 Sunday....**Market Rasen**, Ripon, **Stratford**
22 Monday....Carlisle, Redcar, **Towcester**, Leicester, Windsor
23 Tuesday.... Brighton, Newcastle, Nottingham, **Hexham**, **Huntingdon**
24 Wednesday....Ayr, Lingfield, Yarmouth, Kempton, **Southwell**
25 Thursday....Catterick, Goodwood, **Warwick**, Chelmsford City, Sandown
26 Friday....Bath, Goodwood, Haydock, Musselburgh, Pontefract, **Worcester**
27 Saturday ....**Cartmel**, Chester, Goodwood, Haydock, York, **Ffos Las**, Salisbury
28 Sunday....**Fontwell**, **Kelso**, **Uttoxeter**
29 Monday....**Cartmel**, Chelmsford City, **Huntingdon**, Leicester, Redcar, Windsor
30 Tuesday....Leicester, Lingfield, Redcar, **Newton Abbot**, Wolverhampton
31 Wednesday.... Beverley, **Cartmel**, Nottingham, Ayr, Kempton

June

1 Thursday....Hamilton, Lingfield, Wolverhampton, Chelmsford City, **Ffos Las**, Newcastle
2 Friday....Catterick, Epsom, **Market Rasen**, Bath, Doncaster, Goodwood
3 Saturday ....Doncaster, Epsom, **Hexham**, Musselburgh, **Worcester**, Lingfield, Newcastle
4 Sunday....**Fakenham**, **Perth**
5 Monday.... Leicester, **Newton Abbot**, Thirsk, Ayr, Windsor
6 Tuesday....Chepstow, Wetherby, Yarmouth, **Fontwell**, **Southwell**
7 Wednesday.... Hamilton, **Uttoxeter**, Wolverhampton, Kempton, Ripon
8 Thursday.... **Bangor**, Haydock, Ripon, Carlisle, Sandown
9 Friday.... Brighton, Carlisle, Wolverhampton, Goodwood, Haydock, **Stratford**
10 Saturday ....Beverley, Catterick, Chester, Haydock, Newmarket, Chepstow, **Stratford**
11 Sunday.... Goodwood, Nottingham
12 Monday....Ayr, Brighton, Pontefract, Windsor
13 Tuesday....Salisbury, Yarmouth, Lingfield, **Southwell**
14 Wednesday....Haydock, **Worcester**, Yarmouth, Hamilton, Kempton
15 Thursday.... **Fontwell**, Newbury, Nottingham, Haydock, **Uttoxeter**
16 Friday....**Newton Abbot**, Sandown, York, **Aintree**, Chepstow, Goodwood

17 Saturday ....Bath, **Hexham**, Musselburgh, Sandown, York, Leicester, ...Lingfield
18 Sunday............Doncaster, Salisbury
19 Monday............Carlisle, Wetherby, Nottingham, Windsor
20 Tuesday............Royal Ascot, **Stratford**, Thirsk, Beverley, Brighton
21 Wednesday...... Royal Ascot, Hamilton, **Uttoxeter**, Chelmsford City, Ripon
22 Thursday............Royal Ascot, Chelmsford City, Ripon, **Ffos Las**, Lingfield
23 Friday............Royal Ascot, **Market Rasen**, Redcar, Ayr, Bath, Newmarket
24 Saturday ....Royal Ascot, Ayr, Newmarket, Redcar, Haydock, Lingfield
25 Sunday............**Hexham**, Pontefract, **Worcester**
26 Monday............Chepstow, Wolverhampton, **Southwell**, Windsor
27 Tuesday............Beverley, Brighton, Leicester, **Newton Abbot**
28 Wednesday............Carlisle, Salisbury, **Worcester**, Bath, Kempton
29 Thursday............Newcastle, Newmarket, Nottingham, Hamilton, Newbury
30 Friday..... **Cartmel**, Doncaster, Yarmouth, Chester, Newcastle, Newmarket

July

1 Saturday ....Chester, Newcastle, Newmarket, Windsor, York, Doncaster, ...Lingfield
2 Sunday............**Cartmel**, **Uttoxeter**, Windsor
3 Monday............Pontefract, Wolverhampton, Hamilton, Windsor
4 Tuesday............Brighton, Hamilton, Chepstow, **Stratford**
5 Wednesday............**Perth**, Thirsk, **Worcester**, Bath, Kempton
6 Thursday............Haydock, **Perth**, Yarmouth, Epsom, Newbury
7 Friday............Doncaster, **Newton Abbot**, Sandown, Beverley, ...Chelmsford City, Haydock
8 Saturday .... Beverley, Haydock, Leicester, Sandown, Carlisle, Nottingham
9 Sunday............Ayr, **Market Rasen**
10 Monday............Ayr, **Worcester**, Ripon, Windsor
11 Tuesday............Pontefract, Wolverhampton, Brighton, **Uttoxeter**
12 Wednesday............Catterick, Lingfield, Yarmouth, Bath, Kempton
13 Thursday............Carlisle, Doncaster, Newmarket, Epsom, Newbury
14 Friday............ Ascot, Newmarket, York, Carlisle, Chepstow, Musselburgh
15 Saturday ....Ascot, Chester, Newmarket, York, Hamilton, Salisbury
16 Sunday............**Perth**, **Southwell**, **Stratford**
17 Monday............Ayr, Ffos Las, Windsor, Wolverhampton
18 Tuesday............Bath, Beverley, Thirsk, **Worcester**
19 Wednesday............Catterick, Lingfield, **Uttoxeter**, Sandown, Yarmouth
20 Thursday............ Chepstow, Hamilton, Leicester, Doncaster, Epsom
21 Friday............Haydock, Newbury, Nottingham, Hamilton, Newmarket, ...Pontefract
22 Saturday ....**Cartmel**, **Market Rasen**, Newbury, Newmarket, Ripon, ...Haydock, Lingfield
23 Sunday............**Newton Abbot**, Redcar, **Stratford**
24 Monday............Ayr, **Cartmel**, Beverley, Windsor
25 Tuesday............Ffos Las, Musselburgh, Chelmsford City, Nottingham
26 Wednesday............Bath, Catterick, Lingfield, Leicester, Sandown
27 Thursday............Sandown, **Worcester**, Yarmouth, Doncaster, Newbury
28 Friday............Ascot, Thirsk, **Uttoxeter**, Chepstow, Newmarket, York
29 Saturday ....Ascot, Chester, Newcastle, Newmarket, York, Lingfield, ...Salisbury
30 Sunday............ Pontefract, **Uttoxeter**
31 Monday............Ayr, **Newton Abbot**, Windsor, Wolverhampton

August

1 Tuesday........................ Beverley, Goodwood, Yarmouth, **Perth**, **Worcester**
2 Wednesday........................Goodwood, **Perth**, Redcar, Leicester, Sandown
3 Thursday..................Goodwood, Nottingham, **Stratford**, Epsom, Ffos Las
4 Friday .... **Bangor**, Goodwood, Thirsk, Bath, Musselburgh, ... Newmarket
5 Saturday ....Doncaster, Goodwood, Newmarket, Thirsk, Hamilton, ... Lingfield
6 Sunday... Chester, **Market Rasen**
7 Monday...Ripon, Salisbury, Carlisle, Windsor
8 Tuesday...........................Catterick, Leicester, Chelmsford City, Nottingham
9 Wednesday....................... Bath, Brighton, Pontefract, Kempton, Yarmouth
10 Thursday................. Brighton, Haydock, Yarmouth, Newcastle, Sandown, ... Wolverhampton
11 Friday ....Brighton, Musselburgh, Wolverhampton, Haydock, Newmarket
12 Saturday .... Ascot, Haydock, Newmarket, Redcar, Ayr, Lingfield
13 Sunday..Leicester, Windsor
14 Monday... Ayr, Ripon, Windsor, Wolverhampton
15 Tuesday.............................. Ffos Las, Thirsk, Chelmsford City, Nottingham
16 Wednesday........................... Beverley, **Newton Abbot**, Salisbury, **Bangor**, ... Kempton
17 Thursday.....................Beverley, **Fontwell**, Salisbury, Chepstow, Yarmouth
18 Friday ....Newbury, Nottingham, Wolverhampton, Catterick, Newmarket
19 Saturday ....Doncaster, Newbury, Newmarket, **Perth**, Ripon, Bath, ... **Market Rasen**
20 Sunday.. Pontefract, **Southwell**
21 Monday... Lingfield, Thirsk, **Hexham**, Windsor
22 Tuesday.............................. Brighton, Kempton, **Newton Abbot**, Yarmouth
23 Wednesday................................Bath, Carlisle, York, Kempton, **Worcester**
24 Thursday...........................Chepstow, **Stratford**, York, **Fontwell**, Hamilton
25 Friday........... Ffos Las, Newmarket, York, Goodwood, Hamilton, Salisbury
26 Saturday .... **Cartmel**, Chester, Goodwood, Newmarket, York, Redcar, ... Windsor
27 Sunday.. Beverley, Goodwood, Yarmouth
28 Monday..............................**Cartmel**, Chepstow, Epsom, Ripon, Southwell
29 Tuesday..Epsom, Ripon, Carlisle, **Newton Abbot**
30 Wednesday..........Catterick, Lingfield, Musselburgh, Kempton, **Worcester**
31 Thursday....................... Bath, Chelmsford City, Musselburgh, **Sedgefield**, ... Wolverhampton

September

1 Friday...**Bangor**, Sandown, Thirsk
2 Saturday ....Beverley, Chester, **Newton Abbot**, Sandown, ... Chelmsford City, Hamilton
3 Sunday... Brighton, **Worcester**
4 Monday...Brighton, Ripon, Windsor
5 Tuesday..................................Goodwood, Hamilton, **Hexham**, Kempton
6 Wednesday...............................Chepstow, Lingfield, **Southwell**, Kempton
7 Thursday........................Haydock, Salisbury, **Sedgefield**, Chelmsford City
8 Friday.......................Ascot, Haydock, Newcastle, Kempton, Musselburgh
9 Saturday .... Ascot, Haydock, Kempton, **Stratford**, Thirsk, Wolverhampton
10 Sunday.. **Fontwell**, York

THE ROWLEY MILE: returns after its summer break on September 23

11 Monday..Brighton, **Newton Abbot**, **Perth**
12 Tuesday.................................. Catterick, Leicester, **Worcester**, Newcastle
13 Wednesday..................................Carlisle, Doncaster, **Uttoxeter**, Kempton
14 Thursday.................................... Chepstow, Doncaster, Epsom, **Hexham**
15 Friday.. Chester, Doncaster, Sandown, Salisbury
16 Saturday .... Bath, Chester, Doncaster, Lingfield, Musselburgh
17 Sunday.. Bath, Ffos Las
18 Monday.. Brighton, Carlisle, **Worcester**
19 Tuesday...................................Chepstow, Redcar, Yarmouth, Newcastle
20 Wednesday.................................... Beverley, Sandown, Yarmouth, **Kelso**
21 Thursday................................. Ayr, Pontefract, Yarmouth, Chelmsford City
22 Friday.......................................Ayr, Newbury, **Newton Abbot**, Newcastle
23 Saturday ....Ayr, Catterick, Newbury, Newmarket, Wolverhampton
24 Sunday... **Plumpton**, **Uttoxeter**
25 Monday...Hamilton, Kempton, Leicester

26 Tuesday.............................. Beverley, Lingfield, **Warwick**, Chelmsford City
27 Wednesday.......................................Goodwood, **Perth**, Redcar, Kempton
28 Thursday.......................... Newmarket, **Perth**, Pontefract, Chelmsford City
29 Friday..................................Haydock, Newmarket, Newcastle, **Worcester**
30 Saturday ....Haydock, Chester, **Market Rasen**, Newmarket, Ripon,
.... Chelmsford City

October

1 Sunday...Epsom, Musselburgh
2 Monday... Bath, **Newton Abbot**, **Stratford**
3 Tuesday... Ayr, **Sedgefield**, **Southwell**, Kempton
4 Wednesday.............................. **Bangor**, Nottingham, Salisbury, Kempton
5 Thursday......................**Huntingdon**, Lingfield, **Warwick**, Chelmsford City
6 Friday....................................Ascot, **Fontwell**, **Hexham**, Chelmsford City
7 Saturday .... Ascot, **Fontwell**, Newmarket, Redcar, Wolverhampton
8 Sunday... **Kelso**, **Uttoxeter**
9 Monday...Pontefract, Salisbury, Windsor
10 Tuesday..Brighton, Catterick, Leicester, Newcastle
11 Wednesday.............................**Ludlow**, Nottingham, **Towcester**, Kempton
12 Thursday.......................................Ayr, **Exeter**, **Worcester**, Chelmsford City
13 Friday..................................Newmarket, **Newton Abbot**, York, Kempton
14 Saturday ....**Chepstow**, **Hexham**, Newmarket, York, Kempton
15 Sunday.. **Chepstow**, Goodwood
16 Monday...Musselburgh, Windsor, Yarmouth
17 Tuesday.................................**Hereford**, **Huntingdon**, Leicester, Kempton
18 Wednesday..................................Bath, Nottingham, **Wetherby**, Kempton
19 Thursday.......................................Brighton, **Carlisle**, **Uttoxeter**, Newcastle
20 Friday.......................**Fakenham**, Haydock, Redcar, **Wincanton**, Newcastle
21 Saturday .... Ascot, Catterick, **Ffos Las**, **Market Rasen**, **Stratford**,
.... Wolverhampton
22 Sunday.. **Kempton**, Southwell
23 Monday.. **Plumpton**, Pontefract, Windsor
24 Tuesday..**Exeter**, Newcastle, Yarmouth, Kempton
25 Wednesday....................... Newmarket, **Sedgefield**, **Worcester**, Kempton
26 Thursday...........................**Carlisle**, **Ludlow**, **Southwell**, Chelmsford City
27 Friday......................... **Cheltenham**, Doncaster, Newbury, Wolverhampton
28 Saturday ....**Cheltenham**, Doncaster, **Kelso**, Newbury, Wolverhampton
29 Sunday...**Aintree**, **Wincanton**
30 Monday...**Ayr**, Leicester, Redcar
31 Tuesday........................... **Bangor**, Catterick, **Chepstow**, Wolverhampton

November

1 Wednesday........................... **Fakenham**, Nottingham, **Taunton**, Kempton
2 Thursday........................Lingfield, **Sedgefield**, **Stratford**, Chelmsford City
3 Friday..................................Newmarket, **Uttoxeter**, **Wetherby**, Newcastle
4 Saturday .... **Ascot**, **Ayr**, Newmarket, **Wetherby**, Newcastle
5 Sunday.. **Carlisle**, **Huntingdon**
6 Monday.. Kempton, **Plumpton**, **Southwell**
7 Tuesday.....................................**Exeter**, Redcar, Wolverhampton, Kempton
8 Wednesday...................**Chepstow**, **Musselburgh**, Nottingham, Kempton
9 Thursday...................**Ludlow**, **Market Rasen**, **Newbury**, Chelmsford City
10 Friday...**Fontwell**, **Hexham**, **Warwick**, Newcastle
11 Saturday ....**Aintree**, Doncaster, **Kelso**, **Wincanton**, Wolverhampton

12 Sunday .... **Ffos Las**, **Sandown**
13 Monday .... **Carlisle**, **Kempton**, Southwell
14 Tuesday .... **Hereford**, **Huntingdon**, **Lingfield**
15 Wednesday .... **Ayr**, **Bangor**, **Exeter**, Newcastle
16 Thursday .... **Ludlow**, Southwell, **Taunton**, Chelmsford City
17 Friday .... **Cheltenham**, Lingfield, **Newcastle**, Chelmsford City
18 Saturday ... **Cheltenham**, Lingfield, **Uttoxeter**, **Wetherby**, Wolverhampton
19 Sunday .... **Cheltenham**, **Fontwell**
20 Monday .... **Leicester**, **Plumpton**, Wolverhampton
21 Tuesday .... **Fakenham**, Lingfield, **Southwell**
22 Wednesday .... **Chepstow**, **Hexham**, **Warwick**, Kempton
23 Thursday .... **Market Rasen**, Newcastle, **Wincanton**, Chelmsford City
24 Friday .... **Ascot**, **Catterick**, **Ffos Las**, Newcastle
25 Saturday .... **Ascot**, **Haydock**, **Huntingdon**, Lingfield, Wolverhampton
26 Sunday .... **Exeter**, **Uttoxeter**
27 Monday .... **Ayr**, **Kempton**, **Ludlow**
28 Tuesday .... **Lingfield**, **Sedgefield**, Southwell
29 Wednesday .... **Hereford**, **Wetherby**, Wolverhampton, Kempton
30 Thursday .... **Musselburgh**, **Taunton**, **Towcester**, Newcastle

December

1 Friday .... **Doncaster**, **Newbury**, Southwell, Chelmsford City
2 Saturday .... **Bangor**, **Doncaster**, **Newbury**, **Newcastle**, ... Wolverhampton
3 Sunday .... **Carlisle**, **Leicester**
4 Monday .... **Fakenham**, **Plumpton**, Southwell
5 Tuesday .... **Lingfield**, **Southwell**, Wolverhampton
6 Wednesday .... **Haydock**, Lingfield, **Ludlow**, Newcastle
7 Thursday .... **Leicester**, **Market Rasen**, **Wincanton**, Chelmsford City
8 Friday .... **Exeter**, **Sandown**, **Sedgefield**, Chelmsford City
9 Saturday .... **Aintree**, **Chepstow**, **Sandown**, **Wetherby**, Wolverhampton
10 Sunday .... **Huntingdon**, **Kelso**
11 Monday .... **Fontwell**, **Musselburgh**, Southwell
12 Tuesday .... **Ayr**, Lingfield, **Uttoxeter**
13 Wednesday .... **Hexham**, **Leicester**, Lingfield, Kempton
14 Thursday .... **Newcastle**, **Taunton**, **Warwick**, Chelmsford City
15 Friday .... **Bangor**, **Cheltenham**, **Doncaster**, Chelmsford City
16 Saturday .... **Cheltenham**, **Doncaster**, **Hereford**, Newcastle, ... Wolverhampton
17 Sunday .... **Carlisle**, **Southwell**
18 Monday .... **Ffos Las**, **Plumpton**, Wolverhampton
19 Tuesday .... **Catterick**, **Fakenham**, Southwell
20 Wednesday .... Lingfield, **Ludlow**, **Newbury**, Kempton
21 Thursday .... **Exeter**, Southwell, **Towcester**, Chelmsford City
22 Friday .... **Ascot**, Southwell, **Uttoxeter**, Wolverhampton
23 Saturday .... **Ascot**, **Haydock**, Lingfield, **Newcastle**
26 Tuesday.... **Fontwell**, **Huntingdon**, **Kempton**, **Market Rasen**, **Sedgefield**, ... **Wetherby**, **Wincanton**, Wolverhampton
27 Wednesday .... **Chepstow**, **Kempton**, **Wetherby**, Wolverhampton
28 Thursday .... **Catterick**, **Leicester**, Lingfield
29 Friday .... **Doncaster**, **Kelso**, Southwell
30 Saturday .... **Haydock**, Lingfield, **Newbury**, **Taunton**
31 Sunday .... Lingfield, **Uttoxeter**, **Warwick**

ig-race dates

April

1 Apr	Doncaster	Lincoln (Heritage Handicap)
14 Apr	Lingfield	All-Weather Championship Finals
18 Apr	Newmarket	Nell Gwyn Stakes (Group 3)
19 Apr	Newmarket	Earl of Sefton Stakes (Group 3)
20 Apr	Newmarket	Craven Stakes (Group 3)
22 Apr	Newbury	Fred Darling Stakes (Group 3)
22 Apr	Newbury	Greenham Stakes (Group 3)
22 Apr	Newbury	John Porter Stakes (Group 3)
28 Apr	Sandown	Gordon Richards Stakes (Group 3)
28 Apr	Sandown	bet365 Mile (Group 2)

May

3 May	Ascot	Sagaro Stakes (Group 3)
6 May	Newmarket	2,000 Guineas (Group 1)
6 May	Newmarket	Dahlia Stakes (Group 3)
7 May	Newmarket	1,000 Guineas (Group 1)
7 May	Newmarket	Jockey Club Stakes (Group 2)
10 May	Chester	Chester Cup (Heritage Handicap)
11 May	Chester	Chester Vase (Group 3)
11 May	Chester	Huxley Stakes (Group 3)
12 May	Chester	Ormonde Stakes (Group 3)
13 May	Ascot	Victoria Cup (Heritage Handicap)
13 May	Lingfield	Derby Trial (Group 3)
17 May	York	Duke of York Stakes (Group 2)
17 May	York	Musidora Stakes (Group 3)
18 May	York	Dante Stakes (Group 2)
18 May	York	Middleton Stakes (Group 3)
19 May	York	Yorkshire Cup (Group 2)
20 May	Newbury	Lockinge Stakes (Group 1)
25 May	Sandown	Henry II Stakes (Group 2)
25 May	Sandown	Brigadier Gerard Stakes (Group 3)
27 May	Haydock	Temple Stakes (Group 2)

June

2 Jun	Epsom	The Oaks (Group 1)
2 Jun	Epsom	Princess Elizabeth Stakes (Group 3)
3 Jun	Epsom	The Derby (Group 1)
3 Jun	Epsom	Coronation Cup (Group 1)
10 Jun	Haydock	Sandy Lane Stakes (Group 2)
10 Jun	Haydock	John of Gaunt Stakes (Group 3)
10 Jun	Haydock	Pinnacle Stakes (Group 3)
20 Jun	Royal Ascot	King's Stand Stakes (Group 1)
20 Jun	Royal Ascot	Queen Anne Stakes (Group 1)
20 Jun	Royal Ascot	St James's Palace Stakes (Group 1)
20 Jun	Royal Ascot	Coventry Stakes (Group 2)
21 Jun	Royal Ascot	Prince of Wales's Stakes (Group 1)
21 Jun	Royal Ascot	Queen Mary Stakes (Group 2)
21 Jun	Royal Ascot	Windsor Forest Stakes (Group 2)
21 Jun	Royal Ascot	Jersey Stakes (Group 3)
21 Jun	Royal Ascot	Royal Hunt Cup (Heritage Handicap)
22 Jun	Royal Ascot	Gold Cup (Group 1)

22 Jun	Royal Ascot	Ribblesdale Stakes (Group 2)
22 Jun	Royal Ascot	Norfolk Stakes (Group 2)
23 Jun	Royal Ascot	Coronation Stakes (Group 1)
23 Jun	Royal Ascot	Commonwealth Cup (Group 1)
23 Jun	Royal Ascot	King Edward VII Stakes (Group 2)
23 Jun	Royal Ascot	Albany Stakes (Group 3)
24 Jun	Royal Ascot	Golden Jubilee Stakes (Group 1)
24 Jun	Royal Ascot	Hardwicke Stakes (Group 2)
24 Jun	Royal Ascot	Wokingham (Heritage Handicap)

July

1 Jul	Newcastle	Chipchase Stakes (Group 3)
1 Jul	Newcastle	Northumberland Plate (Heritage Handicap)
1 Jul	Newmarket	Criterion Stakes (Group 3)
8 Jul	Sandown	Coral-Eclipse Stakes (Group 1)
8 Jul	Haydock	Lancashire Oaks (Group 2)
13 Jul	Newmarket	Falmouth Stakes (Group 1)
13 Jul	Newmarket	Cherry Hinton Stakes (Group 2)
14 Jul	Newmarket	Princess of Wales's Stakes (Group 2)
14 Jul	Newmarket	July Stakes (Group 2)
14 Jul	York	Summer Stakes (Group 3)
15 Jul	Newmarket	July Cup (Group 1)
15 Jul	Newmarket	Superlative Stakes (Group 2)
15 Jul	Newmarket	Bunbury Cup (Heritage Handicap)
15 Jul	York	John Smith's Cup (Heritage Handicap)
22 Jul	Newbury	Hackwood Stakes (Group 3)
29 Jul	Ascot	King George VI and Queen Elizabeth Stakes (Group 1)
29 Jul	Ascot	Summer Mile (Group 2)
29 Jul	York	York Stakes (Group 2)

August

1 Aug	Goodwood	Lennox Stakes (Group 2)
1 Aug	Goodwood	Vintage Stakes (Group 2)
2 Aug	Goodwood	Sussex Stakes (Group 1)
2 Aug	Goodwood	Gordon Stakes (Group 3)
2 Aug	Goodwood	Molecomb Stakes (Group 3)
3 Aug	Goodwood	Goodwood Cup (Group 2)
3 Aug	Goodwood	King George Stakes (Group 3)
3 Aug	Goodwood	Richmond Stakes (Group 2)
4 Aug	Goodwood	Betfred Mile (Heritage Handicap)
4 Aug	Goodwood	Oak Tree Stakes (Group 3)
5 Aug	Goodwood	Nassau Stakes (Group 1)
5 Aug	Goodwood	Stewards' Cup (Heritage Handicap)
12 Aug	Ascot	Shergar Cup Day
12 Aug	Haydock	Rose of Lancaster Stakes (Group 3)
12 Aug	Newmarket	Sweet Solera Stakes (Group 3)
17 Aug	Salisbury	Sovereign Stakes (Group 3)
19 Aug	Newbury	Hungerford Stakes (Group 2)
19 Aug	Newbury	Geoffrey Freer Stakes (Group 3)
23 Aug	York	Juddmonte International (Group 1)
23 Aug	York	Great Voltigeur Stakes (Group 2)
23 Aug	York	Acomb Stakes (Group 3)
24 Aug	York	Yorkshire Oaks (Group 1)
24 Aug	York	Lowther Stakes (Group 2)
25 Aug	York	Nunthorpe Stakes (Group 1)
25 Aug	York	Lonsdale Cup (Group 2)

26 Aug	York	Ebor (Heritage Handicap)
26 Aug	York	Lonsdale Cup (Group 2)
26 Aug	Goodwood	Celebration Mile (Group 2)
26 Aug	Goodwood	Prestige Stakes (Group 3)
26 Aug	Windsor	Winter Hill Stakes (Group 3)
27 Aug	Goodwood	Supreme Stakes (Group 3)

September

2 Sep	Sandown	Solario Stakes (Group 3)
9 Sep	Haydock	Sprint Cup (Group 1)
9 Sep	Kempton	Sirenia Stakes (Group 3)
9 Sep	Kempton	September Stakes (Group 3)
14 Sep	Doncaster	May Hill Stakes (Group 2)
14 Sep	Doncaster	Park Hill Stakes (Group 2)
15 Sep	Doncaster	Doncaster Cup (Group 2)
15 Sep	Doncaster	Flying Childers Stakes (Group 2)
16 Sep	Doncaster	St Leger (Group 1)
16 Sep	Doncaster	Park Stakes (Group 2)
16 Sep	Doncaster	Champagne Stakes (Group 2)
16 Sep	Doncaster	Portland (Heritage Handicap)
23 Sep	Ayr	Ayr Gold Cup (Heritage Handicap)
23 Sep	Ayr	Firth Of Clyde Stakes (Group 3)
23 Sep	Newbury	Mill Reef Stakes (Group 2)
23 Sep	Newbury	World Trophy (Group 3)
23 Sep	Newbury	Arc Trial (Group 3)
28 Sep	Newmarket	Somerville Tattersall Stakes (Group 3)
29 Sep	Newmarket	Rockfel Stakes (Group 2)
29 Sep	Newmarket	Joel Stakes (Group 2)
30 Sep	Newmarket	Cambridgeshire (Heritage Handicap)
30 Sep	Newmarket	Middle Stakes (Group 1)
30 Sep	Newmarket	Cheveley Stakes (Group 1)
30 Sep	Newmarket	Royal Lodge Stakes (Group 2)

October

7 Oct	Newmarket	Sun Chariot Stakes (Group 1)
7 Oct	Ascot	Cumberland Lodge Stakes (Group 3)
7 Oct	Ascot	Bengough Stakes (Group 3)
13 Oct	Newmarket	Fillies' Mile (Group 1)
13 Oct	Newmarket	Challenge Stakes (Group 2)
13 Oct	Newmarket	Cornwallis Stakes (Group 3)
13 Oct	Newmarket	Oh So Sharp Stakes (Group 3)
14 Oct	Newmarket	Cesarewitch (Heritage Handicap)
14 Oct	Newmarket	Dewhurst Stakes (Group 1)
14 Oct	Newmarket	Autumn Stakes (Group 3)
14 Oct	Newmarket	Darley Stakes (Group 3)
21 Oct	Ascot	Queen Elizabeth II Stakes (Group 1)
21 Oct	Ascot	Champion Stakes (Group 1)
21 Oct	Ascot	Champions Sprint (Group 2)
21 Oct	Ascot	Champions Filly & Mare Stakes (Group 2)
21 Oct	Ascot	Champions Long Distance Cup (Group 3)
28 Oct	Doncaster	Racing Post Trophy (Group 1)
28 Oct	Newbury	Horris Hill Stakes (Group 3)
28 Oct	Newbury	St Simon Stakes (Group 3)

November

11 Nov	Doncaster	November (Heritage Handicap)

Track Facts

WANT TO size up the layout and undulations of the course where your fancy's about to line up? Over the next 30-odd pages, we bring you three-dimensional maps of all Britain's Flat tracks, allowing you to see at a glance the task facing your selection. The maps come to you courtesy of the Racing Post's website (www.racingpost.com).

We've listed the top dozen trainers and jockeys at each course, ranked by strike-rate, with a breakdown of their relevant statistics over the last five years. We've also included addresses, phone numbers, directions and fixture lists for each track, together with Racing Post standard times for all you clock-watchers.

ASCOT

Ascot, Berkshire SL5 7JX
Tel 0870 7227 227

How to get there Road: M4 junction 6 or M3 junction 3 on to A332. Rail: Frequent service from Reading or Waterloo

Features RH, stiff climb for final mile on round course

2017 Fixtures May 3, 12-13, June 20-24, July 14-15, 28-29, August 12, September 8-9, October 6-7, 21

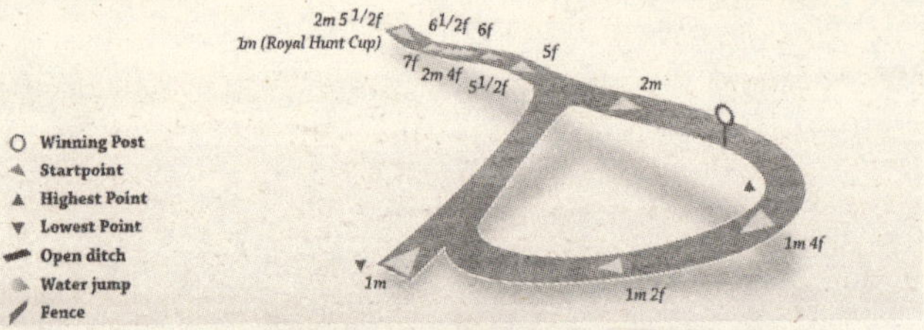

Racing Post standard times

5f	59.5	1m2f	2min5
6f	1min12.4	1m4f	2min28.9
7f	1min25.6	2m	3min22
1m (str)	1min38.8	2m4f	4min20
1m (rnd)	1min39.8	2m5f159yds	4min45

Trainers	*Wins-Runs*	*%*	*2yo*	*3yo+*	*£1 level stks*
John Gosden	35-208	17	5-24	30-184	+14.82
Mark Johnston	25-274	9	5-66	20-208	-63.47
A P O'Brien	23-143	16	6-28	17-115	+40.41
Sir Michael Stoute	22-154	14	1-7	21-147	-8.13
Richard Hannon	20-242	8	13-81	7-161	-121.95
Saeed bin Suroor	20-141	14	5-23	15-118	-5.58
William Haggas	16-176	9	4-35	12-141	-83.13
Richard Hannon Snr	16-167	10	8-77	8-90	-93.26
Roger Varian	15-108	14	3-17	12-91	+18.50
Roger Charlton	15-65	23	2-9	13-56	+14.65
Andrew Balding	13-197	7	0-20	13-177	-107.25
Marco Botti	12-86	14	2-9	10-77	-1.25
Charlie Appleby	10-100	10	4-17	6-83	-25.80

Jockeys	*Wins-Rides*	*%*	*£1 level stks*	*Best Trainer*	*W-R*
Ryan Moore	50-270	19	-20.91	A P O'Brien	12-56
William Buick	33-235	14	-32.13	John Gosden	15-80
James Doyle	26-188	14	-4.15	Roger Charlton	6-27
Jamie Spencer	24-216	11	-27.25	Jamie Osborne	3-7
Richard Hughes	24-209	11	-66.21	Richard Hannon Snr	10-58
Frankie Dettori	21-194	11	-77.46	John Gosden	6-32
Martin Harley	18-170	11	-21.38	Marco Botti	5-32
Tom Queally	16-124	13	+25.62	James Fanshawe	3-16
Adam Kirby	13-141	9	-8.97	Clive Cox	7-50
Joe Fanning	12-143	8	-13.09	Mark Johnston	12-109
Andrea Atzeni	12-128	9	-23.38	Roger Varian	4-32
Paul Hanagan	11-204	5	-145.50	John Gosden	3-15
Jimmy Fortune	11-176	6	-114.25	Brian Meehan	3-45

Favourites

2yo 34% -9.67 | 3yo 32.5% +12.40 | TOTAL 30% -28.50

Whitletts Road Ayr KA8 0JE.
Tel 01292 264 179

AYR

How to get there
Road: south from Glasgow on A77 or A75, A70, A76.
Rail: Ayr, bus service from station on big race days

Features LH

2017 Fixtures
May 8-9, 24, 31, June 5, 12, 23-24, July 9-10, 17, 24, 31, August 12, 14, September 21-23, October 3, 12

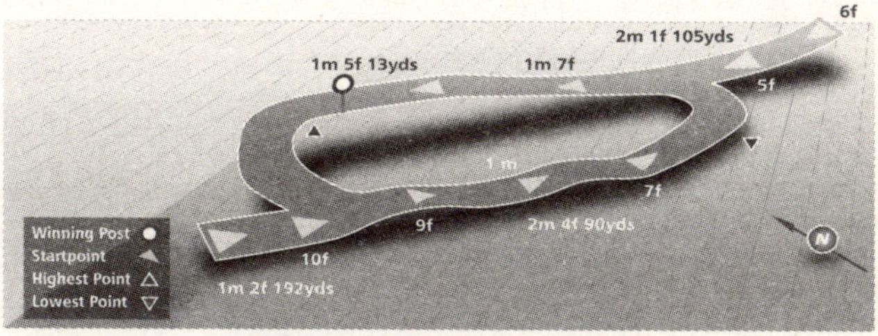

Racing Post standard times

5f	57.7	1m2f192yds	2min17.5
6f	1min10	1m5f13yds	2min47
7f50yds	1min28	1m7f	3min15
1m	1min38	2m1f105yds	3min49
1m1f20yds	1min51	2m4f90yds	4min31
1m2f	2min6		

Trainers	*Wins-Runs*	*%*	*2yo*	*3yo+*	*£1 level stks*
Jim Goldie	56-600	9	0-20	56-580	-105.54
Keith Dalgleish	53-390	14	13-82	40-308	+14.38
Richard Fahey	38-393	10	11-99	27-294	-94.88
David O'Meara	31-182	17	1-17	30-165	-10.08
Linda Perratt	26-353	7	0-8	26-345	-65.75
Michael Dods	26-240	11	5-39	21-201	-33.13
Ruth Carr	19-163	12	0-3	19-160	-20.05
Kevin Ryan	18-185	10	11-65	7-120	-60.40
Mark Johnston	18-158	11	9-69	9-89	-90.00
K R Burke	17-93	18	7-30	10-63	+8.56
Tim Easterby	15-135	11	3-20	12-115	-42.60
John Quinn	15-79	19	5-23	10-56	+9.88
Brian Ellison	14-94	15	0-8	14-86	-30.97

Jockeys	*Wins-Rides*	*%*	*£1 level stks*	*Best Trainer*	*W-R*
Graham Lee	41-352	12	-29.62	Jim Goldie	23-169
Paul Mulrennan	38-251	15	-33.16	Michael Dods	14-102
Daniel Tudhope	36-207	17	-4.18	David O'Meara	17-98
Phillip Makin	35-218	16	+17.35	Keith Dalgleish	18-93
Tom Eaves	30-250	12	+50.25	Keith Dalgleish	12-97
Joe Fanning	29-218	13	-77.96	Mark Johnston	12-85
James Sullivan	21-189	11	-17.55	Ruth Carr	17-108
P J McDonald	19-242	8	-91.50	Alistair Whillans	5-19
Jason Hart	18-121	15	-1.44	Shaun Harris	4-9
Robert Winston	15-73	21	+14.08	Charles Hills	6-13
Tony Hamilton	13-189	7	-94.84	Richard Fahey	12-147
Fergal Lynch	12-107	11	+6.00	Jim Goldie	8-85
Connor Beasley	11-156	7	-79.25	Michael Dods	4-64

Favourites
2yo 33.3% -23.07 3yo 28.8% -16.21 TOTAL 28% -107.69

BATH

Lansdown, Bath, Glos BA1 9BU
Tel 01291 622 260

How to get there
Road: M4, Jctn 18, then A46 south.
Rail: Bath Spa, special bus service to course on race days

Features LH uphill 4f straight

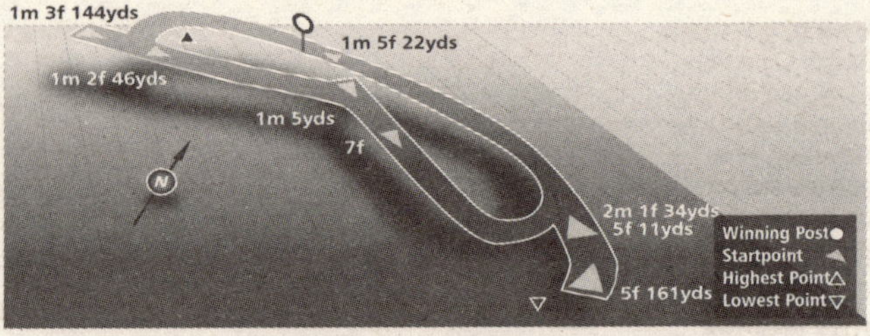

2017 Fixtures April 14, 21, May 1, 10, 17, 26, June 2, 17, 23, 28, July 5, 12, 18, 26, August 4, 9, 19, 23, 31, September 16-17, October 2, 18

Racing Post standard times

5f11yds	1min0.8	1m3f144yds	2min28
5f161yds	1min9.6	1m5f22yds	2min48.5
1m5yds	1min39	2m1f34yds	3min40
1m2f46yds	2min8		

Trainers	*Wins-Runs*	*%*	*2yo*	*3yo+*	*£1 level stks*
Mick Channon	26-225	12	6-62	20-163	-74.05
Clive Cox	26-124	21	7-21	19-103	+15.10
Malcolm Saunders	23-149	15	0-18	23-131	-12.63
Andrew Balding	19-122	16	2-15	17-107	-23.29
Richard Hannon Snr	19-73	26	12-42	7-31	+19.12
David Evans	18-166	11	5-42	13-124	-41.27
Sir Mark Prescott Bt	17-48	35	3-11	14-37	-10.18
Richard Hannon	16-110	15	9-55	7-55	-44.87
Rod Millman	16-91	18	1-15	15-76	+30.68
Tony Carroll	15-144	10	1-12	14-132	-22.25
Roger Charlton	15-57	26	4-9	11-48	+12.71
Ronald Harris	14-220	6	4-47	10-173	-81.75
Jo Hughes	14-107	13	3-34	11-73	+11.38

Jockeys	*Wins-Rides*	*%*	*£1 level stks*	*Best Trainer*	*W-R*
Luke Morris	30-225	13	-79.51	Sir Mark Prescott Bt	15-41
George Baker	24-93	26	-4.22	Mick Channon	3-10
Richard Hughes	24-89	27	+13.73	Richard Hannon Snr	5-15
Steve Drowne	20-156	13	-28.13	Charles Hills	7-17
Adam Kirby	19-95	20	+51.83	Clive Cox	11-36
Cathy Gannon	18-152	12	-36.48	Jo Hughes	4-17
David Probert	17-136	13	-47.25	Andrew Balding	9-46
Silvestre De Sousa	17-88	19	-3.87	Mark Johnston	5-14
Pat Dobbs	15-93	16	-40.59	Richard Hannon Snr	6-23
Liam Keniry	14-147	10	-49.17	David Elsworth	3-7
Martin Dwyer	14-107	13	-7.45	William Muir	4-33
Dane O'Neill	14-104	13	-34.28	Brian Meehan	2-5
Sean Levey	14-94	15	+3.36	Richard Hannon	3-27

Favourites

2yo 42.1% -2.44 3yo 34.8% -56.11 TOTAL 34% -89.91

BEVERLEY

York Road, Beverley, E Yorkshire HU17 8QZ. Tel 01482 867 488

How to get there Road: Course is signposted from the M62. Rail: Beverley, bus service to course on race days

Features RH, uphill finish

2017 Fixtures
April 19, 27, May 1, 16, 31, June 10, 20, 27, July 7-8, 18, 24, August 1, 16-17, 27, September 2, 20, 26

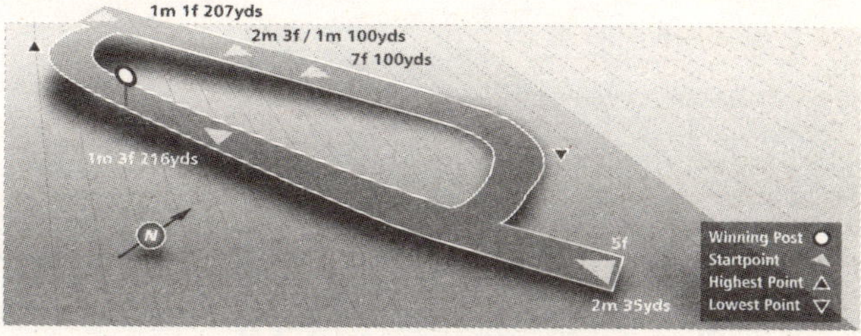

Racing Post standard times

5f	1min1	1m4f16yds	2min34.2
7f100yds	1min30	2m35yds	3min30
1m100yds	1min43	2m3f100yds	4min17
1m1f207yds	2min1.3		

Trainers	*Wins-Runs*	*%*	*2yo*	*3yo+*	*£1 level stks*
Mark Johnston	65-282	23	13-79	52-203	+15.77
Richard Fahey	43-305	14	20-114	23-191	-87.45
David O'Meara	40-209	19	1-32	39-177	+34.07
Tim Easterby	30-352	9	4-116	26-236	-141.13
Brian Ellison	22-132	17	11-33	11-99	+34.19
Kevin Ryan	21-184	11	7-51	14-133	+11.13
Michael Easterby	20-210	10	0-38	20-172	-45.63
David Nicholls	16-95	17	1-3	15-92	+74.17
Ann Duffield	15-134	11	9-73	6-61	-26.61
Richard Guest	14-80	18	3-12	11-68	+34.13
Ollie Pears	13-117	11	2-27	11-90	+16.50
Neville Bycroft	11-94	12	0-0	11-94	-11.88
John Quinn	10-102	10	4-36	6-66	-28.00

Jockeys	*Wins-Rides*	*%*	*£1 level stks*	*Best Trainer*	*W-R*
Joe Fanning	43-219	20	-19.43	Mark Johnston	33-138
Paul Mulrennan	36-244	15	-34.84	Michael Dods	4-23
Daniel Tudhope	32-137	23	+31.92	David O'Meara	18-94
David Allan	27-247	11	-73.58	Tim Easterby	16-136
Tony Hamilton	23-189	12	-77.61	Richard Fahey	19-133
P J McDonald	22-224	10	-83.67	Ann Duffield	9-81
Graham Gibbons	22-198	11	-37.51	David Barron	7-37
Silvestre De Sousa	22-96	23	+27.35	Mark Johnston	9-26
Graham Lee	20-165	12	-51.93	Jedd O'Keeffe	2-10
Barry McHugh	16-192	8	+42.20	Tony Coyle	6-68
Franny Norton	16-110	15	-16.96	Mark Johnston	12-56
Robert Winston	16-105	15	-10.00	Ollie Pears	3-14
Ben Curtis	12-71	17	-4.75	Brian Ellison	5-20

Favourites

2yo 38.4% -12.27 3yo 38.3% -5.25 TOTAL 33% -74.93

BRIGHTON

Freshfield Road, Brighton, E Sussex BN2 2XZ. Tel 01273 603 580

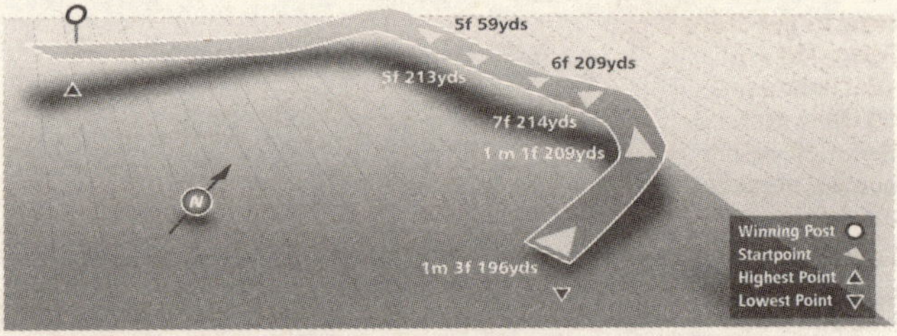

How to get there Road: Signposted from A23 London Road and A27. Rail: Brighton, bus to course on race days

Features LH, undulating, sharp

2017 Fixtures April 15, 25, May 2-3, 15, 23, June 9, 12, 20, 27, July 4, 11, August 9-11, 22, September 3-4, 11, 18, October 10, 19

Racing Post standard times

5f59yds	1min0.4	7f214yds	1min33
5f213yds	1min8.4	1m1f209yds	1min59.4
6f209yds	1min20.5	1m3f196yds	2min28.8

Trainers	*Wins-Runs*	*%*	*2yo*	*3yo+*	*£1 level stks*
Gary Moore	31-184	17	4-12	27-172	-20.95
Tony Carroll	25-120	21	0-2	25-118	+52.60
Mick Channon	21-130	16	6-34	15-96	+19.40
John Bridger	20-154	13	0-4	20-150	-21.29
Richard Hannon	18-83	22	12-44	6-39	-17.09
George Baker	16-94	17	2-12	14-82	+65.75
David Simcock	15-53	28	5-15	10-38	+7.22
David Evans	13-104	13	3-13	10-91	+62.63
John Gallagher	13-69	19	1-5	12-64	+35.75
Mark Johnston	12-81	15	3-29	9-52	-23.52
Ronald Harris	11-83	13	1-15	10-68	+14.25
Andrew Balding	11-64	17	3-12	8-52	-6.60
Sylvester Kirk	11-63	17	3-9	8-54	+4.33

Jockeys	*Wins-Rides*	*%*	*£1 level stks*	*Best Trainer*	*W-R*
Jim Crowley	42-171	25	+0.62	Tony Carroll	5-11
George Baker	30-152	20	+9.73	Gary Moore	11-50
Richard Hughes	29-95	31	+6.08	Richard Hannon	7-20
Luke Morris	25-171	15	-42.65	Sir Mark Prescott Bt	6-22
Adam Kirby	25-100	25	-2.34	Clive Cox	7-15
William Carson	21-182	12	-31.58	John Bridger	14-65
Pat Cosgrave	20-121	17	-5.05	George Baker	7-37
David Probert	19-99	19	+45.43	Andrew Balding	4-19
Silvestre De Sousa	17-91	19	-6.70	Mark Johnston	3-17
Fergus Sweeney	15-130	12	-3.75	J R Jenkins	3-9
Oisin Murphy	13-100	13	-33.34	Alan McCabe	2-3
Shane Kelly	13-97	13	-24.00	Richard Hughes	4-16
Martin Lane	13-78	17	+49.14	David Simcock	5-15

Favourites

2yo 45.9% -11.75 3yo 32.7% -52.55 TOTAL 36.7% -39.74

Durdar Road, Carlisle, Cumbria,
CA2 4TS. Tel 01228 554 700

CARLISLE

How to get there Road: M6 Jctn 42, follow signs on Dalston Road. Rail: Carlisle, 66 bus to course on race days

Features RH, undulating, uphill finish

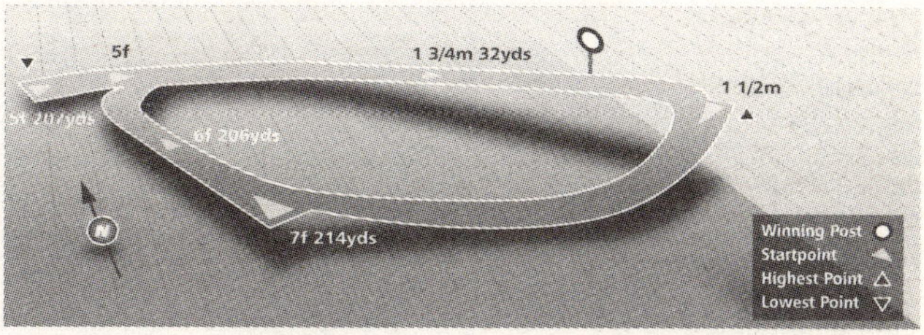

2017 Fixtures May 22, June 8-9, 19, 28, July 8, 13-14, August 7, 23, 29, September 13, 18

Racing Post standard times

5f	1min	1m1f61yds	1min55.2
5f193yds	1min12.2	1m3f107yds	2min23.5
6f192yds	1min25.7	1m6f32yds	3min2.5
7f200yds	1min38.5	2m1f52yds	3min46

Trainers	*Wins-Runs*	*%*	*2yo*	*3yo+*	*£1 level stks*
Keith Dalgleish	31-229	14	3-46	28-183	-28.58
Tim Easterby	28-196	14	6-57	22-139	+0.23
Mark Johnston	23-138	17	7-41	16-97	-8.93
Richard Fahey	21-217	10	6-78	15-139	-122.43
K R Burke	14-58	24	10-28	4-30	+23.45
Alan Swinbank	13-108	12	0-11	13-97	-8.50
Kevin Ryan	13-88	15	7-42	6-46	+17.25
Brian Ellison	13-79	16	1-12	12-67	-24.82
Michael Dods	11-102	11	4-31	7-71	-23.88
Ann Duffield	11-76	14	6-39	5-37	-10.02
David O'Meara	10-88	11	2-11	8-77	-20.00
David Nicholls	9-37	24	0-1	9-36	+21.50
Bryan Smart	7-66	11	3-31	4-35	-11.00

Jockeys	*Wins-Rides*	*%*	*£1 level stks*	*Best Trainer*	*W-R*
Joe Fanning	23-168	14	-6.18	Mark Johnston	16-88
Paul Mulrennan	21-149	14	-68.13	Michael Dods	7-47
Graham Lee	20-136	15	-6.90	James Tate	2-2
Ben Curtis	18-73	25	+100.48	Alan Swinbank	6-27
Phillip Makin	16-118	14	-14.98	Keith Dalgleish	10-51
P J McDonald	15-124	12	-31.41	Ann Duffield	8-50
David Allan	13-85	15	-14.03	Tim Easterby	10-60
Tony Hamilton	12-125	10	-60.89	Richard Fahey	10-91
Franny Norton	11-54	20	-4.00	Mark Johnston	6-33
Dale Swift	11-40	28	+65.25	Brian Ellison	4-12
Tom Eaves	9-154	6	-99.42	Keith Dalgleish	6-64
Daniel Tudhope	9-64	14	-16.04	David O'Meara	5-29
Duran Fentiman	8-83	10	+7.38	Tim Easterby	7-52

Favourites

2yo 42.7% +3.21 3yo 40.2% +9.60 TOTAL 32.8% -35.73

CATTERICK

Catterick Bridge, Richmond, N Yorks
DL10 7PE. Tel 01748 811 478

How to get there Road: A1, exit 5m south of Scotch Corner. Rail: Darlington or Northallerton and bus

Features LH, undulating, tight

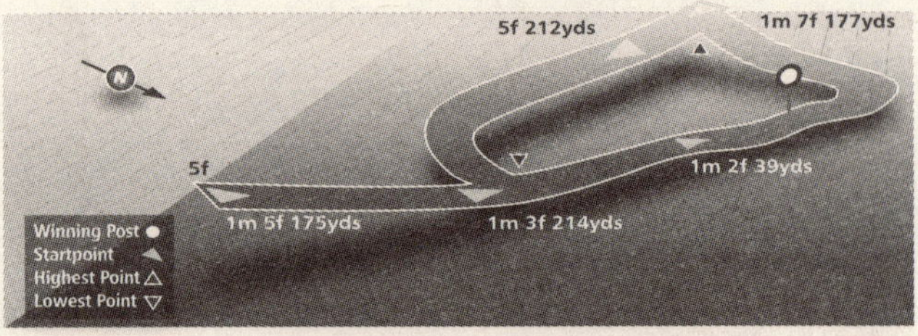

2017 Fixtures
April 12, 26, May 11, 25, June 2, 10, July 12, 19, 26, August 8, 18, 30, September 12, 23, October 10, 21, 31

Racing Post standard times

5f	58.3	1m3f214yds	2min33
5f212yds	1min11.3	1m5f175yds	2min57
7f	1min23.3	1m7f177yds	3min23

Trainers	*Wins-Runs*	*%*	*2yo*	*3yo+*	*£1 level stks*
Richard Fahey	42-180	23	24-72	18-108	+27.30
Mark Johnston	29-143	20	11-64	18-79	-35.96
David O'Meara	25-198	13	4-25	21-173	-59.91
Tim Easterby	22-222	10	4-63	18-159	-71.75
John Quinn	22-131	17	5-43	17-88	+3.91
Brian Ellison	21-103	20	2-10	19-93	+58.40
David Nicholls	18-172	10	2-8	16-164	-54.30
Ruth Carr	18-126	14	0-4	18-122	+7.25
Michael Easterby	15-155	10	0-31	15-124	-9.00
Kevin Ryan	15-98	15	7-32	8-66	-15.61
Ann Duffield	14-127	11	3-59	11-68	-44.54
Keith Dalgleish	12-77	16	4-27	8-50	-26.92
Paul Midgley	11-116	9	1-19	10-97	-16.38

Jockeys	*Wins-Rides*	*%*	*£1 level stks*	*Best Trainer*	*W-R*
P J McDonald	32-235	14	-5.19	Ann Duffield	10-61
Daniel Tudhope	29-163	18	-5.76	David O'Meara	17-92
Graham Lee	25-182	14	-50.18	Ed Dunlop	2-2
Joe Fanning	24-151	16	-22.13	Mark Johnston	13-70
Paul Mulrennan	23-147	16	-33.97	Conor Dore	3-5
David Allan	19-159	12	+5.66	Tim Easterby	10-91
Tony Hamilton	19-119	16	-32.46	Richard Fahey	18-81
Graham Gibbons	16-148	11	-46.07	Michael Easterby	4-39
James Sullivan	15-198	8	-87.13	Ruth Carr	12-81
Phillip Makin	15-103	15	-39.66	Keith Dalgleish	5-23
Silvestre De Sousa	15-54	28	+5.79	Mark Johnston	5-14
Ben Curtis	14-81	17	-15.92	Brian Ellison	5-23
Robert Winston	12-79	15	-1.34	Marjorie Fife	3-6

Favourites

2yo 44.6% -2.79 3yo 33.7% -22.40 TOTAL 32.7% -60.71

CHELMSFORD

Great Leighs, CM3 1QP.
Tel 01245 362 412

How to get there Road: M11 Jctn 8, A120 towards Chelmsford, signposted from A131. Rail: Chelmsford, bus to course on racedays

Features LH, Polytrack, 1m circuit with wide sweeping bends

2017 Fixtures April 1, 6, 13, 27, May 2, 8, 10, 25, 29, June 1, 21-22, July 7, 25, August 8, 15, 31, September 2, 7, 21, 26, 28, 30, October 5-6, 12, 26, November 2, 9, 16-17, 23, December 1, 7-8, 14-15, 21

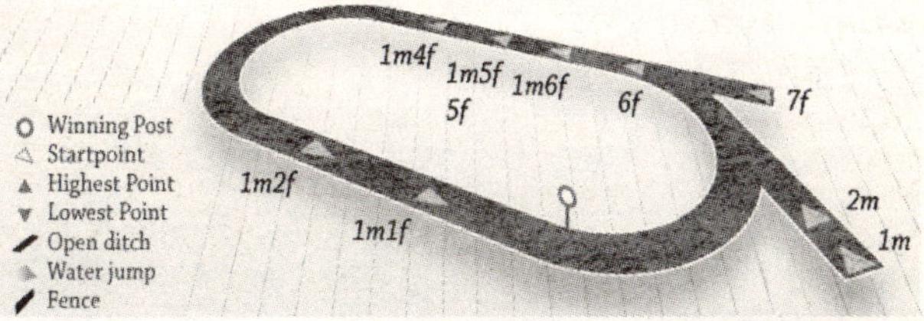

Racing Post standard times

5f	59.6
6f	1min12.3
1m	1min39
1m2f	2min6.5
1m6f	3min0.6
2m	3min28

Trainers	Wins-Runs	%	2yo	3yo+	£1 level stks
Mark Johnston	25-163	15	12-60	13-103	-41.80
Chris Dwyer	25-126	20	1-15	24-111	+62.41
Stuart Williams	23-127	18	3-9	20-118	+37.88
David Simcock	22-97	23	2-11	20-86	+23.70
Marco Botti	20-137	15	7-45	13-92	-25.01
Saeed bin Suroor	20-57	35	8-15	12-42	+4.68
John Gosden	19-61	31	3-14	16-47	-5.44
Michael Appleby	18-173	10	0-6	18-167	-70.47
Derek Shaw	18-138	13	1-19	17-119	+6.50
Richard Hannon	18-121	15	8-60	10-61	-20.08
Hughie Morrison	16-49	33	3-9	13-40	+20.64
Roger Varian	13-64	20	1-12	12-52	-10.14
James Tate	13-62	21	4-18	9-44	-10.93

Jockeys	Wins-Rides	%	£1 level stks	Best Trainer	W-R
Luke Morris	42-309	14	-97.60	Sir Mark Prescott Bt	12-48
Silvestre De Sousa	39-168	23	+32.06	Chris Dwyer	14-46
Jim Crowley	32-143	22	+45.18	Hugo Palmer	6-13
Adam Kirby	31-190	16	-44.73	Ian Williams	3-6
Oisin Murphy	22-126	17	-0.19	Andrew Balding	5-20
Martin Harley	21-167	13	-43.38	Marco Botti	3-16
Martin Lane	19-129	15	+26.20	David Simcock	4-10
Kieren Fox	18-88	20	+35.50	John Best	10-47
Joe Fanning	14-101	14	-29.59	Mark Johnston	10-60
Paul Hanagan	14-67	21	+11.17	Saeed bin Suroor	2-4
Andrew Mullen	13-101	13	-23.88	Michael Appleby	10-82
Jamie Spencer	13-77	17	-26.62	David Simcock	6-20
Robert Havlin	13-73	18	-23.83	John Gosden	8-28

Favourites

2yo 41.9% +5.22 3yo 35.2% -51.63 TOTAL 35.5% -85.88

CHEPSTOW

Chepstow, Monmouthshire, NP16 6BE. Tel 01291 622 260

How to get there Road: M4 Jct 22 on west side of Severn Bridge, A48 north, A446. Rail: Chepstow, bus to course on race days

Features LH, undulating

2017 Fixtures May 5, 16, June 6, 10, 16, 26, July 4, 14, 20, 28, August 17, 24, 28, September 6, 14, 19

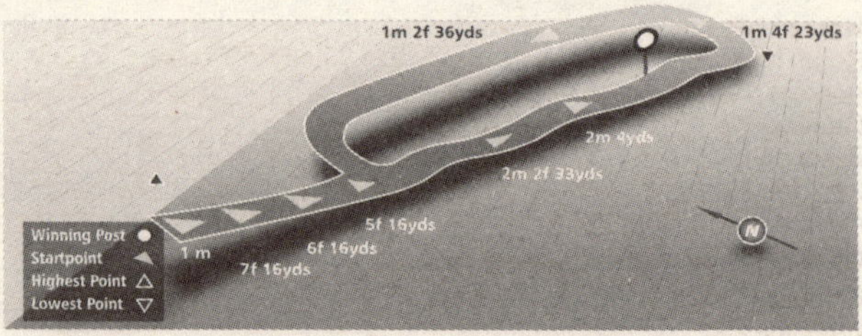

Racing Post standard times

5f16yds	58.3	1m2f36yds	2min6.5
6f16yds	1min9.8	1m4f23yds	2min34
7f16yds	1min21.5	2m49yds	3min28
1m14yds	1min33.5	2m2f	3min52

Trainers	*Wins-Runs*	*%*	*2yo*	*3yo+*	*£1 level stks*
Andrew Balding	22-112	20	2-14	20-98	-12.84
David Evans	21-186	11	5-56	16-130	-18.73
Richard Hannon	21-95	22	12-38	9-57	-11.83
Bernard Llewellyn	20-148	14	0-0	20-148	+0.25
Ronald Harris	19-222	9	3-50	16-172	-57.25
Ralph Beckett	16-59	27	2-17	14-42	-11.41
John O'Shea	15-106	14	0-0	15-106	-10.38
Mick Channon	13-97	13	4-39	9-58	-24.33
George Baker	12-63	19	1-10	11-53	+42.75
Richard Hannon Snr	12-54	22	7-27	5-27	-10.34
David Simcock	11-45	24	4-11	7-34	-0.32
Eve Johnson Houghton	10-44	23	6-17	4-27	+27.93
Malcolm Saunders	9-92	10	1-20	8-72	-39.63

Jockeys	*Wins-Rides*	*%*	*£1 level stks*	*Best Trainer*	*W-R*
David Probert	25-156	16	-31.30	Andrew Balding	9-42
Cathy Gannon	19-149	13	-29.88	Malcolm Saunders	4-26
Tom Marquand	18-86	21	+27.38	Richard Price	7-18
Pat Dobbs	17-67	25	-4.26	Richard Hannon Snr	7-14
Luke Morris	15-171	9	-74.89	John O'Shea	5-24
Richard Hughes	15-82	18	-31.51	Richard Hannon Snr	3-12
Oisin Murphy	14-87	16	-9.00	Andrew Balding	3-17
Jim Crowley	14-63	22	+28.75	Ed de Giles	3-4
Fergus Sweeney	12-84	14	+12.08	David Simcock	4-5
Franny Norton	12-53	23	+33.63	Paul Henderson	4-6
Pat Cosgrave	11-70	16	+19.99	George Baker	7-27
Dane O'Neill	10-79	13	-33.21	Richard Hannon	2-3
John Fahy	10-68	15	-13.13	Eve Johnson Houghton	4-17

Favourites

2yo 40.7% -6.23 3yo 39.1% -13.55 TOTAL 35.2% -43.01

CHESTER

Steam Mill Street, Chester, CH1 2LY
Tel 01244 304 600

How to get there
Road: Inner Ring Road and A458 Queensferry Road.
Rail: Chester General, bus to city centre

Features LH, flat, very sharp

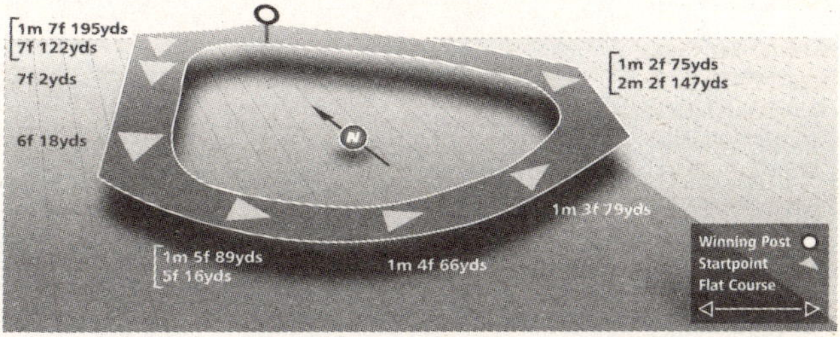

2017 Fixtures May 10-12, 27, June 10, 30, July 1, 15, 29, August 6, 26, September 2, 15-16, 30

Racing Post standard times

5f16yds	59.6	1m3f79yds	2min22.7
5f110yds	1min5.6	1m4f66yds	2min34.6
6f18yds	1min13.1	1m5f89yds	2min48
7f2yds	1min24.3	1m7f195yds	3min24
7f122yds	1min31.4	2m2f147yds	4min1
1m2f75yds	2min7.9		

Trainers	*Wins-Runs*	*%*	*2yo*	*3yo+*	*£1 level stks*
Richard Fahey	57-449	13	16-83	41-366	-78.51
Mark Johnston	40-276	14	15-78	25-198	-29.72
Andrew Balding	34-154	22	4-24	30-130	+33.96
Tom Dascombe	32-241	13	14-80	18-161	-54.73
Tim Easterby	11-115	10	2-16	9-99	-48.25
William Haggas	11-42	26	5-8	6-34	-7.90
A P O'Brien	11-25	44	0-0	11-25	+2.78
David Evans	10-158	6	1-65	9-93	-47.50
Mick Channon	10-113	9	2-31	8-82	-35.00
Kevin Ryan	10-88	11	4-17	6-71	-25.00
Sir Michael Stoute	10-46	22	1-4	9-42	-14.87
Roger Varian	10-43	23	1-3	9-40	+6.41
John Quinn	9-64	14	2-13	7-51	-13.00

Jockeys	*Wins-Rides*	*%*	*£1 level stks*	*Best Trainer*	*W-R*
Franny Norton	49-283	17	+13.74	Mark Johnston	26-125
Richard Kingscote	38-196	19	+1.48	Tom Dascombe	26-137
Ryan Moore	19-66	29	+3.27	A P O'Brien	7-14
Graham Lee	16-74	22	+25.29	James Tate	2-2
Joe Fanning	15-126	12	-48.25	Mark Johnston	9-75
David Probert	14-106	13	-30.75	Andrew Balding	13-71
Graham Gibbons	12-77	16	-1.13	David Barron	5-21
J F Egan	10-71	14	+27.50	David Evans	3-24
Sean Levey	10-65	15	-27.32	Richard Hannon Snr	4-11
David Nolan	9-87	10	-12.00	Richard Fahey	7-62
Paul Hanagan	9-50	18	-2.28	Richard Fahey	4-18
Martin Harley	9-44	20	+10.46	Mick Channon	3-9
Patrick Mathers	8-61	13	+2.75	Richard Fahey	8-48

Favourites
2yo 40.7% -3.42 3yo 30.2% -36.77 TOTAL 31.2% -59.71

DONCASTER

Leger Way, Doncaster
DN2 6BB. Tel 01302 320066/7

How to get there
Road: M18 Jct 3, A638, A18 to Hull.
Rail: Doncaster Central

Features LH, flat

2017 Fixtures
April 1-2, 28-29, May 6, 20, June 2-3, 18, 30, July 1, 7, 13, 20, 27, August 5, 19, September 13-16, October 27-28, November 11

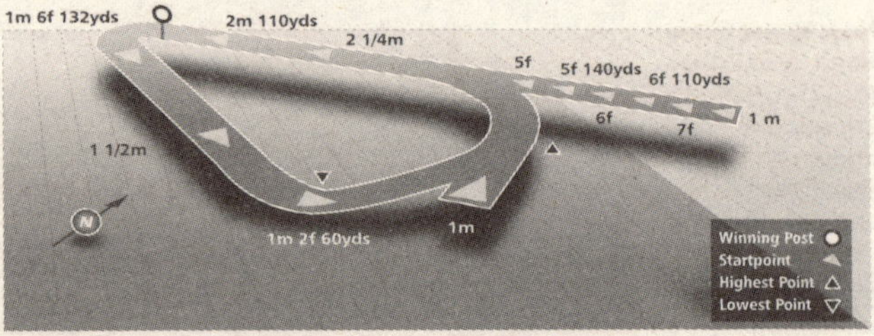

Racing Post standard times

5f	57.9	1m (Rnd)	1min36.2
5f140yds	1min6.2	1m2f60yds	2m6
6f	1min10.5	1m4f	2min29
6f110yds	1min17	1m6f132yds	3min3
7f	1min23.3	2m110yds	3min33
1m (Str)	1min36	2m2f	3min52

Trainers	*Wins-Runs*	%	*2yo*	*3yo+*	*£1 level stks*
Richard Fahey	50-448	11	14-113	36-335	-21.91
John Gosden	35-168	21	9-35	26-133	-31.28
Roger Varian	30-128	23	4-29	26-99	+33.20
David O'Meara	25-256	10	4-14	21-242	-65.59
Richard Hannon	23-173	13	11-88	12-85	-15.50
Saeed bin Suroor	23-108	21	7-24	16-84	-20.66
Charles Hills	22-154	14	6-45	16-109	+7.35
Luca Cumani	21-104	20	1-15	20-89	-12.39
Charlie Appleby	21-100	21	9-45	12-55	-1.90
William Haggas	20-112	18	9-32	11-80	-20.90
David Simcock	20-86	23	1-18	19-68	+58.46
Mark Johnston	19-207	9	9-81	10-126	-106.16
Sir Michael Stoute	19-76	25	4-16	15-60	+14.42

Jockeys	*Wins-Rides*	%	*£1 level stks*	*Best Trainer*	*W-R*
Andrea Atzeni	44-188	23	+90.34	Roger Varian	15-50
William Buick	35-182	19	-18.25	John Gosden	10-53
Paul Hanagan	34-236	14	-31.70	Richard Fahey	8-64
Jamie Spencer	32-166	19	+58.49	David Simcock	7-23
Silvestre De Sousa	27-152	18	+8.29	Saeed bin Suroor	8-23
Graham Lee	21-234	9	-73.42	Jim Goldie	5-21
Ryan Moore	20-129	16	-54.11	Sir Michael Stoute	8-25
Tony Hamilton	19-153	12	+20.66	Richard Fahey	16-129
Daniel Tudhope	18-164	11	+16.25	David O'Meara	9-107
Graham Gibbons	16-165	10	-5.75	David Barron	9-71
James Doyle	16-124	13	-62.06	Charlie Appleby	4-9
Dane O'Neill	15-76	20	+43.27	Charles Hills	2-5
Oisin Murphy	14-73	19	+16.33	Andrew Balding	5-14

Favourites
2yo 43.3% +7.44 3yo 30.6% -55.03 TOTAL 32% -82.39

EPSOM

Epsom Downs, Surrey, KT18 5LQ
Tel 01372 726 311

How to get there Road: M25 Jct 8 (A217) or 9 (A24), 2m south of Epsom on B290. Rail: Epsom and bus, Epsom Downs or Tattenham Corner

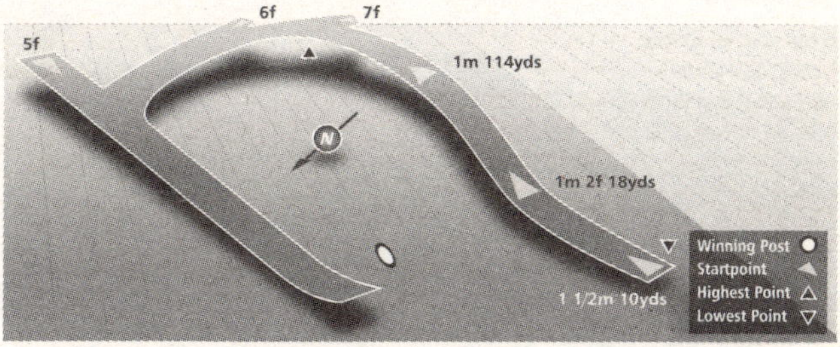

Features LH, undulating

2017 Fixtures April 26, June 2-3, July 6, 13, 20, August 3, 28-29, September 14, October 1

Racing Post standard times

5f	54.9	1m114yds	1min41.8
6f	1min7	1m2f18yds	2min5.3
7f	1min20	1m4f10yds	2min33.6

Trainers	*Wins-Runs*	*%*	*2yo*	*3yo+*	*£1 level stks*
Andrew Balding	20-133	15	7-25	13-108	+1.74
Mark Johnston	16-141	11	6-30	10-111	-59.25
Mick Channon	16-95	17	5-32	11-63	+9.57
Richard Fahey	14-100	14	3-15	11-85	+15.38
Ralph Beckett	12-53	23	3-7	9-46	+19.32
Richard Hannon Snr	11-59	19	6-23	5-36	-17.93
John Gosden	11-45	24	1-2	10-43	-6.96
Richard Hannon	10-57	18	5-19	5-38	-11.04
Pat Phelan	9-76	12	0-12	9-64	+40.63
Roger Varian	9-42	21	0-5	9-37	-3.77
David Simcock	9-34	26	1-3	8-31	+12.25
Stuart Williams	8-54	15	0-1	8-53	+3.94
A P O'Brien	8-42	19	0-0	8-42	+46.93

Jockeys	*Wins-Rides*	*%*	*£1 level stks*	*Best Trainer*	*W-R*
Silvestre De Sousa	25-112	22	+8.57	Mark Johnston	6-44
Richard Hughes	19-91	21	+7.86	Richard Hannon Snr	6-36
Jim Crowley	13-84	15	-15.23	Ralph Beckett	3-17
Ryan Moore	13-83	16	-12.34	Roger Varian	2-2
David Probert	11-74	15	-6.75	Andrew Balding	8-52
James Doyle	9-65	14	-33.30	Roger Charlton	2-7
Neil Callan	9-42	21	+9.25	James Tate	3-8
Charles Bishop	8-25	32	+33.25	Mick Channon	6-20
Jamie Spencer	7-71	10	-34.13	Ed de Giles	2-3
William Buick	7-59	12	-37.00	John Gosden	5-27
Kieren Fallon	7-54	13	+13.50	Mark Johnston	2-8
Jimmy Fortune	7-53	13	-4.00	Eve Johnson Houghton	3-7
Pat Dobbs	7-40	18	+12.75	Richard Hannon	2-10

Favourites

2yo 39% -13.57 3yo 29.3% -30.41 TOTAL 29.8% -64.84

FFOS LAS

Trimsaran, Carmarthenshire, SA17 4DE
Tel: 01554 811092

How to get there
Road: M4 Jctn 48 and follow the A4138 to Llanelli. Rail: Llanelli, Kidwelly or Carmarthen

Features LH, flat, galloping

2017 Fixtures
July 17, 25, August 3, 15, 25, September 17

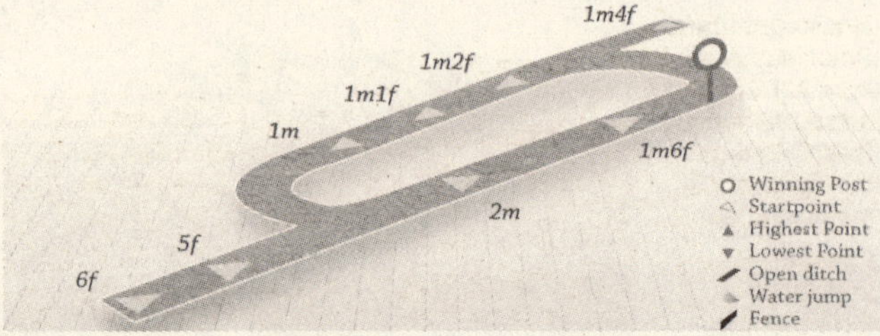

Racing Post standard times

5f	57	1m4f	2min34
6f	1min8.5	1m6f	3min
1m	1min38	2m	3min28.5
1m2f	2min6		

Trainers	*Wins-Runs*	*%*	*2yo*	*3yo+*	*£1 level stks*
David Evans	23-135	17	5-30	18-105	+92.33
Andrew Balding	15-49	31	3-11	12-38	+42.18
Rod Millman	9-52	17	2-13	7-39	-7.75
Mick Channon	8-50	16	3-20	5-30	-16.92
Ronald Harris	7-66	11	4-20	3-46	-25.00
William Muir	7-40	18	2-12	5-28	+17.25
Richard Price	6-30	20	0-2	6-28	+18.25
Roger Charlton	6-26	23	2-6	4-20	-9.11
Ralph Beckett	6-22	27	1-6	5-16	+9.24
Bernard Llewellyn	5-49	10	0-0	5-49	-14.00
Daniel Mark Loughnane	5-30	17	0-2	5-28	-1.75
Richard Hannon	5-25	20	4-15	1-10	-2.25
William Knight	5-22	23	1-4	4-18	-0.50

Jockeys	*Wins-Rides*	*%*	*£1 level stks*	*Best Trainer*	*W-R*
David Probert	13-69	19	+13.84	Andrew Balding	7-23
Steve Drowne	11-64	17	+58.00	Peter Makin	4-9
William Twiston-Davies	10-61	16	-3.92	Nigel Twiston-Davies	3-7
Declan Bates	10-43	23	+20.42	David Evans	7-28
Liam Keniry	9-45	20	+25.75	Rod Millman	2-4
Jim Crowley	9-26	35	+12.88	David Evans	2-3
Martin Harley	8-24	33	+17.50	Mick Channon	4-7
Oisin Murphy	7-45	16	-14.79	Andrew Balding	3-7
Chris Catlin	7-20	35	+16.13	David Simcock	1-1
Cathy Gannon	6-39	15	+29.00	David Evans	2-6
Richard Hughes	6-27	22	+0.08	Richard Hannon	2-2
Martin Dwyer	5-40	13	-3.00	William Muir	5-15
Luke Morris	5-35	14	-7.65	Sir Mark Prescott Bt	2-6

Favourites
2yo 42.9% -9.90 3yo 31.4% -33.28 TOTAL 31.2% -72.70

Chichester, W Sussex,
PO18 0PS. Tel 01243 755 022

GOODWOOD

How to get there
Road: signposted from A27 south and A285 north. Rail: Chichester, bus to course on race days

Features RH, undulating

2017 Fixtures
May 6, 25-27, June 2, 9, 11, 16, August 1-5, 25-27, September 5, 27, October 15

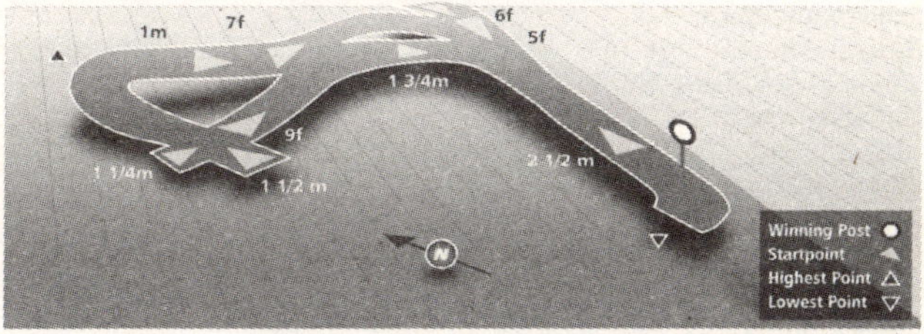

Racing Post standard times

5f	57	1m3f	2min21
6f	1min9.7	1m4f	2min34
7f	1min24	1m6f	2min58.5
1m	1min36.7	2m	3min21
1m1f	1min51.4	2m4f	4min14
1m1f192yds	2min4		

Trainers	*Wins-Runs*	*%*	*2yo*	*3yo+*	*£1 level stks*
Mark Johnston	46-280	16	16-81	30-199	+116.12
Richard Hannon	35-277	13	17-115	18-162	-76.76
Richard Hannon Snr	28-205	14	13-100	15-105	-17.88
Sir Michael Stoute	24-114	21	2-11	22-103	-19.30
Mick Channon	21-252	8	11-94	10-158	-92.22
John Gosden	21-113	19	7-26	14-87	-11.53
Amanda Perrett	19-207	9	1-23	18-184	-76.25
William Haggas	19-76	25	3-13	16-63	+12.21
Charlie Appleby	15-78	19	7-29	8-49	+5.96
Andrew Balding	14-157	9	3-33	11-124	-70.39
Roger Charlton	13-77	17	2-7	11-70	-9.63
David Simcock	12-116	10	1-13	11-103	-41.38
Richard Fahey	11-163	7	3-36	8-127	-46.75

Jockeys	*Wins-Rides*	*%*	*£1 level stks*	*Best Trainer*	*W-R*
Richard Hughes	52-265	20	-21.73	Richard Hannon Snr	19-100
William Buick	35-177	20	+90.38	John Gosden	10-49
Ryan Moore	31-192	16	-73.12	Sir Michael Stoute	9-50
James Doyle	24-181	13	-30.46	Roger Charlton	5-33
Joe Fanning	23-150	15	+33.65	Mark Johnston	20-109
Jim Crowley	21-240	9	-105.18	David Simcock	4-21
Pat Dobbs	19-189	10	-51.67	Amanda Perrett	8-52
Andrea Atzeni	18-112	16	+18.63	Roger Varian	4-29
Frankie Dettori	16-111	14	-34.56	John Gosden	4-17
Franny Norton	15-107	14	+36.25	Mark Johnston	8-65
Adam Kirby	14-114	12	-12.17	Luca Cumani	3-13
George Baker	14-87	16	+11.63	William Haggas	2-2
Silvestre De Sousa	13-140	9	-26.10	Mick Channon	8-25

Favourites

2yo 36.4% -13.78 3yo 32.4% -8.31 TOTAL 33.9% -5.33

HAMILTON

Bothwell Road, Hamilton, Lanarkshire
ML3 0DW. Tel 01698 283 806

How to get there Road: M74 Jct 5, off the A74. Rail: Hamilton West

Features RH, undulating, dip can become testing in wet weather

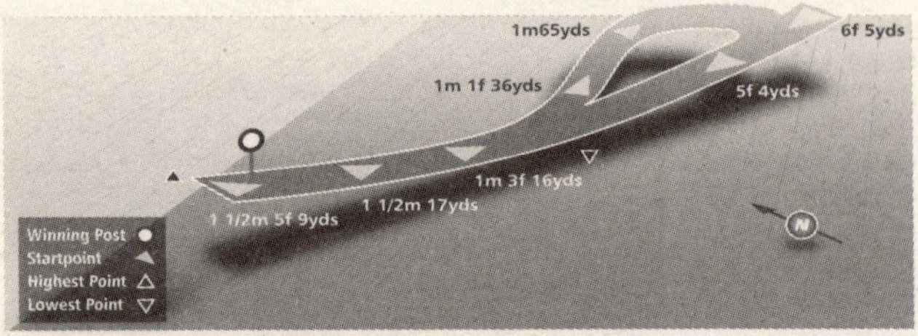

2017 Fixtures
May 7, 19, June 1, 7, 14, 21, 29, July 3-4, 15, 20-21, August 5, 24-25, September 2, 5, 25

Racing Post standard times

5f4yds	58.2	1m3f16yds	2min20
6f5yds	1min10	1m4f17yds	2min33.7
1m65yds	1min45	1m5f9yds	2min47.5
1m1f36yds	1min55.5		

Trainers	*Wins-Runs*	*%*	*2yo*	*3yo+*	*£1 level stks*
Keith Dalgleish	53-378	14	10-63	43-315	-26.21
Mark Johnston	51-224	23	17-65	34-159	-12.37
Richard Fahey	33-248	13	6-70	27-178	-80.55
Kevin Ryan	32-155	21	7-47	25-108	-3.14
David O'Meara	21-112	19	1-16	20-96	-26.03
Jim Goldie	19-207	9	0-2	19-205	-49.10
Alan Berry	18-176	10	1-5	17-171	+48.00
Alan Swinbank	18-124	15	1-3	17-121	-11.58
Eric Alston	18-99	18	0-3	18-96	+30.70
Ann Duffield	15-107	14	5-40	10-67	-27.95
David Nicholls	14-71	20	0-1	14-70	+36.88
Linda Perratt	11-305	4	0-5	11-300	-206.00
Bryan Smart	11-99	11	5-29	6-70	+31.25

Jockeys	*Wins-Rides*	*%*	*£1 level stks*	*Best Trainer*	*W-R*
Joe Fanning	53-268	20	-49.40	Mark Johnston	40-144
Graham Lee	35-230	15	-57.32	Jim Goldie	5-57
P J McDonald	25-203	12	-46.38	Ann Duffield	9-56
Paul Mulrennan	23-188	12	-40.98	Michael Dods	5-20
Phillip Makin	23-168	14	-47.11	Keith Dalgleish	12-70
Tom Eaves	20-267	7	-136.63	Keith Dalgleish	7-77
Jason Hart	19-160	12	-35.30	Eric Alston	11-67
Daniel Tudhope	18-92	20	-8.00	David O'Meara	11-47
Joey Haynes	15-62	24	+74.33	K R Burke	8-20
James Sullivan	14-140	10	-26.75	Ruth Carr	5-52
Connor Beasley	13-116	11	-31.00	Michael Dods	5-25
Tony Hamilton	12-93	13	-13.33	Richard Fahey	8-61
Fergal Lynch	11-52	21	+43.63	Jim Goldie	5-30

Favourites
2yo 36.1% -16.75 3yo 45.6% +34.81 TOTAL 35.5% -30.06

Newton-Le-Willows, Merseyside
WA12 0HQ. Tel 01942 725 963

HAYDOCK

How to get there
Road: M6 Jct 23, A49 to Wigan. Rail: Wigan & 320 bus or Newton-le-Willows

Features LH, flat, easy turns, suits the galloping type

2017 Fixtures
April 29, May 13, 26-27, June 8-10, 14-15, 24, July 6-8, 21-22, August 10-12, September 7-9, 29-30, October 20

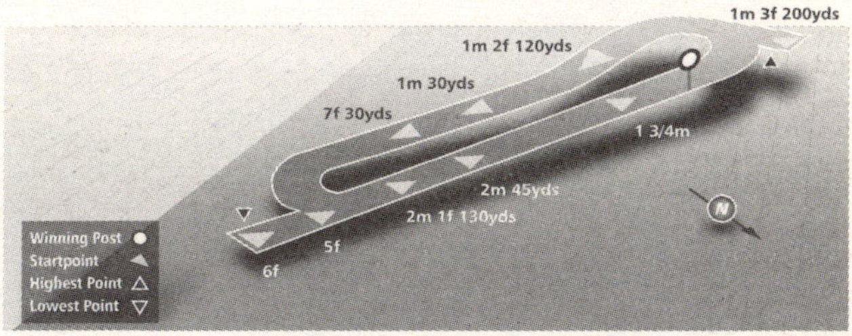

Racing Post standard times

5f	58.5	1m2f95yds	2min9
5f (Inner)	58	1m3f200yds	2min26.5
6f	1min11	1m6f	2min54
6f (Inner)	1min10.3	2m45yds	3min24
7f	1min26	2m1f130yds	3min51
1m	1min38		

Trainers	Wins-Runs	%	2yo	3yo+	£1 level stks
Tom Dascombe	52-283	18	12-103	40-180	+97.48
Richard Fahey	37-379	10	11-101	26-278	-153.92
Mark Johnston	34-268	13	10-86	24-182	-34.42
David O'Meara	29-217	13	0-11	29-206	+6.76
William Haggas	29-98	30	8-24	21-74	+21.51
John Gosden	27-89	30	11-29	16-60	+34.82
Roger Varian	26-114	23	5-28	21-86	-3.30
Kevin Ryan	25-189	13	8-60	17-129	+101.63
Richard Hannon	19-151	13	8-68	11-83	-20.40
Tim Easterby	18-204	9	2-41	16-163	-65.90
K R Burke	16-135	12	3-47	13-88	+1.25
Charles Hills	15-105	14	4-36	11-69	-20.08
Andrew Balding	13-84	15	4-13	9-71	-20.73

Jockeys	Wins-Rides	%	£1 level stks	Best Trainer	W-R
Richard Kingscote	48-282	17	+20.00	Tom Dascombe	40-208
Paul Hanagan	35-164	21	+0.34	Richard Fahey	9-32
Daniel Tudhope	32-182	18	+47.83	David O'Meara	23-107
Graham Lee	25-204	12	-5.21	Kevin Ryan	6-20
Franny Norton	22-151	15	-16.38	Mark Johnston	14-76
Joe Fanning	21-162	13	+29.04	Mark Johnston	13-105
Ryan Moore	21-88	24	-19.48	Sir Michael Stoute	5-24
Graham Gibbons	17-142	12	+24.17	David Barron	6-43
Paul Mulrennan	16-139	12	+7.42	James Tate	2-3
Andrea Atzeni	16-100	16	-2.01	Roger Varian	6-36
Jamie Spencer	15-130	12	-63.31	Kevin Ryan	3-26
Sean Levey	15-114	13	+1.00	Richard Hannon	9-54
Silvestre De Sousa	15-91	16	-6.31	Saeed bin Suroor	3-15

Favourites
2yo 39.7% -13.87 3yo 35.7% -15.78 TOTAL 32.6% -86.06

KEMPTON

Staines Rd East, Sunbury-On-Thames
TW16 5AQ. Tel 01932 782 292

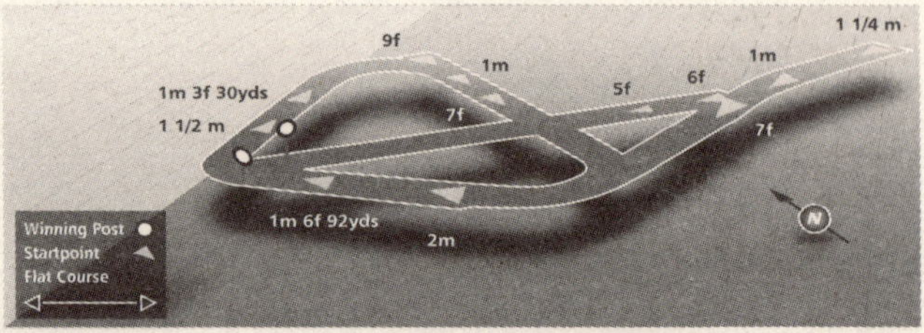

How to get there Road: M3 Jct 1, A308 to Kingston-on-Thames. Rail: Kempton Park from Waterloo

Features RH, Polytrack, sharp

2017 Fixtures
April 1, 5, 7, 12, 15, 24, May 24, 31, June 7, 14, 28, July 5, 12, August 9, 16, 22-23, 30, September 5-6, 8-9, 13, 25, 27, October 3-4, 11, 13-14, 17-18, 24-25, November 1, 6-8, 22, 29, December 13, 20

Racing Post standard times

5f	58.8	1m2f	2min4
6f	1min10.6	1m3f	2min17
7f	1min23.7	1m4f	2min30
1m	1min36.6	2m	3min22.5

Trainers	Wins-Runs	%	2yo	3yo+	£1 level stks
John Gosden	71-332	21	26-146	45-186	-25.89
James Fanshawe	68-308	22	6-44	62-264	+60.97
Saeed bin Suroor	66-248	27	24-82	42-166	+34.63
Ralph Beckett	62-321	19	29-130	33-191	+9.63
Charlie Appleby	61-240	25	36-141	25-99	+7.81
Andrew Balding	60-454	13	7-83	53-371	-83.13
Richard Hannon Snr	56-358	16	29-186	27-172	-20.23
Tony Carroll	52-593	9	0-20	52-573	-223.84
Marco Botti	47-361	13	12-127	35-234	-140.92
Gary Moore	45-354	13	7-37	38-317	-108.61
Mark Johnston	42-360	12	13-99	29-261	-139.56
Richard Hannon	40-346	12	21-184	19-162	-138.84
Sir Michael Stoute	40-207	19	16-87	24-120	-47.55

Jockeys	Wins-Rides	%	£1 level stks	Best Trainer	W-R
Jim Crowley	151-991	15	-86.84	Ralph Beckett	34-136
Adam Kirby	123-875	14	-164.36	Clive Cox	18-97
Luke Morris	113-1117	10	-341.85	Ronald Harris	15-104
George Baker	112-727	15	-90.91	Gary Moore	20-114
William Buick	83-377	22	-71.25	Charlie Appleby	24-70
Richard Hughes	71-419	17	-109.22	Richard Hannon Snr	31-137
Silvestre De Sousa	67-377	18	+4.03	Saeed bin Suroor	11-50
James Doyle	64-382	17	-82.94	Saeed bin Suroor	10-36
Ryan Moore	63-274	23	+6.78	Sir Michael Stoute	17-60
David Probert	56-521	11	-52.46	Andrew Balding	27-168
Martin Harley	55-447	12	-76.23	Marco Botti	18-94
Liam Keniry	54-730	7	-288.83	Neil Mulholland	8-40
Andrea Atzeni	54-329	16	+68.74	Roger Varian	12-66

Favourites
2yo 37.9% -49.29 | 3yo 37% -73.77 | TOTAL 34.5% -217.06

LEICESTER

London Road, Oadby, Leicester, LE2 4QH. Tel 0116 271 6515

How to get there Road: M1 Jct 21, A6, 2m south of city. Rail: Leicester, bus

Features RH, straight mile is downhill for first 4f, then uphill to finish

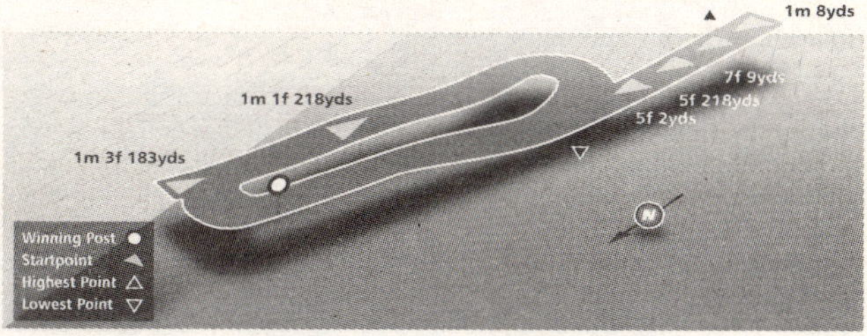

2017 Fixtures April 7, 29, May 9, 22, 29-30, June 5, 17, 27, July 8, 20, 26, August 2, 8, 13, September 12, 25, October 10, 17, 30

Racing Post standard times

5f2yds	59	1m60yds	1min42.5
5f218yds	1min10.5	1m1f218yds	2min4.5
7f9yds	1min23	1m3f183yds	2min29.3
1m8yds	1min41		

Trainers	*Wins-Runs*	*%*	*2yo*	*3yo+*	*£1 level stks*
Richard Fahey	28-135	21	9-48	19-87	+103.78
Sir Michael Stoute	21-76	28	6-32	15-44	-8.72
Mark Johnston	18-144	13	8-61	10-83	-53.22
Richard Hannon	18-123	15	11-65	7-58	-29.25
Charles Hills	18-78	23	9-36	9-42	+1.68
Richard Hannon Snr	18-73	25	13-40	5-33	+24.25
Mick Channon	17-96	18	9-49	8-47	-7.65
Roger Varian	15-73	21	3-28	12-45	-11.98
John Gosden	13-61	21	5-24	8-37	-4.47
Rae Guest	13-48	27	4-13	9-35	+57.75
David O'Meara	12-57	21	0-3	12-54	-4.45
Luca Cumani	12-53	23	3-17	9-36	-6.78
Roger Charlton	12-40	30	2-11	10-29	+4.51

Jockeys	*Wins-Rides*	*%*	*£1 level stks*	*Best Trainer*	*W-R*
Paul Hanagan	38-168	23	+49.10	Richard Fahey	7-31
Silvestre De Sousa	34-131	26	+40.27	Mark Johnston	8-34
Ryan Moore	31-119	26	-16.64	Sir Michael Stoute	11-33
James Doyle	21-94	22	+68.39	Roger Charlton	4-7
Andrea Atzeni	16-94	17	-3.01	Roger Varian	7-27
Richard Hughes	16-67	24	-3.22	Richard Hannon Snr	8-24
Adam Kirby	15-132	11	-69.42	Clive Cox	4-42
William Buick	15-80	19	-25.03	John Gosden	5-23
Martin Dwyer	13-108	12	-16.62	James Tate	4-6
Jamie Spencer	12-91	13	-39.85	Michael Bell	2-15
Tom Queally	11-111	10	-39.39	Barry Leavy	2-3
Sean Levey	11-74	15	-5.50	Richard Hannon	5-29
Jim Crowley	11-68	16	+48.50	Ralph Beckett	3-13

Favourites

2yo 41.9% +0.94 3yo 39.3% -0.42 TOTAL 36.7% -30.50

LINGFIELD turf

Racecourse Road, Lingfield
RH7 6PQ. Tel 01342 834 800

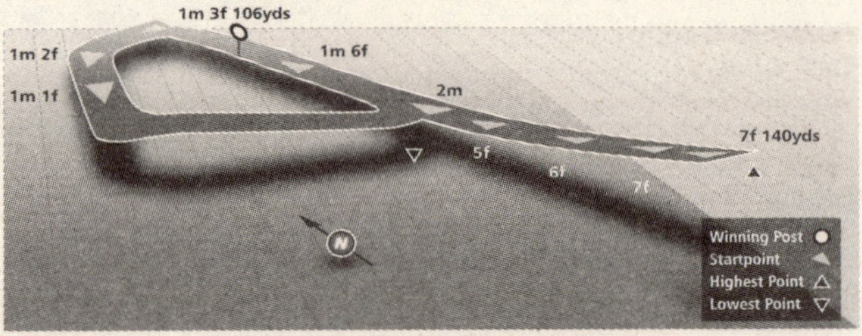

How to get there Road: M25 Jctn 6, south on A22, then B2029. Rail: Lingfield from London Bridge or Victoria

Features LH, undulating

2017 Fixtures
May 12-13, 24, June 1, 17, 24, July 1, 12, 19, 22, 26, 29, August 5, 12, 21, 30, September 6, 16

Racing Post standard times

5f	56.9	1m2f	2min6.7
6f	1min9.4	1m3f106yds	2min27
7f	1min21	1m6f	3min
7f140yds	1min28	2m	3min27.5
1m1f	1min53		

Trainers	*Wins-Runs*	*%*	*2yo*	*3yo+*	*£1 level stks*
J R Jenkins	13-65	20	1-3	12-62	+11.38
William Haggas	13-38	34	4-15	9-23	+7.80
David Evans	11-75	15	5-23	6-52	+7.70
Richard Hannon	11-71	15	6-35	5-36	-10.45
Roger Varian	11-39	28	3-8	8-31	+2.81
Mick Channon	10-90	11	4-33	6-57	+12.00
Andrew Balding	9-44	20	1-6	8-38	-9.93
Ralph Beckett	9-39	23	2-16	7-23	+7.61
Roger Charlton	9-23	39	3-8	6-15	-0.23
John Bridger	8-94	9	1-14	7-80	-14.00
Jim Boyle	8-35	23	1-6	7-29	+35.00
Patrick Chamings	8-28	29	1-2	7-26	+31.83
Richard Hannon Snr	7-46	15	6-24	1-22	-21.27

Jockeys	*Wins-Rides*	*%*	*£1 level stks*	*Best Trainer*	*W-R*
Jim Crowley	24-90	27	+0.89	David Evans	2-2
Richard Hughes	19-92	21	-20.00	Richard Hannon	4-14
Adam Kirby	15-86	17	-15.36	David Evans	3-8
Pat Cosgrave	14-72	19	-17.63	William Haggas	4-9
Silvestre De Sousa	14-65	22	-12.08	Ed Dunlop	3-5
Luke Morris	13-104	13	-57.67	Sir Mark Prescott Bt	3-8
David Probert	12-56	21	+38.28	Andrew Balding	5-15
George Baker	11-72	15	-13.39	Roger Charlton	3-5
Harry Bentley	11-51	22	+3.98	Ed Vaughan	3-6
Andrea Atzeni	10-64	16	-9.45	Roger Varian	6-17
Oisin Murphy	10-59	17	-26.41	Andrew Balding	3-9
James Doyle	10-46	22	-2.81	Roger Charlton	3-6
Martin Dwyer	9-51	18	-12.14	Brian Meehan	2-2

Favourites
2yo 50.9% +19.89 3yo 37.5% -18.07 TOTAL 40% +2.25

LINGFIELD sand

Features LH, Polytrack, tight

2017 Fixtures
April 8, 11, 14, 20, 24, 26, May 4-5, 30, June 22, September 26, October 5, November 2, 17-18, 21, 25, December 6, 12-13, 20, 23, 28, 30-31

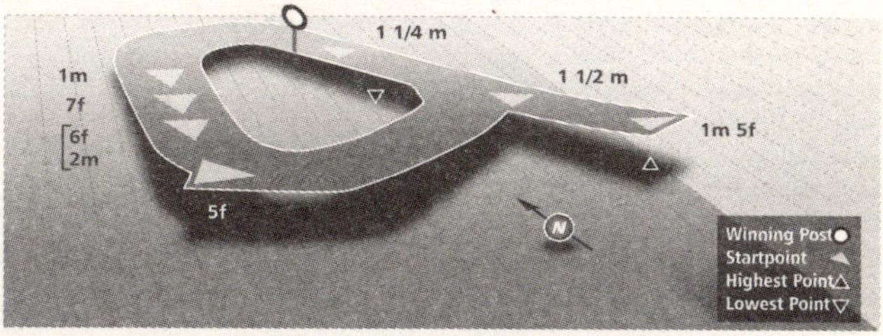

Racing Post standard times

5f	57.5	1m2f	2min1.8
6f	1min9.6	1m4f	2min28
7f	1min22.2	1m5f	2min40.5
1m	1min35.3	2m	3min16

Trainers	*Wins-Runs*	*%*	*2yo*	*3yo+*	*£1 level stks*
David Evans	72-510	14	6-49	66-461	-133.49
Mark Johnston	60-417	14	8-54	52-363	-142.71
John Gosden	56-281	20	11-74	45-207	-57.53
David Simcock	50-229	22	2-13	48-216	+12.51
Andrew Balding	49-304	16	9-41	40-263	-39.38
Stuart Williams	45-220	20	2-11	43-209	+43.01
Charlie Appleby	44-144	31	7-36	37-108	+10.59
William Haggas	43-167	26	10-53	33-114	-3.93
Gary Moore	42-361	12	4-30	38-331	-107.58
Richard Hannon	41-238	17	15-66	26-172	-16.44
Ralph Beckett	35-160	22	6-31	29-129	-6.91
Jeremy Noseda	34-125	27	5-22	29-103	-12.28
Marco Botti	32-230	14	5-44	27-186	-68.67

Jockeys	*Wins-Rides*	*%*	*£1 level stks*	*Best Trainer*	*W-R*
Adam Kirby	172-805	21	+62.31	David Evans	27-111
Luke Morris	132-1051	13	-339.01	Sir Mark Prescott Bt	26-109
Jim Crowley	132-723	18	-72.44	Ralph Beckett	17-61
George Baker	117-689	17	-92.63	Gary Moore	21-138
Joe Fanning	73-482	15	-27.55	Mark Johnston	40-258
Ryan Moore	70-223	31	+17.95	Sir Michael Stoute	19-37
Shane Kelly	62-491	13	-145.13	Peter Crate	9-77
Andrea Atzeni	54-297	18	+26.34	Stuart Williams	9-29
Liam Keniry	53-554	10	-86.38	J S Moore	8-51
William Carson	51-577	9	-255.45	John Bridger	7-113
David Probert	51-426	12	-121.26	Andrew Balding	20-114
Jamie Spencer	51-264	19	-30.23	David Simcock	12-41
Robert Havlin	43-484	9	-252.05	John Gosden	23-110

Favourites
2yo 37.7% -51.49   3yo 40.1% -97.09   TOTAL 37.8% -196.51

MUSSELBURGH

Linkfield Road EH21 7RG
Tel 0131 665 2859

How to get there Road: M8 Jct 2, A8 east, follow Ring Road, A1 east. Rail: Musselburgh from Edinburgh Waverley

Features RH, flat, tight

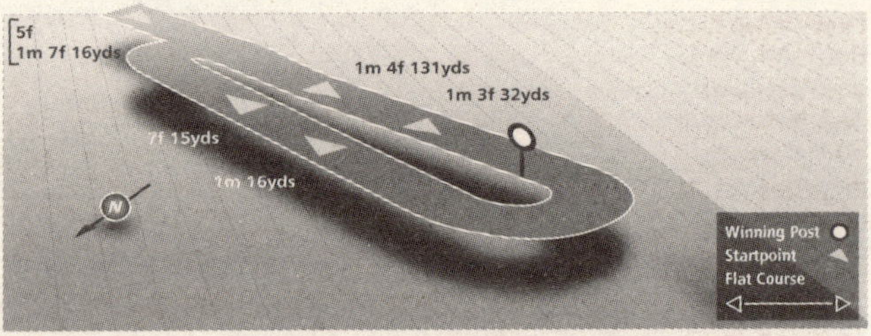

2017 Fixtures April 15, May 4-5, 26, June 3, 17, July 14, 25, August 4, 11, 30-31, September 8, 16, October 1, 16

Racing Post standard times

5f	58	1m3f32yds	2min22
7f30yds	1min26.8	1m4f100yds	2min40
1m	1min38.8	1m6f	1min59.2
1m1f	1min51.1	2m	3min25

Trainers	*Wins-Runs*	*%*	*2yo*	*3yo+*	*£1 level stks*
Mark Johnston	55-268	21	19-77	36-191	+1.15
Richard Fahey	46-231	20	15-63	31-168	+40.94
Keith Dalgleish	36-294	12	12-74	24-220	-14.69
Jim Goldie	31-400	8	0-8	31-392	-107.72
David O'Meara	24-147	16	2-29	22-118	-26.01
Kevin Ryan	20-110	18	9-32	11-78	-0.83
Tim Easterby	17-145	12	4-23	13-122	-26.80
Philip Kirby	14-74	19	0-2	14-72	+26.56
Alan Swinbank	14-74	19	1-3	13-71	-0.63
Michael Dods	14-62	23	4-17	10-45	-1.25
Linda Perratt	13-281	5	0-4	13-277	-83.50
Alistair Whillans	13-102	13	0-2	13-100	-16.79
Brian Ellison	13-99	13	2-15	11-84	-4.75

Jockeys	*Wins-Rides*	*%*	*£1 level stks*	*Best Trainer*	*W-R*
Joe Fanning	54-294	18	-34.72	Mark Johnston	44-166
Graham Lee	30-237	13	-40.52	Jim Goldie	13-98
Paul Mulrennan	24-185	13	-44.22	Paul Midgley	4-9
Tom Eaves	23-251	9	-25.82	Keith Dalgleish	8-79
Phillip Makin	23-177	13	-59.96	Keith Dalgleish	11-55
Connor Beasley	22-97	23	+55.75	Michael Dods	8-18
David Allan	17-100	17	+27.38	Tim Easterby	7-51
Daniel Tudhope	17-95	18	+7.07	David O'Meara	12-54
P J McDonald	16-210	8	-66.00	Alistair Whillans	4-33
James Sullivan	16-153	10	-3.00	Ruth Carr	8-58
Tony Hamilton	16-121	13	-55.88	Richard Fahey	14-86
Graham Gibbons	13-84	15	-15.88	David Barron	8-38
Robert Winston	13-64	20	+16.25	Alan Swinbank	6-20

Favourites

2yo 38% -8.72 3yo 37.7% -7.30 TOTAL 32.5% -70.45

NEWBURY

Newbury, Berkshire, RG14 7NZ
Tel: 01635 400 15 or 01635 550 354

How to get there Road: M4 Jct 13 and A34 south. Rail: Newbury Racecourse

Features LH, wide, flat

2017 Fixtures April 21-22, May 19-20, June 15, 29, July 6, 13, 21-22, 27, August 18-19, September 22-23, October 27-28

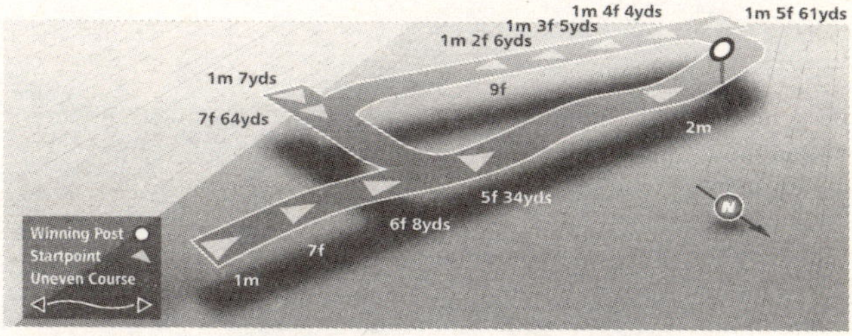

Racing Post standard times

5f34yds	59.6	1m1f	1min50
6f8yds	1min10.5	1m2f6yds	2min3
7f	1min22.8	1m3f5yds	2min17
7f64yds	1min28	1m4f4yds	2min30.3
1m	1min35.8	1m5f61yds	2min47.5
1m7yds	1min36.5	2m	3min23.5

Trainers	*Wins-Runs*	*%*	*2yo*	*3yo+*	*£1 level stks*
John Gosden	34-188	18	9-48	25-140	-10.82
Richard Hannon	33-319	10	18-172	15-147	-120.47
Richard Hannon Snr	30-249	12	23-139	7-110	-72.47
William Haggas	30-148	20	9-58	21-90	+1.79
Andrew Balding	21-163	13	4-52	17-111	-37.22
Ralph Beckett	18-125	14	4-43	14-82	-9.09
Luca Cumani	17-68	25	0-5	17-63	+5.25
Charles Hills	16-189	8	8-89	8-100	-79.13
Saeed bin Suroor	15-70	21	2-13	13-57	-4.51
Brian Meehan	14-164	9	6-88	8-76	-39.25
Clive Cox	14-146	10	5-53	9-93	-55.70
Roger Charlton	14-120	12	4-51	10-69	-27.18
Sir Michael Stoute	13-98	13	3-19	10-79	-31.15

Jockeys	*Wins-Rides*	*%*	*£1 level stks*	*Best Trainer*	*W-R*
Richard Hughes	44-246	18	-18.67	Richard Hannon Snr	20-104
James Doyle	30-223	13	-58.71	Roger Charlton	7-51
William Buick	29-175	17	-36.87	John Gosden	12-63
Paul Hanagan	29-167	17	+11.93	William Haggas	7-20
Silvestre De Sousa	27-158	17	+47.54	Saeed bin Suroor	8-23
Ryan Moore	26-170	15	-56.30	Sir Michael Stoute	9-57
Jim Crowley	21-188	11	-42.25	Ralph Beckett	8-49
Frankie Dettori	20-108	19	+22.52	John Gosden	6-29
Pat Dobbs	18-177	10	-18.00	Richard Hannon	6-65
Adam Kirby	18-166	11	-13.25	Clive Cox	7-70
Andrea Atzeni	17-126	13	+9.10	Roger Varian	5-28
George Baker	17-122	14	+38.63	Roger Charlton	3-29
Jamie Spencer	14-124	11	-18.63	David Simcock	2-13

Favourites

2yo 32.6% -20.30 3yo 27.3% -47.02 TOTAL 28.9% -97.56

NEWCASTLE

High Gosforth Park NE3 5HP
Tel: 0191 236 2020 or 236 5508

How to get there Road: Signposted from A1. Rail: Newcastle Central, metro to Regent Centre or Four Lane End and bus

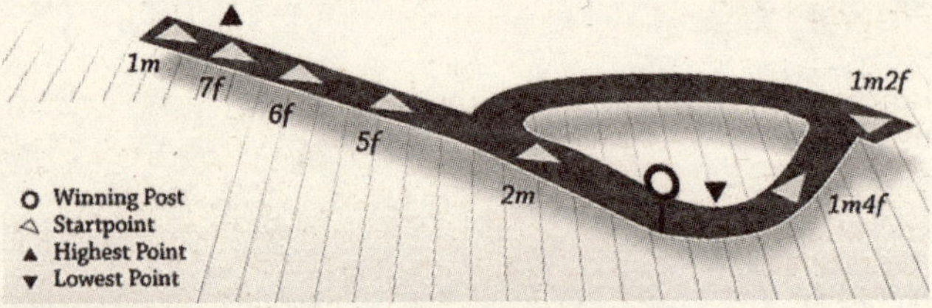

Features LH, Tapeta, easy bends with uphill straight

2017 Fixtures April 14, May 19, 23, June 1, 3, 29-30, July 1, 29, August 10, September 8, 12, 19, 22, 29, October 10, 19-20, 24, November 3-4, 10, 15, 23-24, 30, December 6, 16

Racing Post standard times

5f	58	1m4f98yds	2min36.5
6f	1min10.2	2m56yds	3min27
7f	1min24		
1m	1min36.5		
1m2f	2min6		

Trainers	*Wins-Runs*	*%*	*2yo*	*3yo+*	*£1 level stks*
Richard Fahey	12-114	11	7-45	5-69	-29.63
Michael Easterby	11-63	17	2-10	9-53	+28.83
Kevin Ryan	11-56	20	5-19	6-37	+36.21
David O´Meara	10-77	13	0-7	10-70	-17.00
Mark Johnston	8-64	13	5-41	3-23	-27.64
Richard Guest	8-60	13	0-5	8-55	+15.25
David Simcock	8-26	31	5-14	3-12	+1.89
James Bethell	7-29	24	1-8	6-21	+31.95
Alistair Whillans	6-40	15	1-4	5-36	+22.00
Roger Varian	6-33	18	1-11	5-22	-14.40
Richard Whitaker	6-31	19	0-5	6-26	+9.50
Sir Mark Prescott	6-24	25	1-5	5-19	+1.69
Hugo Palmer	6-20	30	5-14	1-6	+5.41

Jockeys	*Wins-Rides*	*%*	*£1 level stks*	*Best Trainer*	*W-R*
Graham Gibbons	15-81	19	+5.84	David O´Meara	3-10
Luke Morris	11-84	13	-13.56	Sir Mark Prescott Bt	5-20
P J McDonald	10-108	9	-10.38	James Bethell	4-15
Nathan Evans	10-75	13	+5.00	Michael Easterby	7-34
Connor Beasley	9-127	7	-65.25	Richard Guest	5-24
Paul Mulrennan	9-126	7	-75.45	Michael Dods	4-33
David Nolan	9-48	19	+10.63	Richard Fahey	3-15
Tom Eaves	8-106	8	-46.59	David Simcock	2-5
Joe Fanning	8-67	12	-25.46	Mark Johnston	3-25
Barry McHugh	8-55	15	-4.00	Richard Whitaker	5-11
Josephine Gordon	8-49	16	-6.71	Hugo Palmer	4-12
Kevin Stott	8-41	20	-10.45	Kevin Ryan	3-18
Ben Curtis	7-91	8	-49.89	Brian Ellison	4-38

Favourites

2yo 53.1% +16.82 3yo 38.9% +10.91 TOTAL 37.2% +11.71

Westfield House, The Links,
Newmarket, Suffolk. CB8 0TG

NEWMARKET

Rowley Mile

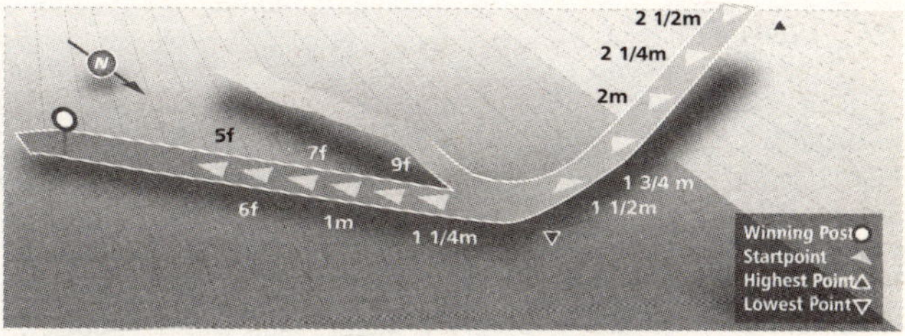

How to get there Road: from south M11 Jct 9, then A11, otherwise A14 and A11. Rail: Newmarket

Features RH, wide, galloping, uphill finish

2017 Fixtures April 18-20, May 6-7, 18-20, September 23, 28-30, October 7, 13-14, 25, November 3-4

Racing Post standard times

5f	57.5	1m2f	2min0.5
6f	1min10.1	1m4f	2min28
7f	1min22.5	1m6f	2min53.5
1m	1min35.1	2m	3min19
1m1f	1min47.8	2m2f	3min45

Trainers	Wins-Runs	%	2yo	3yo+	£1 level stks
John Gosden	52-287	18	17-93	35-194	-23.26
Mark Johnston	32-257	12	15-95	17-162	+25.21
Saeed bin Suroor	29-169	17	12-53	17-116	-8.13
Charlie Appleby	29-134	22	12-62	17-72	+41.67
Richard Hannon	28-217	13	9-92	19-125	-0.96
Richard Hannon Snr	21-170	12	9-78	12-92	-21.52
William Haggas	20-194	10	7-83	13-111	-33.90
Roger Varian	18-157	11	8-58	10-99	-34.42
Sir Michael Stoute	17-156	11	3-47	14-109	-59.76
A P O'Brien	17-83	20	10-46	7-37	+32.18
Charles Hills	16-184	9	7-71	9-113	-60.43
Richard Fahey	15-179	8	3-44	12-135	-70.70
Andrew Balding	14-165	8	2-49	12-116	-37.63

Jockeys	Wins-Rides	%	£1 level stks	Best Trainer	W-R
Ryan Moore	48-309	16	-41.44	A P O'Brien	11-44
William Buick	47-319	15	-20.48	Charlie Appleby	15-66
Paul Hanagan	36-282	13	-115.57	John Gosden	8-22
Frankie Dettori	34-198	17	+8.93	John Gosden	16-49
Andrea Atzeni	25-241	10	-41.34	Roger Varian	9-73
Silvestre De Sousa	25-178	14	+57.73	Mark Johnston	6-29
James Doyle	22-197	11	-84.53	Saeed bin Suroor	10-44
Richard Hughes	21-168	13	-31.68	Richard Hannon Snr	7-52
Jim Crowley	21-163	13	-4.68	Ralph Beckett	7-30
Joe Fanning	18-198	9	-11.65	Mark Johnston	13-125
Jamie Spencer	16-191	8	-94.15	Kevin Ryan	4-30
Tom Queally	16-170	9	-54.34	Sir Henry Cecil	6-26
Mickael Barzalona	15-105	14	-17.86	Charlie Appleby	6-29

Favourites

2yo 39.6% -6.63 3yo 32.8% -13.67 TOTAL 33.6% -25.46

NEWMARKET

Westfield House, The Links, Newmarket, Suffolk. CB8 0TG

July Course

How to get there See previous page

Features RH, wide, galloping, uphill finish

2017 Fixtures June 10, 23-24, 29-30, July 1, 13-15, 21-22, 28-29, August 4-5, 11-12, 18-19, 25-26

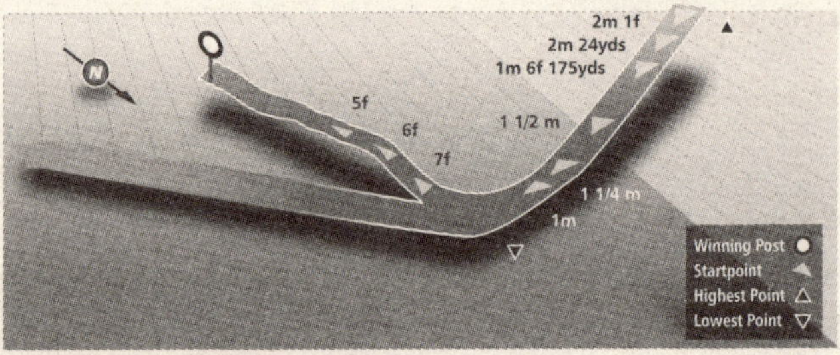

Racing Post standard times

5f	57.2	1m110yds	1min43	1m6f175yds	3min3
6f	1min10.1	1m2f	2min1.5	2m24yds	3min20
7f	1min23	1m4f	2min26.5		
1m	1min36	1m5f	2min40		

Trainers	*Wins-Runs*	*%*	*2yo*	*3yo+*	*£1 level stks*
Mark Johnston	45-235	19	10-68	35-167	+49.14
John Gosden	45-215	21	14-73	31-142	+69.67
Richard Hannon	34-256	13	26-140	8-116	-53.58
Saeed bin Suroor	34-157	22	15-59	19-98	+1.64
Charlie Appleby	29-159	18	18-81	11-78	-27.03
Richard Hannon Snr	27-185	15	16-97	11-88	+0.81
Richard Fahey	26-162	16	6-38	20-124	+45.38
Charles Hills	19-162	12	6-58	13-104	-42.05
William Haggas	19-149	13	4-39	15-110	-57.29
Sir Michael Stoute	18-133	14	4-45	14-88	-62.08
Ralph Beckett	16-101	16	2-31	14-70	-22.97
Mick Channon	14-117	12	6-52	8-65	+39.00
Brian Meehan	14-104	13	4-48	10-56	-43.33

Jockeys	*Wins-Rides*	*%*	*£1 level stks*	*Best Trainer*	*W-R*
William Buick	44-208	21	+20.19	John Gosden	19-62
Ryan Moore	43-208	21	-10.72	Sir Michael Stoute	8-48
Paul Hanagan	37-222	17	+4.06	Richard Fahey	7-31
Mickael Barzalona	35-127	28	+47.87	Saeed bin Suroor	12-36
James Doyle	32-185	17	+1.48	Saeed bin Suroor	7-30
Richard Hughes	26-139	19	-24.72	Richard Hannon Snr	11-56
Frankie Dettori	22-198	11	-98.56	John Gosden	6-24
Silvestre De Sousa	22-166	13	-51.63	Mark Johnston	8-29
Dane O'Neill	21-144	15	+27.10	Mark Johnston	5-15
Adam Kirby	17-116	15	-20.08	Charlie Appleby	5-9
Jim Crowley	17-98	17	+10.60	Mark Johnston	2-6
Harry Bentley	17-95	18	-3.09	Ralph Beckett	3-6
Joe Fanning	15-88	17	-15.83	Mark Johnston	9-53

Favourites

2yo 42% +15.96 3yo 35.7% -10.78 TOTAL 36.2% +4.44

LUMIERE: added to Mark Johnston's great July Course record last year

NOTTINGHAM

Colwick Park, Nottingham, NG2 4BE. Tel 0115 958 0620

How to get there Road: M1 Jct 25, A52 east to B686, signs for Trent Bridge, then Colwick Park. Rail: Nottingham

Features LH, flat, easy turns

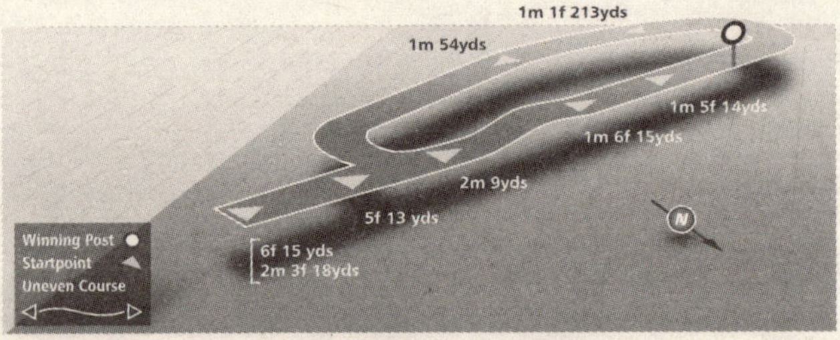

2017 Fixtures April 12, 22, May 2, 12-13, 23, 31, June 11, 15, 19, 29, July 8, 21, 25, August 3, 8, 15, 18, October 4, 11, 18, November 1, 8

Racing Post standard times

5f13yds	58.4	1m2f50yds (Inner)	2min8.6
5f13yds (Inner)	59.8	1m6f15yds	2min57
6f15yds	1min12.2	2m9yds	3min24
1m75yds	1min42	2m9yds (Inner)	3min32
1m75yds (Inner)	1min43.5	2m2f18yds	3min55
1m2f50yds	2min6		

Trainers	*Wins-Runs*	*%*	*2yo*	*3yo+*	*£1 level stks*
Michael Appleby	30-190	16	0-11	30-179	+63.00
Richard Fahey	29-173	17	11-44	18-129	+13.80
John Gosden	22-117	19	9-42	13-75	+3.84
Mark Johnston	16-137	12	10-63	6-74	-54.29
Mick Channon	16-126	13	7-42	9-84	-37.85
Saeed bin Suroor	16-61	26	9-28	7-33	-1.27
Richard Hannon	15-105	14	9-51	6-54	-32.16
Roger Varian	14-82	17	3-28	11-54	+4.08
Clive Cox	14-78	18	2-21	12-57	+9.70
Richard Guest	13-111	12	1-10	12-101	+29.50
Ralph Beckett	13-82	16	2-30	11-52	-6.98
James Fanshawe	12-65	18	1-15	11-50	+11.09
Luca Cumani	12-59	20	3-22	9-37	+0.42

Jockeys	*Wins-Rides*	*%*	*£1 level stks*	*Best Trainer*	*W-R*
Silvestre De Sousa	24-149	16	-10.78	Saeed bin Suroor	6-19
Andrew Mullen	24-132	18	+87.50	Michael Appleby	18-90
Jim Crowley	19-78	24	+50.54	Ralph Beckett	4-18
James Doyle	18-90	20	-19.97	Saeed bin Suroor	3-6
William Buick	18-67	27	+13.82	John Gosden	6-21
Luke Morris	17-144	12	-15.40	Ed Walker	2-5
Frederik Tylicki	17-97	18	-2.41	James Fanshawe	5-19
Paul Hanagan	17-88	19	-6.37	Richard Fahey	4-10
Graham Lee	15-167	9	-71.09	Robert Cowell	2-3
Tom Queally	15-104	14	+46.63	Sir Henry Cecil	3-10
Adam Kirby	14-84	17	-0.25	Clive Cox	5-28
Andrea Atzeni	13-89	15	-4.39	Roger Varian	5-23
Jamie Spencer	13-74	18	-29.73	Ralph Beckett	2-2

Favourites

2yo 38.9% -12.99 3yo 32.7% -42.24 TOTAL 32.1% -90.30

33 Ropergate, Pontefract,
WF8 1LE. Tel 01977 703 224

PONTEFRACT

How to get there Road: M62 Jct 32, then A539. Rail: Pontefract Monkhill or Pontefract Baghill from Leeds

Features LH, undulating, sharp home turn, last half-mile all uphill

2017 Fixtures April 11, 24, May 3, 26, June 12, 25, July 3, 11, 21, 30, August 9, 20, September 21, 28, October 9, 23

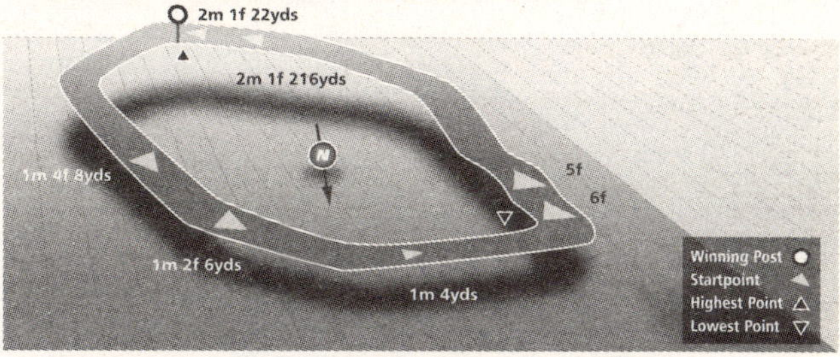

Racing Post standard times

5f	1min1.8	1m4f8yds	2min35.5
6f	1min14.6	2m1f22yds	3min41
1m4yds	1min42.6	2m1f216yds	3min51
1m2f6yds	2min9.4	2m5f122yds	4min41

Trainers	*Wins-Runs*	*%*	*2yo*	*3yo+*	*£1 level stks*
Richard Fahey	50-252	20	19-75	31-177	+43.47
Mark Johnston	32-193	17	9-59	23-134	-65.21
Tim Easterby	19-183	10	3-44	16-139	-29.67
Kevin Ryan	14-125	11	6-42	8-83	+1.88
Michael Dods	13-113	12	1-17	12-96	-24.33
Paul Midgley	13-105	12	0-9	13-96	+40.50
William Haggas	12-45	27	3-16	9-29	-4.68
Charlie Appleby	12-33	36	5-14	7-19	+1.32
Micky Hammond	11-143	8	1-9	10-134	-23.25
Michael Easterby	11-87	13	0-5	11-82	-5.92
David Barron	11-61	18	2-9	9-52	-10.54
Sir Michael Stoute	11-50	22	0-4	11-46	-13.57
Luca Cumani	11-30	37	0-1	11-29	+5.30

Jockeys	*Wins-Rides*	*%*	*£1 level stks*	*Best Trainer*	*W-R*
Silvestre De Sousa	34-170	20	-8.41	Mark Johnston	13-45
Graham Lee	23-196	12	-7.25	Jedd O'Keeffe	4-14
Paul Mulrennan	23-177	13	-0.83	Michael Dods	9-54
Tony Hamilton	23-127	18	-8.99	Richard Fahey	22-91
Paul Hanagan	19-105	18	+16.23	Richard Fahey	8-41
Franny Norton	18-91	20	+28.21	Mark Johnston	10-44
Graham Gibbons	16-120	13	-39.93	David Barron	6-34
P J McDonald	15-162	9	-43.67	Ann Duffield	4-29
Robert Winston	14-102	14	+4.87	David Barron	3-4
David Allan	13-114	11	+11.33	Tim Easterby	8-75
Phillip Makin	12-88	14	-31.31	Charlie Appleby	3-6
William Buick	12-47	26	-12.74	Charlie Appleby	4-9
Daniel Tudhope	11-117	9	-47.38	David O'Meara	5-66

Favourites

2yo 38.4% -1.33 3yo 36.7% -10.82 TOTAL 33.7% -22.73

REDCAR

Redcar, Teesside,
TS10 2BY. Tel 01642 484 068

How to get there
Road: A1, A168, A19, then A174. Rail: Redcar Central from Darlington

Features LH, flat, galloping

2017 Fixtures
April 10, 17, May 4, 22, 29-30, June 23-24, July 23, August 2, 12, 26, September 19, 27, October 7, 20, 30, November 7

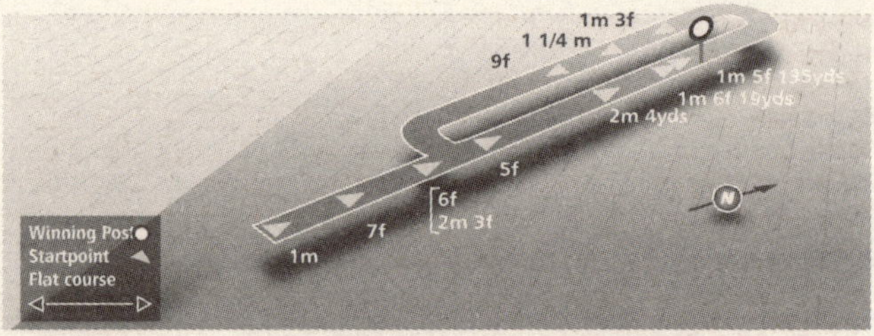

Racing Post standard times

5f	57	1m3f	2min16
6f	1min9.5	1m5f135yds	2min51
7f	1min22	1m6f19yds	2min57.5
1m	1min35	2m4yds	3min22
1m1f	1min48	2m3f	4min8
1m2f	2min3		

Trainers	*Wins-Runs*	*%*	*2yo*	*3yo+*	*£1 level stks*
Richard Fahey	41-260	16	16-107	25-153	-17.07
David O'Meara	39-245	16	8-50	31-195	-4.44
Tim Easterby	26-393	7	6-127	20-266	-202.58
Michael Dods	24-188	13	7-50	17-138	-31.50
Kevin Ryan	19-140	14	8-62	11-78	-18.25
Ruth Carr	17-141	12	0-2	17-139	-9.00
David Barron	17-86	20	3-19	14-67	+67.63
Mark Johnston	16-109	15	4-39	12-70	-19.77
John Quinn	13-112	12	2-50	11-62	-62.93
Michael Easterby	12-151	8	0-33	12-118	-69.75
Paul Midgley	12-116	10	1-20	11-96	-50.58
David Nicholls	12-94	13	0-6	12-88	-16.25
Tracy Waggott	11-162	7	0-5	11-157	-48.50

Jockeys	*Wins-Rides*	*%*	*£1 level stks*	*Best Trainer*	*W-R*
Paul Mulrennan	32-230	14	-8.09	Michael Dods	10-57
Daniel Tudhope	30-145	21	+46.00	David O'Meara	21-92
Graham Lee	29-224	13	-60.15	Paul Midgley	5-25
David Allan	27-255	11	-19.46	Tim Easterby	13-138
Graham Gibbons	26-151	17	+20.54	David Barron	10-39
Tony Hamilton	25-170	15	-49.46	Richard Fahey	22-104
P J McDonald	18-220	8	-65.40	Ann Duffield	5-59
James Sullivan	18-211	9	-19.00	Ruth Carr	12-88
Phillip Makin	18-142	13	-3.75	Keith Reveley	2-2
Tom Eaves	15-240	6	-131.13	Michael Dods	3-22
Jason Hart	14-123	11	-10.50	Shaun Harris	2-5
Ben Curtis	12-99	12	-34.19	Alan Swinbank	4-33
Silvestre De Sousa	12-77	16	-16.68	Mark Johnston	3-11

Favourites

2yo 40.5% +0.97 3yo 31.8% -15.79 TOTAL 34% +1.71

77 North Street, Ripon, N Yorkshire
HG4 1DS. Tel 01765 602 156 or 01765 603 696

RIPON

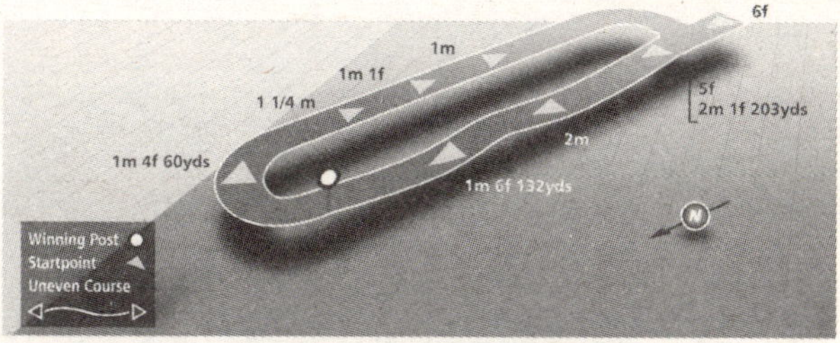

How to get there
Road: A1, then B6265. Rail: Harrogate, bus to Ripon centre, 1m walk

Features RH, sharp

2017 Fixtures
April 20, 29, May 12, 21, June 7-8, 21-22, July 10, 22, August 7, 14, 19, 28-29, September 4, 30

Racing Post standard times

5f	58	1m2f	2min4.5
6f	1min10.3	1m4f10yds	2min33.4
1m	1min38.1	2m	3min26.5
1m1f	1min52	2m1f203yds	3min53
1m1f170yds	2min1.3		

Trainers	*Wins-Runs*	*%*	*2yo*	*3yo+*	*£1 level stks*
David O'Meara	44-264	17	4-36	40-228	+1.78
Richard Fahey	40-299	13	15-87	25-212	-78.55
Tim Easterby	36-392	9	7-120	29-272	-115.26
Mark Johnston	35-201	17	11-50	24-151	+8.83
David Barron	18-121	15	2-17	16-104	-9.65
William Haggas	18-49	37	5-14	13-35	-1.21
Richard Whitaker	15-99	15	1-13	14-86	+27.75
Kevin Ryan	11-142	8	3-33	8-109	-67.88
Ann Duffield	11-88	13	10-45	1-43	-15.21
David Nicholls	9-121	7	1-8	8-113	-74.54
Micky Hammond	9-100	9	0-5	9-95	-24.00
Paul Midgley	9-95	9	3-20	6-75	-35.63
Mick Channon	9-59	15	6-23	3-36	-24.54

Jockeys	*Wins-Rides*	*%*	*£1 level stks*	*Best Trainer*	*W-R*
Tony Hamilton	30-155	19	-13.93	Richard Fahey	26-124
Daniel Tudhope	28-136	21	+11.22	David O'Meara	24-104
David Allan	26-231	11	-63.80	Tim Easterby	19-193
P J McDonald	25-209	12	-42.83	Ann Duffield	8-57
Graham Lee	23-160	14	-17.82	William Haggas	3-5
Graham Gibbons	23-157	15	-48.38	David Barron	10-65
Paul Mulrennan	21-154	14	-37.67	Paul Midgley	3-14
Phillip Makin	17-136	13	-22.13	Keith Dalgleish	5-22
Silvestre De Sousa	16-60	27	+24.81	Mark Johnston	7-18
Franny Norton	14-111	13	-17.56	Mark Johnston	12-76
Adrian Nicholls	13-93	14	+6.83	David Nicholls	7-55
George Chaloner	11-95	12	-32.00	Richard Whitaker	8-41
Richard Kingscote	11-44	25	+14.13	Tom Dascombe	9-33

Favourites

2yo 37.3% -4.04 3yo 39.6% +10.65 TOTAL 35.5% +5.29

SALISBURY

Netherhampton, Salisbury, Wilts SP2 8PN. Tel 01722 326 461

How to get there Road: 2m west of Salisbury on A3094. Rail: Salisbury, bus

Features RH, uphill finish

2017 Fixtures April 30, May 18, 27, June 13, 18, 28, July 15, 29, August 7, 16-17, 25, September 7, 15, October 4, 9

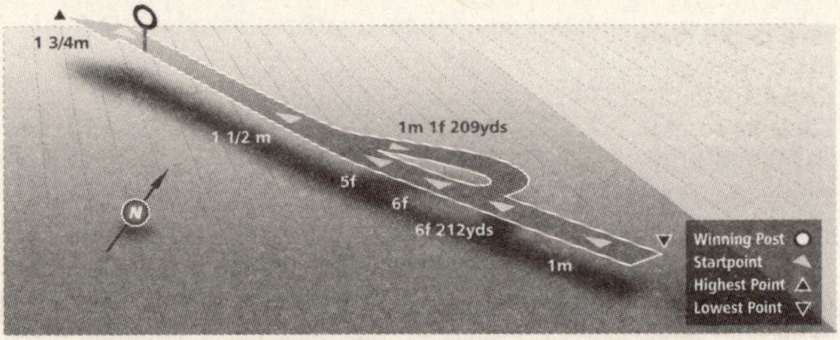

Racing Post standard times

5f	59.8	1m1f198yds	2min5.8
6f	1min12.3	1m4f	2min33
6f212yds	1min26.5	1m6f21yds	3min
1m	1min39.5		

Trainers	*Wins-Runs*	*%*	*2yo*	*3yo+*	*£1 level stks*
Richard Hannon	40-256	16	28-126	12-130	-25.91
Richard Hannon Snr	37-165	22	21-88	16-77	-9.04
Andrew Balding	27-180	15	9-49	18-131	-56.15
Ralph Beckett	27-154	18	7-58	20-96	+1.14
David Evans	17-124	14	8-55	9-69	+123.16
Sir Michael Stoute	15-88	17	2-27	13-61	-7.29
Clive Cox	14-114	12	5-41	9-73	-50.84
John Gosden	13-53	25	3-12	10-41	+22.14
Rod Millman	12-129	9	4-36	8-93	+7.05
Mick Channon	11-150	7	3-62	8-88	-86.04
Roger Varian	11-53	21	1-10	10-43	+11.33
Charles Hills	10-88	11	2-36	8-52	-46.90
David Simcock	10-40	25	3-8	7-32	+29.20

Jockeys	*Wins-Rides*	*%*	*£1 level stks*	*Best Trainer*	*W-R*
Richard Hughes	46-192	24	+1.90	Richard Hannon Snr	26-82
Pat Dobbs	25-178	14	-40.23	Richard Hannon	11-59
James Doyle	23-95	24	+83.42	Roger Charlton	4-24
Jim Crowley	20-142	14	+44.20	Ralph Beckett	7-41
Paul Hanagan	16-75	21	-1.12	Roger Varian	3-5
Oisin Murphy	15-105	14	+24.63	Andrew Balding	4-25
Silvestre De Sousa	14-86	16	-0.83	Saeed bin Suroor	3-8
Dane O'Neill	13-122	11	-21.38	Henry Candy	4-30
George Baker	13-83	16	+10.13	Ed Walker	3-8
Martin Dwyer	13-79	16	+47.83	William Muir	6-20
Andrea Atzeni	13-76	17	-9.84	Luca Cumani	3-5
David Probert	12-114	11	-52.95	Andrew Balding	10-64
Sean Levey	12-80	15	+3.62	Richard Hannon	9-54

Favourites

2yo	40.1%	-15.03	3yo	32%	-41.99	TOTAL	35%	-56.70

Esher, Surrey, KT10 9AJ.
Tel 01372 463 072 or 01372 464 348

SANDOWN

How to get there Road: M25 Jct 10 then A3. Rail: Esher from Waterloo

Features RH, last 7f uphill

2017 Fixtures April 28, May 25, June 8, 16-17, July 7-8, 19, 26-27, August 2, 10, September 1-2, 15, 20

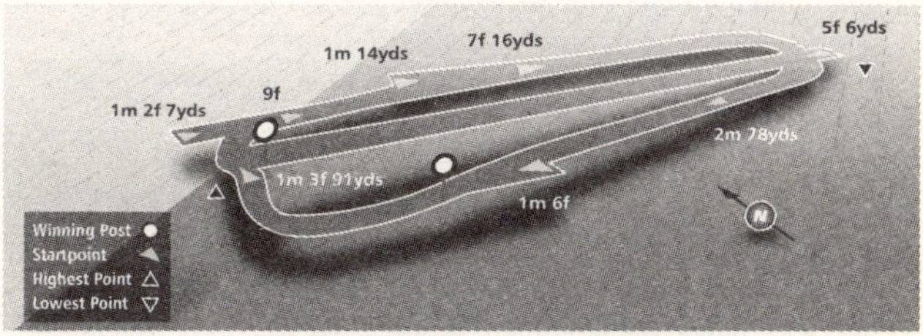

Racing Post standard times

5f6yds	59.8	1m2f7yds	2min5.8
7f16yds	1min27	1m3f91yds	2min23
1m14yds	1min39.9	1m6f	2min58.3
1m1f	1min52.9	2m78yds	3min34

Trainers	*Wins-Runs*	*%*	*2yo*	*3yo+*	*£1 level stks*
John Gosden	32-148	22	8-31	24-117	-9.07
Sir Michael Stoute	30-140	21	2-21	28-119	-9.06
Richard Hannon Snr	28-155	18	16-57	12-98	-1.34
Andrew Balding	24-185	13	5-43	19-142	-25.74
Richard Hannon	22-180	12	13-74	9-106	-33.91
William Haggas	16-68	24	4-16	12-52	+2.88
Saeed bin Suroor	13-77	17	2-15	11-62	-27.32
Roger Charlton	13-64	20	2-14	11-50	-10.89
Clive Cox	12-98	12	2-18	10-80	-14.60
Roger Varian	12-79	15	2-13	10-66	-37.98
Mick Channon	10-95	11	5-31	5-64	-7.70
Ralph Beckett	10-73	14	1-16	9-57	-11.80
Henry Candy	10-55	18	1-8	9-47	+12.42

Jockeys	*Wins-Rides*	*%*	*£1 level stks*	*Best Trainer*	*W-R*
Ryan Moore	51-251	20	-40.06	Sir Michael Stoute	21-81
Richard Hughes	36-178	20	-16.29	Richard Hannon Snr	16-66
William Buick	33-196	17	-49.60	John Gosden	15-75
James Doyle	28-168	17	-26.59	Roger Charlton	6-30
Frankie Dettori	19-99	19	-0.97	John Gosden	4-22
Pat Dobbs	17-132	13	+8.52	Richard Hannon Snr	6-26
Dane O'Neill	17-127	13	-45.42	Henry Candy	6-25
Jim Crowley	16-144	11	+15.50	Ralph Beckett	3-21
George Baker	15-84	18	+9.16	Roger Charlton	3-5
David Probert	14-104	13	-7.06	Andrew Balding	11-72
Jamie Spencer	14-75	19	+1.23	Jamie Osborne	3-5
Andrea Atzeni	13-122	11	-74.44	Roger Varian	4-26
Oisin Murphy	12-83	14	-0.38	Stuart Kittow	2-2

Favourites

2yo 46.9% +4.07 3yo 34% -29.33 TOTAL 37.4% -8.64

SOUTHWELL

Rolleston, Newark, Notts
NG25 0TS. Tel 01636 814 481

How to get there Road: A1 to Newark, then A617 or M1 to Nottingham, then A612. Rail: Rolleston

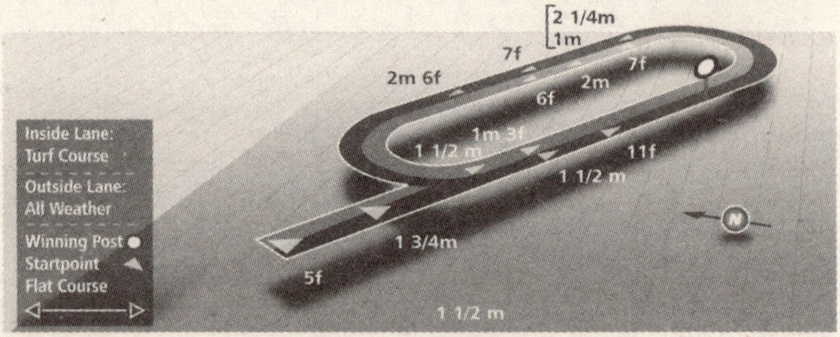

Features LH, Fibresand, sharp

Please note there are no turf fixtures scheduled for 2017 Stats relate to all-weather only

2017 Fixtures April 4, 6, 16, 18, May 8, August 28, October 22, November 13, 16, 28, December 1, 4, 11, 19, 21-22, 29

Racing Post standard times

5f	58	1m4f	2min35
6f	1min14	1m5f	2min50.5
7f	1min27	1m6f	3min2
1m	1min39.8	2m	3min34
1m3f	2min22.3	2m2f	4min4

Trainers	*Wins-Runs*	*%*	*2yo*	*3yo+*	*£1 level stks*
Michael Appleby	108-570	19	2-24	106-546	-31.19
Mark Johnston	48-201	24	8-35	40-166	+1.35
Scott Dixon	45-401	11	3-37	42-364	-36.60
Alan McCabe	35-239	15	5-36	30-203	+10.08
J R Jenkins	34-284	12	0-5	34-279	-31.70
Brian Ellison	34-218	16	4-19	30-199	-62.19
Derek Shaw	29-241	12	0-18	29-223	-56.10
Roy Bowring	28-208	13	0-3	28-205	-17.40
David O'Meara	28-196	14	2-18	26-178	-63.91
Conor Dore	27-200	14	2-5	25-195	-33.00
James Given	26-167	16	6-27	20-140	+38.82
Alan Swinbank	26-137	19	0-0	26-137	-25.63
Kevin Ryan	25-165	15	7-35	18-130	-58.31

Jockeys	*Wins-Rides*	*%*	*£1 level stks*	*Best Trainer*	*W-R*
Luke Morris	63-435	14	-122.14	Scott Dixon	14-81
Joe Fanning	63-372	17	-68.98	Mark Johnston	37-129
Andrew Mullen	58-366	16	-91.16	Michael Appleby	43-256
Tom Eaves	43-367	12	-53.00	Keith Dalgleish	13-37
Ben Curtis	34-207	16	+48.71	Alan McCabe	6-25
Graham Lee	32-213	15	-74.94	James Given	10-44
Hayley Turner	31-170	18	+28.86	Conor Dore	15-93
Alistair Rawlinson	30-144	21	+28.62	Michael Appleby	24-106
Robert Winston	29-193	15	-30.44	Alan Swinbank	5-17
Daniel Tudhope	29-158	18	-22.77	David O'Meara	15-83
Dale Swift	24-155	15	-0.35	Derek Shaw	10-43
Tony Hamilton	23-164	14	-27.76	Richard Fahey	12-76
Graham Gibbons	23-156	15	-10.92	David Barron	8-35

Favourites

2yo 39.8% -24.44 3yo 39.3% -48.93 TOTAL 38.1% -84.78

THIRSK

Station Road, Thirsk, N Yorkshire, YO7 1QL. Tel 01845 522 276

How to get there
Road: A61 from A1 in the west or A19 in the east. Rail: Thirsk, 10min walk

Features LH, sharp, tight turns

2017 Fixtures
April 22, 30, May 6, 13, 20, June 5, 20, July 5, 18, 28, August 4-5, 15, 21, September 1, 9

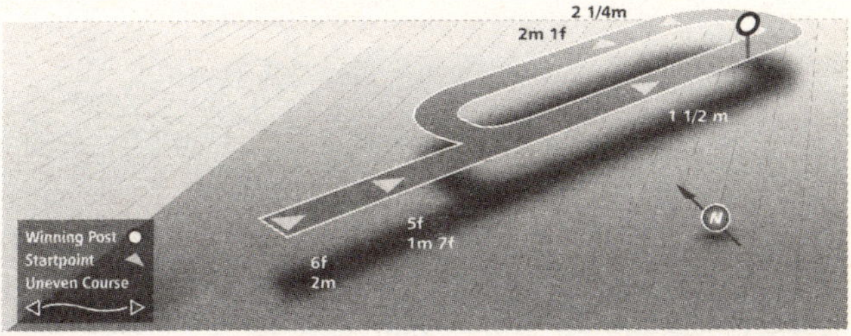

Racing Post standard times

5f	58	1m	1min36.5
6f	1min10.6	1m4f	2min32
7f	1min24	2m	3min23

Trainers	*Wins-Runs*	*%*	*2yo*	*3yo+*	*£1 level stks*
Richard Fahey	40-272	15	13-94	27-178	-6.34
Tim Easterby	30-357	8	9-108	21-249	-89.60
David O'Meara	28-227	12	7-30	21-197	-28.30
Kevin Ryan	26-206	13	9-64	17-142	-6.96
Michael Dods	21-215	10	3-38	18-177	-46.60
Ruth Carr	16-183	9	0-3	16-180	-26.80
David Barron	16-120	13	4-28	12-92	-28.94
Brian Ellison	15-111	14	1-19	14-92	+29.75
Michael Easterby	14-144	10	0-27	14-117	-11.25
David Nicholls	10-157	6	1-10	9-147	-102.25
Declan Carroll	10-106	9	1-8	9-98	+26.50
Richard Guest	10-97	10	1-22	9-75	-16.27
Alan Swinbank	10-83	12	0-6	10-77	-11.88

Jockeys	*Wins-Rides*	*%*	*£1 level stks*	*Best Trainer*	*W-R*
Paul Mulrennan	35-267	13	-24.10	Michael Dods	12-89
Graham Gibbons	28-171	16	+12.70	David Barron	10-61
Daniel Tudhope	28-147	19	+51.40	David O'Meara	19-84
David Allan	22-189	12	-31.10	Tim Easterby	9-111
P J McDonald	19-254	7	-94.55	Ann Duffield	5-43
Tom Eaves	18-221	8	-12.38	Keith Dalgleish	3-13
Graham Lee	17-183	9	-78.06	Mick Channon	2-5
Tony Hamilton	17-170	10	-79.71	Richard Fahey	15-115
Phillip Makin	15-147	10	-36.08	Kevin Ryan	3-27
James Sullivan	14-223	6	-61.80	Ruth Carr	10-122
Robert Winston	13-108	12	-41.02	Mel Brittain	3-9
Jason Hart	13-108	12	+39.73	Declan Carroll	3-14
Ben Curtis	11-92	12	+11.75	Alan Swinbank	5-27

Favourites
2yo 40.2% +1.32 3yo 34% -25.32 TOTAL 32.6% -39.78

WETHERBY

York Road, Wetherby, West Yorks
L22 5EJ. Tel: 01937 582 035

How to get there Road: A1, A58 from Leeds, B1224 from York. Rail: Leeds, Harrogate, York.

Features LH, 1m4f circuit

2017 Fixtures May 15, June 6, 19

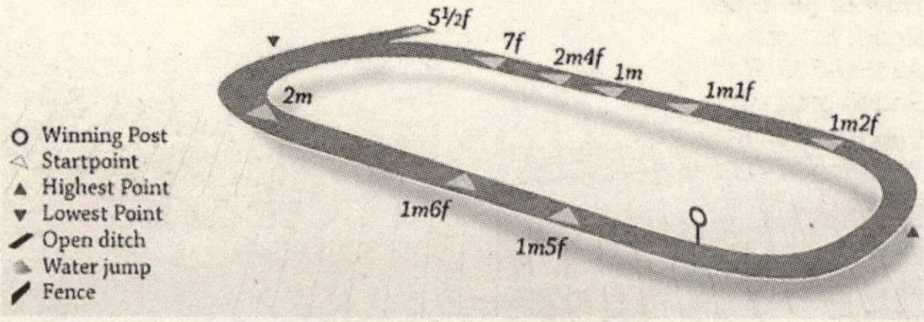

Racing Post standard times

Insufficient data

Trainers	Wins-Runs	%	2yo	3yo+	£1 level stks
Kevin Ryan	2-12	17	1-2	1-10	+26.00
David O'Meara	2-12	17	0-2	2-10	+1.50
Tim Easterby	2-12	17	0-3	2-9	-1.20
Ruth Carr	2-11	18	0-0	2-11	+1.50
Eric Alston	2-5	40	0-0	2-5	+18.00
Mark Johnston	2-5	40	1-2	1-3	+8.10
George Margarson	2-3	67	1-1	1-2	+18.00
David Brown	2-2	100	0-0	2-2	+26.00
Alan Swinbank	1-13	8	0-0	1-13	-1.00
Richard Fahey	1-11	9	0-3	1-8	-2.00
Ann Duffield	1-8	13	0-3	1-5	-5.00
Michael Dods	1-8	13	0-0	1-8	+0.00
John Quinn	1-8	13	1-2	0-6	-5.13

Jockeys	Wins-Rides	%	£1 level stks	Best Trainer	W-R
Paul Mulrennan	5-14	36	+17.10	John Mackie	1-1
Tom Eaves	3-17	18	+45.00	David Brown	2-2
David Allan	3-17	18	+5.80	Alan Swinbank	1-1
Joe Fanning	3-16	19	+25.00	George Margarson	1-1
James Sullivan	3-15	20	+14.50	Ruth Carr	2-8
P J McDonald	3-14	21	+22.00	Antony Brittain	1-1
Tony Hamilton	2-14	14	-2.50	Sally Hall	1-1
Phillip Makin	2-10	20	+3.50	David O'Meara	2-2
Patrick O'Donnell	2-3	67	+15.00	Lawrence Mullaney	1-1
Ben Curtis	1-12	8	-8.00	Brian Ellison	1-2
Tom Queally	1-11	9	+6.00	David Evans	1-1
Paul Hanagan	1-10	10	-8.33	William Haggas	1-2
Neil Farley	1-9	11	-3.00	Eric Alston	1-3

Favourites

2yo 40% -0.02   3yo 33.3% -2.28   TOTAL 29.5% -4.94

Maidenhead Road, Windsor, Berks
SL4 5JJ. Tel 01753 498 400

WINDSOR

How to get there Road: M4 Jctn 6, A355, A308. Rail: Paddington to Windsor Central/ Waterloo to Windsor Riverside

Features Figure of eight, flat, long straight

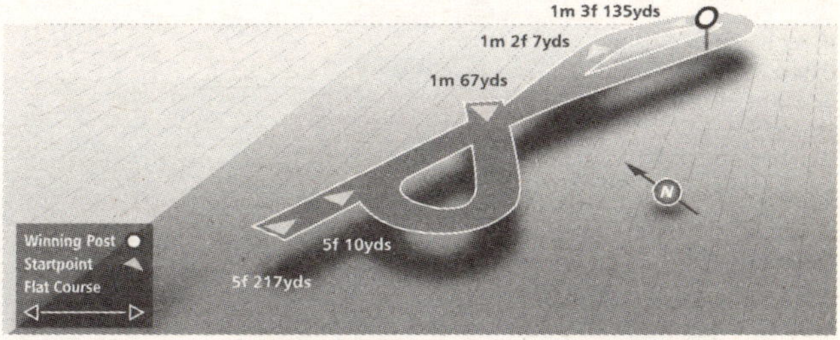

2017 Fixtures April 10, 24, May 1, 8, 15, 22, 29, June 5, 12, 19, 26, July 1-3, 10, 17, 24, 31, August 7, 13-14, 21, 26, September 4, October 9, 16, 23

Racing Post standard times

5f10yds	59.2	1m2f7yds	2min5
6f	1min10.5	1m3f135yds	2min25
1m67yds	1min41.1		

Trainers	*Wins-Runs*	*%*	*2yo*	*3yo+*	*£1 level stks*
Richard Hannon Snr	42-183	23	25-80	17-103	-16.67
Richard Hannon	34-263	13	20-117	14-146	-92.55
Roger Varian	29-99	29	2-12	27-87	+19.46
Andrew Balding	28-164	17	9-26	19-138	-10.10
Clive Cox	28-163	17	8-37	20-126	-37.13
Ralph Beckett	28-137	20	6-43	22-94	-1.94
David Evans	21-177	12	13-65	8-112	-59.80
Roger Charlton	20-109	18	3-31	17-78	+12.81
Henry Candy	19-113	17	4-21	15-92	+4.50
William Haggas	19-74	26	5-24	14-50	-10.97
Saeed bin Suroor	19-49	39	4-9	15-40	+22.08
Gary Moore	18-131	14	3-17	15-114	+14.33
Charles Hills	17-139	12	6-51	11-88	+9.88

Jockeys	*Wins-Rides*	*%*	*£1 level stks*	*Best Trainer*	*W-R*
Richard Hughes	65-295	22	-80.86	Richard Hannon Snr	27-90
Ryan Moore	48-190	25	-18.22	Sir Michael Stoute	10-51
Adam Kirby	46-240	19	-25.68	Clive Cox	19-88
Andrea Atzeni	37-128	29	+58.90	Roger Varian	13-35
George Baker	35-189	19	+29.89	Roger Charlton	6-24
James Doyle	35-178	20	+22.28	Roger Charlton	10-40
Jim Crowley	34-256	13	-72.96	Ralph Beckett	11-52
Jamie Spencer	23-118	19	+12.20	Jamie Osborne	3-7
William Buick	21-114	18	-4.75	Jeremy Noseda	4-8
David Probert	19-181	10	-78.45	Andrew Balding	10-65
Pat Cosgrave	19-153	12	-2.58	William Haggas	7-25
Jimmy Fortune	18-143	13	-18.50	Andrew Balding	4-24
Oisin Murphy	18-132	14	-16.65	Andrew Balding	6-32

Favourites

2yo 52.5% +28.61 3yo 42.4% +31.10 TOTAL 41.3% +65.75

WOLVES

Dunstall Park, Gorsebrook Road, Wolverhampton, West Midlands. WV6 0PE. Tel 08702 202 442

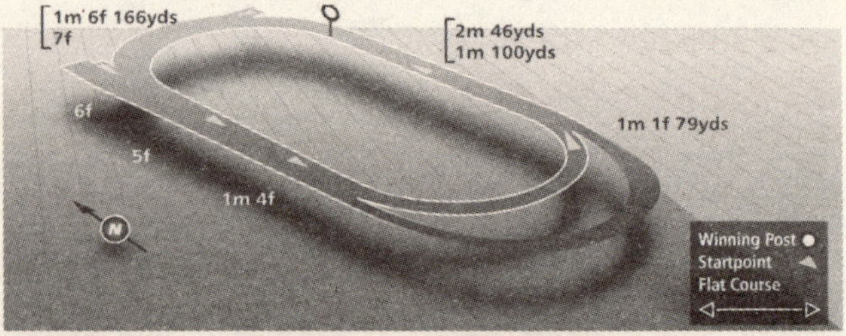

How to get there Road: A449, close to M6, M42 and M54. Rail: Wolverhampton

Features LH, sharp, relaid with Tapeta in 2014

2017 Fixtures April 5, 8, 17, 19, 22, 25, 29, May 2-3, 30, June 1, 7, 9, 26, July 3, 11, 17, 31, August 10-11, 14, 18, 31, September 9, 23, October 7, 21, 27-28, 31, November 7, 11, 18, 20, 25, 29, December 2, 5, 9, 16, 18, 22, 26-27

Racing Post standard times

5f20yds	1min0.5	1m1f103yds	1min57.3
5f216yds	1min13.2	1m4f50yds	2min35.3
7f32yds	1min27	1m5f194yds	2min58.5
1m141yds	1min46.7	2m119yds	3min36

Trainers	*Wins-Runs*	*%*	*2yo*	*3yo+*	*£1 level stks*
David Evans	105-839	13	18-153	87-686	-147.03
Mark Johnston	103-555	19	13-118	90-437	-126.66
Marco Botti	81-392	21	25-125	56-267	+31.20
Richard Fahey	74-575	13	13-144	61-431	-64.36
Jamie Osborne	61-365	17	22-110	39-255	-54.62
Tom Dascombe	60-406	15	19-145	41-261	-103.57
Michael Appleby	57-519	11	1-12	56-507	-179.92
James Tate	53-281	19	14-92	39-189	-10.99
John Gosden	52-138	38	18-47	34-91	+9.34
Daniel Mark Loughnane	50-508	10	0-24	50-484	-140.26
Charlie Appleby	50-166	30	12-62	38-104	-40.81
Tony Carroll	48-532	9	0-13	48-519	-236.56
Michael Easterby	47-370	13	0-34	47-336	-19.41

Jockeys	*Wins-Rides*	*%*	*£1 level stks*	*Best Trainer*	*W-R*
Luke Morris	217-1585	14	-345.37	Sir Mark Prescott Bt	34-151
Adam Kirby	171-803	21	-114.28	Marco Botti	20-54
Joe Fanning	148-911	16	-141.53	Mark Johnston	61-331
Silvestre De Sousa	82-385	21	-13.24	Saeed bin Suroor	14-29
Graham Gibbons	79-597	13	-97.33	Michael Easterby	25-112
Richard Kingscote	78-472	17	-34.81	Tom Dascombe	48-247
Martin Harley	73-422	17	+110.80	Marco Botti	22-76
Shane Kelly	72-603	12	-198.64	Mike Murphy	14-49
George Baker	67-348	19	-28.68	David Lanigan	7-17
Robert Winston	65-397	16	+25.80	Dean Ivory	11-42
Graham Lee	61-459	13	-141.96	James Given	7-41
Tom Eaves	59-756	8	-295.13	Keith Dalgleish	9-68
Franny Norton	55-399	14	-36.18	Mark Johnston	17-72

Favourites

2yo 38.6% -58.71 3yo 40% -43.37 TOTAL 37.4% -168.45

YARMOUTH

North Denes, Great Yarmouth, Norfolk
NR30 4AU. Tel 01493 842 527

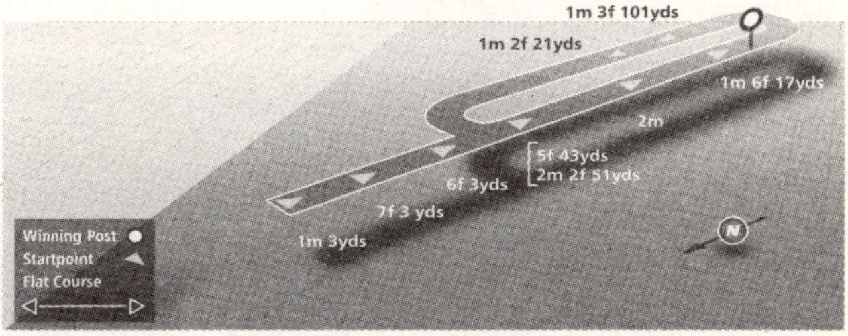

How to get there
Road: A47 to end, A1064. Rail: Great Yarmouth, bus

Features LH, flat

2017 Fixtures
April 25, May 2-3, 17, 24, June 6, 13-14, 30, July 6, 12, 19, 27, August 1, 9-10, 17, 22, 27, September 19-21, October 16, 24

Racing Post standard times

5f43yds	1min0.5	1m2f21yds	2min5
6f3yds	1min11	1m3f101yds	2min23.5
7f3yds	1min23.6	1m6f17yds	2min59
1m3yds	1min36.5	2m	3min24.5
1m1f	1min50	2m2f51yds	3min56

Trainers	*Wins-Runs*	*%*	*2yo*	*3yo+*	*£1 level stks*
William Haggas	34-109	31	9-42	25-67	+14.56
Chris Wall	22-90	24	1-13	21-77	+14.53
David Simcock	19-75	25	4-14	15-61	+92.75
Luca Cumani	16-78	21	6-26	10-52	+11.59
Roger Varian	16-71	23	7-28	9-43	-6.20
John Gosden	16-61	26	6-20	10-41	-4.30
Mark Johnston	15-83	18	4-19	11-64	+51.05
Julia Feilden	14-126	11	0-8	14-118	-28.25
Phil McEntee	14-121	12	1-7	13-114	+6.63
Marco Botti	14-96	15	7-31	7-65	-11.90
J R Jenkins	13-127	10	0-9	13-118	+9.75
Rae Guest	13-66	20	1-12	12-54	-3.18
Sir Michael Stoute	12-68	18	4-25	8-43	-33.42

Jockeys	*Wins-Rides*	*%*	*£1 level stks*	*Best Trainer*	*W-R*
Paul Hanagan	33-136	24	+23.57	William Haggas	6-15
Jamie Spencer	28-176	16	-38.01	David Simcock	6-18
Ryan Moore	28-115	24	-15.72	Sir Michael Stoute	4-25
Ted Durcan	21-154	14	-38.18	Chris Wall	12-50
Silvestre De Sousa	21-110	19	-4.90	Mark Johnston	6-26
Luke Morris	20-186	11	-49.35	Sir Mark Prescott Bt	6-33
William Buick	20-99	20	-27.24	John Gosden	4-24
Tom Queally	19-145	13	+7.26	Sir Henry Cecil	4-9
Andrea Atzeni	19-125	15	-51.86	Roger Varian	6-27
Kieren Fallon	18-99	18	-1.06	Brendan Powell	3-4
Martin Harley	17-103	17	+6.35	Marco Botti	4-21
Chris Catlin	15-63	24	+83.95	Rae Guest	6-19
Pat Cosgrave	14-73	19	+31.96	George Baker	4-8

Favourites
2yo 49.6% +7.42 3yo 39.4% +9.98 TOTAL 37.6% -31.76

YORK

Knavesmire Road, York, YO23 1EX
Tel 01904 620 911

How to get there
Road: Course is south of city. From north, A1, A59 to York, northern bypass from A19 to A64. Otherwise, A64. Rail: York, bus

Features LH, flat

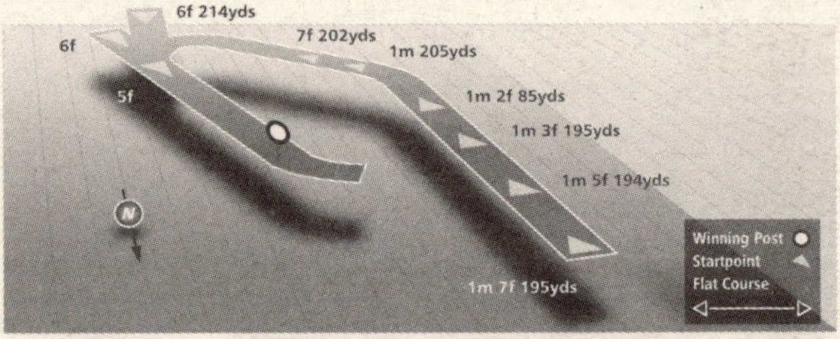

2017 Fixtures May 17-19, 27, June 16-17, July 1, 14-15, 28-29, August 23-26, September 10, October 13-14

Racing Post standard times

5f	57.5	1m208yds	1min49
5f89yds	1min2.7	1m2f88yds	2min7
6f	1min10	1m4f	2min28.1
7f	1min22.3	1m6f	2min57
1m	1min37	2m88yds	3min29

Trainers	*Wins-Runs*	*%*	*2yo*	*3yo+*	*£1 level stks*
David O'Meara	42-396	11	1-26	41-370	-54.75
Richard Fahey	40-643	6	18-196	22-447	-215.46
William Haggas	34-164	21	12-48	22-116	+36.12
Kevin Ryan	27-280	10	19-109	8-171	-74.03
Tim Easterby	18-345	5	4-70	14-275	-189.75
Sir Michael Stoute	17-82	21	2-3	15-79	-16.00
John Gosden	17-80	21	0-5	17-75	+12.59
Mark Johnston	14-258	5	6-102	8-156	-131.40
Saeed bin Suroor	14-101	14	2-12	12-89	-17.40
Luca Cumani	13-70	19	2-4	11-66	+31.50
Brian Ellison	12-179	7	0-22	12-157	-61.25
David Barron	10-140	7	4-26	6-114	-58.17
Mick Channon	9-113	8	5-46	4-67	-60.58

Jockeys	*Wins-Rides*	*%*	*£1 level stks*	*Best Trainer*	*W-R*
Daniel Tudhope	26-213	12	-39.25	David O'Meara	21-169
Paul Hanagan	25-216	12	-34.43	Richard Fahey	11-100
Ryan Moore	23-152	15	-5.53	Sir Michael Stoute	8-34
Phillip Makin	21-177	12	-0.54	David O'Meara	5-27
William Buick	20-145	14	+27.00	John Gosden	6-35
Frankie Dettori	18-107	17	-3.46	John Gosden	5-17
Jamie Spencer	17-171	10	-41.17	Kevin Ryan	5-44
Andrea Atzeni	17-109	16	+23.88	Roger Varian	6-22
Kieren Fallon	16-112	14	+18.00	Luca Cumani	5-18
James Doyle	16-102	16	-3.94	Saeed bin Suroor	5-18
Graham Gibbons	15-199	8	-90.51	David Barron	5-69
Silvestre De Sousa	14-178	8	-28.90	Mark Johnston	4-57
Paul Mulrennan	13-163	8	-13.17	Michael Dods	5-36

Favourites
2yo 28.8% -30.24 3yo 31.9% +1.39 TOTAL 27.9% -54.50

AJAYA: a third Gimcrack winner in 2015 for William Haggas, who loves York

Win - free form!

THIS YEAR'S QUIZ could hardly be more simple, and the prize should prove invaluable to our lucky winner. We're offering a free subscription to The Flat Form Book, the BHA's official form book – every week from May to November, you could be getting the previous week's results in full, together with notebook comments highlighting future winners, adjusted Official Ratings and Racing Post Ratings. The winner will also get a copy of last year's complete form book.

All you have to do is this: identify the three horses pictured on the following pages. And the clue is that all three were Group 1 winners for northern trainers in Britain last season. If you think you know the answer, write their names in the box below in the order in which they appear.

Send your answers along with your details on the entry form below, to:

2017 Flat Annual Competition, Racing & Football Outlook,
Floor 23, 1 Canada Square, London, E14 5AP.

Entries must reach us no later than first post on April 28. The winner's name and the right answers will be printed in the RFO's May 2 edition.

Six runners-up will each receive a copy of last year's form book.

Name..

Address..

....

Town..

Postcode..

In the event of more than one correct entry, the winner will be drawn at random from the correct entries. The Editor's decision is final and no correspondence will be entered into.

BETTING CHART

ON	ODDS	AGAINST
50	Evens	50
52.4	11-10	47.6
54.5	6-5	45.5
55.6	5-4	44.4
58	11-8	42
60	6-4	40
62	13-8	38
63.6	7-4	36.4
65.3	15-8	34.7
66.7	2-1	33.3
68	85-40	32
69.2	9-4	30.8
71.4	5-2	28.6
73.4	11-4	26.6
75	3-1	25
76.9	100-30	23.1
77.8	7-2	22.2
80	4-1	20
82	9-2	18
83.3	5-1	16.7
84.6	11-2	15.4
85.7	6-1	14.3
86.7	13-2	13.3
87.5	7-1	12.5
88.2	15-2	11.8
89	8-1	11
89.35	100-12	10.65
89.4	17-2	10.6
90	9-1	10
91	10-1	9
91.8	11-1	8.2
92.6	12-1	7.4
93.5	14-1	6.5
94.4	16-1	5.6
94.7	18-1	5.3
95.2	20-1	4.8
95.7	22-1	4.3
96.2	25-1	3.8
97.2	33-1	2.8
97.6	40-1	2.4
98.1	50-1	1.9
98.5	66-1	1.3
99.0	100-1	.0.99

The table above (often known as the 'Field Money Table') shows both bookmakers' margins and how much a backer needs to invest to win £100. To calculate a bookmaker's margin, simply add up the percentages of all the odds on offer. The sum by which the total exceeds 100% gives the 'over-round' on the book. To determine what stake is required to win £100 (includes returned stake) at a particular price, just look at the relevant row, either odds-against or odds-on.

RULE 4 DEDUCTIONS

When a horse is withdrawn before coming under starter's orders, but after a market has been formed, bookmakers are entitled to make the following deductions from win and place returns (excluding stakes) in accordance with Tattersalls' Rule 4(c).

	Odds of withdrawn horse	*Deduction from winnings*
(1)	3-10 or shorter	75p in the £
(2)	2-5 to 1-3	70p in the £
(3)	8-15 to 4-9	65p in the £
(4)	8-13 to 4-7	60p in the £
(5)	4-5 to 4-6	55p in the £
(6)	20-21 to 5-6	50p in the £
(7)	Evens to 6-5	45p in the £
(8)	5-4 to 6-4	40p in the £
(9)	13-8 to 7-4	35p in the £
(10)	15-8 to 9-4	30p in the £
(11)	5-2 to 3-1	25p in the £
(12)	100-30 to 4-1	20p in the £
(13)	9-2 to 11-2	15p in the £
(14)	6-1 to 9-1	10p in the £
(15)	10-1 to 14-1	5p in the £
(16)	longer than 14-1	no deductions

(17) .... When more than one horse is withdrawn without coming under starter's orders, total deductions shall not exceed 75p in the £.

**Starting-price bets are affected only when there was insufficient time to form a new market.*

Feedback!

If you have any comments or criticism about this book, or suggestions for future editions, please tell us.

Write

Nick Watts/Dylan Hill
2017 Flat Annual
Racing & Football Outlook
Floor 23
1 Canada Square
London E14 5AP

email rfo@rfoutlook.com

Horse index

All horses discussed, with page numbers, except for references in the Group 1 and two-year-old form sections (pages 80-111), which have their own indexes